"As has often been said, the Psalms reflect every aspect of the human soul. Without them, our worship would be impoverished and less honest, lacking the elements of righteous anger, confusion, and dejection that so often permeate the Psalms. Bruce Waltke and Fred Zaspel have provided us with a gem of a book that opens up fresh insights into the structure, meaning, and purpose of the Psalms. This book crystallizes the fruit of long careers of devoted scholarship with clarity, insight, and skill. Hopefully this book will drive the church back to the Psalms to gain much-needed courage and nourishment. What a wonderful gift to the church."

**Derek W. H. Thomas,** Senior Minister, First Presbyterian Church, Columbia, South Carolina; Chancellor's Professor, Reformed Theological Seminary; Teaching Fellow, Ligonier Ministries

"The most obvious virtue of *How to Read and Understand the Psalms* is its scope. An appropriate subtitle for the book might be *What You Always Wanted to Know about the Psalms.* As part of this admirable scope, detailed explications of specific psalms balance the chapters that explore the topics important to scholarship on the Psalms."

**Leland Ryken,** Emeritus Professor of English, Wheaton College

"This work by Waltke and Zaspel is a milestone achievement, encapsulating a lifetime of study in an accessible form that will serve students, pastors, and anyone else who wants to deepen and enrich their understanding of the book of Psalms."

**Iain M. Duguid,** Professor of Old Testament, Westminster Theological Seminary

"Bruce Waltke and Fred Zaspel have provided the academy and the church with a rich and comprehensive book on how to read and understand the Psalms. Years of scholarship and devotion come to fruition in this masterpiece. It is an essential read for those studying the Psalms."

**Mark D. Futato,** Robert L. Maclellan Professor of Old Testament, Reformed Theological Seminary, Orlando

"What better way to encounter the book of Psalms—a book with such a wide range of topics, emotions, and types of psalms—than through the eyes of a skilled interpreter like Bruce Waltke, assisted by experienced pastor and writer Fred Zaspel. Waltke has spent the better part of a lifetime pondering the Psalms and wisdom literature, and it shows in this eminently readable introduction. It is at once engaging, insightful, and uplifting. I heartily recommend it."

**David M. Howard Jr.,** Professor of Old Testament, Bethlehem College & Seminary; author, *The Structure of Psalms 93–100*; coeditor, *The Psalms: Language for All Seasons of the Soul and Reading the Psalms Theologically*

"A few years ago, I visited the Jeita Grotto in Lebanon. Hidden beneath a nondescript hillside of rock and scrub lies a vast underground cavern, a gallery of dizzying vistas, towering earth sculptures, and precarious chasms—all of it stunningly beautiful. This book feels like that. Waltke and Zaspel take us into and under the Psalter and show a huge, dazzling world teeming there. I'm stumped to know what else could have gone into this monumental book. It is scholarly, highly readable, instantly useful, spilling with insight, and massively comprehensive. The material on David alone is worth the price of the book. Every serious reader, teacher, and preacher of the Psalms needs a copy."

**Mark Buchanan,** author, *David: Rise* and *David: Reign*

*How to Read and Understand the Psalms*

# How to Read and Understand the Psalms

Bruce K. Waltke and Fred G. Zaspel

CROSSWAY®
WHEATON, ILLINOIS

*How to Read and Understand the Psalms*

Published by Crossway
1300 Crescent Street
Wheaton, Illinois 60187

Cover design: Jordan Singer

Cover image: Unsplash, the MET, rawpixel, NYPL

First printing 2023

Printed in the United States of America


All emphases in Scripture quotations have been added by the authors.

Hardcover ISBN: 978-1-4335-8433-6
ePub ISBN: 978-1-4335-8436-7
PDF ISBN: 978-1-4335-8434-3

**Library of Congress Cataloging-in-Publication Data**

Names: Waltke, Bruce K., author. | Zaspel, Fred G., author.
Title: How to read and understand the Psalms / Bruce K. Waltke and Fred G. Zaspel.
Description: Wheaton, Illinois : Crossway, 2023. | Includes bibliographical references and index.
Identifiers: LCCN 2022033632 (print) | LCCN 2022033633 (ebook) | ISBN 9781433584336 (hardcover) | ISBN 9781433584343 (pdf) | ISBN 9781433584367 (epub)
Subjects: LCSH: Bible. Psalms—Criticism, interpretation, etc.
Classification: LCC BS1430.52 .W355 2023 (print) | LCC BS1430.52 (ebook) | DDC 223/.206—dc23/eng/20230103
LC record available at https://lccn.loc.gov/2022033632
LC ebook record available at https://lccn.loc.gov/2022033633

Crossway is a publishing ministry of Good News Publishers.

LB 32 31 30 29 28 27 26 25 24 23
15 14 13 12 11 10 9 8 7 6 5 4 3 2 1

*For Reformed Baptist Church*
*Franconia, Pennsylvania*

# Contents

# Foreword

IT IS A PRIVILEGE TO SERVE as herald to Drs. Bruce Waltke and Fred Zaspel as they step forward to offer this outstanding volume to all lovers of the book of Psalms. Do not let its workmanlike title dampen either your interest or enthusiasm; you are in for a treat in the almost six hundred pages that follow. Although I am neither a prophet nor a prophet's son, I think I can safely predict that *How to Read and Understand the Psalms* is a book you will return to frequently and treasure permanently.

The conception, birth, and maturation of this work are explained by the authors in their preface. Together they bring to its pages an array of gifts and graces: Bruce Waltke has for many years been regarded as a prince, perhaps even a king, among Old Testament scholars; Fred Zaspel has put many of us in his debt through his outstanding works on the great Princeton theologian Benjamin B. Warfield. Perhaps there is something more than merely whimsical in the thought that their collegial work echoes some of the conversations that the great Old Testament theologian Geerhardus Vos shared with Warfield on their regular constitutionals around Princeton Seminary. At any rate, the combination of Old Testament theologian and systematic theologian is an irresistible one!

Here, then, in their combined labors we are given rich exposition of the Psalms rooted in careful study of the Hebrew text, distilled through a well-matured and reflective mind, and brought together in this form by two humble lovers of Scripture. This is the work of two disciples of the one who, more than any other, knew, loved, understood, and applied to himself the book of Psalms. For this reason alone, even were there no others, a book such as this, on the words that helped shape and inform both our Lord's self-understanding and his own emotional and affective life and experience, deserves to become our regular companion along the pilgrim way to the heavenly Zion.

Readers familiar with the work of either or both of these two "doctors of the church" will open these pages with high confidence and anticipation of finding good things. To that confidence I would like to add a word of personal testimony.

I have the privilege of being what the older writers would have quaintly called a "sometime colleague" to Professor Waltke at Westminster Theological Seminary in Philadelphia. Three scenes come to mind that may help readers catch a glimpse of the man himself. Dr. Waltke will remember none of them—underlining the fact that his impact on others has been far greater than he himself could ever imagine.

The first well-remembered scene is of a "water fountain" (or, more accurately, "coffee pot") conversation at the beginning of a new academic year. As though talking to himself as much as to me, Professor Waltke commented on the way he had been praying for the help of the Holy Spirit as he looked forward to teaching his students in the coming semester. They, I am sure, believed that his expertise far surpassed the sum total of their knowledge. Yet the abiding memory is of his dependence on the Lord—a reminder to a junior colleague, as well as to his students, that while one plants and another waters, only God can give the increase.

A second remembered scene takes me back to a dinner conversation at the table of friends whose guests we both were. Dr. Waltke was, at that time, writing his magisterial two-volume commentary on the book of Proverbs. As we talked about various things it was clear Proverbs was much on his mind. What was evident to me was that C. H. Spurgeon's famous words about John Bunyan ("Prick him anywhere; and you will find that his blood is Bibline")[1] could be reapplied to my fellow dinner guest: "Prick him anywhere, and you will find that his blood is Proverbine!" Sacred Scripture had—as Paul put it to the Thessalonians—been received by him "not as the word of men but as what it really is, the word of God, which is at work in you" (1 Thess. 2:13).

The third scene is directly related to the theme of this book. It is the memory of an unspoken aspiration experienced while sitting listening to Dr. Waltke expound Psalm 51: "Would that, somehow, this richly satisfying exposition, and many more like it, were available to a wider public!" In view of his many commitments my hope was, confessedly, not accompanied by great faith. But now, thankfully, the sight of these pages is a rebuke I gladly welcome ("O you of little faith"!).

Dr. Fred Zaspel has also been a friend over many years—a friendship initiated (I suspect) by a common concern for pastoral exposition that combines biblical exegesis with biblical theology and is given depth by the penetration of biblical logic that leads to health-giving theology and fruitfulness in ministry. With many others I am indebted to, and have derived benefit from, his important contributions to the study of the multifaceted writings of B. B. Warfield. He has also been a means of encouraging the people of God to understand that in some measure "we are what we read." With all this Dr. Zaspel has been an encourager of other authors and at times their editor, thus exercising a ministry to his fellow Christians that has often been hidden from public view.

From a more personal viewpoint as someone belonging to the circle of friends who have known Dr. Zaspel and his wife, Kim, for many years, I have witnessed the ways that they have walked together with grace over the sometimes rough and testing pilgrim path and followed in the footsteps of the psalmist. It has been moving to watch from a distance as they have found God's strength and provision to be as real for them as it was for David. And as surely as he was able to echo the

1 Charles Spurgeon, *The Autobiography of Charles H. Spurgeon, Compiled from His Diary, Letters, and Records by His Wife and His Private Secretary*, vol. 4, *1878–1892* (Chicago: Fleming H. Revell, 1900), 268.

Patriarch Jacob's testimony that the Lord had been his lifelong shepherd, so too Fred and Kim have relied on and known the Lord's sure presence.

There is something especially fitting, therefore, that the gifts, graces, and experiences of our two doctors have combined to provide this exposition of the book that John Calvin stated contains "an Anatomy of all the Parts of the Soul."[2] In this exposition of the Psalms, then, these pages present spiritual instruction for the mind and medicine for the soul.

But the herald must refrain from detaining readers any longer by adding to these introductory fanfares! So with these words of introduction to the authors who will guide you through the varied spiritual terrain of the Psalter, I happily exit stage left and leave you to enjoy and profit from *How to Read and Understand the Psalms*. As you make the ascent of the hill of the Lord you will, I feel sure, frequently retain the services of your expert guides, Bruce Waltke and Fred Zaspel, until, by God's grace, the summit is in sight for us all.

Sinclair B. Ferguson
Chancellor's Professor of Systematic Theology
Reformed Theological Seminary

2 John Calvin, *Commentary on the Book of Psalms*, vol. 1, trans. James Anderson (Edinburgh: Calvin Translation Society, 1845), xxxvii.

# Preface

THIS BOOK WAS A JOINT EFFORT, but the bulk of the work was done by Bruce over many decades. Bruce began teaching the Psalms on the graduate level in 1958, the year I (Fred) was born. Many have profited from his long years of focused study. His and James Houston's *The Psalms as Christian Worship*, *The Psalms as Christian Lament*, and *The Psalms as Christian Praise*; his various published articles; his sermons; and his classroom and online lectures all are gold mines of Psalms exposition. His *Concise Commentary on the Psalms* is forthcoming also, to be published online at The Gospel Coalition. Bruce tells the story of his life teaching and learning of the Psalms in his "Biblical Theology of the Psalms Today: A Personal Perspective."[1]

Bruce and I became acquainted when I was editing the Concise Bible Commentary Series for The Gospel Coalition and invited him to write the commentary on the Psalms. Our acquaintance since has been mutually enriching. When I was pursuing Psalms studies in preparation for my own preaching responsibilities, I began listening to his online lecture series at BiblicalTraining.org (also at BiblicalLearning.org), and after hearing only a few lectures I proposed this book project. I was delighted when he so eagerly agreed. I did all the writing, Bruce then combed through it all and gave further input, and so on the process went. The book is a joint effort based primarily on his lecture material,

1 Published in *The Psalms: Language for All Seasons of the Soul*, ed. Andrew J. Schmutzer and David M. Howard Jr. (Chicago: Moody Publishers, 2013), chap. 1.

but much more has been added.[2] We both take full responsibility for the accuracy of our book.

Preaching the Psalms is the frequent privilege and responsibility of pastors, and the Psalter is in many ways uniquely suited to enrich the hearts of God's people. Our goal in this book is to equip Christians to read the Psalms profitably. We have sought to keep the material at the lay level for wide accessibility, but our leading hope is that those who preach and teach the word of God will be equipped by this book to read, teach, and preach the Psalms with greater insight and confidence. To accomplish this we will address matters ranging from authorship and historical setting to psalm forms, Hebrew poetry, rhetorical techniques, the psalms' liturgical use in ancient Israel, and the final shape of the Psalter as we have it. We provide exposition and theology primarily as illustrative examples. Our aim is to enable the lay person as well as the preacher to "get behind" the Psalms, as it were, and into the minds of the psalmists to grasp how they themselves conceived their work and how they shaped and stated their message. If God will use this effort to enrich pastoral expositions of the Psalter and the spiritual life of its readers, we will be most grateful to him for it.

2 For extensive bibliography see J. Kenneth Kuntz, "Continuing the Engagement: Psalms Research Since the Early 1990s," *Currents in Biblical Research* 19 (2012): 321–78; William P. Brown, ed., *The Oxford Handbook of the Psalms* (Oxford: Oxford University Press, 2014); Beat Weber, "Bibliography of Psalms and the Psalter since 1990," Academia.edu (website), accessed September 27, 2022, https://www.academia.edu/5910732/BiblioPss1990ff_Bibliography_of_Psalms_and_the_Psalter_since_1990.

1

# Introduction to the Psalms

## The Psalms and the People of God

The book of Psalms is the most popular book of the Old Testament in both the Jewish community and the Christian community. The Psalter is the most represented corpus in the Qumran community also. In fact, the Psalms is a favorite of the biblical writers as well. Its language is taken up by later Old Testament writers, and it is the most frequently quoted Old Testament book in the New Testament. The Lord Jesus Christ probably memorized the book. He quoted it often—in his teaching ministry, in his debates with the Jewish leaders, in his final hours on the cross, and in his resurrection ministry to his apostles. And in all these scenarios he demonstrated that the Psalms spoke of him. The apostles cited the Psalms often, and as they had learned from their Master, they understood it as speaking of him. Quotations and allusions to the Psalms are found in every book of the New Testament, except 1 Thessalonians, Philemon, and 2–3 John—more than four hundred times total.[1] Most of these writers were not formally educated—they were not scribes—and yet they had such an instinctive grasp of the Psalter that they were able to use it adeptly and with keen exegetical insight and illuminating application in light of the person and work

1 See "Index of Quotations" and "Index of Allusions and Verbal Parallels" in Barbara Aland et al., eds., *The Greek New Testament*, 5th rev. ed. (New York: American Bible Society, 2014), 858–59, 871–74.

of Jesus. That these unlettered men—mostly fishermen—had this kind of knowledge astounded the scribes and the lawyers and the educated such that they asked, "Where did these men get this knowledge?" Of course, they had the advantage of divine inspiration, but in inspiring these men, the Holy Spirit used what was already there. It seems they had memorized these Scriptures. Most of them were "laymen" without a formal education who had spent their lives in the Psalms thoughtfully and piously, and because of that they could breathe the Psalms when they prayed and when they sang.

We see this in the book of Revelation. When John hears the angel singing, he hears the book of Psalms. Mary's Magnificat is another example. These early Christians clearly lived with the Psalms. Paul says in Romans 8:36, "We are regarded as sheep to be slaughtered"—that is Psalm 44:22. The New Testament writers held the Psalms close always—the Psalter was deeply a part of them.

This love of the Psalter continued in the early church of postapostolic times. "Early Christian schools, especially monastic schools, introduced young initiates to the study of Scripture through the psalms and selected New Testament texts. Once admitted to the monastery, the neophyte had to commit psalms to memory and recite them while performing his daily chores."[2] When Marco Polo (1254–1324) discovered "a certain manner of people" without Buddhist idols or Zoroastrian fire, they represented themselves with the book of Psalms and identified themselves as Christians; they numbered more than 700,000 families.[3] The book of Psalms was the first book printed on the Gutenberg press, and as the Bible came to be cast in the vernacular it became the most widely translated book in sixteenth- and seventeenth-century England. Today, Psalm 23 is probably the best-known text in the world. Still today, when the New Testament is published separately, the book of Psalms is often included with it. As Christian mission makes its advance, the book of Psalms is often one of the first books to be translated. It was the first for

2 Alan Cooper, "Some Aspects of Traditional Jewish Psalms Interpretation," in *The Oxford Handbook of the Psalms*, ed. William P. Brown (Oxford: Oxford University Press, 2014), 258.

3 Laurence Bergreen, *Marco Polo* (New York: Vintage, 2007), 231–32.

Jerome in his translating of the Bible into Latin, in what became known as the Vulgate.[4] For centuries, the church sang only the Psalms in their corporate meetings; and still today renditions of and references to the Psalms pervade our hymnals. Martin Luther's rendering of Psalm 46, "A Mighty Fortress Is Our God," is still used regularly in our churches, as is Isaac Watts's rendering of Psalm 72, "Jesus Shall Reign," the much beloved "Old One Hundredth," and of course Psalm 23 and others. The customary "call to worship" in our church meetings finds precedent in the Psalms, and, in fact, the Psalms are still routinely used for that purpose. The Psalter is the book we turn to in times of anxiety and grief and stress—and of blessing and joy. And in committing Scripture to memory, Christians today have probably memorized more verses from the Psalms than any other book—Psalm 1, Psalm 23, Psalm 46, Psalms 90–91, Psalm 100, Psalm 121, selections from Psalm 119, and Psalm 139, to name a few examples.

All this to say, with a fair amount of certainty, that the book of Psalms is the most popular Old Testament book within the Christian community, and it has been so for centuries. It is quite remarkable that songs and prayers written three thousand or so years ago are still in such demand and use today all over the world. We are privileged to be studying them, and as we do, we participate in a community and a long history of study and reflection.

## Approaching the Psalms

### *Title*

The Hebrew Bible provides no title to the book of Psalms. Old Testament books in the Hebrew text are sometimes named according to the first words of the book. For example, the title Genesis is "In the Beginning," and the title of Exodus is "These Are the Names." And the prophetic books are named after the prophet himself. But the book

4 Jerome actually made three translations of the Psalms: the first based on old Latin texts; the second on the Septuagint (the Gallican Psalter), which was memorized by the monks; and a third on the Hebrew text. The monks balked at rememorizing the third, and so the second, the Gallican Psalter, is used in the Vulgate.

of Psalms has no title in the Hebrew text. Psalm 72:20 may hint of an early collection of some of the Psalms when it says, "The prayers of David, the son of Jesse, are ended"—it may be that an early collection of psalms was named "The Prayers of David."[5]

The title of the book in Rabbinic and subsequent Hebrew literature is *Sepher Tehillim* (סֵפֶר תְּהִלִּים, "Book of Praises") or simply *Tehillim* ("Praises"). Although this word (in the singular) is used to title just one psalm (Ps. 145), its later use as a title for the book itself derives from its content—the book of Psalms is a book of praises. There are praise hymns, individual songs of grateful praise, and even the lament or complaint psalms are couched in praise. Each of the Psalms (except Ps. 88) contains expressions of praise, so this title is entirely appropriate. The Hebrew word for "psalm" (מִזְמוֹר) occurs dozens of times in the book (e.g., 3:1), and the Septuagint (Codex Vaticanus) picks this up in the plural as the title of the book—*Psalmoi* (ψαλμοῖ). In Codex Alexandrinus, the title given is *Psalterion* (an ancient stringed instrument), from which we have the name "Psalter." Then in Jerome's Latin Vulgate, it became *Libra Psalmorum*, "The Book of Psalms." So the English title, "The Book of Psalms," comes to us from the Greek through the Latin. The Hebrew word "psalm" denotes "a song sung to an instrumental accompaniment,"[6] but because the note of praise is so dominant in these psalms, the word has come to denote simply a song of praise, a sacred song, or a hymn.

### *The Psalms as Music*

The praises of the Psalms, then, were intended to be sung to musical accompaniment. They must be understood as poetry also, and we will examine this important aspect of our study in a later chapter. But

5 David C. Mitchell challenges this assumption vigorously in *The Message of the Psalter: An Eschatological Programme in the Book of Psalms* (Newton Mearns, Scotland: Campbell, 2003), chap. 2.

6 Sigmund Mowinckel, *Offersang og sangoffer; salmediktningen i Bibelen* 9 (Oslo: Aschehoug, 1951), 492; Delekat, *Zeitschrift für die alttestamentliche Wissenschaft*, 280, cited in Ludwig Koehler, Walter Baumgartner, and Johann J. Stamm, *The Hebrew and Aramaic Lexicon of the Old Testament*, 4 vols., trans. and ed. under the supervision of Mervyn E. J. Richardson (Leiden: Brill, 1994–1999), 566 (s.v. מִזְמוֹר).

we should be aware of the role of both in the psalter. The Psalms are prayers of petition and praise expressed in music and poetry. Music and poetry seem always to have been a chosen means of expressing the deep moving of the heart, and the Psalms are no exception. We will note this at times throughout this book, and the Psalter itself reminds us of its musical orientation with its frequent designation "To the choirmaster." As we will see, at least the majority of the Psalms were composed specifically for use in the temple to accompany the Mosaic ceremonies. The frequent "Selah" is probably another musical notation, perhaps to signal an interlude, although no one knows its precise meaning (some sixty definitions have been proposed!). Other musical designations appear in the superscripts also—although, again, the precise meanings of many have been lost to us. And many of the psalms themselves call for enthusiastic engagement in song and musical accompaniment.

We have all experienced the stimulating effects of music, both emotionally and intellectually. Music has an ability to inspire and enthuse the listener and performer, and music in David's time, as now, served the important function of attaching truth to emotion. Most of us who have had a long experience in the church have found that the great hymns we have sung have burrowed deep into our hearts such that, as needed, they arise in our memory with great spiritual power and with encouragement. Not just the words but the words set to music has a profound effect. So also with the Psalms. Both the laments and the joys of the Psalter were set to music to enhance their messages, and we do well to keep this musical atmosphere of the temple in mind as we read them.

### *The Psalter's "Five Books"*

We will address this important topic at some length in the final chapter, but it will be helpful to note up front that the Psalter, as we have it, is a final product. It is a "hymnbook" of one hundred and fifty psalms carefully arranged and divided by doxologies at the end of Psalms 41, 72, 89, and 106 into five "books":

Book 1: Psalms 1–41
Book 2: Psalms 42–72
Book 3: Psalms 73–89
Book 4: Psalms 90–106
Book 5: Psalms 107–150

Just briefly, for now, we should note that these five books represent the history of Israel from the united monarchy to the exile.

Books 1–2 are principally by David and represent the triumph of the king. Here very often David is in crisis, but his psalms usually end in praise.

Book 3 anticipates Israel's exile. This is known as the "dark book" of the Psalter. Here Israel's kings—the house of David—fail, and the sanctuary is destroyed. This book climaxes in Psalm 89 and its lament of the seeming collapse of the Davidic covenant.

Book 4 is oriented to Israel in exile. She has no king, but here the psalms fall back on God in trust that he is their king. Hope is still alive because God is Israel's eternal refuge.

Book 5 praises God for Israel's restoration and return from exile, and here praise is offered to him from among the nations.

## Studying and Understanding the Psalms

It is often pointed out that the Psalms reflect virtually every human emotion. They are "mirrors of the soul," as Calvin famously remarked.[7] This is a valuable observation, particularly in that in the Psalms we find these emotions as they are brought before the Lord. Our fears, our anger, our distress, our joy, our anxiety—in the Psalms we find how to bring these to God in prayer and in song. And because of this

7 J. A. De Jong, "'An Anatomy of All Parts of the Soul': Insights into Calvin's Spirituality from His Psalm Commentary," in *Calvinus Sacrae Scripturae Professor*, ed. W. H. Neuser (Grand Rapids, MI: Eerdmans, 1994), 121–41, cited in Bruce K. Waltke and James M. Houston, *The Psalms as Christian Worship: A Historical Commentary* (Grand Rapids, MI: Eerdmans, 2010), 64.

the Psalter is often seen as a sort of spiritual and emotional "pick-me-up." This is good, as far as it goes, and it explains in some measure the Psalms' popularity. But the message of the Psalms goes far deeper, addressing the entire range of human existence in its relationship to God, and we must seek in our reading of the Psalter to go beyond the emotional pick-me-up and uncover its message in its fullness for the metanarrative of the Bible and for our own spiritual lives.

The Book of Psalms is not only the Bible's most popular book. It is also one of the longest and most complex books, containing a collection of religious Hebrew poetry extending over a period of about one thousand years, from Moses (Ps. 90) to the exilic era (Ps. 137). It achieved its final shape before the time of the New Testament. The book of Psalms contains a variety of genres. Some psalms are prayers. Some are praises, both individual and community oriented. Some express praise for who God is and what he has done in the past and will do in the future. Others ("new songs") express praise for recent personal intervention and deliverance. And still others praise God for his self-revelation of his nature, for his saving deeds, for Torah, and for Zion. Some psalms, by contrast, lament or complain and cry out to God for help in current crises. Some psalms ask for God to destroy the enemy without mercy. Some psalms are marked by exuberant joy, and others are marked by deep soul anguish and suffering. Some are prayers, and some are prophecies. Some express robust trust in God's providential care. Some provide historical narrative. Some sing of Zion, the place of God's dwelling. Some are "didactic," teaching through meditating on the law, through historical narratives, or sounding like the books of Proverbs, Job, and Ecclesiastes. In some psalms the psalmist speaks to God; in others, he speaks of God to others. The Psalter consists of a wide array of genres indeed.

This present book attempts to enable better reading and understanding of these psalms in their own context as intended by their authors. It is one (wonderful) thing to read the Psalms quickly and hope to pick up a devotional gem along the way, but it is quite another to read with insight to the psalm's message. The complexities of the book of Psalms present unique challenges to interpretation, and even its poetry requires thoughtful reflection. The historical setting of the Psalms themselves is distant from ours, and even the (old covenant) religious setting differs considerably from ours. All this requires significant learning on our part to maximize our understanding.[8]

The attempt here is not a commentary, although there is quite a bit of that. The attempt is not to produce a biblical theology of the Psalter, although there is much of that also. The attempt here is something preliminary to all that. We want to enter the preunderstandings, the mind of the psalmists, as it were, and gain the proper lenses for reading the psalms so that we can interpret more faithfully, understand more precisely, develop our theology more firmly, and expound more fully. The concern here is with fundamentals of understanding and interpreting the Psalms. It is a truism: the meaning of a text cannot be known until it is known *how* it means, and so we explore just how the various psalms go about establishing their message. We want to understand how the various psalms "work"—how the psalmists structured them and how they intended them to be read and used. In brief, we want to find just how the psalmists go about conveying their message.

To accomplish this goal, we must learn to approach the Psalms from various angles simultaneously:

Chapter 1 introduces the Psalter in broad terms.
Chapter 2 sketches out the leading factors necessary for a responsible interpretation of the Psalter.
Chapter 3 examines the historical setting of the Psalms—specifically, the superscripts, the question of Davidic authorship.
Chapter 4 demonstrates the royal orientation of the Psalter, its focus on the Davidic king, which forms the ground of its messianic outlook.

8 For significant contributions to the study of Psalms in the last half century, see Willem A. VanGemeren, "Entering the Textual World of the Psalms: Literary Analysis," in *The Psalms: Language for All Seasons of the Soul*, ed. Andrew J. Schmutzer and David Howard Jr. (Chicago: Moody Publishers, 2013), 29–48.

Chapter 5 examines the liturgical setting of the psalms and their use in temple worship.

Chapter 6 examines the various poetic devices employed by the psalmists to convey their message. Here we consider how parallelism and imagery, for example, convey meaning.

Chapters 7–11 highlight "form criticism" and examine the various genres of psalms and their respective forms—hymns of praise, petition psalms, songs of grateful praise, and psalms of trust. Recognizing these forms is basic to understanding the psalmist's message.

Chapter 12 surveys how the Psalms point us to Christ.

Chapter 13 examines didactic psalms.

Chapter 14 examines how a text establishes its meaning through various rhetorical devices and conventions.

Chapter 15 examines how the book of Psalms was put together and considers the message of its ordering and final arrangement.

Our method to achieving our goal will be, first, to learn how to read the Psalms with these various lenses in place. Then, at each step, we will examine a variety of representative psalms with the new lenses and provide selected expositions. In each category we have arranged the selected psalms not in numerical order but according to their respective treatments. First we highlight some psalms briefly to demonstrate a given psalm form, and then we progress to "exceptional" cases and fuller expositions.

The words of the psalmists are by the Spirit's inspiration of the word of God to us. Combining these various interpretive approaches, and trusting the Spirit's illumination, we hope to gain a clear understanding of this ancient and beloved book—and then to internalize them and so increase our knowledge and love for the triune God who inspired them, and to grow in righteousness to his glory. In this way, it is hoped, our own sacrifice of praises and petitions to God will become ever more pleasing to him.

## PSALM 1

## WICKET GATE TO THE PSALTER

As we have noted, not all psalms are alike. There is a variety of psalm genres, and there are subvarieties also. One comparatively small but important group of psalms is the didactic psalms, psalms given to moral and ethical instruction directing God's people in faithful living before him. A subgroup is the Torah psalms, which commend the law as a source of authoritative instruction. We will examine this genre in a later chapter, but we meet a didactic-torah psalm immediately as we open the Psalter. Psalm 1 is not praise as such, and it is not petition. It is instruction to embrace the law for faithful living before God, and with this instruction, this opening psalm prepares the reader for entering the book of Psalms as a whole.

We do not know who wrote this psalm. All we know about him (as we will see) is that he is a covenant partner with the Lord God, that he treasures God's law, that he is an inspired sage, and that he is a literary artist.

1 Blessed is the man[9] who walks not in the counsel of the wicked
    nor stands in the way of sinners,
    nor sits in the seat of scoffers;
2 but his delight is in the law of the Lord,
    and on his law he meditates day and night.
3 He is like a tree
    planted by streams of water
that yields its fruit in its season,
    and its leaf does not wither.
In all that he does, he prospers.
4 The wicked are not so,
    but are like chaff that the wind drives away.
5 Therefore the wicked will not stand in the judgment,

9 Note that the Hebrew term for "man" here signifies a person, an individual within a social context, not a male in contrast to a female.

nor sinners in the congregation of the righteous;
6 for the LORD knows the way of the righteous,
but the way of the wicked will perish.[10]

**Structure**

Rhetorical criticism has to do with the logic of the psalm and how it is put together. This psalm may be structured in a number of ways. One approach is to highlight the way the psalm is "stitched" together by contrasting positive and negative ideas.

"Does not walk in step with the wicked" (1:1)
versus "His delight is in the law of the LORD" (1:2).

"He is like a tree" (1:3)
versus "The wicked . . . / are like chaff" (1:4).

"The way of the righteous"
versus "the way of the wicked" (1:6).

"The LORD knows the way of the righteous"
versus "the way of the wicked will perish" (1:6).

Or this psalm may be structured in two halves, based on the two "ways":

The way of the righteous (1:1–3)
The way of the wicked (1:4–6)

**Survey Exposition**[11]

The psalm begins similarly to Jesus's "Beatitudes" (Matt. 5:3–12). It pronounces the blessedness of the person who is devoted to the LORD's law. It has become popular to translate the word "blessed" (אַשְׁרֵי) as

10 In some places throughout this book, poetry line breaks in the ESV have been altered to better reflect the original language and meaning of the psalm at hand.

11 See also Waltke and Houston, *Psalms as Christian Worship*, chap. 4.

- "happy," but this is inadequate and relatively trite. God's "blessing" ultimately results in happiness, but the two concepts are not the same. We probably do not have an exact equivalent for this word in English. The Hebrew word usually refers to the future and indicates a blessed destiny based on your relationship with God and his favor. In Job 5:17–18, for example, we read,

> blessed is the one whom God reproves; therefore despise not
> the discipline of the Almighty.
> For he wounds, but he binds up; he shatters, but his hands heal.

The idea is that you will have a blessed future, favored by God. This sense is conveyed in the New Testament in the Beatitudes of Jesus in Matthew 5. The "blessed" (μακάριος) person may be one who mourns and suffers and is persecuted or even put to death, but he is "blessed" nonetheless. The "blessed" person is one who is favored by God for being faithful to him; rather than cursed, he will be rewarded. "Happy" fails to capture this sense, but in English we have no exact equivalent. Perhaps "How rewarding" or "How favored" would come closest.

So the Psalter opens with the prospect of divine favor—surely the highest hope any person could entertain. Psalm 1:1–2 describes the reason for that blessedness, explaining in terms of this person's behavior and ideals. The blessed person is one "who walks not in the counsel of the wicked, / nor stands in the way of sinners, / nor sits in the seat of scoffers" (1:1), but rather "delights" in and "meditates" on "the law of the LORD" (1:2). The metaphor of the two divergent "ways" dominates this psalm, as it does the book of Proverbs. "The way" in 1:1 and 1:6 brackets Psalm 1 (an *inclusio*), and by this metaphor life is pictured as a journey—a common figure in both Psalms and Proverbs. "Way" connotes the context, conduct, and consequences of a particular direction taken in life, and this psalm stresses that the "way" of the righteous differs from the "way" of the wicked in these respects.

In 1:1, the expression "stand in the way of sinners" presents a challenge in translation. To "stand in the way" frequently means to obstruct or oppose. Those of us who grew up in the church are so familiar with Psalm 1:1 that we scarcely notice that this can be—and in fact often is—confusing to the new convert reading the psalm. Many have taken "does not stand in the way of sinners" to mean "does not interfere" with sinners in their course of sin. To avoid this confusion, the NIV translates it as "does not . . . stand in the way that sinners take," adding the idea of "take" to clarify. That is, the blessed person is the one who does not "go the same way" as sinners. Nor does he heed the counsel of the wicked or give ear to those who scoff at divine wisdom.

As commentators commonly observe, 1:1 reflects a sense of progression, a hardening in sin on several levels:

- The nouns "counsel . . . way . . . seat" moves from sinful advice to sinful behavior and then to settled association with sin.
- "Wicked . . . sinners . . . scoffers" likewise moves from "wicked," a broad term for those who violate God's law and incur guilt, to "sinners," a term for criminals, and then to "scoffers," who mock the teachings of Scripture.
- The verbs slow down, as it were, from "walking" to "standing" and finally to "sitting," indicating again a progressive hardening in sin.

Together this well-ordered terminology reflects "a gradual descent into evil, in which one first walks alongside, then stops, and ultimately takes up permanent residence in the company of the wicked.[12] James Smith explains,

> Sin takes a downward course. Adoption of the principles of the wicked ("walked in the counsel of wicked men") leads to persistence in the practices of notorious offenders ("stood in the way of sinners").

12 Gerald H. Wilson, *Psalms Volume 1*, The NIV Application Commentary (Grand Rapids, MI: Zondervan, 2002), 94.

> This in turn leads to deliberate association with those who openly mock at faith ("sit in the seat of the scorners.").[13]

The blessed person does not think like the wicked, behave like the wicked, or take part in wickedness in any way. He or she will not take one step onto this slippery "way" to destruction. The "blessed" person takes a different route in life entirely, pursuing the way directed by "the law of the LORD" (1:2). "Law" here is *Torah*, which in the book of Psalms invariably refers to the Mosaic Law and essentially connotes catechetical instruction, not the "commanding" aspects of the law only but the law's entire direction for living. It is instruction for living. It has to do with a way of life, the way you live because you believe God has redeemed you. The psalmist insists that the "blessed" person is the one who lives by God's direction and is not influenced by the ungodly.

Those who are blessed "delight" in this divine instruction (1:2a). They do not merely conform outwardly. They understand the value of God's revealed will and prize it accordingly, with zeal and affection. It is not a drudgery but a joy to live by divine instruction—they find it rewarding. Thus, they "meditate" on it continuously (1:2b). This is not the meditation of mysticism in search of inner lights. It is careful, prolonged contemplation, poring over the Scriptures eagerly to know God in his self-revelation and to live unto him faithfully. Implicit is the idea of trust: the blessed are those who trust God's direction for life; convinced that this instruction is best, they entrust their lives to it.[14] Obedience, therefore, is not begrudging but joyful and confident. A regenerate heart is obviously presupposed. This person is "righteous" (1:6) and has godly appetites. This is not legalism but childlike dependence upon God in recognition of his law's ideal. And by extension we must of course understand this in terms of the believer's delight in all the word of God, climaxing in the supreme revelation of God in Christ. This is what distinguishes the righteous from the wicked—their

13 James E. Smith, *The Wisdom Literature and Psalms* (Joplin, MO: College Press, 1996), 216.

14 James L. Mays, *Psalms*, Interpretation: A Commentary for Teaching and Preaching (Louisville: John Knox, 1994), 42.

attitude toward and response to God's word. The righteous recognize God's wisdom and authority, and so they approach his word worshipfully and submit to it gratefully. This entails both the negative and the positive: the godly will not follow the way of sin but will delightfully pursue the way of God's word. The wicked think they will find joy in the pursuit of sin. The righteous know better: they understand the value of God's word and so are eager to know it and be shaped by it. Thus they "meditate" on it continuously, "day and night." They pay attention to it and accept it and prayerfully seek by God's enabling grace to live by it.

Psalm 1:3–4 draws out the contrast between the wicked and the righteous, a contrast already implicit in 1:1–2. The wicked delight in the way of sin and devote themselves to it. Those who are blessed reject the way of sin and love the way of righteousness; they value and delight in God's instruction for life, devote themselves to it, and seek to live accordingly.

As a consequence of this delighted reception of God's word, the godly person "is like a tree / planted by streams of water / that yields its fruit in its season, / and its leaf does not wither. / In all that he does, he prospers" (1:3). The picture is that of a tree transplanted (שָׁתַל) and placed next to an irrigation channel (פֶּלֶג) where it receives continuous nourishment and so is strong, is stable, and produces fruit (cf. Ps. 92:12–15; Jer. 17:5–8). The metaphor points us to the word of God as nourishing and invigorating. Like a tree by a canal, the blessed person is well nourished, stable, and fruitful (cf. John 15:1–6), enjoying eternal life here and now. This person who pursues God's law and who is nourished by it "prospers" and succeeds in life under God (Ps. 1:3; cf. Josh. 1:8).

The "blessed" person of the first stanza is the "righteous" person of the second (Ps. 1:5–6) and here stands in contrast to the "wicked." The psalmist does not describe the wicked with the same detail as it does the righteous, but he does set them in stark contrast: The wicked are "not so" (1:4). This contrast reaches back to 1:1–3. The righteous treasures God's law and is faithful to it; the wicked do not treasure it and, in fact, oppose it. They are "wicked." Nor do the wicked have a fruitful, stable existence, as the righteous do; rather, they are unstable, worthless, and fleeting—"like chaff that the wind drives away." Artur Weiser comments perceptively that

> in the opinion of the poet the life of the wicked, a life lived apart from God, is just as empty, just as meaningless and worthless as the chaff. To anyone holding such a view God means indeed everything, and everything else which life could offer in other respects and which from the human point of view might be a matter of temptation is nothing in comparison with it.[15]

The self-directed life is indeed chaff-like and worthless, as the book of Ecclesiastes argues at length. This is likely entailed in the psalmist's imagery. But what his simile ultimately signifies ("therefore," Ps. 1:5) is that in the final judgment: "the wicked will not stand [their ground]" or "pass muster,"[16] or have part "in the assembly of the righteous." Like worthless chaff that is blown away, the wicked will not endure judgment (1:4, 6). Unlike Psalm 73, this psalm turns a blind eye to the present prosperity of the wicked; it looks only at the end of the way, how it turns out. The righteous and the wicked come to two very different ends, and the difference turns on their response to God's word. Here, along with 1:6, the psalm links to a prominent theme of Scripture—that of eschatological judgment. The climactic establishing of the kingdom of God will be marked by the final blessedness of the righteous and destruction of the wicked (cf. Dan. 12:2; Matt. 3:11–12; 7:13–27; 24:37–41; 25:13–46; 2 Thess. 1:5–10; Rev. 19–22).

Many have observed further hints of an eschatological perspective here. The "judgment" and "perish[ing]" in view (Ps. 1:5–6) is certainly, at least ultimately, eschatological, and "chaff" is a familiar

15 Artur Weiser, *The Psalms: A Commentary*, The Old Testament Library (Philadelphia: Westminster, 1962), 106.

16 A. H. McNeile, *The Psalms*, vol. 1 of *A New Commentary on Holy Scripture*, ed. C. Gore, H. L. Goudge, and A. Guillaume (New York: Macmillan, 1942), 345.

symbol employed in that context (cf. Matt. 3:11–12; 7:21–27). The precise language of the Edenic allusions of Ps. 1:3 is taken up in Ezekiel's vision of the eschatological temple (Ezek. 47:12). So also the "new creation" connotations of the well-nourished tree planted by the water (cf. Ps. 92:13–14; Isa. 30:25; 32:2; Ezek. 17:1–23; 19:10, 13; 47). "Transplanted upon [עַל] rivers of waters" (Ps. 1:3, authors' translation) may echo in Ps. 2:7, the king enthroned "upon Zion." This considered, the "it shall come to pass" (1:3, וְהָיָה) just may have eschatological overtones.[17]

Psalm 1:6 summarizes. On the one hand, "the LORD knows the way of the righteous." To "know" in Scripture often signifies knowing with favor (cf. Ps. 31:7; 37:18; Amos 3:2; Matt. 7:23; Rom. 11:2; 2 Tim. 2:19), and that is plainly its connotation here. The righteous person, the one who treasures God's word, enjoys God's favor, and will have a sure standing in judgment. The righteous are "blessed"—God regards them with favor and watches over them accordingly. And so in the day of judgment they will "stand." "But the way of the wicked will perish" (Ps. 1:6)—they will end in ruin (cf. 2:10–12). God does not "know" them.

This psalm is one of sustained contrast between the righteous and the wicked, and the difference between them is graphically portrayed in the first and last words: "Blessed . . . perish." The two ways differ greatly in life and in death, in time and for eternity. "So the two ways, and there is no third, part for ever."[18]

We may outline the psalm as follows:

I. The two ways (1:1–2)
II. The two ways pictured (1:3–4)
III. The two ends (1:5–6)

17 See Robert L. Cole, "Psalms 1–2: The Psalter's Introduction," in Schmutzer and Howard, *The Psalms*, 189–92. See also James M. Hamilton Jr., *Psalms*, vol. 1, Evangelical Biblical Theology Commentary (Bellingham, WA: Lexham Academic, 2021), 94–96.

18 Derek Kidner, *Psalms 1–72*, Tyndale Old Testament Commentaries (London: Inter-Varsity Press, 1973), 66.

## Psalm 1 in the Psalter

The instruction of Psalm 1 opens the Psalter and prepares the reader for entering. It also identifies those for whom the Psalter is intended—the righteous. The Psalter is for those pronounced "blessed," who refuse the way of sin and devote themselves to divine revelation. God does not want the feigned worship of the wicked—he despises it and finds it repugnant. He accepts only the worship of the righteous, those who honor him with their life as well as their lips. Since the days of the early church, Christian have recognized that Psalm 1 functions as a gateway to the Psalter—the way in. In his masterful allegory, *Pilgrim's Progress*, John Bunyan presents one Pilgrim fleeing from the City of Destruction. This pilgrim realizes that the city is doomed, and he wants to escape. And he soon learns that he has to go through the wicket gate to enter the road to the Celestial City. If he will not go through the gate, then he must return to the City of Destruction. There is no third way. That is how Psalm 1 functions in the Psalter. There is no third way. We either enter as "the righteous" that Psalm 1 describes or we have no place in the book of Psalms at all. "Psalm 1 stands like a Levitical gatekeeper, warning the wicked to proceed no further."[19] "Just as one must reject profane and wicked conduct to enter a holy area (cf. Isa. 55 and Prov. 9:1–6), so one must reject wicked companions to pray the sacred psalms."[20]

The Psalter therefore begins by declaring that godliness is essential to worship. God does not want worship from unclean people (cf. Ps. 24:3–4). Such "worship" would be abominable to him. Obedience is required. Nor are these didactic psalms concerned with mere external adherence to the law (legalism); they are concerned with a heart for God and a dependence upon him to live faithfully.

In a later chapter we will examine Psalm 2, a psalm of the messianic King. But we should note here that along with Psalm 1, Psalm 2 completes the "gateway" to the Psalter. There are significant verbal links between

19 Tremper Longman III, *Psalms: An Introduction and Commentary*, Tyndale Old Testament Commentaries (Downers Grove, IL: IVP Academic, 2014), 55.

20 Richard J. Clifford, *Psalms 1–72*, Abington Old Testament Commentaries (Nashville: Abingdon, 2002), 41.

Psalm 1 and Psalm 2 that together indicate that these two psalms were intended by the final editors of the Psalter to be together. For example, Psalm 1 begins by pronouncing "blessed" (אַשְׁרֵי) the person who adheres to God's law; Psalm 2 ends with the same pronouncement regarding those who submit willingly to his rule (2:12). Psalm 1:1 warns of the "seat" (מוֹשָׁב) of the mockers; Psalm 2:4 reassures us that God is "seated" on his throne. In 1:2 the blessed man "meditates" (הָגָה) on the law of the Lord; in 2:1 the nations "plot" their vain rebellion. Both psalms employ words for mocking: in Psalm 1 the wicked mock the righteous, and in Psalm 2 God mocks the wicked. The key word "way" of Psalm 1 (דֶּרֶךְ, 1:1, 6) concludes Psalm 2 also (2:12). The warning that the wicked will "perish" (אָבַד) concludes both psalms (1:6; 2:12). The wicked in Psalm 1 who reject God's law and therefore "perish" are the ones who in Psalm 2 oppose God's King and so will be destroyed by him. The wicked who reject God's law in Psalm 1 are the "heathen" (KJV), rebellious nations, of Psalm 2 who rage and conspire against God and his king. Psalm 1 is about the law, and Psalm 2 is prophecy—law and prophecy, the twin "foci around which the whole of the Old Testament moves."[21] Psalm 1 directs the reader to a right attitude toward the law, and Psalm 2 "gives the essence of prophecy."[22] These verbal and conceptual links indicate an intended unity of these two psalms that together form an introduction or gateway to the Psalter.[23]

The parallels go further. Psalm 1 counsels regarding morals and righteousness, describing the kind of person who may enter and profit from the Psalter. Psalm 2, a psalm of the great King, presents us with the subject and hero of the Psalter who is celebrated throughout. Put more simply, Psalm 1 tells us *for whom* the Psalter is intended (the righteous), and Psalm 2 tells us *about whom* it speaks (the King). "While Psalm 1 provides us with insight into the purpose of the book of Psalms

21 W. Graham Scroggie, *The Psalms* (Ada, MI: Revell, 1978), 48.

22 H. C. Leupold, *Exposition of the Psalms* (Grand Rapids, MI: Baker, 1969), 31.

23 Some early manuscripts of Acts 13:33 identify our Ps. 2 as "the first psalm." Metzger here summarizes impressive evidence that the editors intended for Pss. 1–2 to form a unit. See Bruce Metzger, *Textual Commentary on the New Testament*, 2nd ed. (New York: American Bible Society, 1994), 363–64.

[instruction in the law of the LORD], Psalm 2 provides us a window on the message of the whole" (the Lord's reign).[24] The Psalter, like the rest of the Bible, is principally concerned with the establishing of God's kingdom in the earth through his appointed King, the Lord Jesus Christ. So we might say that if Psalm 2 tells us of the King's foreign policy, then Psalm 1 provides his domestic policy, describing his kingdom ideals. And if Psalm 2 presents the King in his royal rule, Psalm 1 presents his character. Psalm 1:3 makes unmistakable allusion to Joshua 1:8, only with the obvious difference that Joshua's prosperity and success is conditional, while that of the blessed man of Psalm 1:3 is certain.[25] In this way the "prosperous" man of Psalm 1:3 is parallel to the one in Psalm 2 who is enthroned and brings God's kingdom to full realization.

These observations seem to indicate clearly that these two psalms, though independent, were brought together by the final editors to open the door and provide entrance to the Psalter as a whole. They have a uniform message—the pious and righteous are fully rewarded, and in the time of judgment they triumph over the wicked in the presence of the king.[26]

Moreover, these two psalms set a trajectory that continues through the Psalms and the entire biblical canon. Psalm 1 may resonate with the redeemed heart and excite joy by its ideal and love for God's word: this is what God's will done on earth as in heaven looks like! Yet this idealized portrait of the righteous person may also arouse feelings of guilt for our failures to live up to that ideal. This psalm indeed presses its ideal on us, and it is the mark of God's people that we make it our goal. Yet it is a goal that not one of us attains—not David, not Moses, not Abraham.

Ultimately, in the larger flow of Scripture and even within the Psalter itself, Psalm 1 points us to another Joshua who delights and meditates

24 Mark D. Futato, *Interpreting the Psalms: An Exegetical Handbook*, Handbooks for Old Testament Exegesis (Grand Rapids, MI: Kregel, 2007), 59.

25 Cole, "Psalms 1–2," 190. Cf. Hamilton, *Psalms*, 96.

26 See Bruce K. Waltke, *An Old Testament Theology: An Exegetical, Canonical, and Thematic Approach* (Grand Rapids, MI: Zondervan, 2007), 884–85.

on God's law (1:2–3; cf. Josh. 1:8) and therefore leads the people of God aright.[27] Psalm 1 introduces us to the great King of Psalm 2 who as our representative and as the very embodiment of the righteous person of Psalm 1 ascends the hill of the LORD with "clean hands and a pure heart" (24:3–4)—the one who steadfastly refused the counsel of the wicked (Matt. 4:1–11), the one who (unlike King Saul; 1 Sam. 15:22–23) delighted in the law of the Lord supremely (Matt. 3:17; John 4:34) and followed it perfectly (John 8:44), the one who took our sin to himself and became for us all the righteousness God requires of us (1 Cor. 1:30; 2 Cor. 5:21), the one who by his Spirit writes God's law on our hearts (Jer. 31:31–34) and enables us to bear fruit unto God (John 15:1–6; 17:17), and the one who shares his glorious reign with all those who submit to his rule and take refuge in him (Ps. 2:10–12).

27 Patrick D. Miller, *Interpreting the Psalms* (Philadelphia: Fortress, 1986), 84.

2

# Hermeneutics

## Interpreting the Psalms as Believers

*"Open my eyes, that I may behold*
*wondrous things out of your law!"*

WHAT IS REQUIRED of us to understand the Psalter and gain spiritual profit from it? How can we enter the mind of the authors and the text itself so as to grasp its intended meaning and benefit from its message?

A right understanding of any object of study demands that we seek to understand it on its own terms. So also an understanding of the Psalter (and of the Bible itself) hinges on an understanding of its authors and a certain sympathy with them. Our precommitments and theirs must coincide. "The fear of the LORD is the beginning of wisdom" (Ps. 111:10; Prov. 9:10) and of knowledge (Prov. 1:7); this attitude and positioning of ourselves before God presupposes regeneration. Moreover, Scripture insists that divine illumination is necessary for understanding (1 Cor. 2:11–14). So the interpretive process hinges on the working of God in us. And yet Scripture also requires diligent study (2 Tim. 2:15; cf. Acts 17:11). Understanding is sovereignly given, but not apart from concentrated effort on our part. How does all of this work out in experience and practice?

A consideration of the two leading biblical statements on the nature of Scripture provides a helpful frame of reference. In 2 Timothy 3:16, the apostle Paul affirms *that* "all Scripture is breathed out by God"—the text is inspired of God. Then in 2 Peter 1:20–21 the apostle Peter tells us *how* the inspired Scriptures came about: "no prophecy was ever produced by the will of man, but men spoke from God as they were carried along by the Holy Spirit." These verses affirm that God is the ultimate author of Scripture and that it came to us through the writings of inspired human authors, and they underline the inspiration of both the biblical writers and the biblical text itself. To interpret Scripture rightly we must have a sympathetic understanding of God, the divine author, the human authors, and the text itself.[1]

### Scripture's Divine and Human Authors

That Scripture is the word of God through human authors is the Bible's claim throughout. The famous summary statements of 2 Timothy 3:16 and 2 Peter 1:19–21 are just that—crisp and definitive summary statements of what the biblical writers unanimously assert, from the characteristic "Thus says the LORD" of the prophets to the designation of their writings as "Scripture," "oracle," "law," and "word of the LORD." This is no less true of the Psalms and of David in particular.

> 1 Now these are the last words of David:
>
> The oracle of David, the son of Jesse,
> the oracle of the man who was raised on high,
> the anointed of the God of Jacob,
>     the sweet psalmist of Israel:
> 2 "The Spirit of the LORD speaks by me;
>     his word is on my tongue.

1 See also Bruce K. Waltke, *An Old Testament Theology: An Exegetical, Canonical, and Thematic Approach* (Grand Rapids, MI: Zondervan, 2007), chap. 3.

> The God of Israel has spoken;
> the Rock of Israel has said to me." (2 Sam. 23:1–3)

Two assertions here are important for our purposes:

1. David was Israel's premier psalmist: "the sweet psalmist of Israel."
2. David was an inspired spokesman for God: "The Spirit of the LORD speaks by me; his word is on my tongue."

This second assertion is emphasized in two ways: it is a claim that David himself makes plainly (22:2–3), and it is how the narrator characterizes David's words: "oracle" (23:1). This word (נְאֻם), used twice here, refers to prophetic speech, words spoken by God's Spirit through his spokesman, the prophet. That is, "oracle" is "prophetic" speech. David's words recorded here (22:2–7) are in fact not his last words spoken (cf. 1 Kings. 1–2) but his final prophetic oracle.

Jesus and the New Testament writers understood David's words as inspired also:

- David spoke "in the Spirit" (Matt. 22:43–44, citing Ps. 110:1).
- The Holy Spirit spoke through David (Acts 1:16, citing Ps. 69:25 and 109:8; also Acts 4:25, citing Ps. 2:1).
- David was a "prophet" (Acts 2:30, citing Ps. 16:9–11).
- David's words are "Scripture" (Mark 12:10, citing Ps. 118:22; John 13:18, citing Ps. 41:9; John 19:24, citing Ps. 22:18; cf. Luke 24:44–45).
- David's word was authoritative divine "law" (John 10:34–35, citing Ps. 82:6).

Just as Scripture comes to us from God, so also our understanding of it depends on his enablement (1 Cor. 2:11–14). That is to say, "The Holy Spirit, Scripture's divine Author, both authenticates it to us by His inward witness and opens our minds to understand its meaning."[2] This is the divine side in the interpretive process.

Moreover, God's revelation cannot be received apart from a spiritual commitment to him in faith, hope, and love. The doctrine of illumination entails the responsibility on our part to read Scripture "in a spirit that is harmonious with God's Spirit," and it "demands that we stand under the text to respond in service to its Author, not to stand in judgment above it in order to critique the text."[3] Anselm's "faith seeking understanding"[4] has long been the recognized dictum of Christian theologians, so also Augustine's famous "I believe, in order to understand."[5] As a result of Enlightenment thinking, this spiritual dimension of interpretation was deemed incompatible with the scientific method of interpreting of Scripture. Prayer and piety had no role. But if God is God, and if he is, in fact, the ultimate author of Scripture, then a commitment to him in submissive trust is indispensable. "The Holy Scriptures call us to surrender our wills to its claims" and approach "with open hands of faith."[6] A lack of devotion obstructs understanding. "The fear of God" is the foundation of all learning, not least in understanding his word. For this we are dependent upon God's initiative and work in us, but it correspondingly requires that we commit to him in trust as is appropriate to him. We must come to Scripture prayerfully and in trust. "Open my eyes, that I may behold / wondrous things out of your law" (Ps. 119:18). David Steinmetz writes,

> Scripture is not in our power. It is not at the disposal of our intellect and is not obliged to render up its secrets to those who have theologi-

2 "The Chicago Statement on Biblical Inerrancy," Short Statement 3 (1987), https://www.etsjets.org/files/documents/Chicago_Statement.pdf.

3 Waltke, *Old Testament Theology*, 81, 82.

4 "Saint Anselm," *Stanford Encyclopedia of Philosophy* (website), May 18, 2000; rev. December 8, 2020, https://plato.stanford.edu/index.html.

5 Quoted in Tom Hoopes, "'I Believe in order to Understand': *Fides et Ratio*, Chap. 2," *Ex Corde* (website), May 7, 2017, https://excorde.org/.

6 Bruce K. Waltke, *The Dance between God and Humanity: Reading the Bible Today as the People of God* (Grand Rapids, MI: Eerdmans, 2013), 184.

cal training, merely because they are learned. Scripture imposes its own meaning; it binds the soul to God through faith. Because the initiative in the interpretation of Scripture remains in the hands of God, we must humble ourselves in His presence and pray that He will give understanding and wisdom to us as we meditate on the sacred text. While we may take courage from the thought that God gives understanding of Scripture to the humble, we should also heed the warning that the truth of God can never coexist with human pride. Humility is the hermeneutical precondition for authentic exegesis.[7]

An understanding of the inspired human authors likewise requires a distinct sympathy with them. Advanced learning should not be neglected, but to understand the biblical authors rightly we cannot stand above them as their judges but must position ourselves sympathetically as their students and disciples. We must enter the world and context of these writers, understanding their setting, their covenantal context, their faith in the God of those covenants, and share with them in it all. Apart from this established fellowship with them in a common faith we will err in our interpretation of their writings. Even in the case of those biblical passages—like many of the Psalms—whose human authors are not specifically identified, we may be sure they were written "for our instruction" (1 Cor. 10:11; cf. 1 Tim. 3:15–17; Heb. 12:5).

Patrick Fairbairn's discussion of this point merits citing at length.

> *He* [the interpreter] *must endeavour to attain to a sympathy in thought and feeling with the sacred writers, whose meaning he seeks to unfold.* Such a sympathy is not required for the interpretation alone of the inspired writings; it is equally necessary in respect to any ancient author. Language is but the utterance of thought and feeling of one person to another, and the more we can identify ourselves with the state of mind out of which that thought and feeling arose, the more manifestly

7 David C. Steinmetz, "Luther as an Interpreter of the Bible," in *Archiv für Reformationgeschichte* 70 (Beiheft: Literaturbericht, 1973), 71.

shall we be qualified for appreciating the language in which they are embodied, and reproducing true and living impressions of it. . . .

Not a few of them [interpreters] have given proof of superior talents, and have brought to the task also the acquirements of a profound and varied scholarship. The lexicography and grammar, the philology and archaeology of Scripture, have been largely indebted to their inquiries and researches; but, from the grievous mental discrepancy existing between the commentator and his author, and the different points of view from which they respectively looked at Divine things, writers of this class necessarily failed to penetrate the depths of the subjects they had to handle, fell often into jejune and superficial representations on particular parts, and on entire books of Scripture never once succeeded in producing a really satisfactory exposition. . . .

Hence it is laid down as a fundamental point by a distinguished German theologian—by Hagenbach in his Encyclopedia, that "An inward interest in the doctrine of theology is needful for a Biblical interpreter. As we say, that a philosophical spirit is demanded for the study of Plato, a political taste for the reading of Homer or Pindar, a sensibility to wit and satire for the perusal of Lucian, a patriotic sentiment for the enjoyment of Sallust and Tacitus, equally certain is it, that the fitness to understand the profound truths of Scripture, of the New Testament sentiment of piety, an inward religious experience."[8]

### Understanding the Biblical Text

Until we approach the Scripture with a sense of humble devotion to the God who gave it, we will miss the depths of its message. But with these pre-understandings in place, we are ready to do the work of studying the text. "We must approach our hymnbook as both scientist and saint."[9]

8 Patrick Fairbairn, *Hermeneutical Manual; or, Introduction to the Exegetical Study of Scriptures of the New Testament* (Edinburgh: T. & T. Clark, 1858), 63–66; emphasis original. Cited in Waltke, *Old Testament Theology*, 84–85.

9 Waltke, *Dance between God and Humanity*, 186.

We must resolve to do the hard work of "the scientific method" in the context of "faith seeking understanding." A learning of the Scriptures—and of the Psalms in particular—does not come by prayer alone but requires thoughtful study of the text. We come to the text humbly, for it is the word of God, and yet we come determined to apply all the tools of learning at our disposal—objectively, yet believingly.

In this book, we will emphasize the need to uncover the historical setting of the Psalms—their authors, their original settings and liturgical use, their poetry, their literary genres and corresponding structures, their final arrangement, and their overall orientation and theme. We will examine words, phrases, lines/versets, verses, strophes, stanzas, whole psalms, various collections of psalms, their place in the flow of progressive revelation, and ultimately their place in the canon. All this requires intellectual diligence on our part, and it is all necessary to ascertain the intended meaning of the Psalms. We want, as far as we are able, to enter the mind of the psalmists as they wrote their psalms in order to ascertain their meanings.

**Perspectives**

All this pertains to both our spirit of approach to the Psalms and our devotion to intellectual rigor. That intellectual rigor entails maintaining other perspectives that we will be considering in the following chapters: the historical (chapter 3), the royal (chapter 4), the liturgical (chapter 5), the poetic (chapter 6), the form-critical (chapters 7–13), the rhetorical (chapter 14), the editorial (chapter 15), and the canonical (appendix 2). Here we highlight three perspectives that were not recognized until recently. First, the "editorial" perspective that takes note of the place of individual psalms within the Psalter. That is, we must seek to ascertain the perspective of the editors of the Psalter and the placement and arrangement of the individual psalms in the Psalter's final form. The Psalter tells a story. This story or message and the individual psalms that tell it are mutually informing. We will note this at points throughout this book, but the subject requires a discussion of its own that we take it up in chapter 15. We mention it here as a heads-up.

Next, the "royal" perspective recognizes the Psalter's extensive focus on the king, not just in those psalms that mention the king. The prominence in the Psalter of David, the Davidic kings, and God's "anointed," reminds us continually that the Psalms have a distinct royal orientation. In the Psalms we encounter God's king throughout, and we must be careful to keep him in mind. "The human subject in most of the psalms is the king/King, and we shall never enter fully into rich devotional material until we realize this."[10] We will develop this further in chapter 4 and throughout the book, but we note in this context that a vital aspect of a right understanding the Psalms is a recognition of their royal subject. The "I" and "me" of the Psalms is not Mr. Everyman; pervasively, it is the king. To interpret the Psalms as though the point of reference is us or any pious Israelite is to miss the point.

Finally, the "canonical" perspective seeks to read the Psalms within the perspective of the full biblical canon. The Davidic king in view throughout the Psalter foreshadows the great King, the Lord Jesus Christ. We have it on his word that the Psalms were written about him (Luke 24:44), and so we must look to see just how this is so. To read the Psalms otherwise is to misunderstand them and miss the benefit of an acquaintance with our Lord that is intended for us there. We have it on his authority that the great King in view in the Psalter is both David's son and David's Lord (Matt. 22:41–45), a puzzle that finds resolution only in Jesus Christ himself, the incarnate Son of God. And so following our Lord's lead we will pursue our study of the Psalms to find just how the Davidic king anticipates the Messiah (see chapter 12). And we will do this to learn how Israel's royal hymnbook becomes the church's hymnbook to guide us in singing of Christ. This effort demands thorough, thoughtful, and careful scrutiny of the text, yet we do it as faithful disciples in the joyful expectation that God will, in grace, open our eyes so that we may behold wondrous things in his law (Ps. 119:18).[11]

10 Waltke, *Dance between God and Humanity*, 186.

11 See also appendix 2.

## Summary

To interpret the Psalms in an accredited way, we come as believers humbly receiving God's word to us and prayerfully seeking enlightenment from him. We read thoughtfully, applying every intellectual and academic resource to determine the meaning of the authors within the Psalter itself and within the larger biblical canon. We remain aware of the Psalms' orientation to the Davidic king and, in turn, their anticipation of Christ. And with this approach we trust God to give us understanding.

3

# The Historical Setting of the Psalms

*"A Psalm of David"*

LIKE ANY PIECE OF LITERATURE the Bible must be understood in light of its own historical context, and for the study of the Psalms this discussion focuses on the superscripts (headings) that appear at the top of individual psalms—in particular, the expression "of David" that appears above seventy-three of them and the fourteen (3; 7; 18; 30; 34; 51; 52; 54; 56; 57; 59; 60; 63; 142) that link these psalms to specific incidents in David's life as recorded in the books of Samuel and Chronicles. Traditionally the superscripts were taken at face value, but only until historical criticism came to dominate Old Testament studies in the nineteenth century.[1] "Historical criticism" is grounded in a skepticism toward the historical reliability of Scripture, including its own claims to authorship, as we will discuss in chapter 7, and it has become so pervasively accepted that it is difficult to find in academic studies today any acknowledgment of the Davidic background to the Psalter. This skepticism is not

1 See Bruce K. Waltke and James M. Houston, *The Psalms as Christian Worship: A Historical Commentary* (Grand Rapids, MI: Eerdmans, 2010), 79.

uncommon among even evangelical scholars. And in Bible publication the superscripts are routinely printed in italics, inevitably leaving the impression that they are not part of the original text. This against all textual evidence, for no ancient manuscript lacks these superscripts.

Much is at stake in the discussion, and we will touch on these issues here. But our specific interest is the reliability of the historical background that these superscripts provide, apart from which we would often be left without context, and the Davidic-royal orientation of the Psalter would be almost completely lost.[2]

**Superscripts and Postscripts**

The superscripts and postscripts are designed to provide information about the composition of the psalm—authorship, historical setting, genre, and intended use. By the expression "to the choirmaster," for example, the author of the psalm indicates his intention for its use or performance in temple worship. Some clarification is necessary here, however. In our printed Bibles this expression ("To the choirmaster") in all its fifty-five occurrences appear in superscripts, but in all probability these should be understood as a *postscripts to the previous psalms*. It was through textual error that these postscripts became attached instead to the succeeding psalms. The superscripts pertain to the psalm's composition, and the postscripts pertain to the psalm's performance ("To the choirmaster," etc.). We have reserved the fuller discussion of this for appendix 1, but we will highlight the argument here.

First, the use of superscripts and postscripts is not unique to the Psalter. It was a common practice in ancient Near Eastern literature, and it finds parallels in the Septuagint and the Dead Sea Scrolls. One biblical example is found the hymn of Habakkuk in Habakkuk 3:

2 This material is largely adapted from Waltke and Houston, *Psalms as Christian Worship*, 86–92. See also Bruce K. Waltke, *An Old Testament Theology: An Exegetical, Canonical, and Thematic Approach* (Grand Rapids, MI: Zondervan, 2007), 870–74.

Habakkuk 3:1 records the superscript, informing the reader of the form and authorship of the following verses—"A prayer of Habakkuk."

Habakkuk 3:2–19 records the prayer itself, concluding in 3:19a, "GOD, the Lord, is my strength; / he makes my feet like the deer's; / he makes me tread on my high places."

Then 3:19b adds the postscript: "To the choirmaster: with stringed instruments." Here we find that this prayer is in fact a hymn to be delivered to the choirmaster for use in public worship.

This would seem to be the standard pattern employed originally by the psalmists:

Superscript
Psalm/poem
Postscript

Isaiah 38:9–20 provides a striking parallel:

38:9, superscript: "A writing of Hezekiah king of Judah, after he had been sick and had recovered from his sickness."

38:10–19, hymn: "I said, In the middle of my days. . . ."

38:20, postscript or liturgical conclusion regarding performance: "and we will play my music on stringed instruments / all the days of our lives, / at the house of the LORD."

Again, this pattern seems to be standard:

Superscript
Body of hymn
Postscript

This understanding resolves the otherwise inexplicable problem of the superscript of Psalm 88, which illogically specifies two genres and two authors. This pattern would also explain why the expression "To the choirmaster" always appear as the first terms in the superscript[3] and never without a superscript in the preceding psalm.

Explanation for this conflation may be found in both unintentional scribal error and deliberate scribal editorial activity on the part of scribes. The attempted but mistaken translation of this expression on the part of the Septuagint translators reveals that they were unaware of its meaning. This plus the lack of versification in at least many of the manuscripts, with the poetry of the psalm and the prose of the prose postscripts butting up against the prose superscripts of the next psalm, rendered the conflation virtually inevitable. All considered, though the expression "To the choirmaster" (plus musical instrument) appears in the superscript of fifty-five psalms, the evidence points strongly to understanding them in connection with (postscripts to) the previous psalms.[4]

## Superscripts

Evidence of the antiquity and genuineness of the superscripts is abundant.[5] These superscripts are present in every ancient manuscript that we possess and every ancient version of the Psalms—none omits them. And as we have seen, they appear to be standard issue for prayers and hymns outside the Psalter (cf. Ex. 15:1; Judg. 5:2; 2 Sam. 22:1; Isa. 38:9; Hab. 3). With this in view it is astounding that the New English Bible omits the superscripts altogether; such an omission runs contrary to the textual and historical evidence. Sumerian and Akkadian ritual texts dating from the third millennium BC contain elements corresponding to those in the Psalter superscripts.[6] So also Egyptian hymns from the eighteenth dynasty (the time of Moses) and later contain superscripts

3 Except in the superscript of Psalm 88, where a scribal gloss for Psalm 87 may have later been misunderstood as the superscript of Psalm 88.

4 See appendix 1.

5 See also Robert Dick Wilson, "The Headings of the Psalms," in *The Princeton Theological Review* 24, no. 1 (January 1926): 1–37.

6 Gerald Henry Wilson, *The Editing of the Hebrew Psalter*, Society of Biblical Literature Dissertation Series (Chico, CA: Scholars Press, 1985), 13–24.

identifying the "cultic occasion; . . . the official appointed to utter the [hymn], the type of composition (prayer, incantation, lamentation), the title of the composition, the instrument(s) to accompany it, the mode of utterance (singing, reciting)".[7] Additionally, *no hymn in the Old Testament outside of the Psalter lacks a superscript*.[8] This evidence provides presumptive orientation that the superscripts of the Psalms are indeed genuine.

In fact, some of the psalms ascribed to David appear in themselves to be quite ancient. We will see the Canaanite-Baal background of Psalm 29, for example, in chapter 8, in which certain words, images, and parallelism that appear in the Psalms are attested in the Ugaritic texts (ca. 1400 BC).[9] This is a major factor that has persuaded much of modern scholarship to acknowledge that many psalms are indeed much older than the second temple.

It is also significant that many technical terms in the superscripts are obscure to Greek (ca. 150 BC) and Aramaic translators, which suggests an extended gap of time between their composition and the Tannaitic period (AD 70–220).[10] "The fact that these Hebrew technical terms were no longer understood can only lead to the conclusion that these particular words had fallen out of use so long before the second century BC that the true meaning had been completely forgotten."[11] And yet their presence in the text led these ancient translators to accept their genuineness, and so they were preserved. Similarly, linguistic, stylistic, structural, thematic, and theological differences are so great between the Psalter and its imitative thanksgiving psalms at Qumran as to leave no doubt of the far greater antiquity of the Psalter. The psalms at Qumran are quite

7 J. B. Pritchard, *Ancient Near Eastern Texts Relating to the Old Testament*, 3rd ed. (Princeton: Princeton University Press, 1969), 365–81.

8 Cf. Ex. 15:1; Judg. 5:1; 1 Sam. 2:1; 2 Sam. 23:1 [cf. Ps. 18 superscript]; Isa. 38:9; Hab. 3:1.

9 Mitchell Dahood, *Psalms I, 1–50: Introduction, Translation, and Notes*, Anchor Bible (Garden City, NY, Doubleday, 1965), xxix–xxx.

10 The Tannaim are rabbinic sages whose views are recorded in the Mishnah.

11 Gleason L. Archer, *A Survey of Old Testament Introduction*, rev. ed. (Chicago: Moody Press, 1974), 444.

different from the Psalms of the Old Testament, again suggesting a significant gap in time between them.

Finally, references to salvation history in psalms by David extend from Abraham to the exodus and to the conquest, but not beyond. Nor is there in the Davidic psalms any mention of a divided kingdom. By all accounts the superscripts are part of the biblical text, and no compelling empirical evidence exists to question their genuineness.

### "Of David": A Defense of Davidic Authorship

That the expression "of David" (לְדָוִד) in the superscript was, in fact, intended to assign authorship is its most obvious understanding. This is indisputably the meaning of the preposition (לְ) in Isaiah 38:9, Habakkuk 3:1, and Psalm 18. This Davidic superscript appears in seventy-three of the psalms. It seems plausible to assume that the preposition has the same meaning with other names: Moses (Ps. 90), Solomon (72; 127), the guilds and priests associated with David: the sons of Korah (42–49; 84–87), Asaph (50; 73–83), Heman (88), and Ethan (89).

Psalm 18:1 is instructive here in that it makes Davidic authorship unmistakably explicit. Note the superscript, here printed in italics for clarity:

> *A Psalm of David, the servant of the Lord, who addressed the words of this song to the Lord on the day when the Lord delivered him from the hand of all his enemies, and from the hand of Saul. He said*: I love you, O LORD, my strength.

"A psalm of David. . . . He said" leaves no room for misunderstanding. This Psalm is recorded again, along with a similar superscript, in 2 Samuel 22:1, and neither case leaves room for doubt that "A Psalm of David" is meant to indicate authorship.

Fourteen of the "of David" superscripts describe historical settings from David's life that are recorded in the books of Samuel. David's time of exile (1 Sam. 16–31) is mentioned in Psalms 34, 52, 54, 56, 57, 59, and 142. His time of blessing (2 Sam.1–10) is referred to in Psalms 18 and 60. And his time under divine displeasure (2 Sam. 11–20) finds reference in Psalms 3, 51, and 63. These all are entirely consistent with Davidic authorship.

David's Life in the Psalms

| Psalm | Incident | 1 Samuel |
|---|---|---|
| | **The Time of David's Election and Exile (1 Sam. 16–31)** | |
| 59 | House surrounded | 19:11 |
| 56 | Seized by Achish | 21:10–11 |
| 34 | Escape from Achish | 21:12–22:1 |
| 52 | Doeg | 22:7, 9, 18–20 |
| 54 | Betrayed by Ziphites | 23:19 |
| 57, 142 | In cave | 22 Adullam / 24 Engedi |
| | **The Time of David's Blessing (2 Sam. 1–10)** | **2 Samuel** |
| 60 | Victory over Transjordan | 8:5–13 |
| 18 | Victory over all enemies | 22 |
| | **David Under Divine Displeasure (2 Sam. 11–20)** | |
| 51 | Against the House of Uriah | 11–12 |
| 3 | Absalom's revolt | 15–17 |
| 63 | Desert of Judah | 15–17 |
| | **Unclassified (2 Sam. 21–24)** | |
| 30 | For the dedication of the temple at the time of numbering the people. | 24 |
| 7 | Cush the Benjaminite | (unknown) |

On the other hand, some of the superscripts introduce historical settings unknown in the earlier biblical record (7, 30, 60). The superscript for Psalm 7, for example, reads, "A Shiggaion of David, which he sang to the Lord concerning the words of Cush, a Benjaminite." Nothing is known of this man, Cush, in the biblical record, and so we are left to ask if the superscript is not genuine why later editors would have inserted such a reference. For that matter, Why would they have left fifty-nine of the Davidic psalms without historical notices, particularly when many of them could easily have been assigned to some event in David's life? Why would they introduce historical information in Psalms 7, 30, and 60 that is not found in the historical books or in the psalms themselves? And why should we allow superscripts for psalms outside the Psalter and not in the Psalter itself?[12] Only a Davidic origin provides satisfactory explanation to these questions.

It is not at all surprising, then, but expected, that an understanding of the Davidic origin of the Psalms is reflected elsewhere in the Old Testament (1 Sam. 16:14–23; 1 Chron. 23:4–5; 2 Chron. 29:25–30; Neh. 12:36; Amos 6:5). Evidence that David was a poet is abundant; indeed, David is the one who by the institution of psalm singing transformed the worship system given by Moses (1 Chron. 15–16). "In the Chronicler's day . . . it can scarcely be doubted that the meaning [of the expression "of David"] was 'by David.'"[13] Nor is it surprising that this understanding continues in the intertestamental literature (Sirach 47:8–10), the Qumran scrolls (11QPsa), Josephus,[14] and the rabbis.[15]

Most importantly, this understanding of Davidic authorship of the Psalms is confirmed by the Lord Jesus himself (Matt. 22:43–45; Mark 12:36–37; Luke 20:42), the apostle Peter (Acts 1:16; 2:25, 34), the early church (Acts 4:24–25), the apostle Paul (Rom. 4:6; 11:9), and the writer to the Hebrews (Heb. 4:7). In fact, in our Lord's debate with the Pharisees in Matthew 22, the reliability of the superscript and Davidic authorship of Psalm 110 forms the very ground of his argument:

12 Cf. Ex. 15:1; Deut. 31:30 (cf. 32:44); Judg. 5:1; 2 Sam. 22:1; Jonah 2; Is. 38:9. Cf. Waltke, *Old Testament Theology*, 874; Waltke and Houston, *Psalms as Christian Worship*, 92.

13 J. F. A. Sawyer, "An Analysis of the Context and Meaning of the Psalm-Headings," *Transactions of the Glasgow University Oriental Society* 22 (1970): 26–38.

14 Flavius Josephus, *The Antiquities of the Jews*, 7.12.3, trans. William Whiston, Project Gutenberg (website), accessed October 12, 2022, https://gutenberg.org/.

15 Charles A. Briggs, *A Critical and Exegetical Commentary on the Book of Psalms* (New York: C. Scribner's Sons: 1906–1907), liv.

Now while the Pharisees were gathered together, Jesus asked them a question, saying, "What do you think about the Christ? Whose son is he?" They said to him, "The son of David." He said to them, "How is it then that David, in the Spirit, calls him Lord, saying,

"'The Lord said to my Lord,
"Sit at my right hand,
until I put your enemies under your feet"'?

If then David calls him Lord, how is he his son?" (Matt. 22:41–45).

Apart from the reliability of the superscript of Psalm 110, and apart from a conviction that "of David" indicates Davidic authorship, Jesus's argument would fail. Jesus clearly considered the superscript to be part of the authoritative text.

Peter's argument for the messiahship of Jesus likewise hangs on the reliability of the superscript and Davidic authorship of Psalm 16:

For David says concerning him,

"'I saw the Lord always before me,
for he is at my right hand that I may not be shaken;
therefore my heart was glad, and my tongue rejoiced;
my flesh also will dwell in hope.
For you will not abandon my soul to Hades,
or let your Holy One see corruption.
You have made known to me the paths of life;
you will make me full of gladness with your presence.'"

Brothers, I may say to you with confidence about the patriarch David that he both died and was buried, and his tomb is with us to this day. Being therefore a prophet, and knowing that God had sworn with an oath to him that he would set one of his descendants on his throne, he foresaw and spoke about the resurrection of the Christ, that he was not abandoned to Hades, nor did his flesh see corruption. This Jesus God raised up, and of that we all are witnesses. (Acts 2:25–32)

It is similarly worth noting regarding the composite psalm of 1 Chronicles 16[16] that the chronicler seems to attribute Davidic authorship to Psalms 96, 105, and 106. And if Psalm 96, then probably Psalm 98 also.[17] It is also noteworthy that Hebrews 4:7 attributes Psalm 95 to David, following the superscript of the Septuagint and though lacking in the Hebrew text.

The textual evidence, the historical witness, the inspired writers of both the Old and New Testaments, and our Lord himself unanimously attest to the Davidic authorship of the psalms attributed to him.

## Responding to Arguments against Davidic Authorship

Some have alleged that the inclusion of additional superscripts in the Psalter of the Septuagint, as compared to the Psalter of the Masoretic (Hebrew) Text, leaves all superscripts under suspicion. But this conclusion just does not follow; it is a different question altogether. The attribution of more psalms to David in textual traditions other than those attested in the Masoretic Text does not disprove the originality of the superscripts in the Masoretic Text. The manuscript evidence in favor of the superscripts of the Masoretic Text is unanimous; that there may be additional psalms attributed to David is a separate, intertextual question. We might mention that the Dead Sea Scrolls attribute even more psalms to David than the Septuagint does. But this does not disprove the genuineness of the superscripts so strongly attested in the Hebrew text. Indeed, there are strong reasons to accept the additional "of David" superscripts of the Septuagint Psalter as genuine also.[18] Hebrews 4:7, for example, as we mentioned above, attributes Psalm 95

16 1 Chron. 16:8–22 = Ps. 105:1–15; 1 Chron. 16:23–33 = Ps. 96:1–13; 1 Chron. 16:34–36 = Ps. 106:1, 47–48.

17 David M. Howard Jr., *The Structure of Psalms 93–100*, Biblical and Judaic Studies from the University of California, San Diego 5 (Winona Lake, IN: Eisenbrauns, 1997), 178.

18 This at least in book 4 of the Psalter. See Bruce K. Waltke and James M. Houston, *Psalms as Christian Praise: A Historical Commentary* (Grand Rapids, MI: Eerdmans, 2019), 13–16.

to David, following the Septuagint. In brief, the presence of additional superscripts in the Septuagint implies nothing about the genuineness of the unanimously attested superscripts of the Masoretic Text.

Rejection of Davidic authorship of the psalms is grounded—often entirely—on the mention of "temple" and "holy mountain" in the "Davidic" psalms. It is assumed that such Solomonic references in connection with David would be anachronistic. But this is too simplistic. "Temple" means "house of God," not necessarily Solomon's temple (cf. 24:7, 9). Wherever God resides, it is a "temple." Reference to the "tent" of meeting as a "temple" (lit., "large house") goes back to the time of Eli (1 Sam. 1:9; 3:3). In his song of deliverance, David testifies,

> In my distress I called upon the Lord;
>   to my God I called.
> From his temple [lit., "large house"] he heard my voice,
>   and my cry came to his ears. (2 Sam. 22:7)

"Temple" is not merely a Solomonic structure; it is an institution. The significance of the tent-tabernacle was that it was a "temple," the residence and throne room of God. And given that the ark was in Jerusalem under David's reign, "holy mountain" is a very appropriately Davidic expression also.

It is worth observing in this vein that in Psalm 15:1, "A Psalm of David," we read, "O LORD, who shall sojourn in your tent?" In David's day he built his own tent for the ark, years before Solomon built the temple. He did not say "temple," but "tent." This would appear to evidence Davidic authorship.

It is further objected that the superscript of Psalm 30 is anachronistic: "A Psalm of David. A song at the dedication of the temple" (30:1). However, there is good reason to believe that David, as Israel's poet laureate, composed the dedicatory prayer for the temple (Ps. 30), just as he designed it and prepared beforehand for its building (1 Chron. 28).[19]

19 Waltke, *Old Testament Theology*, 873.

David was aware that Solomon would oversee the construction of the temple, and David saw to it that financial resources were provided in abundance. Moreover, this dedicatory prayer includes a confession of David's sin of numbering the people: "As for me, I said in my prosperity, / 'I shall never be moved'" (Ps. 30:6). That is, in his feeling of his own strength and resources he felt secure. But in light of this sinful sense of self-sufficiency he now confesses that it was indeed the Lord who made him strong (30:7) and so pleads to him for mercy (30:8). The superscript is no anachronism but consistent with the historical setting and with the psalm itself.

Another argument against Davidic authorship of the psalms is the presence of certain Aramaisms in the text—seen most famously in Psalm 139—expressions that betray (purportedly later) Aramaic origins. This is perhaps the strongest argument against Davidic authorship. And yet the major study on this topic by Abraham Hurvitz concludes that Aramaisms do not, in fact, prove a late date: "Evidence of Aramaic influence alone cannot serve as decisive proof for arguing for a late date of a given text."[20] Contact between the Jews and the Aramaeans has a history prior to that of David, and as Gleason Archer notes, David had "extensive contact" with Aramaic-speaking peoples to his north (cf. 2 Sam. 10).[21]

We might add that there are broad considerations that argue that the Psalms in large measure originated in the period of David or the monarchy. First, by the time of David psalms had already been in long use in Israel (Ex. 15; Deut. 32, 33; Judg. 5; 1 Sam. 2), and we know from Samuel that David wrote psalms (2 Sam. 1:17; 22:1; 23:1). The situation reflected throughout is that of the united monarchy (Pss. 68:26–27; 133). Even the Psalms of Ascents, as we will see in a later chapter, often considered postexilic, reflect the time period when the nation is still united (133) under one Davidic king (122, 132) in Jerusalem (120–134) in time of peace (122). The Aaronic priest ministered in the temple to pronounce blessing (128:5; 133:2; 134:3). Professor Margolioth cites

20 Avi Hurvitz, "The Chronological Significance of 'Aramaisms' in Biblical Hebrew," *Israel Exploration Journal* 18 (1968): 234.

21 Archer, *Survey of Old Testament Introduction*, 441.

several observations that militate against a postexilic timeframe for the Psalms:

- There is no sign of a divided kingdom (68:28).
- There is no sign of a restoration of the kingdom. "The Psalmists who verify the sacred history must have known of the glories of the Solomonic era, and of the splitting of the nation, if they lived after the close of the monarchical period; why, then, do they become vague after the accession of David or earlier? If they belong to the period of the divided kingdom, why do we find no trace of the hostility which ordinarily prevailed between the two divisions of Israel? Why are Ephraim and Manasseh given an honored place beside Judah and Benjamin?"
- There is no mention of postexilic heroes. "In Ben Sira's 'Praise of the Fathers,' Nehemiah and Zerubbabel are as highly honored as Samuel. If the Psalms are post-exilic, how is it that these heroes of the restoration are ignored?"
- Any restoration in fact is regarded as future. Such a great event would surely be prominent in the Psalms, if it had, in fact, occurred. "The turning of the captivity of Zion, on the other hand, is an event still in the uncertain future (126:4; 53:6; 79:11; 106:47)."[22]

**Summary and Conclusion**

Against the prevalent skepticism of an academic consensus regarding the originality, and so the veracity, of the Psalms' superscripts, both the universal tradition of Davidic authorship and empirical evidence support the traditional understanding that "of David" means "by David"—that David authored the psalms attributed to him and that the historical notices that associate fourteen psalms with his career are credible.

In support of the historical reliability of the superscripts generally, we may summarize in brief:

22 Cited in Parke P. Flournoy, "The Psalms Not Post-Exilic," *The Bible Student* 3, no. 1 (January 1901): 60.

- The textual evidence for the genuineness of the superscripts is unanimous.
- All the other psalms and hymns of the Old Testament have superscripts; the Psalter is no exception. The evidence indicates that the use of superscripts was standard.
- The expression "of David" (לְדָוִד) can mean "by David."
- The superscript of Psalm 18 is explicit in its attribution of the psalm to David. This, along with the entire psalm, finds explicit verification in 2 Samuel 22 also.
- Religious Ugaritic texts from Ras Shamra, from a timeframe even earlier than David's, parallel the Psalms.
- Jesus and the New Testament writers built their arguments on the historical accuracy of the superscripts.
- The meaning of some of the technical terms in the superscripts were already lost to Greek translators around 200 BC, suggesting a significant gap of time between them.[23] Only because of recent archaeological discoveries do we understand the meaning of some of these terms today.

Next we consider Psalm 3, whose superscript makes explicit the historical situation. Then we consider Psalm 4, whose historical context can be inferred.

---

## PSALM 3

[Superscript:] A Psalm of David, when he fled from Absalom his son.

1 O Lord, how many are my foes!
Many are rising against me;
2 many are saying of my soul,
"There is no salvation for him in God." *Selah*

23 Waltke, *Old Testament Theology*, 872.

3 But you, O LORD, are a shield about me,
  my glory, and the lifter of my head.
4 I cried aloud to the LORD,
  and he answered me from his holy hill. *Selah*
5 I lay down and slept;
  I woke again, for the LORD sustained me.
6 I will not be afraid of many thousands of people
  who have set themselves against me all around.
7 Arise, O LORD!
  Save me, O my God!
For you strike all my enemies on the cheek;
  you break the teeth of the wicked.
8 Salvation belongs to the LORD;
  your blessing be on your people! *Selah*
[Postscript:] To the choirmaster: with stringed instruments.

Psalm 3 is the first of twelve psalms composed of ten prayers of two groups of five (3–7; 9–13), with a sixth that characterizes the human condition (8; 14).[24] Psalms 1–4 reflect a theological journey: trust of God's people in God's word (1) to the king's trust in particular in God's covenantal promise (2) despite the challenges to that promise (3–4). Psalm 3 is a morning prayer (3:5), and Psalm 4 an evening prayer (4:8). In both, David learns to view the external circumstances in light of God's promise and so will sleep peacefully and unafraid (3:5–6; 4:8).

## Setting

Our focus here is on the historical approach and the significance of the superscripts in providing a setting for the Psalms, and we take up Psalms 3 and 4 as examples of the importance of interpreting the psalms in their own historical perspective. Psalm 3 is the first of the fourteen psalms that in the superscription identify the historical situation that prompted David to write. He identifies this psalm as written during

24 *NIV Study Bible: Fully Revised Edition* (Zondervan, 2020), 890.

his flight from his son Absalom, who had usurped David's throne. His own kingdom, previously so appreciative of him and loyal to him, is now in rebellion against him. He is the king, but his kingdom is no longer safe for him. Now for his life he must flee from his own palace and from his capital city.

David writes this psalm away from Jerusalem yet praying toward the holy mountain (3:4) and with the temple in view. Several details in the psalm itself draw attention to this situation. In 3:3 David poetically describes God as a "shield about me," "my glory," and "the lifter of my head." Any believer could use this king language with reference to God, but in conjunction with "I will not be afraid of many thousands of people [or troops] / who have set themselves against me all around" (3:6; cf. 3:1–2), it leads us to picture King David. This is a military scene and not mere metaphor, which fits with the superscript's mention of David's flight from Absalom. Still, the imagery is graphic in its depiction of David's grief and sunken spirits.

The mention of this historical setting assumes an understanding of the chapter of David's life recorded in 2 Samuel 14–18, and a review of that setting is necessary to illuminate the psalm. Lying further in the background is the tragic episode of David's adultery with Bathsheba and murder of her husband Uriah (2 Sam. 11–12) and the consequences of that sin in his own family and kingdom. God forgives him of his sins, but this is a turning point in David's career. The consequences are severe. First, his eldest son Amnon, the heir apparent, models his father's sexual passions and rapes his sister, Tamar. David fails to act in response, and so his next oldest son, Absalom, kills Amnon for what he had done—again, modeling his father's sin. As a result, Absalom is forced into exile. Eventually, David invites him back, but there is never a clear confession or righting of the wrong. And the relationship between them remains strained until finally Absalom seeks the kingdom for himself and leads a revolt against his own father. David is forced to flee from Jerusalem in the late afternoon, wondering whether he will live to see the next day (2 Sam. 15–16). After making it safely through the night, he is persuaded of God's safekeeping (Ps. 3:5).

Usurping his father's throne and seeking to assassinate him is an evil of the highest order, and Absalom's wickedness shows itself throughout the details of the story. Deceit and pretense mark the entire episode, particularly in his feigned spiritual concerns used as an occasion to gain his following. Attempting a coup in Jerusalem would not succeed, so he decides instead on Hebron. He lies to his father and claims that he has made a vow to offer sacrifices at Hebron, which David approves. But it is a pretense. Absalom has another agenda in mind altogether. The people know only that the king's son is going to Hebron to offer a sacrifice. But during the offering of the sacrifice Absalom's messengers make their way among the people, telling them that Absalom is the king. As in *The Godfather* movie when the godfather was baptizing the baby he was actually murdering all his rivals, so while Absalom is offering up his sacrifice he is actually working to undermine David and destroy him. He is misusing God's name, and it is extreme evil.

Then as he is offering the sacrifice, he secures the number one intellect in the country—Ahithophel, the Gilonite. It seems Ahithophel is Bathsheba's grandfather—the father of Eliam, who was the father of Bathsheba. And it seems he never forgave David for what he had done. So he is very willing to conspire with Absalom to overthrow David, and now he becomes Absalom's counselor. And a brilliant advisor he is. David considers him equal to a prophet because of his insight and ability to discern events and how people would behave (2 Sam. 16:23). So when David learns that Ahithophel is part of the conspiracy, he immediately prays that God will frustrate his counsel (2 Sam. 15:31).

Ahithophel's first counsel is for Absalom to take his father's harem and rape his father's wives on the roof of the palace where all could see. This would serve as the news broadcast that the revolt was on. Further, Absalom steals the hearts and loyalty of the people. Like the stereotypical politician he lies about his father, make great promises, and proclaim all the good he would do as king.

The evil of David's enemy is extreme, and the nation is taken in. This is what David faces as he writes Psalm 3. It is a spiritual war as well as a military war. And by stating this setting in the superscript David wants us to read this history and understand this context. It is a war, but it is a battle between good and evil, and between justice and injustice. It is no hyperbole when David describes his enemies as "wicked" (3:7).

When David learns of the coup, he decides that Jerusalem is no longer safe for him. There will be many spies, and acts of treason or attempted assassination would be too easy. So he leaves the city, opting rather to settle the matter on the battlefield, should it become necessary.

In God's providence David has a number of personal encounters as he leaves the city. For one, Ittai the Gittite joins him with complete loyalty. This is a happy but unexpected providence. David's own people are rejecting him, but here a Gentile, the Gittite from Gath, home of Goliath, is loyal to him—all prospective of Jesus and the church, which by the second century AD had become mostly Gentile.

Then David meets Zadok, the priest, whom David enlists as a spy and a counselor. He sends Zadok back to Jerusalem with the ark of the covenant. Note that in Psalm 3:4, David anticipates that God will answer him "from his holy hill." And David links Zadok with another priest by the name of Abiathar and his son Jonathan, and with another priest by the name of Abiathar and his son Ahimaaz. These together form David's counter spy system. Zadok will be his eyes and ears to keep him abreast of Absalom's plans. The younger men, Jonathan and Ahimaaz, will serve as runners to report to David.

Then in answer to David's prayer (2 Sam. 15:31), Hushai joins David's cause also. He too is a brilliant counselor, and so David sends him undercover to Absalom with a mission to frustrate the counsel of Ahithophel. Again in God's providence, Absalom is entering the city as Hushai enters also. As he sees Absalom, Hushai says, "Long live the king!"—which he means very sincerely in reference to David, but which Absalom in his pride hears as praise for him. The spy ring is in place.

Ahithophel's counsel is to take the army and strike David quickly, while he is still weak. Hushai knows that Ahithophel's counsel is perceptive, and so he offers contrary advice. He reminds Absalom of his father's military prowess and convinces him that once David kills a few of Absalom's soldiers, they will all abandon him for fear. He also convinces him that David is already in hiding and that striking his army now will be useless because David, the one they need to kill, will not be among them. So Hushai counsels Absalom to wait until he has gathered together all the fighting men of the entire land—then they can find David and overwhelm him wherever he may be.

Absalom takes Hushai's counsel over that of Ahithophel. For his part, Ahithophel is perceptive enough to see the folly of this plan, so he goes home and hangs himself, knowing that Absalom will now fail and that he will be put to death. David will win as a result of Hushai's successful counsel.

All this lies in the background of Psalm 3, and when David praises God for the victory that will come, it is praise for his providence at work through the cunning of Zadok, Hushai, and the entire spy ring. The message of the psalm, then, is not simply "sit back and trust God." Trusting God through the clever actions and even risks of faithful men is in view.

The superscript directs us to think of King David, the author, as he flees from Absalom, and with that episode in mind we now can better read the psalm.

### Form and Structure

The opening direct address, "O LORD!" (3:1), signals immediately that this is a lament psalm. In later chapters we will examine various genres of the psalms and their respective forms, but we will point out here that Psalm 3 follows the standard petition or lament form:

The **address** is up front and brief:

> "O LORD . . . !" (3:1)

3:1–2 states the **lament**:

> how many are my foes!
> Many are rising against me;
> many are saying of my soul,
> "There is no salvation for him in God." *Selah*

3:3–6 expresses David's **confidence**:

> But you, O LORD, are a shield about me,
> my glory, and the lifter of my head.
> I cried aloud to the LORD,
> and he answered me from his holy hill. *Selah*
> I lay down and slept;
> I woke again, for the LORD sustained me.
> I will not be afraid of many thousands of people
> who have set themselves against me all around.

In 3:7, David makes his **petition**, and the "imprecation" also:

> Arise, O LORD!
> Save me, O my God!
> For you strike all my enemies on the cheek;
> you break the teeth of the wicked.

Finally, 3:8 states the **conclusion**, which in this case is praise:

> Salvation belongs to the LORD;
> your blessing be on your people! *Selah*

This form is not slavishly followed by the psalmists, but it is relatively standard, and we will come across it often. With regard to structure we might note also that 3:2 and 3:7–8 form an *inclusio*, framing the psalm with the theme of deliverance:

3:2: deliverance denied
3:7–8: deliverance affirmed

## Survey Exposition[25]

### *3:1–2: David's Lament*

1 O LORD, how many are my foes!
Many are rising against me;
2 many are saying of my soul,
"There is no salvation for him in God." *Selah*

We will discuss Hebrew poetry and parallelism in chapter 6, but the parallelism in 3:1 is rare, almost completely synonymous, and thus highly emphatic: David's "many foes" (cf. 3:6, 7; 2 Sam. 15:13; 17:11) are those who are "rising against me." But there is some escalation: not only are they enemies at heart; they are actively on the attack. In 3:2, David laments his enemies' unbelief and rejection of their king. David is the anointed king, established by God himself, and everyone knows it. But now they abandon it all. This is the man who had defeated Goliath and had secured and extended their kingdom from the Euphrates River to the Nile. Now, despite all he had accomplished for them, they turn on him, and so quickly, and they would see him put to death. The pathos of 3:2 is obvious: They say, "God will not deliver him" (NIV; cf. Matt. 27:42). They have lost faith in him and in God. And yet what his enemies say seems to be so—God is not saving him. This is likely the most painful aspect of David's lament. The lament, then, has several layers: the enemy is too numerous and too strong for him, and God has not helped.

### *3:3–6: David's Confidence*

Although perilously outnumbered by his enemies (3:1, 6, 7; cf. 2 Sam. 15:12–14), David refuses to come to terms with them. Instead, he turns to the Lord who chose and appointed him, with his trust unabated, and

25 See also Waltke and Houston, *Psalms as Christian Worship*, chap. 6.

in 3:3–6 he expresses his confidence. This confidence is stated in two parts. First is his affirmation of confidence in God (3:3–4):

3 But you, O Lord, are a shield about me,
my glory, and the lifter of my head.
4 I cried aloud to the Lord,
and he answered me from his holy hill.

The exposed king, surrounded by his enemies, signals his confidence by the unequivocal mark of faith: "But you." David contrasts his foes not with his own seeming helplessness but with God himself, and here he finds confidence.

The "shield" in view (3:3) is the round, lightweight infantry shield, a familiar metaphor employed in the Old Testament to describe God's protective presence.[26] David says that the Lord is his shield all around him (cf. 2 Sam. 22:2–3). David's confidence is grounded in God's electing grace: "you bestow glory on me and lift up my head" (3:3, authors' translation[27]). When David fled Jerusalem he was forced to do so "barefoot and with his head covered" (2 Sam. 15:30), hiding for his life. But he will return with head lifted high. With this figure, David asserts his trust that the God who appointed him as king will cause him to prevail against his foes. David knows God and trusts his promises, and so he is convinced that God will hear his prayer and grant his petition.

In 3:4 David testifies that when he "cried aloud to the Lord" for help, he "answered me from his holy hill"—Zion, the location of the ark and the dwelling place of God. Zion was God's appointed place of meeting with his people, and his presence was symbolized in the ark. David was not superstitious, however, and he declined to have the ark taken with him in his flight (2 Sam. 15:24–27). Yet in response to his prayer God gave assurance "from his holy hill" that he would be with David.

26 Cf. Leland Ryken et al., eds., *Dictionary of Biblical Imagery* (Downers Grove, IL: InterVarsity Press, 1998), 785.

27 Waltke and Houston, *Psalms as Christian Worship*, 202.

The scenic depiction of this moment conveys more than geographical information. Psalm 3:4 pictures God atop holy Mount Zion, twenty-five hundred feet above sea level. As he prays this psalm David is in the Jordanian Rift, nearly twenty-five hundred feet below sea level—literally the lowest point on earth. God is on high; David is in the depths. The geography matches the depths to which David has fallen. Physical distance, of course, makes no difference to God—he is near his people always (139:7–12). But the language is intended to draw attention both to the depths of David's plight and to the transcendent God who rules over all. "He answered me from his holy hill" (3:4) expresses David's confidence boldly. He does not explain the "answer" received at that point, only that it gave such assurance that he was able to sleep (3:5).

Psalm 3:5–6 forms the second part of David's confidence. Here he validates or proves his confidence by sleeping serenely in exile, presumably out in the open, still amid danger.

> 5 I lay down and slept;
> I woke again, for the LORD sustained me.
> 6 I will not be afraid of many thousands of people
> who have set themselves against me all around.

To sleep securely in trust (3:5) is unique in the ancient Near East. For example, Pharaoh counsels his son, "Even when you sleep, guard your heart because no man has adherents on the day of distress."[28] That is, never go to sleep because you have no one who will stand with you. By contrast, David trusts the Lord God, and so he sleeps. In such circumstances this is remarkable, but such is David's confidence in God (cf. Mark 4:36–40). As Scroggie comments, "He is speaking of the morning after a night of refreshing sleep—not in bed! but out in the open and beneath the stars, hunted by foes! It is not the sleep of exhaustion, but of trust in God."[29] Commentators regularly point

28 Pritchard, *Ancient Near Eastern Texts*, 418.
29 W. Graham Scroggie, *The Psalms* (Revell, 1978), 57.

out that the "emphatic 'I'" of 3:5 is fronted to sharpen the contrast in thought: "I [emphatic in Hebrew] lay down and slept." H. C. Leupold remarks that in such circumstances this remark by itself could seem triumphalistic bravado—"idle boasting, cheap heroics"—but coming as it does after the divine encouragement of 3:4, it is the sincere "boldness of true faith."[30] David had failed in many ways, but his trust in God remains. And after the good night's sleep, he wakes up refreshed and ready to meet the enemy (3:6).

*3:7: David's Petition*

> 7 Arise, LORD!
> Deliver me, my God!
> Strike all my enemies on the jaw;
> break the teeth of the wicked. (NIV)[31]

The bold call for God to "arise" is common in the Psalter (7:6; 9:19; 10:12; 17:13; 74:22; 82:8; 132:8; cf. 12:5; 68:1; 102:13) and connotes a call to action on God's part, divine intervention in light of the psalmist's helplessness. This generally has military connotations, a call to attack echoing Moses's war cry in Numbers 10:35. His mention of deliverance here (3:7, "save me"; 3:8, "Salvation belongs to the LORD") is the crucial *inclusio* that frames and defines the psalm. The psalm began with the enemy saying, "God will not deliver him" (3:2). But David does not despair, and now at the end of the psalm he petitions God in affirmation that he is indeed "my God" who will, in fact, deliver.

Deliverance has two senses, military and juridicial. That is, the deliverance he cries for is in the interests of what is right. The one who is wronged raises his voice in a cry for help, whereupon the one who hears is obliged to intervene in the interests of justice (Deut. 22:24, 27). If the Lord fails to help, the afflicted is put to shame (Ps. 44:15). It is therefore

30 H. C. Leupold, *Exposition of the Psalms* (Grand Rapids, MI: Baker, 1969), 63.

31 "Strike" and "break": interpreting the Hebrew perfect as a precative perfect. See Bruce K. Waltke and M. O'Connor, *Introduction to Biblical Hebrew Syntax* (Winona Lake, IN: Eisenbrauns, 1990), 494.

the responsibility of the one wronged to cry out. This responsibility fell particularly upon the king (1 Sam. 10:27; 2 Kings. 6:26). Failure to cry out would amount to abdicating his throne. Frequently, the psalmist will "cry aloud" (cf. Ps. 3:4), and when he does the responsibility is now the Lord's (20:6; 9:7, 10).

With the petition comes the imprecation. "Strike" (3:7) signifies scornful humiliation (cf. Ps. 78:66; 1 Kings 22:24; Job 16:10; Lam. 3:30; Micah 5:1; 4:14), the climactic insult of utter defeat.[32] In this case the enemy has no defense. "Break the teeth" (Ps. 3:7) signifies that the enemy, who like wild beasts had been eager to devour him, has been rendered harmless, with no ability to go on the offensive (cf. Ps. 56:6; Job 29:17). David's petition is that God will render his enemies defenseless and bring them to utter defeat. He does not quite ask for their death, but he does ask that they be neutralized.

*3:8: David's Praise*

David concludes his psalm with a praise for deliverance, a deliverance he is confident will come.

> 8 Salvation belongs to the LORD;
> your blessing be on your people!

This is the key to the psalm: "salvation belongs to LORD," hence David's petition and his confidence. But the king does not pray for his own deliverance only; the deliverance of his people is tied up with his own, and his thoughts are for them also. They have been divided by this rebellion, and some unrest doubtless remains. So he prays for "blessing . . . on your people." As Derek Kidner explains,

> The psalm ends by looking beyond the "I" and "me" of all the previous verses, to thy people (not even "my people"), and to thy blessing,

32 A. F. Kirkpatrick, *The Book of Psalms: Book I* (Cambridge: Cambridge University Press, 1892), 16.

> which goes as far beyond victory as health and fruitfulness go beyond survival. Without this, even a reunited people will lack the breath of life; with it, they can bless the world.[33]

We today as God's people continue to be the beneficiaries of this prayer for blessing. And giving his psalm "to the choirmaster" David intends for us to sing this psalm with him. Matthew Henry writes,

> In singing this, and praying it over, we should possess ourselves with an apprehension of the danger we are in from the multitude and malice of our spiritual enemies, who seek the ruin of our souls by driving us from our God, and we should concern ourselves in the distresses and dangers of the church of God, which is every where spoken against, every where fought against; but, in reference to both, we should encourage ourselves in our God, who owns and protects and will in due time crown his own interest both in the world and in the hearts of his people.[34]

### Final Reflections

This psalm illustrates well both the form of the lament psalms and the importance of the superscripts, directing us to understand the psalm with the narrative of 2 Samuel in mind. As a point of "practical theology," it is surely worth noting that God's deliverance did not come apart from David's active involvement. Without the superscript informing us of the fuller story we might have been left with the impression that all David did was pray. But the superscript leads us to consider more, and the historical account in Samuel supplies details of David's own shrewdness. Faith and works are not separated for David here. He trusted God for deliverance, and so he strategized. Yet when he writes the psalm he does not indulge in self-congratulation. He does not even praise Hushai. Rather, he

33 Derek Kidner, *Psalms 1–72* (London: Inter-Varsity Press, 1973), 71.

34 Matthew Henry, *Matthew Henry's Commentary on the Whole Bible: Complete and Unabridged in One Volume* (Peabody, MA: Hendrickson, 1994), 747.

sees God at work behind and through it all, and he praises him accordingly.

Psalm 3 begins the so-called Davidic Psalter (Pss. 3–41). All through these Davidic Psalms, we see David in prayer, and often in lament, as here in Psalm 3. And yet according to the postscript he intends for us to sing this with him. How so?

We cannot claim the very same "kingship" promise that God gave to the house of David, but we do have his covenant promise of salvation that he alone can give (3:8), and in this promise he is our "shield" (3:3) and defender also. "Salvation belongs to the LORD" (3:8). "It is his sovereign prerogative and gift, and, once given, it is never withdrawn."[35] He will keep his people safe forever. And yet there are dangers that threaten, and we learn from David that in the face of these dangers we must look to God, petition him for help, and trust him for it.

Moreover, as we have noted, the Psalter is a royal hymnbook whose leading figure is the Davidic king who, in turn, characteristically foreshadows David's greater son, the Lord Jesus Christ. This first psalm of lament is no exception. Like David, Christ recognized his own kingship. Like David, he was hated without cause, rejected by his own people, and then received by the Gentiles (Rom. 9–11). Like David, he was driven into the wilderness to be tested. Like David, the Lord Jesus was taunted with shouts, "He saved others; he cannot save himself" (Matt. 27:42). Like David, he entrusted himself to him who judges righteously (1 Pet. 2:23); God alone was his only shield, his glory, and the one who lifted up his head. Like David, the Lord Jesus also cried out in distress, "My God!" Yet unlike David, our Lord suffered for the sins of others, not his own. The early church understood Psalm 3:5 as foreshadowing Christ's death and resurrection—like David, he lay down and rose again, trusting God for vindication. And like David, the Lord Jesus Christ also rejoiced in vindication and in that vindication pronounced blessing on all the people of God.[36]

35 Alec Motyer, *Treasures of the King: Psalms from the Life of David* (Nottingham, UK: Inter-Varsity Press, 2007), 137.

36 Cf. Waltke and Houston, *Psalms as Christian Worship*, 204.

*Outline*

We may outline the psalm as follows:

I. Address with lament (3:1–2)
  A. Enemies too many
  B. God will not deliver
II. Confidence (3:3–6)
  A. Affirmation of his trust (3:3–4)
  B. Validation of his faith (3:5–6)
III. Petition (3:7)
  A. Deliver from the enemy
  B. Punish the enemy
IV. Praise (3:8)

## PSALM 4

A Psalm of David.

1 Answer me when I call, O God of my righteousness!
You have given me relief when I was in distress.
Be gracious to me and hear my prayer!
2 O men, how long shall my honor be turned into shame?
How long will you love vain words and seek after lies? *Selah*
3 But know that the LORD has set apart the godly for himself;
the LORD hears when I call to him.
4 Be angry, and do not sin;
ponder in your own hearts on your beds,
and be silent. *Selah*
5 Offer right sacrifices,
and put your trust in the LORD.
6 There are many who say, "Who will show us some good?
Lift up the light of your face upon us, O LORD!"
7 You have put more joy in my heart
than they have when their grain and wine abound.

8 In peace I will both lie down and sleep;
for you alone, O LORD, make me dwell in safety.
To the choirmaster: for the flutes.

**Form**

Psalm 4 is another petition-lament psalm with the usual components:

- address: my righteous God (4:1a)
- introductory petition that God will be favorable (4:1b)
- lament: turned my glory to shame (4:2)
- confidence: seven admonitions (4:3–5)
- petition: favor, harvests (4:6–7)
- confidence and praise (goes to sleep) (4:8)

**Exposition**[37]

Psalm 4 provides another example of the importance of interpreting the psalms in their own historical setting. The superscript of this psalm credits king David as the author; the importance of this will become evident as we proceed. This is another crisis psalm. Psalm 4 is related to Psalm 3 in a general theme: David laments the opposition he faces, yet with a robust trust in God's safekeeping he is able to sleep (cf. 3:5 and 4:8).

*4:1: David's Address and Introductory Petition*

1 Answer me when I call, O God of my righteousness!
You have given me relief when I was in distress.
Be gracious to me and hear my prayer!

The opening of this psalm presents David in a time of "distress" in which he petitions God for help, expressed in the three lines. The ESV translates the second line as a statement of fact: "You have given me relief." The form of this verb can also be understood as an imperative: "Give me relief." In parallel to the petition of the first and third lines,

37 See also Waltke and Houston, *Psalms as Christian Worship*, chap. 7.

this seems to make more sense here. So in 4:1 David offers three petitions: "Answer. . . . Give relief. . . . Be gracious."

At the outset there is the direct address ("O God"), the typical characteristic of the lament psalm. Later in the psalm David uses the divine name, Yahweh, to refer to God (4:3, 6). Yahweh is God's personal name and in God's own mouth means I AM (Ex. 3:13–15). It is his covenant name to Israel. Here in 4:1 David appeals to "God," the title that sets him apart as transcendent and supreme. The NIV translation—"my righteous God"—is preferred here and is particularly appropriate. By adding the pronoun "my God," David implies his covenant relationship with God, and by adding "my righteous God," he calls God to witness, as it were, that this particular suffering is undeserved. His appeal, then, is for God to set things right that have gone wrong, and positioning himself as helpless he asks this as a favor of grace: "be gracious." David grounds his petition in God's righteousness and mercy.

*4:2: David's Lament*

2 O men, how long shall my honor be turned into shame?
How long will you love vain words and seek after lies? *Selah*

The identity of the "men" is determinative for understanding the psalm, and so we must consider a point of translation. Almost all English versions translate the Hebrew term simply "men": "How long, men?" But this fails to recognize the significance of this Hebrew expression (בְּנֵי אִישׁ, "sons of [a] man"). This expression does not have ordinary men in view but specifically "highborn" men. The term "denotes such as stand prominently forward out of the multitude"[38] or "men of rank."[39] It is the king's leadership that are in view—his nobles, the aristocracy and powerful. This Hebrew expression differs from a related expression (בְּנֵי־אָדָם) that connotes "sons of mankind." We can see this difference in Psalm 49:2, which employs both terms: "both low and high" (גַּם־בְּנֵי אָדָם גַּם־בְּנֵי־אִישׁ).

38 C. F. Keil and F. Delitzsch, *Commentary on the Old Testament*, vol. 5 (Peabody, MA: Hendrickson, 1996), 67.

39 Dahood, *Psalms I*, 23.

The difference is evident in Psalm 62:9 also: "Those of low estate [בְּנֵי־אָדָם] are but a breath; / those of high estate [בְּנֵי אִישׁ] are a delusion." These in 4:2 (בְּנֵי אִישׁ) are highborn men, the influential and powerful.

So the problem David faces is that his highborn men—his leadership—are "turning his glory into shame" (4:2). The king who has been victorious and successful and whose "glory" is divinely appointed—they now criticize and undermine him. Leaders are beginning to defect. Moreover, in their turning against the king they are turning against God also: "How long will you love delusions and seek false gods?" (NIV). David is the divinely appointed king, and to turn from him inevitably entails religious and theological apostasy; hence, the NIV rendering, "seek false gods." So now the nature of the crisis comes into focus. David's leadership has lost faith in him, and they are turning against him. Only when we recognize who the speaker in the psalm is—namely, the king—and that it is his glory in view, can we read and apply the psalm rightly. David is facing apostasy within his own leadership. It is not about people who turn *our* glory into shame and oppose *us*. It is about opposition to the king, which in David's case is inseparable from turning away from God also.

So Psalm 4 reflects a crisis in Israel. David's cabinet, so to speak, has lost faith in his leadership, and so they are looking elsewhere. Now David wants to restore their confidence, and so he addresses these who are abandoning him in the imperative (4:3–5):

> 3 But know that the Lord has set apart the godly for himself;
> the LORD hears when I call to him.
> 4 Be angry, and do not sin;
> ponder in your own hearts on your beds, and be silent. *Selah*
> 5 Offer right sacrifices,
> and put your trust in the LORD.

Then he cites the people at large (4:6):

> 6 There are many who say, "Who will show us some good?
> Lift up the light of your face upon us, O LORD!"

Then in 4:7 the king himself speaks:

7 Fill my heart with joy
when their grain and wine abound. (NIV)

Our understanding of 4:7 is critical to our understanding of the psalm, so we should examine it at this point. It is the *crux interpretum* that determines the meaning of the entire psalm. And again we must consider a point of translation. The question is whether 4:7 should be translated, "You have put *more* joy in my heart / *than* when their grain and new wine abound" (cf. ESV, NASB), or "Fill[40] my heart with joy / *when* their grain and new wine abound" (NIV). The issue is whether the Hebrew compound מֵעֵת means "more than the time" or "from the time." Elsewhere the Hebrew preposition (מִן, *min*) in this construction (מֵעֵת, "from the time") is always temporal, not comparative. In Isaiah 48:16, for example, we read "from the time it came to be" (see also 1 Chron. 9:25; Ezek. 4:10, 11). There is no exception to this. This is crucial. The king is not praying for something that will give "more joy than" that of fruitful harvest. He is praying for joy *in* fruitful harvest: "Fill my heart with joy / *when* their grain and new wine abound." In other words, the crisis at hand is that of a drought. This is the historical context of the psalm.

Note further that, unlike almost all other lament psalms, there is no mention of an enemy. There are about sixty psalms of lament; this is one of only three that make no mention of an enemy. Commentators here routinely refer David's remarks to his "enemies," but there is no mention of them in the psalm. David makes no mention of impending attack, only of verbal opposition and important people becoming disaffected. The nation's leadership is losing confidence in the king and in God, not because of external threat but because of a famine (cf. 2 Sam. 21:1–14; cf. 1 Kings 8:35–37). The problem is that there is no rain and

40 The grammatical form is interpreted as a precative perfect. See Waltke and O'Connor, *Introduction to Biblical Hebrew Syntax*, 30.5.4c, 494.

so no harvest of the crops for food in the spring and of the grapes for wine and oil in the fall. A drought in an ancient agrarian culture is devastating. The food supply has run short, and the fearful people are turning against the king and against his God. And so David prays for God to give joy in the time of harvest.

This explains "the good" of Psalm 4:6: "There are many who say, 'O that we may see some good?'" (NRSV). The "good" they seek is that of fruitful harvest. Psalm 85:12 speaks similarly but more definitively:

> Yes, the LORD will give what is good,
> and our land will yield its increase.

Notice in this parallelism that the second line defines the first—the "good" sought for is that of harvest (cf. Deut. 28:12; Isa. 9:3; Jer. 5:24–25; 17:6). And so in recognition of this crisis the king prays for his people: "Lift up the light of your face upon us, O LORD" (Ps. 4:6). He is praying that God will supply food for his people. Recognizing all this here in 4:6, Dahood translates "good" (טוֹב) rather freely as "rain"—"Who will show us rain?"[41]

This crisis of drought is compounded by the fact that the king in the ancient world was responsible for rain. This explains the leaders' loss of confidence in David at this point. John Eaton's *Kingship and the Psalms* provides valuable historical background here. Kings in the ancient Near East commonly took credit for rich harvest, boasting that their prayers were always effective, that the gods would always hear. "'Everything proceeding from the lips of his Majesty,' it was said of the Pharaoh, 'his father (the god) Amon causes to be realized there and then.' The sun god 'rises in the horizon each day to hear all his prayer.'"[42] Eaton demonstrates that similar boasts are found among Assyrian and Hittite kings also. In the ancient world the king was expected to be effective in prayer. In these religious environments

41 Dahood, *Psalms I*, 25.

42 John H. Eaton, *Kingship and the Psalms*, Studies in Biblical Theology, 2nd ser., 32 (Naperville, IL: Alec R. Allenson, n.d.), 195.

the king could boast that he could just "name it and claim it"—"As soon as I pray, I get the answer." That is pagan religion. Our psalm is of Israel's king who reigns under the true God, but even in Israel "it was thought that a good king in favour with heaven should ensure fertility (72.3, 6, 16)."[43] But in Psalm 4 the prayers of King David go unheard. This is reflected in the "How long?" of 4:2. So now because of drought the leadership is losing confidence in their king and turning to false gods—presumably the Canaanite storm god, Baal, who, they believed, drove the clouds across the sky and whose voice was heard in the thunder.

King David, then, is in a great crisis. And though he is faithful and looks to God for help, no help comes. God does not answer David's prayer for rain. In this respect it is the age-old problem of why the righteous suffer. David's virtue does not seem to result in observable favor from God. His faithfulness does not seem to pay off.

### *4:3–5: David's Confidence*

David's faith does not waver, and in 4:3–5 he gives seven admonitions, reflecting his confidence. The first sets the tone for the others:

> 3 But know that the LORD has set apart the godly for himself;
> the LORD hears when I call to him.

Here the king challenges his detractors to consider carefully that he (David) belongs uniquely to God. Know your king! He is God's covenant partner, the divinely appointed king. David's admonition of 4:3 is designed to give his would-be opponents pause before undermining and opposing him: "the LORD hears when I call to him." This claim may have seemed hollow, given the circumstances—it was precisely because God did *not* hear David's prayers that these leaders were losing confidence in their king. But such was David's trust in God.

43 John Eaton, *The Psalms: A Historical and Spiritual Commentary with an Introduction and New Translation* (New York: Continuum, 2005), 71.

Further reflecting David's confidence, in 4:4–5 he gives six more admonitions, which are stated in three pairs.

> 4 Be angry, and do not sin;
> ponder in your own hearts on your beds, and be silent. *Selah*
> 5 Offer right sacrifices,
> and put your trust in the LORD.

The first pair admonishes to dread the consequences of apostasy. The ESV renders this "Be angry and do not sin." Here again we must consider a point of translation. The verb translated "Be angry" (רָגַז, 4:4a) means to "tremble" or "shake" in trauma. Context must determine the precise connotations of this "trembling." Is David admonishing his leaders to anger (ESV) or fear (cf. NIV, NASB, KJV, the usual connotation of the verb)? The Septuagint opts for anger (ὀργίζω), and in Ephesians 4:26 Paul cites the Septuagint rendering. This apostolic rendering may seem to settle the matter (hence the ESV). But we must ask two questions: (1) What is indicated by the "trembling" in Psalm 4? And (2), When Paul quotes the Septuagint translation, is he thereby giving it "official" sanction? Or is he simply borrowing its language?[44] If the latter, it would resemble the way many of us who grew up with the King James Version cite its language at times—not intending to convey interpretation or fulfillment, just borrowing the language. If this is the case, then Paul's words are appropriate, of course, but not intended to convey the meaning of Psalm 4:4a in context.

So the first question is what David meant by this word, "tremble." This word occurs four other times in the Psalms, and in each, the connotation is that of fear (18:8; 77:17, 19; 99:1), not anger. This is its sense in the majority of its occurrences elsewhere in the Old Testament also. More to the point, it does not seem in the context of Psalm 4 that a command to "be angry" would make as much sense as "to tremble in fear." David has no cause to command his leadership to be angry. But he does have cause

44 In the biblical world, the Greco-Roman world, as sometimes today, writers could cite works in a way to advance their argument without attempting to represent accurately the cited author's intended meaning.

to call them to fear the consequences of their apostasy. "Tremble," that is, "before God, not before me, and sin not against him."[45] "Tremble, and do not sin by forsaking the king and opposing the God who appointed him" is the sense. They should be very afraid of the consequences of turning against this king and this God, and of embracing false gods. "Tremble and do not sin" is a hendiadys:[46] as a result of their trembling in fear of God, they will cease running headlong in their rebellion against God. David is warning them that in opposing him they are opposing God.

This warning reflects an understanding of the king's anointing that is seen commonly in the Old Testament. We will come across it again, particularly in Psalm 2. By the prophetic anointing the king came under God's protection as his peculiar property. To oppose him was to oppose God. "Touch not my anointed ones, / do my prophets no harm" (105:15). This finds application in the New Testament—to oppose the people of Christ is to oppose him (Acts 9:4). But David belongs to God in an exceptional sense as the divinely appointed and anointed king and covenant partner. To oppose him is to oppose God. So "be afraid, and do not sin [by opposing God]" is the sense here.

The second pair of admonitions (Ps. 4:4b) continues in the same vein:

> ponder in your own hearts on your beds, and be silent.

"Ponder in your own hearts on your beds" connotes "Instead of hardening your hearts, search them," and "Be silent" again suggests a trembling fear (cf. Ex. 15:16; Job 31:34). With this pair of commands David counsels his leaders to consider their decisions carefully in the quiet contemplation of the night, and let their conscience confirm their faith.

The final pair of admonitions is given in Psalm 4:5:

> 5 Offer right sacrifices,
>   and put your trust in the LORD.

45 J. J. Stewart Perowne, *The Book of Psalms*, vol. 1 (Andover: Warren F Draper, 1879), 104.

46 I.e., a figure of speech in which two words are joined to express a single idea.

The admonition continues in its Godward orientation. The reference here is to the communal meal associated with certain sacrifices in Israel's worship. David is calling his leaders back to the faithful worship of the Lord God. "Trust in the Lord and offer sacrifices to him—not to Baal, the rain god."

We may summarize these seven admonitions as follows:

- Know your king (4:3).
- Understand the consequences of your sin (4:4a).
- Let your conscience confirm you or condemn you (4:4b).
- Remain faithful to the Lord (4:5).

Implicit in this admonition is a call to repentance, and by these admonitions David seeks to restore the confidence of his leadership.

*4:6–7: David's Petition*

Finally, in Psalm 4:6–7 we have the petition for rain. First, the prayer of the people:

> 6 There are many who say, "Who will show us some good?
> Lift up the light of your face upon us, O Lord!"

Then the king's own prayer:

> 7 Fill my heart with joy
> when their grain and new wine abound. (NIV)

By his petition David expresses his dependence upon God for the "good" he desires. Yet his request is bold in asking for this good in "abundance."

*4:8: David's Confidence and Praise*

At the end of the psalm the prayer is still unanswered. David is still in crisis. Yet he concludes with a resolve to go to sleep, a sleep explained in terms of confidence in God. We saw in our study of Psalm 3 that in 3:5 David reflects on the previous night's sleep that God gave him in that crisis; it was his morning prayer. Psalm 4, now, is an evening prayer, offered as he is about to retire:

> 8 In peace I will both lie down and sleep;
> for you alone, O LORD, make me dwell in safety.

This is clearly the climax of the psalm. The crisis remains, and the king is disturbed by the defection of his leaders. Indeed, if he does not remain awake and alert, he is left vulnerable. But his trust in God remains also, a trust so robust that he can lie down and sleep. Here David "returns to the tone of his prayer in 4:1, only that petition has given place, as it should, to possession and confident thankfulness."[47] David's trust in God's care is firm, and there are "no fears or anxieties delaying slumber."[48]

Vern Poythress finds in this verse a "figural analogy" that is meant to imply more than a night's rest. David needs sleep from physical exhaustion, to be sure. But his lying down to sleep at such a time reflects a larger scope of trust, a committing of himself to God's safekeeping, even in the face of death.[49] Augustine understands 4:8 somewhat similarly and links it to 1 Corinthians 15:54–55.[50] Others in the early church understood 4:8 with reference to the sleep of death also. Martin Luther likewise expressed his desire for this psalm, particularly 4:8, to be the last words he would hear sung to him when it came time to die.[51] Sleep in the midst of life-threatening crisis—this is what a person who trusts God can do (cf. Ps. 127:2; Isa. 26:3; Phil. 4:6–7). No longer fretting and no longer worrying, the king's heart is quiet. He is at peace because he trusts God to be his shield.

47 Alexander MacLaren, *The Psalms*, vol. 1 (New York: A. C. Armstrong and Son, 1904), 36.

48 Kirkpatrick, *Psalms: Book 1*, 20.

49 Vern Poythress, *Reading the Word of God in the Presence of God: A Handbook for Biblical Interpretation* (Wheaton, IL: Crossway, 2016), 380–38.

50 Augustine, *The Confessions of St. Augustine* (New York: Wiley and Putnam, 1844), 150–51.

51 Rowland E. Prothero, *The Psalms in Human Life* (1903; repr., Vestavia Hills, AL: Solid Ground Christian Books, n.d.), 13, 94.

## Reflections

The postscript tells us that David gives his psalm to the choirmaster for the people of God to sing with him. At this point it becomes our prayer and our song. This psalm is not just for David; he has explicitly given it to the people so that they all can sing it with him.

But just how may we sing this psalm? Where do we find ourselves in it? It may be that we can best identify not with David but with those who doubted him. Facing crisis they began to lose confidence in their king, and they began to defect. In our crises we may lose faith also, and at such times we need very much to hear David's admonitions, singing them to ourselves, as it were: "Know your king! Understand the consequences of faithlessness! Be very afraid of turning away your trust from him!" In every event of life, we owe God our trust and must count on our King always to do what is right and best for us.

Christians of course will want to identify not with his defectors but with David himself and sing his song of faith with him:

> They may sing it while they cling more and more every day to Jehovah, as their all-sufficient heritage, now and in the age to come. They may sing it, too, in the happy confidence of faith and hope, when the evening of this world's day is coming, and may then fall asleep in the certainty of what shall greet their eyes on the Resurrection morning.[52]

We may also sing this psalm of Christ, who trusted God supremely. In the midst of danger the Lord Jesus slept peacefully and afterward exhorted his disciples to greater faith (Mark 4:35–41). Under the severest of opposition he "entrust[ed] himself to him who judges justly" (1 Pet. 2:23) and laid down in the sleep of death, confident of God's safekeeping (Luke 23:46). This peaceful and restful peace he gives to us also (John 14:27), and he exhorts us to trust God's safekeeping always

52 Andrew Bonar, *Christ and His Church in the Book of Psalms* (London: James Nisbet, 1859), 15.

(Phil. 4:6; 1 Pet. 5:7), even in the face of death. Like David, our prayer for deliverance rests on the righteousness of God and divine mercy (Ps. 4:1).[53] And like David, we can rest peacefully also, singing of Jesus's uninterrupted kingship, of the continued advance of his kingdom, and of our safety under his protective care forever.

53 J. A. Motyer, "The Psalms," in D. A. Carson et al., eds., *New Bible Commentary* (Downers Grove, IL: InterVarsity Press, 1994), 490.

# 4

# The Royal Orientation of the Psalms

*"O Lord, save the king!"*

ONE IMPORTANT UPSHOT of this historical approach is the royal orientation of the Psalter. By "royal orientation" we mean that the king is the central figure. Fundamentally, the Psalms are both *by* and *about* the king. The Psalter can be thought of as a royal hymnbook, and its individual psalms have the house of David as its subject matter and point of reference. Obviously, not all the psalms are about the king; many are about Israel without reference to the king. This is especially true in the fourth and fifth books (e.g., Pss. 90; 93; 113; 114; 115). But ideally, Israel is to be ruled by the king. According to David Carr, "The education of scribes in the biblical world was designed to train in them royal values and national culture."[1] But "it was the king, not the scribe, who embodied the fullest ideal of humanity."[2] The royal orientation anticipates David's greater son promised to him in 2 Samuel 7:8–16 and finally realized in the Lord Jesus Christ. At this point we want to

1 David M. Carr, *Writing on the Tablet of the Heart: Origin of Scripture and Literature* (Oxford: Oxford University Press, 2005), cited in Gordon J. Wenham, *Psalms as Torah: Reading Biblical Song Ethically* (Grand Rapids, MI: Baker Academic, 2012), 45.

2 Carr, *Writing on the Tablet of the Heart*, 31, cited in Wenham, *Psalms as Torah*, 42.

establish that this is indeed the orientation of the Psalter and just how it is so.[3]

The importance of this discussion is immediately evident: it determines how we ought to read and understand the Psalms. Is the Psalter in fact oriented toward the king? Who is the "I," the "me," the "my," and the "he" who speaks in the Psalms? If these refer to "everyman" or even "every pious man," that is one thing. But if they refer to David or the Davidic king who represents the kingdom of God and the people of God, quite another understanding arises.

For example, as we have just seen, Psalm 4, "A Psalm of David," is not about personal opposition and interpersonal conflict; opposition to the king is in view. The difference is important and determines how we are to understand the psalm. Or if Psalm 63 was in fact written by David during his flight from Absalom, then his reflections on the sanctuary (63:2) take specific significance; the superscript provides this context, and without it we are left with no context.

As we will see in chapter 7, Hermann Gunkel identified ten or eleven "royal" psalms—Psalms 2, 18, 20, 21, 45, 72, 101, 110, 132, 144:1–11, and possibly 89 (cf. 89:47–52). Gunkel's determination was based on each psalm's obvious reference to the king. And indeed, these psalms pertain to some specific aspect of the king's career: his coronation (2; 110), his marriage (45), his leading the nation into battle (20) and his victorious return (21), the qualities of his person and rule (18; 72; 144), intercessions that the king would be righteous and prosper (72) and that God would remember his covenant with David and his resolve to bring the ark to Jerusalem (132). But in most psalms the king serves the national interests, not his own, and in that sense they too are royal. According to the superscripts fully half of the Psalter is Davidic, and therefore royal. Moreover, on the one hand, the somewhat random scattering of these "royal" psalms suggests

3 See Bruce K. Waltke, "A Canonical Process Approach to the Psalms," originally published in John S. Feinberg and Paul D. Feinberg, *Tradition and Testament: Essays in Honor of Charles Lee Feinberg* (Chicago: Moody Press, 1981), 3–18; republished in Waltke, *The Dance between God and Humanity: Reading the Bible Today as the People of God* (Grand Rapids, MI: Eerdmans, 2013), 58–74.

a royal orientation; on the other hand, as we will see in chapter 15, when we examine the final arrangement, shape, and message of the Psalter, these uniquely royal psalms were placed strategically to signal just this Davidic/royal perspective. As we have already mentioned, Psalm 2, the psalm in which God's anointed is commanded to ask for the nations as his inheritance, is placed up front to help introduce the Psalter and establish its leading figure. In Psalm 3 we hear the king in prayer surrounded by his enemies. Similarly, the uniquely royal psalms are placed at the seams of the five "books" of the Psalms to remind us of the same. The entire first book is Davidic (Pss. 3–41), as is most of the second. The editors added more psalms of David in the other three books. The large number of psalms by David and the strategic placing of uniquely royal psalms in the Psalter's editing seem to justify this understanding of its orientation.

John Eaton's landmark work, *Kingship and the Psalms*, peruses many Psalms and demonstrates that this royal orientation goes further and is, in fact, pervasive. His work begins with the most obvious clue, the superscripts' explicit identification of David, and proceeds to display further evidence from the rest of the Psalter. Here we will summarize his primary lines of evidence:[4]

1. The heading "Of David" appears over seventy-three of the psalms (eighty-four in the Septuagint).
2. Strong biblical tradition (1 Chron. 15–16; 25:1–8; 2 Chron. 29:25–26; Neh. 12:36; Amos 6:5, etc.) and later Jewish tradition also, including one of the Dead Sea Scrolls, unanimously attribute the Psalter to David.
3. Throughout the ancient Near East the king was responsible for the temple worship, and David took this initiative also (1 Chron 15–16; cf. Hezekiah, 2 Chron 29; Isa. 38:20).
4. The only identifiable "situation" in the "psalms of the individual" ("I") is that of the king.

4 John H. Eaton, *Kingship and the Psalms*, Studies in Biblical Theology, 2nd ser., 32 (Naperville, IL: Alec R. Allenson, n.d.), 20–26.

5. "Coupled with the preceding point is the general homogeneity of the psalms. . . . There is a prevailing similarity which is in accord with an origin within a restricted royal and national cultus."
6. The "enemies" in view in various psalms are frequently nations (e.g., Pss. 18:43; 20; 21; 28; 61; 63; 89; 144), indicating again that the king is in view. Psalm 21, for example, opens with the king's rejoicing in victory.
7. In some of the psalms the "I" and "we" alternate (e.g., 9–10; 44; 60; 66; 75; 102). This interpretive problem is easily resolved by a recognition of the representative character of the king.
8. Royal references occur frequently throughout the "psalms of the individual." Here he cites Gunkel: "All nations attend to the psalmist's thanksgiving (18:49; 57:9; 138:1, 4; 119:46). His deliverance has vast repercussions (22:27–31). He invokes a world-judgment to rectify his cause (7:7–8; 56:7; 59:5, 8; cf. 43:1). He depicts himself as victorious over the nations through God's intervention (118:10). He confronts armies (3:6; 27:3; 56:2; 59; 109:3; 120:7; 140:2, 7–8). He is like a bull raising horns in triumph (Ps. 92:10; 1 Sam. 2:1). He is God's son (Ps. 2:7)."
9. "In many cases the royal interpretation is especially to be preferred because it allows the psalm as it stands to be seen as a consistent and meaningful whole."
10. "It is almost unthinkable that a collection of hymns stemming from the royal temple—one large court enclosed . . . both the LORD's Temple and the king's palace—should not include the petitions and praises of the king."

Each of Eaton's ten points may be expanded at some length. Eaton comments further:

> The speaker vows continual psalmody. He stands out before the vast festal congregation (22:33, 26; 40:10f.). His head is raised on high. . . . His glory receives special mention. . . . He is blessed with superabun-

> dant life. . . . His designations of God as his helper are often related to warfare. . . . Enemies, military and national in character, aim at him personally rather than at his country and people.[5]

All of this reflects a royal orientation. And we should keep in mind those that mention David and his house (18:50; 78:70; 89:3, 20, 35, 49; 132:1, 10–11, 17; 144:10; cf. 122:5). The psalmist's concern for the fate of his people, as in Psalm 94, is best accounted for with reference to the king. Some of the Psalms are prayers of intercession for the king (cf. 28:8; 61:6–7; 63:11; 84:8–9; 72). Ethan's lament in Psalm 89 is all about the king. In Psalm 84, the pilgrims make their way to Jerusalem for the festival, and when they arrive, they sing of their king:

> 9 Behold our shield, O God;
> look on the face of your anointed! (84:9)

The "shield" is the king, God's anointed, and the prayer is for him, and he represents to the covenant congregation who is in corporate solidarity with him—David and his kingdom and proleptically Christ the true King and his church. The covenant people participate in the king's defeat and victories. If we read the psalms as pertaining to "everyman," we miss that the psalms speak of the king's battle: "Behold our shield, O God!" It is not our battle—it is his. Our hope hangs on *his* success.

So also in Psalm 44, the sons of Korah sing of the king:

> 5 Through you we push down our foes;
> through your name we tread down those who rise up against us.
> 6 For not in my bow do I trust,
> nor can my sword save me.
> 7 But you have saved us from our foes
> and have put to shame those who hate us.

5 Eaton, *Kingship and the Psalms*, 23–24.

8 In God we have boasted continually,
and we will give thanks to your name forever. *Selah.*
(44:5–8)

Is it not most likely that the king represents the defeated army of Israel in prayer before God? Who is a more likely candidate than the king as the speaker of the line "I do not trust in my bow, I do not count on my sword to save me" (44:6 NLT)? It is also instructive to note that in this psalm, as in many others, there is a fluid interchange between the plural pronoun "we" and the singular pronoun "I." This psalm begins, for example, "We have heard with our ears / our fathers have told us what you did in their days" followed by "You are my King, O God" (44:4). This change can best be explained on the assumption that the human subject is the king representing the people. In short, although the psalm is assigned to the sons of Korah, the human subject is a king. Does not this also suggest that other Psalms not assigned to David were composed for Israel's king?[6]

James Hutchinson argues at length that the Psalter itself is intended by the editors to be understood as an extended reflection on Psalm 2,[7] and John Woodhouse argues that "the reader of the Psalms is not allowed to forget" Psalm 2 and its promise of the reign of God's anointed. Even the exilic Psalm 137 is about David, he argues: "What else does 'we remembered Zion' (Ps. 137:1) mean? Psalm 137 is about the city of David, and the promises of God associated with it."[8] Many expressions are found throughout the Psalms that are especially appropriate with reference to the king.

From you comes my praise in the great congregation
my vows I will perform before those who fear him (22:25).

6 Waltke, "Canonical Process," 13.

7 James Hely Hutchinson, "The Psalter as a Book," in *Stirred by a Noble Theme: The Book of Psalms in the Life of The Church*, ed. Andrew Shead (Nottingham, UK: Apollos, 2013), chap. 2.

8 John Woodhouse, "Reading the Psalms as Christian Scripture," in Shead, *Stirred*, 54–55.

But you have exalted my horn like that of the wild ox;
you have poured over me fresh oil (92:10).

All nations surrounded me;
in the name of the Lord I cut them off (118:10).

I will also speak of your testimonies before kings
and shall not be put to shame (119:46).

The Davidic covenant, often in view in the Psalms, most prominently in Psalms 89 and 132, indicate that the royal sons remain in view also. Indeed, in light of this promise (2 Sam. 7:12–16), "it would be most surprising if David did not intend his many and varied types of psalms to be used by and for the house of David at the house of the Lord. Almost certainly these royal psalms had a royal significance in Israel's cultus." Each next Davidic king inherited the covenant promise and thus, at least in his ideal, inherits the nations (Ps. 2:8) and reigns in righteousness over the world, and also "suffers on behalf of the kingdom of God and wrestles with God in prayer" for that kingdom.[9]

It is surely significant also that this royal orientation of the Psalter parallels the literature and hymns of the contemporary ancient Near Eastern religions.

## Conclusion

All these themes and more indicate that pervasively it is the king who is in view throughout the Psalter. It is abundantly evident that the subject of the Psalms is not the common man or even the outstandingly pious man. And the many about Israel are about the kingdom of God over which the Lord set the house of David. More basic to an understanding of the Psalms than a recognition of the various psalm types is the recognition that the king is the subject in view throughout—not just in the praise psalms but in the laments and acknowledgment (traditionally,

9 Waltke, "Canonical Process," 13–14.

"thanksgiving") psalms also. And after the fall of the house of David the eschatological dimension of the royal psalms took even sharper focus.

Some (particularly older) commentators were so convinced of the specifically Davidic orientation that they would labor to reconstruct historical background to psalms where none is provided in the superscript. Such a task should be considered tentative at best. There are exceptions to the Davidic orientation, of course, but even in psalms written after the collapse of the Davidic kingship, the Davidic orientation is not necessarily absent, as Psalm 137. The royal orientation of the Psalter is pervasive. It is essentially a royal hymnbook with all the people of God gathered around the king at the temple.

### The Significance of the Psalter's Royal Orientation

The significance of this point is readily apparent. Apart from this royal orientation many of the psalms would lack unity and coherence, as we have seen in Psalm 4. Without a recognition of the Davidic authorship of the psalms attributed to him this royal orientation would be less apparent, and the exposition of those psalms would go astray, as happened after historical criticism hit academics like a tsunami.

The significance of this goes further as we seek to understand the Psalms in canonical perspective. We will explore this at length in chapter 12, but here we can note already that the Davidic king is prospective of David's greater son. And often the Psalms present the king in his ideal, in which case Christ comes into view more directly. Moreover, the king represents the people, Israel—the two were inseparable. And just as the king is prospective of the greater King, so also Israel is prospective of the church. This royal orientation of the Psalter defines its place in the canon and gives us the right to sing the Psalms with reference to Christ. As we understand that the Psalms concern the king, and when we observe that David delivers his psalms "to the choirmaster" to sing about the king, he gives us warrant to sing of the King also. If we miss this, we will individualize the Psalms and read them as though they are talking about us—an interpretive mistake that would rob Christ of his glory and us of their original and canonical significance.

The Psalms are ultimately the prayers of Jesus Christ, the Son of God. He alone is worthy to pray the ideal vision of a king suffering for righteousness and emerging victorious over the hosts of evil. As the corporate head of the church he represents believers in these prayers. Moreover, Christians, as sons of God and as royal priests, can rightly pray these prayers along with their representative head. Dietrich Bonhoeffer also reached the conclusion that Jesus Christ is the one praying in the psalter. "The Psalter," he wrote, "is the prayer book of Jesus Christ in the truest sense of the word."[10]

With this royal understanding we lay a firm foundation for a Christological interpretation of the Psalms. We will see more of this throughout this book and especially in chapter 12. Jesus said the Psalms speak of him, and here we see just how that is so—they speak of the king, and he, the son of David, is the King par excellence. The experiences and emotions of the king in the Psalms—his passions, his sufferings, his struggles, his heartaches—foreshadow the experiences and emotions of the Lord Jesus, the messianic King, the Christ who in fact has taken on all of our sufferings and emotions. Even he, on the cross, felt abandoned by God. He was tempted. And yet he triumphed and in doing so both accomplished our redemption and showed us how we may triumph also. With this historical approach and royal orientation in mind we see our Savior more clearly.

10 Waltke, "Canonical Process," 16; Dietrich Bonhoeffer, *Life Together*, trans. John W. Doberstein (New York: Harper and Brothers, 1954), 46.

# 5

# The Liturgical Setting of the Psalms

*"Enter his courts with praise!"*

IN THIS CHAPTER we examine the origin of the Psalms in relation to the temple and their use in Israel's worship. We will see in chapter 7 that form criticism examines not only the composition or form of the individual psalms but also their "setting in life"; this area of attention is so significant that it becomes a distinct approach of its own.

## Background

At God's direction to Moses at Sinai, some four hundred years before David, Israel constructed a portable temple, an ornate tent-like (tabernacle) structure with three major sections, the center of which was the Holy of Holies or Most Holy Place. This sacred room that housed the ark of the covenant was at the heart of Israel's worship; its sacredness can scarcely be overstated. In this place the transcendent and omnipresent God made his glory uniquely present (cf. Ex. 40:35). We will discuss more fully the symbolic function of the ark of the covenant below. It was the footstool of God's throne. He sat enthroned between the cherubim, winged creatures who guarded his throne (1 Chron. 28:2; Pss. 99:5; 132:7). This was "the house of the LORD" (e.g., Ps. 122:1), his throne room (Jer. 3:16–17), and the place where through sacrifice God met with his people (Ex. 25:22). Covering the ark housing the law was the mercy seat, where sacrificial blood was sprinkled to atone for the covenant people's sin. This tent followed Israel through the wilderness (cf. Num. 10:33–34), and during Joshua's military campaigns the ark was carried in battle to show God's protective and powerful presence. The tent and ark finally found a home in Shiloh, but during Eli's time the ark was captured by the Philistines. After considerable trouble, it was finally taken to Kiriath-jearim (1 Sam. 4–7). The tent was relocated to Nob (1 Sam. 21) and finally to Gibeon (1 Chron. 16:39). The ark remained in Kiriath-jearim during the reign of impious Saul until David, having captured Jerusalem, brought it to his capital city and placed it in a tent he had prepared for it on Mount Zion (2 Sam. 6; 1 Chron. 15–16).

The presence of the ark in Jerusalem was important for David in order to show God's presence there, for it was the LORD who was Israel's King (cf. Ps. 5:2). Because the ark housed the Law of God, its presence in Jerusalem also symbolized the moral character of his kingdom. David had plans to construct a temple for the ark, to replace the tent, but instead God assigned this role to Solomon (2 Sam. 7; 1 Chron. 17). At Solomon's ceremony dedicating the temple (1 Kings 8; 2 Chron. 7) the ark found a permanent home, and according to Josephus the sacred furnishings of the tent, presumably in Gibeon, were then brought to the temple also (1 Kings 8:4).[1] By relocating the ark to Jerusalem David made Jerusalem a sacred place, and Solomon's great temple ensured that it would remain so for centuries. The "holy hill" of Mount Zion (Ps. 15:1) was the Lord's residence (68:16) and, thus, the center of Israel's religion and worship.

## The Function of the Mosaic Cultus

Our focus here is the temple worship itself—its significance and how it functioned—and how this background is evident in the Psalms. The terminology commonly used in academic literature with reference to

1 Flavius Josephus, *The Antiquities of the Jews*, 8.4.1, trans. William Whiston, Project Gutenberg (website), accessed September 12, 2022, https://gutenberg.org/.

the system of old covenant worship is *cult* or *cultus*. This can be confusing to many because "cult" in popular lingo connotes an unorthodox system of religious belief. In academic contexts, however, the term simply refers to the external expression of any given religion. The practice and forms of religion are in view. In Christian contexts discussion of "cultus" would focus on ritual practices such as the gathering of the congregation, the reading of Scripture, the singing of praises, prayer, the observance of the ordinances, and the preaching of the word. The precise ordering or pattern of these practices we would refer to as *liturgy*. In the Old Testament context the focus of this discussion is the temple, the priesthood, the sacrificial system, the offerings, the religious calendar, and so on. In the temple the worshiper enters the sacred space by means of divinely defined covenant structures. The presence of God is not open to just anyone, anytime, and prescribed procedures must be followed. Most importantly, there must be forgiveness via sacrifice. Then, only a certain kind of person may enter. As we have seen, the Psalter restricts its worship to the righteous, and it is in this sense that Psalm 1 functions as its gateway.

### *Symbolism*

The first significance of the Old Testament worship was its *symbolism*. Its visible form portrayed the essentials of their religion. On the one hand, it symbolized the movement of man toward God, from the inner spiritual reality to outward actions that were offered up to God. The ascending smoke, for example, would represent prayers going up to God, and the raising of hands would symbolize offering up gifts to God and receiving his grace. On the other hand, Israel's liturgy symbolized the movement of God to man. The inside of the Holy of Holies was highly symbolic also. Carved on the walls were palm trees and other trees, all reminiscent of the garden of Eden and eternal life. At the very center of the room was the ark of the covenant. In fact, as the high priest would proceed through Solomon's temple, the doorways narrowed—the main door, the entrance way, and then into the Holy of Holies. The roofline dropped, driving attention finally to the ark of the covenant covered in gold. The individual

Israelite could not enter the Holy of Holies; only the high priest could enter there, and that only once a year. And yet these functions of the priest were clearly revealed for all Israel, so they lived in imagination, picturing in their mind's eye the activities of the priest inside.

Inside the ark were the tablets of stone, the Ten Commandments, symbolizing the moral rule of God. Israel's religion in its form resembled other religions of the biblical world, but in terms of theology and religion, there was no resemblance. In pagan religions, there were nature deities. There would be a statue of the sun or the moon; through myth and ritual, voodoo, their priest sought to manipulate the idol to make the people fruitful. But at the heart of Israel's religion was the transcendent will of God—ethics, morals, a way of living. Instead of manipulating the gods to obtain life as in pagan religions, the Israelite religion demanded submission to the Lord's rule of love of God and neighbor to live in the way of life. At the heart of Israel's religion was the reminder that God's kingdom is a righteous kingdom marked by the rule of his law and that the function of the cultus was not mere ceremony. The temple was the beachhead of God's rule in the world.

Then over the top of the ark was the mercy seat where atonement was made by the sprinkling of blood by which a sinful people could enter the presence of God in worship. Overlooking the ark and the mercy seat were the cherubim, sphinxlike figures that guarded the sanctity of that holy place, just as the cherubim protected the garden of Eden from sinners. Then outside of there was the showbread or bread of presence whereby the worshiper could eat and fellowship with God. Then outside of that was the altar of incense symbolizing prayer. Everything about the temple was designed to teach theology through symbolism.

This symbolic function of the temple has a distinct role in Psalm 73, the psalm of Asaph's crisis of faith. In a later chapter we will see that it was through the symbolism of the temple and its visual reminders of the ways of God that his crisis of faith was resolved. The temple symbolism was important to David also, as he expresses in his psalm of repentance (Ps. 51).

Another dimension of the temple's symbolism is its *typology*. Typology is a kind of symbolism, but it is a symbolism that points ahead to the future. It is anticipatory. It portrays or illustrates what will be actualized in the future. Typology is eschatologically oriented. In the progress and unfolding of biblical revelation this temple theme develops significantly, beginning in Genesis and climaxing in Revelation. In Genesis 1–3 the enjoyment of God's presence on earth is established and then lost. In the Mosaic tabernacle and then in the temple, God's presence is reestablished among his people Israel. But God's tabernacle-temple presence in Israel was not an end in itself. Nor was the tabernacle-temple itself the pattern—it was but a "copy" of an eternal heavenly reality.[2] It was a shadow of heaven, as it were. The incarnation of Christ marked a new advance in the reestablishing of God's temple presence in the earth (John 1:14)—he was himself "God with us" (Isa. 7:14; cf. Matt. 1:21–23). But it was not merely his person but by his destroyed and risen body by which Jesus established himself as the meeting place with God (John 2:18–22; cf. Heb. 10:19–20). Pentecost marked a further advance: now the church, God's people by the indwelling Spirit are constituted a temple (1 Cor. 3:16; 6:19; Eph. 2:21; 1 Pet. 2:5). Then all this culminates in the return of Christ and the eternal state where the people of God dwell in God's immediate presence (Rev. 21:22). As wonderful as the Old Testament temple was in itself because of its glory and the presence of God, it was, after all, only anticipatory. It served as a pointer, directing attention to what is ultimately realized in Christ.

### *Sacramental Function*

The Old Testament cultus was also *sacramental* in that by its provisions the worshiper entered communion with God—through sacrifice, the worshiper obtained forgiveness and found fellowship with God.

### *Artistic Propaganda*

Finally, the cultus functioned as *artistic propaganda*—propaganda in the best sense of the word. *Artistic proclamation*, we might call it. That is, by its building and banners and music it proclaimed a particular

2 Cf. Heb. 8–10, see esp. 8:2, 5; 9:1, 11–12, 23, 24; cf. Isa. 6:1; Rev. 4–5.

message and point of view. Architecture can do that. Just as the classic Greek architecture and marble buildings of our nation's capital speak of power and authority, so also did the temple. This is why the church has often built cathedrals—the buildings themselves speak of permanence and authority. This is why following the period of "Enlightenment," universities constructed great cathedral-like buildings with grandiose architecture that was intended to replace the church with the secular state. University libraries, for example, often look much like a cathedral—triple arched, recessed doorways, stained glass windows, and so on. They have statues, not of the apostles but of Rousseau or Voltaire and the Rationalists. It makes a statement and, in their case, a new form of worship. So also Solomon's temple. This magnificent edifice itself with all its trappings made a statement. It symbolized permanence, endurance, authority, and strength, and it proclaimed that the Lord is King. And with its artistic and architectural symbolism, its typological significance remains, anticipating the final day when the Lord's kingship will be fully established over all the earth.

From our distance it may be a bit difficult to enter the atmosphere of Israel's worship under the old covenant. Its expression was more external, physical, and structured, and it entailed more the senses of sight and smell. Solomon's temple was to be seen and appreciated with its gold, brilliant colors, designs, and artistry. The smell of the smoke and the roasting meat of the sacrifice of the altar filled the air. There was the priest in his priestly white garments with bells and pomegranates on the hems. But an acquaintance with Israel's cultus is necessary to an understanding of the Psalms.

**David's Innovations**

Note that in the Mosaic Law, nothing is said about hymnody in the cultus. After crossing the Red Sea, Moses and the people sang, and so did Miriam with a tambourine in hand (Ex. 15:1, 20–21). And after the defeat of the Canaanites so did Deborah and Barak (Judg. 5). But music was not part of an established liturgy. The only prescribed words were those to be spoken when the worshiper brought his firstfruits: "A wandering Aramean was my father" (Deut. 26:5), a reference to Jacob's sojourn in Aram (Syria). The message of the temple was conveyed by its symbolism and ceremonies. It was not verbally or musically oriented.

But with David this changed. He built on the Mosaic provisions and kept that system of worship in place, but he transformed it into something much larger and more dramatic. He provided staging and music to accompany the Mosaic rituals. And the singing of psalms now became part of the atmosphere, along with stringed instruments and the blowing of trumpets. This is the setting of the Psalter.

The moment of this change was David's relocation of the ark to Jerusalem. Both the writer of Samuel and the chronicler describe the carefully planned, festive occasion. Levites carried the ark in procession, and David himself was dressed in white linen, priestly garments, and the entire nation was involved in the celebration. Gatekeepers were appointed for security. Musical guilds were appointed under Asaph's oversight, with singers and musical instruments of all kinds to heighten the celebration. David himself was so overjoyed at the occasion that his wife, like her father, Saul, who had no love for the Lord, despised David. First Chronicles 15–16 reports the event. The entire account is relevant in this connection, but these verses are especially to our point:

> [4] Then he appointed some of the Levites as ministers before the ark
> of the LORD, to invoke, to thank, and to praise the LORD, the God
> of Israel. [5] Asaph was the chief, and second to him were Zechariah,
> Jeiel, Shemiramoth, Jehiel, Mattithiah, Eliab, Benaiah, Obed-edom,
> and Jeiel, who were to play harps and lyres; Asaph was to sound the
> cymbals, [6] and Benaiah and Jahaziel the priests were to blow trum-
> pets regularly before the ark of the covenant of God. [7] Then on that
> day David first appointed that thanksgiving be sung to the LORD by
> Asaph and his brothers. . . . [37] So David left Asaph and his brothers
> there before the ark of the covenant of the LORD to minister regularly
> before the ark as each day required. . . . [39] And he left Zadok the priest
> and his brothers the priests before the tabernacle of the LORD in the

> high place that was at Gibeon [40] to offer burnt offerings to the LORD on the altar of burnt offering regularly morning and evening, to do all that is written in the Law of the LORD that he commanded Israel. (16:4–7, 37, 39–40)[3]

This event marked the change in Israel's worship. Music and singing not only highlighted that occasion—it was now made a permanent fixture in Israel's worship. David instituted singing and music to accompany the temple rituals from that point onward. Essentially, he transformed the sacred ceremonies into opera. The Psalms were composed as libretto to accompany the Mosaic rituals. Psalms now were sung regularly at the daily sacrifices. The sacred personnel associated with Israel's worship were expanded to include music leaders, choirs, and musicians. The sacred personnel were expanded beyond the house of Aaron and the Levites and now included the king and the prophets who represent God to the king and speak to the king for God (cf. Ps. 50). The sacred calendar was expanded also. In addition to the annual, weekly, and daily acts of worship prescribed by Moses—the Day of Atonement, New Year, the sacred feasts, the weekly Sabbaths, the sabbatical year, and so on—the cultus played an important role in "crisis" moments, times of war or drought or plague or earthquake (1 Kings 8:31–53). The innovations David introduced were extensive and reshaped Israel's worship forever.

David was a remarkably multigifted man. He was handsome and athletic. He was a shepherd, a rugged outdoorsman, a fierce warrior, a brilliant military tactician, a successful king and administrator, a master poet and skillful speaker, and an accomplished musician (cf. 1 Sam. 16:18). He was the Mozart of his day who transformed the entire atmosphere of Israel's worship, reshaping the sacred rituals into a grand and glorious praise of God in song with musical instruments accompanying. This is the backdrop of the Psalms and their use in Israel's worship.

3 Cf. 1 Chron. 16:8–22 = Ps. 105:1–5; 1 Chron. 16:23–36 = Pss. 96:1–3 and 106:1, 47. Note that at the time of David, the ark was separated from the tabernacle.

## The Temple Orientation of the Psalms

This temple backdrop is evident throughout the Psalter. The postscript to many of the Psalms make explicit that the Psalms were originally intended for use in temple worship: fifty-five of the psalms are said to be "to the choirmaster." David (and others) wrote psalms for use in the temple and then delivered them to the chief musician for use in public worship. The superscript to Psalm 30 tells us that David composed the psalm specifically for the temple dedication. Just as he had designed and prepared beforehand for the temple construction (1 Chron. 28), so also he composed psalms for use once it was constructed.[4] The call to praise that begins so many of the praise psalms is directed to the temple assembly. The songs of grateful praise have exclusive reference to a group or community setting accompanied by an offering. Likewise, the hymns, the community laments, the battle psalms (20; 21), the royal psalms (2; 110), and the royal wedding psalm (45) all were composed for temple use. The repeated refrains in some of the psalms (e.g., 8:1, 9) indicate corporate use also.

And there are still further indications of the Psalms' liturgical use. Aspects of Israel's liturgy included the sacred site of the temple, sacred objects, sacred personnel, sacred seasons, and sacred institutions such as offerings and sacrifices.[5] One finds frequent reference to the liturgical site "Zion," "house of the Lord," and "holy hill" (e.g., Pss. 2:6; 3:4; 48:1; 63:14; 74:3; 76:2; 92:12–13; 100:4; 114:2; 116:18, 19; 118:19, 20). One also finds a mixture of references to offerings (22:25–26; 96:8; 107:22; 116:14, 17–19), feasts (50:8; 69:22), visitations with friends (22:22–24), and public processions (15; 24; 26:6–8 [cf. 43:4]; 47:1; 59:8; 68:24–27; 84). In addition, there is an entire collection labeled "Songs of Ascent" (120–134). Reference is also made to sacred objects: altar (84:3; 118:27), cup (116:13), banners (20:5), and musical instruments (47:5; 150). Sacred personnel include angels (103:20–21), priests (132:8–9),

4 Bruce K. Waltke, *An Old Testament Theology: An Exegetical, Canonical, and Thematic Approach* (Grand Rapids, MI: Zondervan, 2007), 873.

5 Waltke, *Old Testament Theology*, 458–67.

Levites (135:19–21), warriors and worshipers (20–21), and, above all, the anointed king.[6]

Many of the psalms, of course, did not originate in direct connection with the temple. Some originated with David in his wilderness experience where he was being prepared for kingship and learning a life of faith in his flight from King Saul (cf. 57 and 59). So also in his later flight from Absalom, he composed Psalm 3 apart from any immediate contact with the temple (cf. 74, 79). Psalm 137 was written in the Babylonian exile. But even these reflect a temple orientation. In Psalm 137 the exiles in Babylon respond to the mocking taunt of their captors to sing songs of Zion with a resolve to remember Zion. In Psalm 3, David prays toward God's holy place. In Psalms 42–43 the psalmist in exile anticipates returning to worship at the temple. As Weiser remarks, these psalms that were written in some way apart from the temple are "inwardly so closely related to the sanctuary and its cultic traditions that not many hymns are left over in the Psalter of which it can be said that they are really 'dissociated from the cult' and not many exclusively composed for private edification."[7]

One question that arises at this point is how the sage and the didactic psalms fit in the temple setting. The sage was in the city gate. How would Psalm 1, for example, fit in the temple setting? Psalm 49, another didactic psalm, is one that deals with theodicy and the problem of evil. How does this psalm fit in temple life? Or Psalm 73? The answer seems to be found in the function of the priest as a teacher in Israel, and in this way the didactic psalms have a very appropriate place in temple worship. This is alluded to in Malachi 2:4–6: "So shall you know that I have sent this command to you, that my covenant with Levi may stand, says the Lord of hosts. . . . True instruction was in his mouth, and no wrong was found on his lips."

6 Waltke, "Psalms," in W. VanGemeren, ed., *New International Dictionary of Old Testament Theology and Exegesis*, vol. 4 (Grand Rapids, MI: Zondervan, 1997), 1108.

7 Artur Weiser, *The Psalms: A Commentary*, The Old Testament Library (Philadelphia: Westminster, 1962), 81.

The leading features of Israel's cultus that we highlighted above are reflected in the Psalms also. We will survey them again, now with reference to the Psalter.

*The Sacred Site*

We mentioned above the "statement" made by the architecture of the temple. This is often reflected in the songs of Zion. These psalms celebrate the greatness of Zion and invite all to come and look at these magnificent buildings which themselves proclaim that God is king. Psalm 48 provides a good example here:

1 Great is the LORD and greatly to be praised
in the city of our God!
His holy mountain, 2 beautiful in elevation,
is the joy of all the earth,
Mount Zion, in the far north,
the city of the great King.
3 Within her citadels God
has made himself known as a fortress.
4 For behold, the kings assembled;
they came on together.
5 As soon as they saw it, they were astounded;
they were in panic; they took to flight.
6 Trembling took hold of them there,
anguish as of a woman in labor.
7 By the east wind you shattered
the ships of Tarshish.
8 As we have heard, so have we seen
in the city of the LORD of hosts,
in the city of our God,
which God will establish forever. *Selah*
9 We have thought on your steadfast love, O God,
in the midst of your temple.
10 As your name, O God,

so your praise reaches to the ends of the earth.
Your right hand is filled with righteousness.
11 Let Mount Zion be glad!
Let the daughters of Judah rejoice
because of your judgments!
12 Walk about Zion, go around her,
number her towers,
13 consider well her ramparts,
go through her citadels,
that you may tell the next generation
14 that this is God,
our God forever and ever.
He will guide us forever.

Following the symbolism of the temple further, the contrast between *inside* and *outside* the temple is stark. Within the temple, covenantal benevolences are mediated to the worshiper, including forgiveness through sacrifice. Within it is holy, set apart; without is the profane. When the worshiper would enter the temple complex he entered into a sacred space, the holy sphere of God's presence. Within is what is eternal and infinite, the presence of God; outside is what is finite and temporal, passing away. Within the temple there is perfection; outside the temple there is imperfection and sin. The temple was a "sacred" site in the fullest sense of the term.

This awesome sense of God's presence informs the Psalter at virtually every point. The terms "Zion," "house of the LORD," "holy hill," "sanctuary of God," "dwelling place in Zion" all signal this thinking (e.g., 2:6; 3:4; 63:14; 74:3; 76:2; 79:1; 92:12–13; 100:4; 114:2; 116:18, 19; 118:19, 20). Some psalms celebrate the election of Mount Zion. Just as God chose the house of David, so he also chose Mount Zion (e.g., 46; 48; 76; 84; 87; 122). In pagan religions the god is endemically related to a given place; he is related to that mountain. He cannot move. But Israel's God is transcendent. He met Israel at Mount Sinai and then he elected Mount Zion. He is not inherently connected with Mount Zion but infinite and sovereign over all the world; yet in grace he condescends to reside with Israel in Zion, the place of his choosing. Psalm 46 is an outstanding example of this:

1 God is our refuge and strength,
a very present help in trouble.
2 Therefore we will not fear though the earth gives way,
though the mountains be moved into the heart of the sea,
3 though its waters roar and foam,
though the mountains tremble at its swelling. *Selah*
4 There is a river whose streams make glad the city of God,
the holy habitation of the Most High.
5 God is in the midst of her; she shall not be moved;
God will help her when morning dawns.
6 The nations rage, the kingdoms totter;
he utters his voice, the earth melts.
7 The LORD of hosts is with us;
the God of Jacob is our fortress. *Selah*
8 Come, behold the works of the LORD,
how he has brought desolations on the earth.
9 He makes wars cease to the end of the earth;
he breaks the bow and shatters the spear;
he burns the chariots with fire.
10 "Be still, and know that I am God.
I will be exalted among the nations,
I will be exalted in the earth!"
11 The LORD of hosts is with us;
the God of Jacob is our fortress. *Selah*

Psalm 87 is another psalm that celebrates Zion in a pointed way:

1 On the holy mount stands the city he founded;
2 the LORD loves the gates of Zion
more than all the dwelling places of Jacob.

3 Glorious things of you are spoken,
O city of God.

We noted previously that only the righteous and upright may worship God aright. Accordingly, some psalms are "entrance liturgies" describing the person who is qualified to participate in the worship of the temple.

O Lord, who shall sojourn in your tent?
Who shall dwell on your holy hill? (15:1)

Who shall ascend the hill of the Lord?
And who shall stand in his holy place? (24:3)

Psalm 15 is of particular interest in this regard because here David casts his psalm in the form of the Ten Commandments. The implication seems to be that only those who are loyal to the covenant may enter God's presence. We will examine this psalm further in a later chapter.

*Sacred Seasons*

The Psalms also speak of the sacred seasons and appointed times of worship in Israel's cultus. These are a mixture of individual sacrifice, visitations with friends, public processions, priestly recitations, and sacred actions. The superscript for Psalm 92, for example, reads, "A Psalm. A Song for the Sabbath"—it is a psalm composed for use on the Sabbath day. Psalm 81 was recited at the new moon, the feast of trumpets (81:3). Many of the Psalms were recited at the morning and evening sacrifices. As we have seen, Psalm 3 is a morning prayer, and Psalm 4 is an evening prayer. Psalm 5 is a morning prayer, and Psalm 6 is an evening prayer. It is likely that these psalms were recited in connection with the morning and evening sacrifices respectively.

*Sacred Actions*

The Psalms also speak of sacred activities in the temple, perhaps most prominently the offering of sacrifices:

Ascribe to the Lord the glory due his name;
bring an offering, and come into his courts! (96:8)

Let them thank the Lord for his steadfast love,
for his wondrous works to the children of man!
And let them offer sacrifices of thanksgiving,
and tell of his deeds in songs of joy! (107:21–22)

What shall I render to the Lord
for all his benefits to me?
I will lift up the cup of salvation
and call on the name of the Lord,
I will pay my vows to the Lord
in the presence of all his people. . . .
I will offer to you the sacrifice of thanksgiving
and call on the name of the Lord.
I will pay my vows to the Lord
in the presence of all his people,
in the courts of the house of the Lord,
in your midst, O Jerusalem.
Praise the Lord! (116:12–14, 17–19)

These all are songs of grateful praise, sung in connection with the grateful praise ("thanksgiving") offerings.

The giving of prophetic oracles was another sacred activity in the temple. In Psalm 50, for example, Asaph speaks for God and faults the people for failing to keep covenant and ethics—a prophetic activity:

1 The Mighty One, God the Lord,
speaks and summons the earth
from the rising of the sun to its setting. . . .
7 "Hear, O my people, and I will speak;
O Israel, I will testify against you.

I am God, your God.
8 Not for your sacrifices do I rebuke you;
your burnt offerings are continually before me" (50:1, 7–8)

Psalm 95 combines a hymn with a prophetic warning to the people not to harden their hearts and not praise God in spite of an apparent draught:

6 Oh come, let us worship and bow down;
let us kneel before the LORD, our Maker!
7 For he is our God,
and we are the people of his pasture,
and the sheep of his hand.
Today, if you hear his voice,
8 do not harden your hearts, as at Meribah,
as on the day at Massah in the wilderness,
9 when your fathers put me to the test
and put me to the proof, though they had seen my work.

Sacred processions also marked the sacred activity of the temple. In Psalm 26, David says in protestation of his innocence,

6 I wash my hands in innocence
and go around your altar, O LORD,
7 proclaiming thanksgiving aloud,
and telling all your wondrous deeds.
8 O LORD, I love the habitation of your house
and the place where your glory dwells. (26:6–8)

Then in Psalm 68 he describes the procession, which you can almost see as the tribes enter for worship:

25 the singers in front, the musicians last,
between them virgins playing tambourines:

26 "Bless God in the great congregation,
the LORD, O you who are of Israel's fountain!"
27 There is Benjamin, the least of them, in the lead,
the princes of Judah in their throng,
the princes of Zebulun, the princes of Naphtali. (68:25–27).

Songs of pilgrimage also marked the sacred activity of the temple. Psalms 120–134, "Psalms of Ascents," were sung when Israel made pilgrimage to the temple. Psalm 84 is similar in that it depicts a journey to the temple and the experience along the way. This psalm was composed by the sons of Korah, one of the Levitical guilds:

A Psalm of the Sons of Korah.
1 How lovely is your dwelling place,
O LORD of hosts!
2 My soul longs, yes, faints
for the courts of the LORD;
my heart and flesh sing for joy
to the living God.
3 Even the sparrow finds a home,
and the swallow a nest for herself,
where she may lay her young,
at your altars, O LORD of hosts,
my King and my God. (84:1–3)

The birds could safely build their nests there because there could be no killing at the temple. The picture is one of protection and security. If even a bird could find security there, how much more God's chosen people!

4 Blessed are those who dwell in your house,
ever singing your praise! *Selah*
5 Blessed are those whose strength is in you,
in whose heart are the highways to Zion.

6 As they go through the Valley of Baca
they make it a place of springs;
the early rain also covers it with pools. (84:4–6)

"Baca" means "dry," so 84:6 says that the saints' pilgrimage to Zion fills the dry places with pools of water—at the temple their tears are transformed into springs of life.

7 They go from strength to strength;
each one appears before God in Zion.
8 O Lord God of hosts, hear my prayer;
give ear, O God of Jacob! *Selah*
9 Behold our shield, O God;
look on the face of your anointed! (84:7–9)

"Our shield" (84:9) is a reference to the king, and he prays that God will protect him. Then he reflects on his pilgrimage:

10 For a day in your courts is better
than a thousand elsewhere.
I would rather be a doorkeeper in the house of my God
than dwell in the tents of wickedness.
11 For the Lord God is a sun and shield;
the Lord bestows favor and honor.
No good thing does he withhold
from those who walk uprightly.
12 O Lord of hosts,
blessed is the one who trusts in you! (84:10–12)

In this pilgrimage psalm the psalmist looks forward to being in the presence of God. When he is there he prays for the king, that God will favor him. The psalmist himself is refreshed in worship, and he realizes that there is no place on earth he would rather be than worshiping in the presence of God.

These sacred actions—offering sacrifices, prophetic utterances, processions, and pilgrimages—are prominent in the Psalms. The Psalter immerses us in the temple atmosphere, and so our familiarity with temple worship will inform our reading of the Psalms.

*Sacred Objects*

The various sacred objects of Israel's cultus are prominent in the Psalms also. We have already seen reference to the altar in Psalm 84:3 (cf. 118:27). There is a sacred cup also, "the cup of salvation," that marks the grateful song of praise (116:13). The grateful songs of praise also speak of "banners," as in Psalm 20:5. These banners refer to those unfurled ahead of the tribes as the king led them out to war. Psalm 20 is a prayer for the king as he goes out to battle, and Psalm 21 celebrates his victory upon his return:

> May we shout for joy over your salvation,
> and in the name of our God set up our banners!
> May the LORD fulfill all your petitions! (20:5).

Musical instruments were also among the sacred objects of the temple, as in Psalm 47:5 and Psalm 150. Psalm 150 is the climax of the Psalter, and here the entire orchestra joins in praise:

> 1 Praise the LORD!
> Praise God in his sanctuary;
> praise him in his mighty heavens!
> 2 Praise him for his mighty deeds;
> praise him according to his excellent greatness!
> 3 Praise him with trumpet sound;
> praise him with lute and harp!
> 4 Praise him with tambourine and dance;
> praise him with strings and pipe!
> 5 Praise him with sounding cymbals;
> praise him with loud clashing cymbals!

6 Let everything that has breath praise the LORD!
Praise the LORD!

*Sacred Personnel*

We have already noted that the temple was an expression of heaven. There was no sharp dichotomy between God and heaven and God and the temple. The temple was a replica of heaven, designed to direct thinking toward heaven. And so it is not surprising that we find angels among the sacred personnel of the temple:

20 Bless the LORD, O you his angels,
you mighty ones who do his word,
obeying the voice of his word!
21 Bless the LORD, all his hosts,
his ministers, who do his will! (103:20–21)

The priests were prominent in temple worship, as well as the Levites:

8 Arise, O LORD, and go to your resting place,
you and the ark of your might.
9 Let your priests be clothed with righteousness,
and let your saints shout for joy. (132:8–9)

19 O house of Israel, bless the LORD!
O house of Aaron, bless the LORD!
20 O house of Levi, bless the LORD! (135:19–20a)

Psalm 135:20b then extends the call to worship beyond the priests and Levites: "You who fear the LORD, bless the LORD!" This would include the warriors/worshipers (Ps. 44) and all God-fearers (135:20), as well as the king.

We should recall again that beginning with David, musicians and singers became an important part of the sacred personnel in temple worship. These may include Levitical guilds such as the sons of Korah

(42–49; 84–87), and they may be designated "servants of the Lord, / who stand by night in the house of the Lord!" (134:1; cf. 135:2).

All of this provides the general "cultic" backdrop of the Psalter, and it is essential to hold it all in mind as we read the Psalms. And of course as we do we keep in mind also its significance in pointing us to Christ, the king who fulfills all the types and symbols of the old order, and through whom access to God is accomplished (John 2:19; Heb. 9–10).

Next, we will examine some specific psalms in which this background is prominent.

---

## SONGS OF ASCENTS

### "LET US GO UP!"

One vivid illustration of this temple orientation of the Psalter is the unified collection of the fifteen psalms called the Songs of Ascents, so named after their superscripts. "Ascents" is usually understood to refer to pilgrimages up to the temple on Mount Zion. Deuteronomy 12:5–7 prescribes that the sacrifices were to be offered in Jerusalem:

> [5] But you shall seek *the place that the Lord your God will choose* out of all your tribes to put his name and make his habitation there. *There* you shall go, [6] and *there* you shall bring your burnt offerings and your sacrifices, your tithes and the contribution that you present, your vow offerings, your freewill offerings, and the firstborn of your herd and of your flock. [7] And *there* you shall eat before the Lord your God, and you shall rejoice, you and your households, in all that you undertake, in which the Lord your God has blessed you.

Deuteronomy 16:1–17 further specifies three principal feasts for which Israel was called to come to Jerusalem for observance.

| Deut. 16 | Festival | Time of Year |
|---|---|---|
| 16:1–8 | Passover | Abib = March–April |
| 16:9–12 | Pentecost (Feast of Weeks) | Sivan = May–June |
| 16:13–15 | Booths (Ingathering) | Tishri = early October |
| 16:16–17 | Summary | |

Most scholars agree that the "Songs of Ascents" (Pss. 120–134) were sung at least at the fall festival, the Feast of Booths (traditionally, "Tabernacles"), Sukkot. It was the most festive, and the harvest imagery of these psalms (126:5–6; 127:2; 128:2; 129:6–8; 132:15) seems to indicate that this feast was specifically in view.

The term translated "Ascents" can denote either "going up" or "steps"—David Mitchell argues that both meanings are intended, noting that puns are common in Hebrew literature.[8] According to him, "going up" refers to the approach to Mount Zion (the "pilgrimage"), and "steps" refers to the fifteen steps of the temple, to which these fifteen psalms correspond. The Mishnah[9] says that the Levites sang these fifteen songs as they descended[10] the steps from the court of women to the court of Israel at Sukkoth[11] in a water-drawing ceremony. Mitchell justifies connecting this liturgy of the Herodian temple (destroyed in AD 70) with that of Solomon's, built a thousand years earlier, by three arguments: (1) the visionary temple of Ezekiel had steps (Ezek. 40:6); (2) the step structure of three of the unified ascent psalms; and (3) Israel's conservative traditions of worship.[12] To be sure, the temple visions of Ezekiel, a priest, are informed by Solomon's temple, but the steps in Ezekiel's visionary temple led up to the eastern gate of the temple mount, not from one courtyard to another (Ezek. 40:6,

8 David C. Mitchell, *The Songs of Ascents: Psalms 120 to 134 in the Worship of Jerusalem's Temples* (Newton Mears, Scotland: Campbell, 2015), chap. 3.

9 The Mishnah is the Oral Law that rabbinic scholars passed on generation after generation, and experts in each generation contributed to it with notes. These notes were organized and published ca. AD 190–200.

10 Tosefta Sukkah 4:7–9.

11 Sukkah 5.2 reads, "At sundown of the first festival day of Sukkot they descended to the Court of Women"; see Mitchell, *Songs of Ascents*, 31.

12 Mitchell, *Songs of Ascents*, 32–35, 120.

22, 32–34). Since the Scriptures do not even mention these courts, the argument is not convincing. The step-like structure of Psalms 120–123 (see below) may have suggested using these fifteen psalms for the ritual on the fifteen steps of the Herodian temple; Israel's liturgical traditions are both conservative and innovative.

Nevertheless, the term "Ascents" may still be a pun that refers both to "going up" in pilgrimage and to the "step"-like structure of Psalms 120–123. In this structure, technically called "anadiplosis, a word in the second half of a verse is repeated in the first half of the next; for example, "dwell" (120:5b) / "dwelling" (120:6a), "peace" (120:6b) / "peace" (120:7a).

Mitchell argues persuasively for the unity of the pilgrimage psalms, as has been long recognized. They frequently mention the temple, "the house of the LORD," Zion, Jerusalem, Israel, and various liturgical phrases such as "benedictions of blessing and peace (125:5; 128:5, 6; 134:3), summons to confess and hope (124:1; 129:1; 130:7; 131:3), and confessional terms (121:2; 124:8; 134:3)."[13] In fact, it seems the ordering of these psalms itself reflects the pilgrimage:

In Psalm 120 the worshiper is away in a hostile land longing for Jerusalem.
In Psalm 121 the worshiper looks to Mount Zion and makes his approach.
In Psalm 122 the worshiper rejoices to stand within the gates of the temple.
In Psalm 123 the worshiper is in the temple looking to God in prayer.
In Psalm 124 the worshiper offers praise for God's past protection.
In Psalm 125 the worshiper expresses the blessedness of living under God's protection.
In Psalm 126 the worshiper rejoices in God's past deliverances and prays for further restoration, comparing it to the time of harvest.
In Psalm 127 the worshiper rejoices in God's enablement to build "the house"—evidently an intended pun referring to the family, the Davidic dynasty, and the temple itself.

13 James L. Mays, *Psalms*, Interpretation: A Commentary for Teaching and Preaching (Louisville: John Knox, 1994), 386.

In Psalm 128 the worshiper expresses the blessedness of God's care.
In Psalm 129 the worshiper prays for the thwarting of the enemy.
In Psalm 130 the worshiper praises the Lord for his forgiveness and steadfast love.
In Psalm 131 the worshiper is admonished to hope in the Lord.
In Psalm 132 the worshiper rejoices at his entrance to the temple and in God's promise to David.
In Psalm 133 the worshiper rejoices in the blessed unity of the nation.
In Psalm 134 the worshiper departs from the temple and petitions for continued blessing from Zion.

The arrangement mimics the pilgrimage. The first four pertain to the pilgrims' ascent, the next ten pertain to reflections while on the mount, and the last one refers to departure. This "story" that the Songs of Ascents tell has been recognized for centuries.

Having established the liturgical use of these psalms and their unity as a collection, Mitchell further argued that they were collected by David and Jeduthun for the dedication of the temple in 959 BC. In spite of the many clues he finds within the Songs of Ascents to support his thesis, Psalm 126, which celebrates Israel's restoration from some captivity does not fit Israel's united monarchy. The Assyrians, two centuries after 959 BC, were the first to take people into exile (cf. 2 Kings 17:6). So Mitchell's thesis is not compelling.

The Songs of Ascents not only tell a personal pilgrimage story, as we noted above, but also convey a message of faith, a message the prophet Zechariah expounds in his prophecy. Here again we refer to Mitchell's work where he finds correspondence in the prophecy of Zechariah.[14] In Zechariah 9–10 the prophet speaks of the arrival of the Messiah to restore Israel. In Zechariah 11–13 we read of Messiah the shepherd stricken and pierced and of Israel in mourning over it. Then Zecha-

14 Mitchell, *Songs of Ascents*, 214–15.

riah 14 foretells of the nations going up to Jerusalem to worship at the Feast of Booths. Five times (14:16, 17, 18 [2x], 19) the prophet speaks of the nations going up to Jerusalem for worship (cf. עָלָה, Zech. 14:13; see also Isa. 2:3; Mic. 4:2). This prospect of worldwide blessing in the day of the Messiah seems to echo the Songs of Ascents, and it would seem that the inclusion of these psalms as a distinct group in book 5 of the Psalter reflects such a faith on the part of the final editors.

## PSALM 2

Psalms 2 and 110 provide further examples of the liturgical use of the Psalms. Reflecting the custom in the ancient Near East, these psalms have been recognized as coronation liturgies and as such have their setting in the temple.[15] All of David's sons inherited the Davidic covenant and as such anticipate David's greater son, the Messiah. But these psalms stand out among other psalms that pertain to the Davidic king in that they present exclusively an idealized king far superior to all of David's sons, except the Messiah himself. In this way they find unique fulfillment in the Lord Jesus, as the New Testament writers confirm. Psalms 2 and 110 are the leading "Messianic" psalms of the Psalter—they speak prophetically of Christ (see chapter 12). Yet they were sung as part of the temple liturgy at the coronation of Davidic kings, each of whom stood as an anticipation of the great King who was to come. On the historical horizon, "king" and its metonymies ("son" and "anointed") should be written in lowercase; but on the canonical horizon, where the full deity of the Messiah is revealed, they should be written in uppercase.

### Psalm 2

1 Why do the nations rage
    and the peoples plot in vain?

15 John Eaton, *The Psalms: A Historical and Spiritual Commentary with an Introduction and New Translation* (New York: Continuum, 2005), 65.

2 The kings of the earth set themselves,
and the rulers take counsel together,
against the LORD and against his anointed, saying,
3 "Let us burst their bonds apart
and cast away their cords from us."
4 He who sits in the heavens laughs;
the Lord holds them in derision.
5 Then he will speak to them in his wrath,
and terrify them in his fury, saying,
6 "As for me, I have set my King
on Zion, my holy hill."
7 I will tell of the decree:
The LORD said to me, "You are my Son;
today I have begotten you.
8 Ask of me, and I will make the nations your heritage,
and the ends of the earth your possession.
9 You shall break them with a rod of iron
and dash them in pieces like a potter's vessel."
10 Now therefore, O kings, be wise;
be warned, O rulers of the earth.
11 Serve the LORD with fear,
and rejoice with trembling.
12 Kiss the Son,
lest he be angry, and you perish in the way,
for his wrath is quickly kindled.
Blessed are all who take refuge in him.

## Overview

This Psalm of twelve verses falls into four stanzas, with three verses in each. The stanzas are marked off by different speakers. In the first stanza (2:1–3) the nations speak in collective rebellion against God and against his anointed king. In stanza two (2:4–6) God speaks in response. In stanza three (2:7–9) the king speaks, proclaiming a stipulation of the Davidic covenant. This is the Son of God, the Lord Christ, speaking and relaying words that God the Father had spoken to him. In the final stanza (2:10–12) the psalmist himself speaks, addressing the kings of the earth with words of admonition, both threat and promise. This is the natural outline of the psalm. In the first stanza we are taken into the royal palace of earthly kings, and we hear them announce their resolve to throw off the rule of God and his king. In the second stanza we are taken into the throne room of heaven and allowed to hear God speak of his own resolve to install his king. In the third stanza the enthroned king speaks of his resolve to rule the nations as God has given him authority. And in the final stanza the psalmist steps to the stage and admonishes these hostile kings to submit to the Lord God and his king, warning them of the futility of their rebellion.

- 2:1–3: The nations rebel.
- 2:4–6: God responds.
- 2:7–9: The king asserts his right to rule.
- 2:10–12: The psalmist admonishes the nations accordingly.

## Setting

### *Setting in the Temple*

Psalm 2 is a coronation liturgy that was sung at the Jerusalem temple at the installation of the Davidic king: "I have set my king / on Zion, my holy hill" (2:6). The "today" of 2:7 is presumably the day of the king's coronation, at which appointment he becomes his "Son": "You are my Son; today I have begotten you" (cf. 2 Sam. 7:14). All this is enthronement language reflecting the temple ceremony at the king's accession to the throne. We will see more evidence of this in connection with Psalm 110. Perhaps this psalm was used at the anniversary of his accession also—we can only guess. It seems likely that it was intended to be sung antiphonally according to the voices of the four stanzas.

### *Background*

The backdrop of this psalm is found in the Davidic covenant (2 Sam. 7). David is the psalmist (Acts 4:25), and the terminology of this "king" (Ps.

2:6) as God's "Son" (2:12) who will inevitably triumph links to that covenant promise explicitly (cf. 2 Sam. 7:12–16; 1 Chron. 17; 28:6–7). Describing this king as God's "anointed" (Ps. 2:2) who inherits the nations (2:8) ties the psalm to a stream of Old Testament messianic prophecy (see chapter 12).

*Setting in the Psalter*

This psalm also finds a significant setting in the Psalter. As we noted in our discussion of Psalm 1, Psalms 1 and 2 form the introduction to the Psalter. These psalms together prepare those who meditate on this anthology of petitions, praises, and instruction to interpret the psalms both with respect to the king and to themselves as individuals within his kingdom. The Psalter is to be read on a dual level: it is applicable to the king, and it is applicable to us as individuals in our relationship to him.

*Canonical Setting*

Finally, this psalm finds an important setting within the biblical canon in that it finds its fulfillment uniquely in Christ. The early church understood this psalm as Davidic and as prophetic of the Lord Jesus Christ. In fact, "the kings of the earth" did reject him when he came, and they rejected his apostles Peter and John and warned them to cease speaking of Jesus (Acts 4:1–22).

> 23 When they were released, they went to their friends and reported
> what the chief priests and the elders had said to them. 24 And when
> they heard it, they lifted their voices together to God and said, "Sov-
> ereign Lord, who made the heaven and the earth and the sea and
> everything in them, 25 who through the mouth of our father David,
> your servant, said by the Holy Spirit,
>
> "'Why did the Gentiles rage,
> and the peoples plot in vain?
> 26 The kings of the earth set themselves,
> and the rulers were gathered together,
> against the Lord and against his anointed'—

> [27] for truly in this city there were gathered together against your holy servant Jesus, whom you anointed, both Herod and Pontius Pilate, along with the Gentiles and the peoples of Israel, [28] to do whatever your hand and your plan had predestined to take place." (Acts 4:23–28)

Several observations here are significant. First, these early Christians attributed Psalm 2 to David (Acts 4:25), even though the psalm itself has no superscript. Second, with a touch of irony, they associate "the peoples" (Ps. 2:1) with the people of Israel. Third, they recognize all this rebellion as in keeping with God's sovereign rule to the fulfilment of his own purpose (Acts 4:28). And most significantly, they understood the psalm as finding its point of reference and fulfillment in Christ (4:27), this in keeping with the New Testament writers generally.[16] The New Testament thus sets the model for understanding the Psalms: both in "type" and in direct prophecy the king anticipates the great King, the Messiah (cf. Luke 24:44). As the early French Protestant theologian Moses Amyraut (ca. 1625) is said to have remarked, "We must keep our left eye on the historical king and our right eye on eternal Christ."

Christ is the King against whom the nations rebel (Ps. 2:1), but he is also the King enthroned in Zion (2:6). Christ fulfills this psalm initially in his ascension-coronation, when he took his seat at the right hand of the Father to rule over the ends of the earth, and ultimately in his return in glory to bring God's kingdom to consummation. This psalm looks far beyond David and any Davidic king of the Old Testament.

### Survey Exposition[17]

*Stanza 1: The World Speaks (2:1–3)*

1 Why do the nations rage
    and the peoples plot in vain?

16 Cf. Ps. 2:1/Rev. 11:18; Ps. 2:2/Rev. 19:19; Ps. 2:7/Acts 13:33; Heb. 1:5; 5:5; Ps. 2:8/Heb. 1:2; Ps. 2:8–9/Rev. 2:26–27; 12:5; 19:15.

17 See also Bruce K. Waltke and James M. Houston, *The Psalms as Christian Worship: A Historical Commentary* (Grand Rapids, MI: Eerdmans, 2010), chap. 5.

2 The kings of the earth set themselves,
and the rulers take counsel together,
against the LORD and against his Anointed, saying,
3 "Let us burst their bonds apart
and cast away their cords from us."

In 2:1 the psalmist expresses his amazement and indignation that the peoples "of the earth" would attempt a futile rebellion against the Lord God of heaven and his king. Their rebellion cannot succeed—the attempted overthrow of God's rule is in vain. His inquiry ("Why?") is rhetorical—he is not expecting a reasoned, well-stated response; he is expressing incredulity: Why would anyone make such a foolish, self-defeating attempt?

The Lord's "Anointed" is the king. There were three "anointed" offices in Israel: the prophet, the priest, and the king. The prophet was anointed by the Spirit, and his possession of the Spirit giving prophetic utterance functioned as the seal or badge of his office. The "anointed" one in the Psalms is the king, who was anointed by the prophet, God's spokesman (cf. 1 Sam. 16:1–13). The prophet would designate the king and come to him with a flask, a clay jar, or a ram's horn filled with oil. In the case of the ram's horn the large end would be upward, and then the horn was filled with scented oil. The point of the horn would be hollowed out for pouring over the king's head so that the oil covered him from head to foot. This ritual was performed for the anointing of the priest also. This anointing was the king's seal or badge of authority that set him apart, like the presidential seal in the United States.

The king's anointing with oil was his validation, without which he would not be recognized as a legitimate king. Recall, for example, that when Adonijah set himself up as the king, even though he had Joab, the great general, he had no prophetic designation or anointing (1 Kings 1:5–8). Solomon had the prophet Nathan's designation and anointing and thus was validated as king (1 Kings 1:28–53). During the divided monarchy, the minor prophets at times cite the northern and the southern kings, but they will not mention the kings who set themselves up on the throne like Pekahiah, Pekah, or Hoshea. They set themselves up with no prophetic designation or anointing and thus were illegitimate.

As God's anointed, the king "is designated and appointed publicly for divine status and with divine authority (1 Sam. 10:1; 15:1, 17; 16:1–13; 2 Sam. 2:4, 7; 5:3, 17) and consecrated as God's property (Ex. 29:7; 40:9–11; Lev. 8:10–11; Num. 7:10–11). This entails the invincibility (Ps. 2:10–12) and divine protection (1 Sam. 24:6–11; 26:9–24; Ps. 105:15; Lev. 10:1–2) and his being qualified and equipped for tasks by [God's] Spirit (1 Sam. 10:6; 16:13; Is. 61:1–3)."[18] To touch or misuse and defile God's property would incur his wrath. An attack on God's anointed is an attack on God's rule and against God himself. This is why David would not dare touch Saul (1 Sam. 24:1–13). By the anointing under Samuel, Saul had become God's property; David must leave him to God's disposition. This was something of an ambiguous situation in which God had anointed two kings, and during this time David was tested as to whether he would live in obedience and faith, trusting God to resolve the situation and not take matters into his own hands. This is also why Paul considered himself the chief of sinners, because in his persecution of Christians he had attacked God's anointed Christ.

Here in the first stanza of the psalm David portrays the world in determined ("set themselves," Ps. 2:2) and collective ("together," 2:2) rebellion against God and against his anointed. They will not have his rule. The Torah, in which the righteous find delight (Ps. 1), the world views as chains on the neck and as shackles that bind them in captivity, and they are determined to throw them off (2:1–3). We have in ancient history an interesting parallel to this. In the El Amarna letters, dating to about 1300 BC, we read the correspondence of the petty kings of Syria and Palestine plotting a revolt against the great king of Egypt, their Suzerain, who, in turn, is unthreatened by such foolish schemes.[19] This is the picture of earth in rebellion against God that Psalm 2 presents.

18 Waltke, *Old Testament Theology*, 887.

19 Mitchel Dahood, *Psalms I, 1–50: Introduction, Translation, and Notes*, The Anchor Yale Bible (Garden City, NY: Doubleday, 1965), 8.

And it has a dreadfully contemporary ring to it, as any Christian observer of our culture will notice. Carl Trueman argues that Sigmund Freud and Karl Marx, both of whom hated Christ, have significantly influenced the thinking of today's influential elites in regarding Christ's teaching as repressive.[20] God allows such evil to thrive, but only for a time. It cannot ultimately succeed.

Yet this rebellion is universal, organized ("set themselves," 2:2), and determined. The world is resolved to throw off any restraints from heaven.

*Stanza 2: The Lord Speaks (2:4–6)*

4 He who sits in the heavens laughs;
the Lord holds them in derision.
5 Then he will speak to them in his wrath,
and terrify them in his fury, saying,
6 "As for me, I have set my King
on Zion, my holy hill."

In the second stanza the Lord confronts his rebels. The stanza is framed, on the one hand, by the Lord God enthroned in the heavens and, on the other hand, by the anointed king enthroned "on Zion, my holy hill" (2:6). The upper frame speaks of God's universal transcendence over all, and the lower frame speaks of his immanent presence through his anointed king through whom his kingdom extends throughout the earth. God has installed his royal king in his chosen royal city.

Secure in his rule over his would-be enemies, God laughs (2:4). Victory is so lopsided as to be comical. But it is not a laugh of sheer amusement but of anger and offense, a laugh of mocking derision (2:4) at such a futile effort. It is also a laugh of the triumph of righteousness over wickedness (2:5; cf. 37:12–13; 59:7–8). Yet something

20 Carl Trueman, *The Rise and Triumph of the Modern Self: Cultural Amnesia, Expressive Individualism, and the Road to Sexual Revolution* (Wheaton, IL: Crossway, 2020).

of a comic element remains. It is not unlike *Gulliver's Travels* when Gulliver washed ashore on the island of Lilliput and fell asleep and the Lilliputians attempted to tie him down—Gulliver plays along with their little scheme for a time. So also God allows the world's rebellion to play itself out to his glory, futile as it is. But forever he reigns over all. He has established his king in Zion (2:6), and his purpose will never fail.

This raises the question of what the Germans refer to as *schadenfreude* ("joy at damage")—laughing at the misfortune of others. Ordinarily, to laugh at the destruction of others would seem inappropriate. Christian and non-Christian ethicists and philosophers have judged this as evil, and certainly we all would agree that *schadenfreude* is a dangerous emotion at best. And when it is injustice that is celebrated it surely is evil. But what should we feel when justice is served? Israel's songs (Ex. 15; Judg. 5) are deemed by the biblical writers as entirely appropriate, as when Lady Wisdom laughs at the destruction of fools (Prov. 1:20–33). Indifference toward matters of justice is no virtue. The righteous recognize right versus wrong. They are committed to what is right and seek the end of wrong. They feel indignation toward injustice and rejoice in the vindication of justice (cf. Rev. 19:1–6). Recognizing that this is a day of grace and the free offer of salvation must surely foster patience—indeed, love and prayer for our own enemies (Matt. 5:44–45). Yet the day of the Lord will come, and in it the righteous will rejoice.

In Psalm 2:6, God speaks. The Hebrew calls attention to the change of speakers—"As for me, I"—as if to say, "You have had your say; now I have something to say." And what he has to say reflects his resolve: "I have set my King on Zion, / my holy hill."

The meaning of the word "Zion" is unknown, but it refers to the hill on the east side of Jerusalem where Solomon's temple stood, where the Dome of the Rock now sits. It was "holy" (2:6) because it was the place of God's residence. It was also therefore considered Israel's stronghold (cf. Ps. 46; 2 Sam. 5:7; 1 Chron. 11:5); God's presence among his people rendered them invincible. The Lord's declaration that he has installed his king (Ps. 2:6) refers ultimately to the ascension of Christ (Acts 2:33–36) to the heavenly Zion where as a consequence of his successful mediatorial work God exalted him above all earthly powers (Phil. 2:5–11; cf. Eph. 1:19–22; 1 Pet. 3:22).[21] Christ has taken his throne and is presently reigning over all things for the advance of his kingdom, which will come to final culmination in his return (Rev. 19).

So the second stanza affirms that God allows evil to go seemingly unchecked for a time, though he is angry with it, and that he remains resolute in carrying out his righteous purpose in the world through the work of his enthroned king.

*Stanza 3: The King Speaks (2:7–9)*

The third stanza is remarkable in that it recites a prior conversation between the Lord and the Messiah. The king is the speaker in this stanza, but what he recites is the decree God had given him to rule over all the earth, a poetic elaboration of 2 Samuel 7:12–16. This decree is framed in terms of the king's relationship to God (Ps. 2:7) and to the nations (2:8–9):

7 I will tell of the decree:
the LORD said to me, "You are my Son;
today I have begotten you.
8 Ask of me, and I will make the nations your heritage,
and the ends of the earth your possession.
9 You shall break them with a rod of iron
and dash them in pieces like a potter's vessel."

"You are my Son; / today I have begotten you" (2:7) is the language of enthronement. This is God's word to his King. This psalm was designed as a coronation liturgy for Solomon and each of the kings of Israel who upon taking the throne became God's "son" (cf. 2 Sam. 7:12–14). "Son of God," then, became a messianic title pointing to David's greater son, whose reign would be universal. He would be the obedient and faithful

21 For parallels to Ps. 2:6–7, see Ps. 110, Dan. 7:13–14, and Rev. 5:9–10; cf. Matt. 26:64; Acts 1:9.

messianic "Son" par excellence—the King whose sonship entailed inferences of eternal deity (Matt. 11:27; 28:19; John 1:14; 5:23, 26). And so the "decree"—that is, the promises stipulated in the covenant God made with David (2 Sam. 7:12–14) as elaborated here in Psalm 2:7–8—pertains uniquely to Christ. And this decree the Son-King pledges to recite. "I will tell" (or "I will recite," authors' translation) is a cohortative of resolve: "I am resolved to recite it" is the idea. When the Lord Jesus would affirm that he is God's promised King, he would do so in the face of the fiercest opposition. But he would not run from it—he was resolved to tell of the decree.

In this decree God, the Creator, bequeaths to this King rulership over the whole earth: "Ask of me, and I will make the nations your heritage, / and the ends of the earth your possession" (2:8). This is the King's inheritance from God. He must "ask," and upon asking, God will grant him the nations. The nations who are presently in rebellion against him (2:1) will be his—to "the ends of the earth." The decree that the king's (and God's) enemies will be smashed to pieces "like a potter's vessel" (2:9) finds graphic depiction in the Egyptian execration texts, which illustrate the Egyptian practice of formally cursing persons and cities. The ritual involved writing the names of the person or city on a pottery figure and/or ceramic bowl, and after the curse was spoken the figures or bowls were smashed. So it will end for those who oppose God.

David's son Solomon anticipated this future King and his universal rule also:

8 May he have dominion from sea to sea,
    and from the River to the ends of the earth!
9 May desert tribes bow down before him,
    and his enemies lick the dust!
10 May the kings of Tarshish and of the coastlands
    render him tribute;
may the kings of Sheba and Seba
    bring gifts!
11 May all kings fall down before him,
    all nations serve him! (72:8–11)

Psalm 2 was sung as part of the coronation liturgy upon the installation of each Davidic king. So just which Davidic king is in view? It is not David, for he was not anointed in Zion. It is not Solomon, for he was apostate. And no other Davidic king extended Israel's rule to the ends of the earth. This divine decree pertains to the Messiah, and the Lord Jesus Christ claims its promise: "All authority in heaven and on earth has been given to me. Go therefore and make disciples of all nations, baptizing them in the name of the Father and of the Son and of the Holy Spirit, teaching them to observe all that I have commanded you" (Matt. 28:18–20).

Having accomplished his mediatorial mission on earth, he earned universal dominion (cf. Phil. 2:5–11), and in his ascension (Luke 24:45–53; Acts 1:1–11), the Lord Jesus Christ took his place at God's right hand (Ps. 110:1; Dan. 7:13–14; Acts 2:33–36; Rev. 5) where he rules over all things (Eph. 1:19–22; 1 Pet. 3:22) until all the world is brought into submission to him (Ps. 2:8; 110:1; Matt. 28:19; Acts 1:8; Phil. 2:9–11; Heb. 2; Rev. 19). The saints share with him in this rule and are destined to reign with him forever (Ps. 110:3; Dan. 7:27; Rom. 8:16–17; Rev. 19–22).

In Christ's inheritance of the nations many will acknowledge his kingship willingly and with joy (Ps. 110:3). This is the mission of the church today (Matt. 28:18–20; Acts 1:8). But Christ's universal dominion is not contingent on human willingness. Today, Christ's rule is extended through the gospel, but it will reach its consummation through judgment:

> 8 "Ask of me, and I will make the nations your heritage,
> and the ends of the earth your possession.
> 9 You shall break them with a rod of iron
> and dash them in pieces like a potter's vessel." (Ps. 2:8–9)

The promise of Psalm 2:9 points to the return of Christ (cf. Rev. 2:26–27; 19:15, "rod of iron"; cf. 2 Thess. 1:8–9). There is a textual problem here in Psalm 2:9a concerning the word "break" (תְּרֹעֵם). The question is whether the root word here means "to break" (רָעַע) or "to shepherd" (רָעָה). A "rod" is not a shepherd's staff but an instrument of authority, as "king" with "rod of iron" makes explicit. Also, the parallel is "dash" or "smash" (2:9b). So "break" seems to be the right translation here, pointing us to the conquering rule of Christ in his return (Rev. 19), at which time all the world will become his (cf. Rev. 11:15).

So in stanza one the nations are in rebellion. In stanza two God is unmoved in his resolve to exercise his rule through his appointed King. In stanza three the King himself recites God's decree that he will reign universally. Now in stanza four David counsels the rebellious nations accordingly.

*Stanza 4: The Psalmist Speaks (2:10–12)*

10 Now therefore, O kings, be wise;
  be warned, O rulers of the earth.
11 Serve the Lord with fear,
  and rejoice with trembling.
12 Kiss the Son,
  lest he be angry, and you perish in the way,
  for his wrath is quickly kindled.
Blessed are all who take refuge in him.

In this final stanza David positions himself as counselor to the rebellious nations, giving important and needed advice. In 2:7 he calls them to wise up and consider what he has written in the psalm. God's decree is sure, his King is enthroned, and their rebellion can never succeed. "Be wise, and submit to his rule willingly, while you may" is the sense of 2:10. In spite of his threatening tone, David's warning contains a large measure of grace. He extends God's salvation beyond the limits of the covenant people Israel to the whole uncircumcised world, concluding his poem with a universal embrace: "Blessed are all who take refuge in him" (2:12).

In 2:11, David calls the rebels to "serve" the Lord. This is the language of worship, as well as submission. Fundamentally, "serve" means to be in subjection to or in a subordinate position to the Lord as master and has to do with a way of life (cf. Josh. 24:15). In the Psalter, however, as sometimes elsewhere, this word further signifies the liturgical notion of serving him in the temple ritual and so may be glossed "worship." Mortals serve some god or gods; the only question is which one(s). And so deliverance by the Lord God entails a change of masters. He delivered Israel from Egyptian bondage to serve him as their new master. But he is a benevolent master, and servitude to him leads to peace, prosperity, and life. Servitude to other masters, by contrast, such as Pharaoh and idols, leads to wretchedness and death. And so there is irony: to free oneself from servitude to the Lord God will lead only to slavery to oppressive masters.

This worship must be "with fear," not mere ritualism, and with faith that God will do as he says. Such faith will entail "fear" and "trembling" awe on the one hand and "rejoicing" on the other, a joyful appreciation of God's rule through his Son.

The significance of "kiss" (Ps. 2:12), of course, varies with context, but in a religious and kingship context it connotes homage and submission (cf. 1 Sam 10:1; 1 Kings 19:18; Hos. 13:2). Seeking "refuge" (Ps. 2:12) is the posture that stands behind fear and trembling (2:11). God is at once a Savior or a Destroyer. We may refuse him and in the end face his wrath (1 Thess. 5:1–3), or we may bow before him now and know his blessed care. And so this coronation liturgy closes with God's mercy in salvation trumping his judgment as David calls the nations into submission to Christ. He extends God's salvation beyond the limits of Israel to the whole uncircumcised world, and he concludes his poem with a universal embrace: "How rewarding is the life of all who take refuge in him" (authors' translation).

Psalm 2 provides, in brief, a graphic portrayal of the outworking of God's purpose in history to reclaim the nations. It looks ahead to the incarnation, cross, resurrection, and ascension of Christ, and ultimately to his return when he will bring the kingdom of God to its consummation. At last it will be known that "the kingdom of the world has become the kingdom of our Lord and of his Christ, and he shall reign forever and ever" (Rev. 11:15).

## PSALM 110

A Psalm of David.

1 The LORD says to my Lord:
"Sit at my right hand,
until I make your enemies your footstool."
2 The LORD sends forth from Zion
your mighty scepter.
Rule in the midst of your enemies!
3 Your people will offer themselves freely
on the day of your power,
in holy garments;
from the womb of the morning,
the dew of your youth will be yours.
4 The LORD has sworn
and will not change his mind,
"You are a priest forever
after the order of Melchizedek."
5 The Lord is at your right hand;
he will shatter kings on the day of his wrath.
6 He will execute judgment among the nations,
filling them with corpses;
he will shatter chiefs
over the wide earth.
7 He will drink from the brook by the way;
therefore he will lift up his head.

### Psalm 110 in Perspective

Psalm 110 is the most prominent psalm in the New Testament writings, particularly the language of the king's session, "seated" (cf. Eph. 1:20) in heaven at "the right hand" of God (110:1). We have it on the authority of the Lord Jesus himself that this psalm speaks of him (Matt. 22:44 = Mark 12:35–36 = Luke 20:41–43; Matt. 26:64 = Mark 14:62 = Luke 22:69). The apostles and early church evidently took their cue from Jesus and followed suit. Peter (Acts 2:33–36; 5:31; 1 Pet. 3:22), Stephen (Acts 7:55–56), Paul (Rom. 8:34; Eph. 1:19–22; Col. 3:1; cf. Eph. 2:6; Phil. 2:9–11), and the writer of the epistle to the Hebrews (1:13; 2:7–8; 8:1; 10:12; 12:2) all cite and interpret Psalm 110:1 with reference to him. The epistle to the Hebrews also makes much of Psalm 110:4 and the Melchizedekian priesthood of Christ (5:6, 10; 6:20; 7:1–28). Indeed, Jared Compton seeks to demonstrate that the very argument of the epistle to the Hebrews is shaped by considerations drawn from Psalm 110:1 and 110:4.[22] All told, this Psalm is cited or alluded to in the New Testament more than twenty-five times. Its shaping influence on the early church's understanding of Christ's enthronement is massive. In fact, within the Old Testament itself, the enthronement scene of Psalm 110:1 is reflected in Daniel's vision of the Son of Man (Dan. 7:13–14; cf. Matt. 26:64), as it is later dramatized in Revelation 5. And so it is no surprise that this psalm has received wide attention throughout the history of the church. From its early centuries the church has recited together, "I believe in Jesus Christ . . . who ascended into heaven and is seated at the right hand of the Father."[23] Martin Luther took 123 pages to expound this psalm, the lengthiest exposition of any psalm in his writings. He concludes, "This beautiful psalm is the very core and quintessence of the whole Scripture. No other psalm prophesies as abundantly and completely about Christ. It portrays the Lord and his entire Kingdom, and is full of comfort for Christians."[24] Psalm 110:1 in particular echoes pervasively in Christian hymnody also. The church's historic teaching and the New Testament writer's own theology of Christ's ascension-exaltation in the heavens grows in large part out of this psalm.

22 Jared Compton, *Psalm 110 and the Logic of Hebrews*, Library of New Testament Studies, 537 (New York: Bloomsbury T&T Clark, 2015).

23 Cf. the Nicene Creed and the Apostles' Creed.

24 Martin Luther, *Selected Psalms II*, vol. 13 of *Luther's Works*, ed. Jaroslav Pelikan, (St. Louis: Concordia, 1955), 348.

## Introductory Considerations

Again, this is a "psalm," a song to be sung with musical accompaniment. And its poetry is again filled with imagery—God's army is likened to the dew of the morning (110:3), for example. And it is full of parallelism, as we have come to expect. And, in fact, this psalm is prophecy, prospective of Christ's ascension to the place of universal authority as judge over the whole earth.

The setting of the psalm, as with Psalm 2, is that of a coronation liturgy: "sit at my right hand" (110:1) is the language of enthronement. The work of John Hilber here has been helpful in identifying this as a coronation liturgy by demonstrating the psalm's similarities to those of Assyrian kings. The parallels are extensive:[25]

- begins with an introduction formula: 110:1
- the subdivision of the oracle marked by a second introduction formula: 110:4
- a change in person, both of the addressee and the divine speaker: 110:4–5, 6–7
- legitimization of relationship between deity and king ("at my right hand"): 110:1
- enemies at the king's feet: 110:1
- promise of the destruction of enemies: 110:2, 5–6
- promise of universal dominion: 110:1, 6
- presence of loyal support: 110:3
- divine promise accompanied by denial of lying: 110:4
- affirmation of priestly responsibility: 110:4
- eternality of royal prerogatives: 110:4

All these features in Psalm 110 are characteristic of the Assyrian coronation poems. As Hilber summarizes, "It is likely that Psalm 110

25 John W. Hilber, *Cultic Prophecy in the Psalms*, Beihefte zur Zeitschrift für die alttestamentliche Wissenschaft 352 (New York: Walter de Gruyter, 2005), 76–79. See also Waltke and Houston, *Psalms as Christian Worship*, 498–99.

was a prophetic oracle originating and subsequently used in conjunction with cultic celebration of the king's enthronement."[26]

Notice in particular the alternating of speakers. The Psalm is divided in two parts: 110:1–3 and 110:4–7. The Lord speaks twice (110:1 and 110:4), marking the two divisions of the psalm. But in 110:2–3, it is David who speaks, and he speaks again in 110:5–7. So the psalm advances with alternating speakers.

In 110:1, God speaks to the King:

> 1 The LORD says to my Lord:
> "Sit at my right hand,
> until I make your enemies your footstool."

Then in 110:2–3, the prophet-psalmist David speaks to the King:

> 2 The LORD sends forth from Zion
> your mighty scepter.
> Rule in the midst of your enemies!
> 3 Your people will offer themselves freely
> on the day of your power,
> in holy garments;
> from the womb of the morning,
> the dew of your youth will be yours.

Then in 110:4, God addresses the King again:

> 4 The LORD has sworn
> and will not change his mind,
> "You are a priest forever
> after the order of Melchizedek."

Finally, in 110:5–7 David again speaks, but here there is another shift. In 110:5, he addresses the King:

26 Hilber, *Cultic Prophecy*, 85.

5 The Lord is at your right hand;
he will shatter kings on the day of his wrath.

And then in 110:6–7 he addresses the congregation, speaking *about* the King:

6 He will execute judgment among the nations,
filling them with corpses;
he will shatter chiefs
over the wide earth.
7 He will drink from the brook by the way;
therefore he will lift up his head.

The psalm is divided evenly in two halves. Although the first stanza consists of three verses (110:1–3), and the second stanza four verses (110:4–7), the Hebrew text consists of seventy-four words in each. This kind of symmetry is not uncommon in the Psalms, as we saw in Psalm 2. The psalm is held together by parallelism in the three major divisions of the two stanzas: an introduction to the divine citation, the citation, and then the prophetic reflection.

As noted, this structure parallels the Assyrian poems. Our point is that it reflects the psalm's use in the temple ceremony. As with Psalm 2, this psalm also would presumably have been sung antiphonally according to the changing voices in the psalm itself. David wrote in prophecy about his greater Son, and this psalm-prophecy, it seems, was used as a part of Israel's cultus at the coronation of each king. The final prophetic reflection spoken to the congregation about the king is presumably intended to embolden and encourage the king who doubtless is overhearing.

**Exposition**[27]

*Stanza 1 (110:1–3)*

As we have noted, 110:1 consists of a citation of God's speech. "The LORD says to my Lord: / 'Sit at my right hand, / until I make your

27 See also Waltke and Houston, *Psalms as Christian Worship*, chap. 15.

enemies your footstool.'" The Hebrew has various words for speaking. The usual words have to do with the act of speaking (דָּבָר) or the content of what is spoken (אָמַר). Another is used to refer to "prophetic" speech (נְאֻם), words spoken by God or by his Spirit through his spokesman. The latter is the word used here—divine-prophetic speech is in view. This is how Jesus understood this word and this psalm: David was speaking "in the Spirit" (Matt. 22:43; cf. 1 Sam. 23:1–2; Acts 1:16; 2:30; 4:25).

The superscript of the psalm is again of controlling significance: it is a psalm of David. The psalm therefore predates the extant similar Assyrian liturgies (seventh c. BC) by more than three hundred years. In 110:1, David recites the words of the LORD, to someone David designates "my Lord" (Adonai), David's master, one to whom David is subordinate. Implications of the deity of the Messiah are indisputable, a point of exegesis that confounded Jesus's enemies (Matt. 22:41–45).

The citation itself authorizes David's Lord to rule: "Sit at my right hand, / until I make your enemies your footstool" (Ps. 110:1). "Sitting" is the posture of authority and "the right hand" the position of authority (cf. Matt. 20:20–24). The footstool was at the feet of the king as he sat on his throne. "Make your enemies your footstool" is a metaphor of complete subjugation, just one of many "triumph of the Messiah" prophecies that dominate the Bible storyline (cf. Gen. 3:15). Although the psalm was composed to be sung to the succeeding Davidic kings in coronation liturgy, it links to a major biblical theme and looks to the greater King to come. David speaks prophetically, an oracle that finds its fulfillment in the resurrection and ascension of Christ and finally its consummation in his return to judge the world (Rev. 19).

The temple in Jerusalem, the Lord's residence, was a copy of heaven, as we have previously noted. The temple faced the East, and on the south side, the right hand, there was the Portico of Justice (1 Kings 7:7) where the king, the son of David, sat enthroned and rendered judgment. Both the temple and the Portico of Justice were in a common enclosure. So in the temple there was the throne room of God where he sat enthroned on the wings of the cherubim who flanked his throne. Inside the ark was the law of God, the Ten Commandments.

Then on the right hand was the king who implemented the covenant and administered its regulations. Again, this is a replica of heaven. God is the lawgiver, and Christ is the administrator of law and justice. God has given his King universal authority, and ascended to God's "right hand" the King upholds God's law and will judge the earth accordingly. He is the one through whom God will subdue all his enemies, putting them all under his feet (1 Cor. 15:25; Eph. 1:22; Heb. 2:6–9).

In Psalm 110:2–3 we have the prophetic reflection on the divine citation of verse 1:

> 2 The LORD sends forth from Zion
> your mighty scepter.
> Rule in the midst of your enemies!
> 3 Your people will offer themselves freely
> on the day of your power,
> in holy garments;
> from the womb of the morning,
> the dew of your youth will be yours.

In 110:2 the prophet speaks, but he is reflecting on the oracle of 110:1. The "scepter" is the symbol of the king's authority, and his is a "mighty" one. This symbol is used in Psalm 2:9 also, an unbreakable "rod of iron" with which the King will break the nations. Here the "sending forth" of the scepter pictures the King's ever-extending sway over the earth. "Zion" prefigures the heavenly Zion to which Christ ascended and whence he rules. In 110:2 the prophet seems to repeat or paraphrase the oracle, highlighting the divine directive to the King to rule over his enemies. He is to initiate holy war and bring all into submission to him. Today this mission is carried out by the sword of the Word and Spirit, the gospel in the hands of a suffering church, and by its prayer, "Your kingdom come, / your will be done, / on earth as it is in heaven" (Matt. 6:10).

The people of God who offer themselves freely to his service are the troops, his soldiers. The word "freely" is the word for a freewill offering

(נְדָבָה), offerings that were not required but voluntary. This army consists wholly of volunteers, not mercenaries or draftees. In Israel's holy wars, there was no forced drafting—the army was of volunteer soldiers only. "And the officers shall speak further to the people, and say, 'Is there any man who is fearful and fainthearted? Let him go back to his house, lest he make the heart of his fellows melt like his own'" (Deut. 20:8). Only those wholly dedicated to the cause could enlist. It was a freewill offering of sorts. So also the "soldiers" of the messianic King. All are volunteers—dedicated, fearless warriors who love, trust, and support their King and joyfully give themselves to his cause in full confidence that their King will prevail (cf. Phil. 2:16–17).

"The day of his power" is the day of his enthronement, the day he obtains and begins to execute his kingly rule. Christ's worldwide rule and conquest begin in his ascension to the right hand of God and his pouring out of the Spirit on his people who, in turn, give themselves freely to his cause, even in the face of martyrdom. Endowed by his Spirit they are arrayed "in holy garments" for their service to him. These soldiers in brilliant military regalia (cf. Ps. 45:3) are priests, holy and righteous in Christ. The metaphor "from the womb of the dawn" (110:3a) signifies the dawn of the great king's rule, which gives birth to his dedicated army. God raises up his own army of energetic ("youth[ful]") volunteers who like the "morning dew" (110:3b) are innumerable (cf. Mic. 5:7). So Christ builds his church (Rom. 16:20; 2 Cor. 2:14–17; Rev. 12:11). Frances Havergal (1836–1879) captures this stanza in her famous hymn:

Who is on the Lord's side? Who will serve the King?
Who will be his helpers, other lives to bring?
Who will leave the world's side? Who will face the foe?
Who is on the Lord's side? Who for him will go?
By thy call of mercy, by thy grace divine,
We are on the Lord's side—Savior, we are thine!

Not for weight of glory, nor for crown and palm,
Enter we the army, raise the warrior psalm;

But for love that claimeth lives for whom He died:
He whom Jesus saveth marches on His side.
By thy love constraining, by thy grace divine,
We are on the Lord's side—Savior, we are thine! . . .

Fierce may be the conflict, strong may be the foe,
But the King's own army none can overthrow;
'Round His standard ranging, vict'ry is secure,
For His truth unchanging makes the triumph sure.
Joyfully enlisting, by Thy grace divine,
We are on the Lord's side—Savior, we are Thine![28]

*Stanza 2 (110:4–7)*

4 The LORD has sworn
and will not change his mind,
"You are a priest forever
after the order of Melchizedek."
5 The Lord is at your right hand;
he will shatter kings on the day of his wrath.
6 He will execute judgment among the nations,
filling them with corpses;
he will shatter chiefs
over the wide earth.
7 He will drink from the brook by the way;
therefore he will lift up his head.

Stanza 2 begins with a declaration of the eternal priesthood of the King and ends with assurance of his eternal victory. Several observations from this verse stand out. First, the King is a priest. This is unprecedented, and it would seem impossible. The priests are from the tribe of Levi, the high priest from Aaron; the Messiah is from the tribe

28 Frances Havergal, "Who Is on the Lord's Side?" (1877), Hymnary.org (website), accessed October 14, 2022, https://hymnary.org/.

of Judah. David implicitly prophesies the eventual obsolescence of the Levitical priesthood. Second, he in fact is not an Aaronic priest because of Melchizedek. The Hebrew expression here (עַל־דִּבְרָתִי) probably does not mean "in the order of" but "for the reason that." The Messiah is a king and a priest because before Aaron's priesthood, Melchizedek, a royal priest, served him. Third, he is a priest "forever." His priestly work will never be left to anyone else. Indeed, his priesthood is given by irrevocable divine oath:

> 4 The LORD has sworn
> and will not change his mind,
> "You are a priest forever
> after the order of Melchizedek." (110:4)

A divine oath differs from a prophecy in that the fulfillment of a given prophecy, as we have seen, may be conditioned on human obedience (Jer. 18:7–11). Judgment may be averted by repentance, and blessing may be forfeited by apostasy. But a divine oath is irrevocable (cf. Heb. 6:13–17).[29] God's oath here is that the King will also be a priest, and he will be so forever. All this the epistle to the Hebrews develops at length with reference to the resurrected and ascended Christ whose mediatorial work continues forever for the eternal preservation of his people (Heb. 7).

Psalm 110:5–7 records the prophet's reflection on the divine decree. We should note that in 110:5 "the Lord" (Adonai) in view is Yahweh himself, "the LORD" who in 110:1 spoke to David's "Lord" (Adonai). Yahweh is "master" (Adonai) of all, and he is the one who has "sworn" in oath to David's greater son, the Messiah. The Lord God himself is at the King's "right hand," and by him he will triumph. He will "execute judgment among the nations" resulting in widespread devastation (110:6). He will lead in the punishment (יָדִין) of the rebellious nations of the earth (cf. Ps. 2).

29 Cf. Richard Pratt, "Historical Contingencies and Biblical Predictions," in *The Way of Wisdom: Essays in Honor of Bruce K. Waltke*, ed. J. I. Packer and Sven K. Soderlund (Grand Rapids, MI: Zondervan, 2000), 180–203.

From the "brook" (110:7, נַחַל, wadi), God will supply the Messiah with abundant refreshment in the execution of his rule so that he will never tire in "the way" of triumph (cf. 2 Cor. 2:14–17; Rev. 19). Neither desert nor fatigue will hinder him in his task, whatever rigors may be demanded of him. Along his march to establish God's kingdom to the ends of the earth, he will "drink from the brook," be refreshed, and persevere until he "lift[s] up his head" in final victory. At last, all the world will acknowledge him as King.

### Final Reflections

As we highlighted at the outset, this psalm heavily influenced New Testament Christology. David foresaw Christ's death (Ps. 22), his resurrection (16), his ascension-enthronement (110:1–3), and his eventual universal triumph (110:5–7). It is not clear that he understood just how Christ's rule would unfold. But following Christ's own lead (Matt. 26:64), the apostles understood Psalm 110 as defining Christ's rule in this inaugurated phase of his kingdom, their message that Jesus is Lord, and the agenda of this age. Enthroned at the Father's right hand, the Lord Jesus has sent his Spirit into the world to advance his kingdom through the gospel (Acts 1:4–5, 8; 2:33–36), and for this kingdom advance, members of his army, emboldened by his Spirit, gladly give themselves to the cause (Ps. 110:3). When this gospel advance is complete, the end will come (Matt. 24:14)—Christ will return and bring his kingdom to consummation (Rev. 19). At last the world will recognize their rightful king: "at the name of Jesus every knee should bow, in heaven and on earth and under the earth, and every tongue confess that Jesus Christ is Lord, to the glory of God the Father" (Phil. 2:10–11).

# 6

# Hebrew Poetry

*"Sing praises with a psalm!"*

AS WE HAVE EMPHASIZED, our goal in this book is to "get behind" the Psalms and understand the mind and preunderstandings of the psalmists. This means we must understand something about Hebrew poetry that the psalmists themselves assume.

## What Is Hebrew Poetry?

Poetry is marked by certain restrictions, a sort of rhythm that does not normally govern prose. Hebrew poetry, however, is not restricted by features commonly associated with our poetry but is restricted in at least these three ways.

### *Parallelism*

The first is parallelism: a verse is divided into two halves. The terminology for the halves of a verse has not been standardized, and so the terminology varies. A half verse has been called a line, a half line, a stich, a hemistich, or a colon. We prefer with Robert Alter the term "verset." The entire verse is composed of two versets, a bicolon (pl. bicola) or, when a verset is further divided into halves, three versets (see above), a tricolon (pl. tricola). A verse with two pairs of parallel lines (that is, two bicola) is a quatrain. Two related verses are a couplet. Consider the two parallel versets of Psalm 2:1, a bicolon:

> Why do the nations rage
> and the peoples plot in vain?

Psalm 1:1 has three versets, a tricolon:

> Blessed is the man who walks not in the counsel of the wicked,
> nor stands in the way of sinners,
> nor sits in the seat of scoffers.

Parallel versets correspond to one another in similar structure and semantics. Take Psalm 2:1 as an example:

> Why do the nations rage
> and the peoples plot in vain?

The rhythm and grammar are similar, and, more importantly, they correspond in meaning: "nations" matches "peoples," and "rage" matches "plot in vain." "Why do the nations rage?" is supplemented with "and the peoples plot in vain?" It aims to give complex information in a unified way so that the message is heard stereophonically. We will examine parallelism further below.

*Brevity and Terseness*

The second restriction is true of all poetry: it is terse and brief—you might even say abbreviated at times. It has been rather humorously remarked that you can tell it's poetry by all the white space on the page. And when you turn to the Psalms you see a lot of white space! Poetry often omits verbal particles, it leaves gaps, and it often states its point in briefest fashion. The focus is on the parallel. It is more like a telegraph than a motion picture. "Not so the wicked" (Ps. 1:4 NIV) is one example of terseness. The psalmist does not go back through the description of the righteous of 1:1–3 and explain now, in specifics, how the wicked differs from them. He just says, "Not so the wicked." Another example is Psalm 4:6, which we have already seen: "Who will show us some good?" The request is for rain, but there is no narrative to spell that out, only brief statements that, taken together, paint a fuller picture and inform us of the meaning of "good" in this verse.

Judges 4:19 provides a vivid example also, where we read of Jael and Sisera: "And he said to her, 'Please give me a little water to drink, for I am thirsty.' So she opened a skin of milk and gave him a drink and covered him." That's prose. Reading the narrative you will notice that she met the request and relieved his thirst, but she did more—she gave him milk instead of water. Now notice how this appears in poetry (Judg. 5:25):

> "Water," he asked. Milk she gave;
>   in a princely bowl she offered curds. (authors' translation)

It is terse, not run-on like prose. And the net effect is that it draws your attention to what she did for him. She met his thirst, but she also gave him milk to help him sleep, and she treated him like a king. Recognizing this poetic device often has profound implications for understanding the emphasis of a given passage.

### *Imagery and Figures of Speech*

The third restriction is also true of all poetry: it employs concrete imagery and various figures of speech. Imagery is suggestive and captivating, and it is one aspect of poetry's terseness. God as a rock (Ps. 18:46) or a shield (7:10) or shade (121:5) or guardian (110:5) are familiar images of the Psalter. Imagery and metaphors stir the imagination and provide vivid clarity. We may speak of God's providence, but figurative expressions such as sheltered under God's "wings" (91:4) and "you hold me by my right hand" (73:23 NIV) drive the point emotively and with vivid effect. So also speaking of God as a "river" that sustains a city (46:4) graphically portrays God's protection and provision. Similarly, many psalms extol the justice of God and anticipate a day of vindication for the righteous, but few stamp the expectation on the imagination like the imagery of 37:6:

> He will bring forth your righteousness as the light,
> and your justice as the noonday.

And David's depiction of God's caring concern for him in Psalm 56:8 evokes both emotion and confidence:

> You have kept count of my tossings;
> put my tears in your bottle.
> Are they not in your book?

Imagery calls for thoughtful reflection to appreciate the point at hand, and we must be alert to it throughout our reading of the Psalms.

### *More on Parallelism*

#### ROBERT LOWTH (1710–1787)

The first scholarly work on parallelism was by Robert Lowth, a British bishop at Oxford. In 1753, he published *De Sacra Poesi Hebraeorum* ("On the Sacred Poetry of the Hebrews"), which influenced virtually all future scholarship on the poetry of the Bible. There were some rabbis earlier, such as Ramban in the eleventh century, who observed parallelism also, but Lowth marks the beginning of modern scholarship on the subject. And it has been recognized since that parallelism is fundamental to understanding the poetry of the Psalms.

Lowth defined parallelism as the correspondence of one line (better, verset) with another. We noted this in Psalm 2. Lowth emphasized the similarities of the versets to one another and thought of them as restatement, not as related statement. The notion of "restatement" dominated until a revolution of our understanding of Hebrew poetry occurred in

1981. James Kugel argued convincingly that the second verset expands and/or emphasizes the first.[1]

Lowth tended to identify three types of parallelism. This oversimplifies the matter, but his "three types" of parallelism (synonymous, antithetical, and synthetic)[2] remain somewhat helpful. In what he calls *synonymous parallelism* the two lines (versets) of the verse seem to say nearly the same thing:

> O Lord, how many are my foes!
> Many are rising against me. (3:1)

*Antithetical parallelism* we saw in Psalm 1:6:

> the Lord knows the way of the righteous,
> but the way of the wicked will perish.

Here "the way of the righteous" contrasts with "the way of the wicked, and "the Lord knows" contrasts with "shall perish." The one way is life, and the other is death. The two lines treat a common point, but they do so in contrasting ways.

In *synthetic parallelism* the second line significantly expands the first. Psalm 1:2, for example:

> his delight is in the law of the LORD,
> and on his law he meditates day and night.

Here the second line adds to the thought of the first—because the psalmist "delights" in God's law, he "meditates" on it "day and night." The second line is not merely a restatement; it advances the thought somewhat. Similarly in Psalm 2:11: "Serve the LORD with fear" is tempered

1 James Kugel, *The Idea of Biblical Poetry: Parallelism and Its History* (New Haven, CT: Yale University Press, 1981).

2 Robert Lowth, *De Sacra Poesi Hebraeorum: Praelectiones Academiae Oxonii Habitae* (Oxonii: E Typographeo Clarendoniano, 1753), 177–96.

by "rejoice with trembling." Both lines repeat the notion of "fear," but the second adds to "serve," "rejoice"; the service that pleases the Lord is reverential and joyful, not reluctant.

A fourth kind of parallelism worth identifying is *formal parallelism*.[3] The two halves are connected by their rhythm and syntax, but not by semantics. For example,

> Turn to me and be gracious to me,
> for I am lonely and afflicted. (25:16)

## POST-LOWTHIAN REFINEMENTS

Since 1980 Lowth's view of Hebrew parallelism has undergone significant refinement with the work of Robert Alter and James Kugel. Lowth thought that synonymous parallelism was standard, but Alter and Kugel argued convincingly that synthetic is the norm. The second line does not aim to repeat the thought of the first but to reinforce it in some way. The second line is not a throwaway shadow of the first: it either says it emphatically or adds something to it. There is statement and then related or emphatic statement, not just restatement. To understand the second line as a mere restatement of the first will often lead us to miss a significant thought. The second line does not merely restate but enriches the first and is often the more important of the two. The difference here is subtle but significant. In the second line different words are used that mean different things, and although the difference may be slight, it does affect meaning.

Reconsider Psalm 2:5:

> Then he will speak to them in his wrath,
> and terrify them in his fury, saying.

"Terrify" intensifies "speak," and "fury" intensifies "anger."

3 Gerald Wilson, calls this "advancing parallelism," but the second verset in synonymous and synthetic parallels also advances the first verset in some way, so this nomenclature does not distinguish mere syntactic advancement from them. Gerald H. Wilson, *Psalms Volume 1*, The NIV Application Commentary (Grand Rapids, MI: Zondervan, 2002), 41–46.

Take the quatrain of Psalm 3:7 as an example. Its first bicolon is

> Arise, O Lord!
> Save me, O my God!

Obviously, there is parallelism, but "arise" (to go to battle) is significantly advanced by its purpose, "save me." On the other hand, "O Lord" and "O God" are probably stock-in-trade parallels.

Its second bicolon reads,

> For you strike all my enemies on the cheek;
> You break the teeth of the wicked.

Both versets pertain to God's salvation of David, but "strike on the cheek" signifies their humiliating defeat, whereas "break the teeth" signifies their inability to harm him anymore. Importantly, the second verset identifies the enemies as wicked. The second verset intensifies the first.

This distinction is important, as Kugel points out: "Overall, [Lowth's view] has had a disastrous effect on subsequent criticism. Because of it, synonymity was often imposed where it did not exist, sharpness was lost, and the real nature of biblical parallelism was henceforth condemned to a perpetual 'falling between two stools.'"[4] Kugel continues,

> B was connected to A, had something in common with it, but was not expected to be (or regarded as) mere restatement. . . .
>
> . . . It is the dual nature of B both to come *after* A and thus to add to it, often particularizing, defining, or expanding the meaning and harken back to A and in an obvious way to connect to it.
>
> . . . What this means is simply: B, being connected to A—carrying it further, echoing it, defining it, restating it, contrasting with it, *it does not matter which*—has an emphatic, "seconding" character, and it is this more than any aesthetic of symmetry or paralleling, which is at the heart of biblical parallelism.

4 Kugel, *The Idea of Biblical Poetry*, 15.

> To state the matter somewhat simplistically, biblical lines are parallelistic not because B is meant to be a parallel of A, but because B typically *supports* A, carries it further, backs it up, completes it, goes beyond it.[5]

Prior to this breakthrough in understanding, dissertations were written attempting to give a taxonomy of all the kinds of parallelism in the Psalms. There are so many that the task became impossible because, simply, the B verset in some way emphasizes or adds to verset A, yielding a different and richer perspective on the A verset.

Psalm 22:18 provides another example:

> They divide my clothes among them
> and cast lots for my garment. (NIV)

From Lowth's viewpoint, "clothes" and "garments" are saying the same thing. From Kugel's viewpoint, these are different things. The apostle John interpreted Hebrew poetry in this way:

> When the soldiers had crucified Jesus, they took his garments and divided them into four parts, one part for each soldier; also his tunic. But the tunic was seamless, woven in one piece from top to bottom, so they said to one another, "Let us not tear it, but cast lots for it to see whose it shall be." This was to fulfill the Scripture which says,
>
> " They divided my garments among them,
> and for my clothing they cast lots." (John 19:23–24)

Notice the soldiers divided the clothes but cast lots for the garment. There is a difference between clothes and cloak. Instead of seeing them as saying the same thing they say different things.

5 Kugel, *The Idea of Biblical Poetry*, 8, 51–52.

Take Zechariah 9:9 as another example. The ESV translates

> 9 Rejoice greatly, O daughter of Zion!
>   Shout aloud, O daughter of Jerusalem!
> Behold, your king is coming to you;
>   righteous and having salvation is he,
> humble and mounted on a donkey,
>   on a colt, the foal of a donkey.

But the Hebrew can be read either normally as "mounted and on a donkey *and* a colt" or less normally as "mounted on a donkey, *even* a colt." Riding on two animals is difficult to imagine. So the translators opted to interpret the poetry as synonymous, understanding donkey and colt as synonymous parallels. But Matthew saw two animals and read the prophecy as referring to two animals.

> Now when they drew near to Jerusalem and came to Bethphage, to the Mount of Olives, then Jesus sent two disciples, saying to them, "Go into the village in front of you, and immediately you will find a donkey tied, and a colt with her. Untie them and bring them to me. If anyone says anything to you, you shall say, 'The Lord needs them,' and he will send them at once." This took place to fulfill what was spoken by the prophet, saying,
>
> "Say to the daughter of Zion,
>   'Behold, your king is coming to you,
> humble, and mounted on a donkey,
>   [and] on a colt, the foal of a beast of burden.'" (Matt. 21:1–5)

Matthew witnessed Jesus as riding on a donkey and on a colt.

So Kugel's view supports Matthew's normal interpretation of Hebrew grammar and poetry. "Synthetic" parallelism is normal, not abnormal, and the variety of possible relations between versets is endless. This view has some precedent also in that some rabbis who composed and developed Hebrew poetry differentiated "B" from "A." It has precedent in the New Testament use of the parallels, as we have just seen. And it yields better exegetical returns, cutting the text with a sharp razor rather than a butter knife.

Let's take a few more examples:

63 I am a companion of all who fear you,
of those who keep your precepts (Ps. 119:63).

Here the parallel second line is broadly synonymous, but it does more than merely repeat the thought of the first—it specifies in practical terms what it means to fear the Lord. To fear the Lord is to obey his word.

Let's consider some verses from Psalm 96:

3 Declare his glory among the nations,
his marvelous works among all the peoples! (96:3)

Both versets constitute a call to praise; this is the mark of a praise psalm (hymn). But the second verset does not merely repeat the thought of the first. It tells us that we declare God's "glory" by proclaiming "his marvelous works." The thought narrows.

So also in 96:9:

9 Worship the Lord in the splendor of holiness;
tremble before him, all the earth!

Here the second verset tells us that worshiping God entails fearing him.

And the verses in 96:11–13 hang together:

11 Let the heavens be glad, and let the earth rejoice;
let the sea roar, and all that fills it;
12 let the field exult, and everything in it!
Then shall all the trees of the forest sing for joy

13 before the LORD, for he comes,
for he comes to judge the earth.
He will judge the world in righteousness,
and the peoples in his faithfulness. (96:11–13)

Here we have several poetic elements at play. Psalm 96:11a, the first verset, calls heaven and earth to rejoice. And 96:11b–12 parallel 96:11a; they expand the thought of "earth rejoicing" with the graphic imagery of the sea, the fields, and the forests joining in joyful praise.

**Additional Note**

We should note that these features of poetry—parallelism, terseness, figurative language, and more—all require thoughtful reflection. To grasp the message of a psalm we must pause and carefully consider its poetic elements. We must emphasize this, and we will be reminded of it repeatedly throughout this book: the Psalms must be read thoughtfully. We are not accustomed to this. We usually want to read linearly and quickly get to the point. But poetry just does not work that way, and we just will never read the Psalms well if we only read them quickly. They require thoughtful consideration. If we are to understand them, we must pause and meditate. We must discern how the lines parallel, even how the stanzas or strophes parallel. We must consider thoughtfully what is conveyed in brief or terse expressions, how the chosen imagery illuminates the point at hand, how the psalm is structured, how the thought progresses, and so on. Without thoughtful meditation we may pick up a devotional gem here and there, but we will miss the full message that the poem in its richness is intended to convey.

Once again, to emphasize, we must read the Psalms thoughtfully. The blessed man is the one who "meditates" on God's word (1:2). The poets of the Psalms composed their poems carefully, in word and structure, as a means of conveying their message. To profit, we must take our time and read accordingly.

## PSALM 133

A Song of Ascents. Of David.

1 Behold, how good and pleasant it is
when brothers dwell in unity!
2 It is like the precious oil on the head,
running down on the beard,
on the beard of Aaron,
running down on the collar of his robes!
3 It is like the dew of Hermon,
which falls on the mountains of Zion!
For there the Lord has commanded the blessing,
life forevermore.

Psalm 133 is a brief psalm that illustrates the use of imagery. This psalm of David has a single theme: unity. The unity of the nation ("brothers," 133:1) is in view. Some have suggested that David wrote this psalm when the twelve tribes came together to acknowledge him as king (2 Sam. 5:1–10), but it may have been composed for use at Solomon's temple dedication at Sukkoth, the festive time when all the tribes worshiped together as one.

By way of overview we may outline the psalm like this:

133:1: *Proposition.* Here David introduces his theme:

1 Behold, how good and pleasant it is
when brothers dwell in unity!

133:2–3a: *Illustration.* Here David illustrates his theme with two similes:

2 It is like the precious oil on the head,
running down on the beard,
on the beard of Aaron,
running down on the collar of his robes!

3 It is like the dew of Hermon,
which falls on the mountains of Zion!

133:3b: *Explanation.* Here David shows the reason underlying his theme:

For there the Lord has commanded the blessing,
life forevermore.

Note that David's theme is not unity simply, but the blessedness of unity. The harmony of the people is "good and pleasant." That is, it is both beneficial and delightful. This is his theme, and to enhance his point he gives two illustrations (133:2–3).

First, he likens the people's unity ("it," 133:2) to oil suffusing Aaron's beard and dripping onto his robes. The reference is to Aaron's anointing for priesthood in which oil was poured on his head (Ex. 29:7; Lev. 8:12) and sprinkled on his robe (Ex. 29:21). Every hair was not just touched by it but completely saturated with it, so much so that it poured off onto his collar also. It was a fragrant aroma and a delightful and joyous event. Elsewhere this oil is referred to as "the oil of gladness" (Ps. 45:7).

The unity of the people is also "like the dew of Hermon, / which falls on the mountains of Zion!" (133:3a). The dew on high Mount Hermon was known to be so heavy that it could appear in the morning as if it had rained. So much dew was both refreshing and invigorating for the crops, a particular blessing in an agrarian culture. The simile here takes an obvious metaphorical dimension when David speaks of the dew of Hermon falling "on the mountain of Zion," some ninety miles to the south. The picture is that of Jerusalem benefitting from such dewfall.

This imagery goes further. The tension between the northern and southern tribes of Israel was long-standing, and after David squelched Absalom's revolt a civil war between the northern tribes and Judah broke out. Still, David had brought the tribes together under his kingship, and he celebrates their unity here. "Hermon was the prominent mountain of the north, as Zion was of the south, and David sees them as no longer in tension but belonging so naturally together that it is as if the dew of Hermon could come and fall on Zion!"[6] David intends for us to understand both the happy, fragrant event of Aaron's anointing and the refreshing, invigorating dew of Mount Hermon as pictures of the experienced unity of the people.

In 133:3b, he explains: "for there the Lord has commanded the blessing, / life forevermore"—that is, harmonious unity in Zion is the place of God's blessing.

In its canonical context, the imagery reaches profound depths. The anointing oil in the Old Testament represents the gift of the Spirit (1 Sam. 16:13; cf. 2 Sam. 23:1–3). Both Aaron himself as high priest and the oil poured out in abundance are prospective of the Lord Jesus Christ, our great high priest (Heb. 4:14) who received the Spirit "without measure" (John 3:34). He, in turn, has baptized us in the Spirit (1 Cor. 12:13), has given us the anointing (1 John 2:20), and has made us priests unto God also (1 Pet. 2:5; Rev. 5:10). Mount Zion represents the church (1 Pet. 2:4–6), the heavenly Zion to which we in Christ have come (Heb. 12:22; Rev. 14:1), and the eschatological place of God's dwelling with his people (Rev. 21:2). The church is one people united in Christ (John 10:16), and our harmonious brotherhood of love is what sets us apart from the world (John 13:34–35). This goal is to be highly valued, as the place of refreshment and joy, and deemed worthy of our every effort to maintain (Eph. 4:3), and this in anticipation of its climactic realization in the eschaton (cf. Eph. 1:10; Rev. 21–22). The church in harmonious unity is the divinely designated place of blessing.

## PSALM 121

A Song of Ascents.

1 I lift up my eyes to the hills.
From where does my help come?
2 My help comes from the Lord,

6 Alec Motyer, *Journey: Psalms for Pilgrim People* (Nottingham, UK: Inter-Varsity Press, 2009), 142–43.

who made heaven and earth.
3 He will not let your foot be moved;
he who keeps you will not slumber.
4 Behold, he who keeps Israel
will neither slumber nor sleep.
5 The LORD is your keeper;
the LORD is your shade on your right hand.
6 The sun shall not strike you by day,
nor the moon by night.
7 The LORD will keep you from all evil;
he will keep your life.
8 The LORD will keep your going out and your coming in
from this time forth and forevermore.

**Poetry and Structure**

In both its construction and its imagery Psalm 121 illustrates well for us the poetic beauty of the Psalms. As are virtually all the Psalms in the Songs of Ascents, this psalm is oriented to the Jerusalem temple. The superscript informs us that it is "A Song of Ascents," a psalm sung by the faithful as they made their journey to the holy city to observe its annual feasts. We looked at these "Pilgrimage Psalms" (120–134) in the previous chapter. They were sung by Israelites as they approached ("ascent") the city for festivities, having the "holy hill" (Mount Zion) and surrounding hills in view. That journey, in turn, becomes a picture of the journey of life under the watchful guardianship of God (121:8).

The atmosphere is one of a potentially dangerous journey; the theme is that of confident trust. "Psalms of trust" is another category of the Psalter we will examine in a later chapter. Here the theme of confidence is developed through the psalm by an overview of God's protective care. Repeatedly he is portrayed as a very personal guardian ("my help," "your keeper," "your shade").[7] The key word of the psalm is "keep" or

7 See Fred Zaspel, "A Psalm of Confidence: Psalm 121," *Credo Magazine*, October 17, 2013, https://credomag.com/.

"keeper," appearing six times (שָׁמַר, 121:3, 4, 5, 7 [2x], 8), essentially synonymous with "help" (121:1, 2). Throughout the psalm it is "the Lord" who gives "help" and who "keeps" (121:2, 3, 4, 5, 7, 8). He is his people's watchful guardian, and the faithful look to him as such.

Alec Motyer notes a distinct progression in the psalm. In 121:1–2 the Lord is presented as Creator. Then in 121:3–4, with its reference to Israel, he is presented as redeemer and covenant Lord. And finally in 121:5–6 he is presented as companion, standing alongside his people to help. "This threefold theology of Creator, Redeemer and Companion, then leads into the climax (vv. 7–8), keeping from all evil (7a), the whole person (7b), in every activity (8a), and for all time, starting now (8b)."[8]

The psalmist states his theme at the outset (121:1–2). Here the pilgrim ("I," "My"), looking up toward the temple mount and considering the difficulty and potential dangers of the trek, affirms his faith in the Lord's protective care. In 121:3–8 the answer is given. Commentators discuss here the question of whether this ("you," "your") indicates a second speaker—a priest, perhaps, pronouncing blessing and assuring a safe journey—or the psalmist's own response to his rhetorical question. In liturgical use, at least, it may signal a change in singers. We will come to this question again in our conclusion, and it may be helpful to keep in mind a possible distinction between the psalm in its original use and in its later use by pilgrims en route to Jerusalem. Here we will just note that throughout we hear the resounding affirmation of God's protective care, first affirmed (121:1–2) and then repeatedly restated with assurance (121:3–8).

The poem is symmetrically constructed in four stanzas with two verses each. The successive stanzas "build on each other, particularly through the repetition of the word *watch*"[9] (or "keep/keeper"). Each verse is a bicolon constructed with two parallel lines in which the second line supplements or completes the thought of the first or heightens it in some way. The two verses of each stanza also parallel one another:

8 Alec Motyer, *A Christian's Pocket Guide to Loving the Old Testament: One Book, One God, One Story*, Pocket Guides (Fearn, Ross-shire, Scotland: Christian Focus, 2015), 99.

9 Tremper Longman III, *Psalms: An Introduction and Commentary*, Tyndale Old Testament Commentaries (Downers Grove, IL: IVP Academic, 2014), 413.

121:2 completes the thought of 121:1, linking them by the catchword "help"; 121:4 extends the thought of 121:3, using the catchword "keep"; 121:6 completes the thought of 121:5 by the association of sun and shade; and 121:8 heightens the thought of 121:7, again linking them by "keep." Let's look at this more carefully.

In verset 121:1a the psalmist looks to the hills; in verset 121:1b we find that he is looking to the hills for help. In verset 121:2a he affirms that his help comes from the Lord, Israel's covenant God; in verset 121:2b he extends the thought by declaring that Israel's God is the Creator of all things. In both verses the second line parallels the first in some kind of completive sense. This is stanza 1. But notice further not just the second lines but that 121:2 itself parallels 121:1, completing its thought:

1 I lift up my eyes to the hills.
    From where does my help come?
2 My help comes from the Lord,
    who made heaven and earth.

So also in stanza 2, the second verse parallels the first by extending its thought:

3 He will not let your foot be moved;
    he who keeps you will not slumber.
4 Behold, he who keeps Israel
    will neither slumber nor sleep.

So also in stanza 3, the second verse parallels the first by completing its thought:

5 The Lord is your keeper;
    the Lord is your shade on your right hand.
6 The sun shall not strike you by day,
    nor the moon by night.

And so also in stanza 4, the second verse parallels the first by heightening its thought.

7 The LORD will keep you from all evil;
he will keep your life.
8 The LORD will keep your going out and your coming in
from this time forth and forevermore.

In all these, the second line of each verse parallels the first, and the second verse of each stanza parallels the first also.

Commentators often point out a further developed parallelism as well—*anadiplosis*, or step parallelism. In this technique a word in one verse is repeated in the next, leaving the effect of "stepping up." This may be illustrated with the use of bold text:

1 I lift up my eyes to the hills.
From where does **my help come**?
2 **My help comes** from the LORD,
who made heaven and earth.
3 He will not let your foot be moved;
**he who keeps** you **will not slumber**.
4 Behold, **he who keeps** Israel
**will neither slumber nor sleep**.
5 **The LORD is your keeper**;
the LORD is your shade on your right hand.
6 The sun shall not strike you by day,
nor the moon by night.
7 **The LORD will keep you** from all evil;
he will keep your life.
8 **The LORD will keep** your going out and your coming in
from this time forth and forevermore.[10]

10 See W. Graham Scroggie, *A Guide to the Psalms*, vol. 3, *A Comprehensive Analysis of the Psalms* (Grand Rapids, MI: Kregel, 1995), 196; see also W. Dennis Tucker Jr. and

The psalmist employs various other poetic devices also. "Heaven and earth" (121:2) is a merism, a figure of speech by which two polar extremes are mentioned to represent the whole: God is the Creator of all things. "By day or by night" (121:6) is a merism for "all the time," and "your going out and your coming in" (121:8) is a merism for all your activities. "He will not let your foot be moved" (121:3) is a metonymy referring to the stability of the whole of life in God's care. "Neither slumber nor sleep" is a pleonasm (redundancy), stressing that God's care is unceasing. Both "your shade" and "at your right hand" (121:5) are metaphors symbolizing God's protection from harm. Psalm 121:6 is a perfect chiasm in the Hebrew, the two halves of the verse pivoting on the verb "will not smite": "By day the sun will not smite you, / nor the moon by night" (121:6 NJB). Both "sun" and "moon" are metaphors of various kinds of dangers. "From all evil" (121:7) is another pivot: "The Lord will keep you from all evil; / he will keep your life." "Your life" here is another metonymy, referring to the person himself. "Your going out and your coming in" (121:8) is a merism descriptive, again, of the whole of life. And throughout the psalm the psalter employs extensive repetition of both verbal terminology and concepts.[11]

All this to note that the poetic work of the psalmist is extensive, both in the construction of the psalm and in the specific devices employed. We do not have the space in this book to analyze the poetry of each psalm in this much detail, but this illustrates the carefulness of the psalmists' work that the interpreter will want to take time to notice.

We may outline the thought of this psalm broadly:

121:1–2: Affirmation of trust (stanza 1)
121:3–8: Assurance of protection (stanzas 2–4)

**Survey Exposition**

In each stanza, indeed, in each verse, the psalmist's theme is reiterated: God our trustworthy guardian. In 121:1–2 the traveler affirms his trust:

---

Jamie A. Grant, *Psalms Volume. 2*, The NIV Application Commentary (Grand Rapids, MI: Zondervan, 2018), 730.

11 See Zaspel, "A Psalm of Confidence."

1 I lift up my eyes to the hills [or "mountains"].
From where does my help come?
2 My help comes from the LORD,
who made heaven and earth.

Scholars differ on the meaning of the plural "mountains." "Lift up" in most Old Testament passages means "to turn the eyes toward with desire" (cf. Gen. 39:7; Ezek. 18:6). So he looks with longing on Zion, called "mountains of Zion" in Psalm 133:3. His question, "From where does my help come?" (121:1), implies that there are multiple dangers in this journey. But the question is not intended to reflect anxiety on the traveler's part but rather to draw attention to the answer: 121:1 raises the question in order to draw attention to the answer given in 121:2.

The second line of 121:2 elaborates on the first: "My help comes from the LORD, / who made heaven and earth." God as Creator is a common theme in the Psalter, often, as here, to highlight his greatness and power as a ground of trust. "Heaven and earth" is a merism: God is the Creator of all that is. "The thought of this verse leaps beyond the hills to the universe; beyond the universe to its Maker."[12] The Creator—and therefore universal sovereign—is himself the "keeper" of his covenant people. Surely such a God, our covenant Lord, is both willing and capable of protecting his people on their journey to their eternal destiny. It is doubtless no coincidence that these Songs of Ascents are followed immediately by Psalm 135, a song of praise to God for his sovereign rule over all things. Surely our anxieties come only as we lose sight of the greatness and goodness of our God. As David Livingstone left for his virgin mission work in Africa he read Psalms 121 and 135 with his family[13]—well-chosen psalms for encouragement on such a venture.

Next, in 121:3–4 the psalmist characterizes God's protective care as faithfully vigilant and unceasing:

12 Derek Kidner, *Psalms 73–150* (London: Inter-Varsity Press, 1975), 467.

13 John Ker, *The Psalms in History and Biography* (1886; repr., Solid Ground Christian Books, 2006), 149.

3 He will not let your foot be moved;
he who keeps you will not slumber.
4 Behold, he who keeps Israel
will neither slumber nor sleep.

Psalm 121:3 affirms God's protective care in the minute details of life—"not even a foot will slip" is the sense. The reference is to the pilgrim in his journey up the hill toward Jerusalem, but the imagery reflects a confidence in God's protection for all misfortune. To our knowledge, biblical Israel was never attacked as they gathered for festivities as Moses had commanded.[14] The psalmist goes further ("Behold," 121:4) to affirm that God's aseity assures us that his care will never cease. He never becomes tired or too weary to care for his people (cf. 1 Kings 18:27; Isa. 40:28), and he is never caught off guard. "Israel's keeper" will surely not fail to care for any Israelite.

In 121:5–6 the psalmist describes the extent of the Lord's protective care:

5 The Lord is your keeper;
the Lord is your shade on your right hand.
6 The sun shall not strike you by day,
nor the moon by night.

Psalm 121:5 combines two images of danger and protection. The Lord is a "shade" from the natural elements, and he is "on your right hand" as a personal bodyguard. In both cases, "the Lord" is fronted, reminding the reader that it is no ordinary shade and no ordinary sentry who protects but the Creator and covenant Lord himself. The idea of protection from natural elements is carried into 121:6. "By day . . . by night" is another merism—the Lord's protection is constant. He is ever vigilant. "Sun" and "moon" may be intended as merisms also—the Lord protects from all kinds of dangers (cf. 121:7, "all evil").

14 On Yom Kippur, 1973, the Arab states led by Syria and Egypt attacked the modern state of Israel. The Syrian tanks reached the plain of Sharon and, fearing a trap, turned back.

In 121:7–8 the verb tense shifts to affirm that the Lord's protective care will continue forever.

> 7 The LORD will keep you from all evil;
> he will keep your life.
> 8 The LORD will keep your going out and your coming in
> from this time forth and forevermore.

"Your going out and your coming in" is yet another merism, signifying that the Lord watches over his people ceaselessly. By itself this may refer to the pilgrim's departure and return from the journey. "From this time forth and forevermore" is a Hebrew idiom for the future. It broadens the affirmation of trust to all of life. And with this final affirmation of trust the Psalm ends. God's protective care is constant and all-encompassing and never-ending. There is no limit either in detail or in time. For all of life and eternity we, his people, are the objects of his diligent care.

Throughout this psalm the psalmist affirms the truth of God's protective care over and over again. He has highlighted various aspects of that protective care, but it is this single theme that he drives repeatedly throughout. Repetition is a common feature of the poetry of the Psalms, but there is a didactic purpose also, as Calvin points out in his closing comments on this psalm:

> Such repetition seems at first sight superfluous; but when we consider how difficult it is to correct our distrust, it will be easily perceived that he does not improperly dwell upon the commendation of the divine providence. How few are to be found who yield to God the honor of being a keeper, in order to their being thence assured of their safety, and led to call upon him in the midst of their perils! On the contrary, even when we seem to have largely experienced what this protection of God implies, we yet instantly tremble at the noise of a leaf falling from a tree, as if God had quite forgotten us. Being then entangled in so many unholy misgivings, and so much inclined to distrust, we

> are taught from the passage that if a sentence couched in a few words does not suffice us, we should gather together whatever may be found throughout the whole Scriptures concerning the providence of God, until this doctrine—"that God always keeps watch for us"—is deeply rooted in our hearts; so that depending upon his guardianship alone we may bid adieu to all the vain confidences of the world.[15]

### Further Reflections

Psalm 121 is a psalm of trust. It expresses a firm confidence in God's protective care. On the face of it, the assurance is absolute, unconditional, and for all of life. Many have puzzled over this psalm, wondering how the idea that "no evil will befall you" corresponds with the reality of the suffering of God's people. Indeed, we might ask if any Israelite who sang this psalm en route to Jerusalem had a misstep along the way (121:3).

But we must recall the royal orientation of the Psalter, and Eaton points us to such a focus here:

> Surely the person in question is most likely to be the king, to whom such elaborate pledges are given elsewhere. Yahweh is at his right hand (v. 5). Corresponding to the style of royal avowals of trust ('Yahweh is my —,'), the minister assures him 'Yahweh is thy keeper, Yahweh is thy shade.' The expression 'go out and come in' is often (though not exclusively) used of kings, especially of warfare. The help will be 'from now and until eternity.'[16]

Bullock notes a striking resemblance of Psalm 121 to Psalm 91, which we will argue is messianic in outlook.[17] If the "I" and "my" of 121:1–2 are the king, then it is his certain success that is assured. We therefore

15 John Calvin, *Commentary on the Book of Psalms*, trans James Anderson, vol. 4 (1847; repr., Grand Rapids, MI: Baker, 2003), 68.

16 John H. Eaton, *Kingship and the Psalms*, Studies in Biblical Theology, 2nd ser., 32 (Naperville, IL: Alec R. Allenson, n.d.), 83.

17 C. Hassell Bullock, *Psalms*, vol. 2, *Psalms 73–150* (Grand Rapids, MI: Baker, 2017), 382.

have ground to read the psalm with messianic overtones also and with assurances of his kingdom advance.

And yet by extension we who follow the king and trust in God's all-encompassing and infallible providence may sing the psalm with him who is the pioneer of our faith (Heb. 12:1). The ancient pilgrim sang this psalm "as he [left] his home to meet the Lord in the Great Congregation at Jerusalem; and the believer (like the Master) sings it as he journeys through earth to the New Jerusalem."[18] The psalm's promise for us "does not imply a cushioned life, but a well-armed one"[19] in the knowledge of God's safe keeping. Its assurance that "no evil" will befall the pilgrim on his journey echoes in our Lord's affirmation of his protective presence with us always through this life (Matt. 28:20; cf. 6:25–34; Phil. 4:19) and forever (John 10:27–30; 17:10–15). God will keep us from falling and infallibly bring us to our appointed goal (Jude 24–25). In the hands of our Redeemer we are assured that we are safe forever (Rom. 8:28–39).

## PSALM 23

A Psalm of David.

1 The LORD is my shepherd;
  I shall not want.
2 He makes me lie down in green pastures.
  He leads me beside still waters.
3 He restores my soul.
  He leads me in paths of righteousness for his name's sake.
4 Even though I walk through the valley of the shadow of death,
  I will fear no evil,
for you are with me;
  your rod and your staff, they comfort me.
5 You prepare a table before me in the presence of my enemies;

18 Andrew Bonar, *Christ and His Church in the Book of Psalms* (London: James Nisbet, 1859), 382.

19 Kidner, *Psalms 73–150*, 468.

you anoint my head with oil; my cup overflows.
6 Surely goodness and mercy shall follow me all the days of my life,
and I shall dwell in the house of the LORD forever.

Psalm 23 is probably the best known piece of literature in the world. It is properly a psalm of trust, a genre we will discuss in a later chapter. Its highly figurative language makes it a fitting sample for us at this point.

**Survey Exposition**[20]

This psalm presents two allegories (a figure of speech in which abstract ideas and principles are described in terms of characters, figures, and events). There are three scenes. The first scene is that of a shepherd with his sheep in the pasture (23:1–4). Here the psalmist images himself as a sheep to illustrate what it means to be under the care of Israel's covenant God (the shepherd). The second scene is that of a sheik at the table in his tent hosting the psalmist as his guest (23:5). And the third scene is that of a temple (23:6), and here we leave imagery behind. The pastureland and the tent are illustrative of the temple. All this suggestive imagery of God as watchful shepherd and generous host points to the reality of God's presence—his goodness and his kindness (חֶסֶד).

Psalm 23:1 is a summary, stating the theme of the Psalm in terms of shepherd-sheep imagery. The imagery will change in 23:5 and 23:6, but this metaphor of God's shepherdlike care sets the theme that carries the entire psalm. In this first scene the metaphor becomes an extended allegory that coheres by following the typical day in the life of a shepherd. In the morning he leads his sheep to green pastures; these "pastures" (דֶּשֶׁא) are not rough Saint Augustine grass but golf-course grass, very tender. Then at noon the shepherd allows the sheep to rest in the grassy pastures by cool and quiet waters where their "vitality" is "restored." The Hebrew word here is usually (and rightly)

20 See also Bruce K. Waltke and James M. Houston, *The Psalms as Christian Worship: A Historical Commentary* (Grand Rapids, MI: Eerdmans, 2010), chap. 13.

translated "soul," but "soul" in the Old Testament does not mean what it means in English or in the New Testament. In the New Testament, you have a body and a soul (or spirit). In the Old Testament, you *are* a soul. The word refers to our desires and appetites. Usually the connotation is that of yearning—"my soul yearns for you" (Isa. 26:9). "My soul makes its boast in the Lord" (Ps. 34:2). The soul hungers and thirsts (42:2) and rejoices (35:9). "Soul" pertains to our vitality, our drives and appetites.

Renewed and refreshed, then, the sheep resume their trek back to their sheepfold for the night. The shepherd leads his sheep out from the sheepfold in the morning along safe paths to the green pastures and refreshing water, and then back to the sheepfold in the evening. Should the shepherd and his sheep confront enemies in the dark ravine, the shepherd is fully armed with club and crook to beat them off, a "comfort" to the sheep (23:4). Not one of his sheep will be lost. Upon return to the sheepfold the shepherd attends to his fevered and/or scratched sheep. "I shall not want" (23:1), or "I lack nothing," does not reflect a theology of material prosperity but "the psalmist's recognition that God's presence is the most valuable blessing any person can have" (cf. Deut. 2:7; 28:48).[21]

So the shepherd provides his sheep with food, water, rest (Ps. 23:2), guidance (23:3), and protection (23:4). He is highly sensitive to the needs of his sheep, and so he leads them to green pastures. He tends them and cares for them. He allows them to lie down and rest, and he gives them an abundant supply of water, having led them "by choice resting places" (authors' paraphrase). And then he brings them home. It is the shepherd's responsibility to "lead" his sheep through safe paths both to and from the sheepfold, even though the way home may be a dark and dangerous ravine. The sheep are well cared for. He restores them and protects them. They walk about securely. Under this shepherd's care the sheep are fully satisfied, content, and refreshed.

21 Jerome Creach, *Psalms: Six Themes Everyone Should Know* (Louisville: Geneva Press, 2019), 12.

In the ancient Near East sheep were utterly dependent on their shepherd for everything. For the ancient peoples themselves, the king was the shepherd of his people. He made decisions for them, (ideally) cared for them, provided for them, represented them, and protected them. Shepherd imagery is common in Israel's prophets also (e.g., Jer. 3:15; 12:10). Above all else, God was Israel's shepherd-king (Ps. 80:1), as we will see later especially in connection with the enthronement psalms. Above King David is God, Israel's ultimate king, who also is commonly portrayed as a shepherd (e.g., Gen. 48:15; Ps. 78:71–72; Isa. 40:11; Mic. 7:14). The Lord is Israel's shepherd-king. Weiser notes that what is unusual here is that this notion of God as king normally has reference to the nation; here David individualizes the concept[22] and by means of this vivid imagery expresses the joy and confidence of living under God's faithful care. It is a psalm of trust. "Under his good care, I walk securely through this life" is his theme. The Lord himself provides for me (John 10:9; Eph. 1:3; Phil. 4:19; 2 Pet. 2:3), he will care for me (1 Pet. 5:7), he will protect me, and I will never be lost (John 10:27–30; 17:11–12, 15; Rom. 8:28–39).

Sinclair Ferguson observes helpfully that the depiction of Psalm 23 commonly in children's books may be entirely misleading.[23] Scenes of a carefree shepherd boy in an idyllic world fail to reflect the "valley of the shadow of death" (Ps. 23:4a) as well as the constant threat of wild animals (Ps. 23:4b; cf. 1 Sam. 17:34–35). It is in this context that David sees himself—safe, satisfied, and comforted, to be sure, but this in the presence of real danger. Augustine therefore designated Psalm 23 as "the hymn of martyrs."[24] Comfort and safety are found in the shepherd's presence—"you are with me." The expression, that God is "with you," appears frequently in one form or another in Scripture and generally connotes the presence of danger (Gen. 26:3;

22 Artur Weiser, *The Psalms: A Commentary*, The Old Testament Library (Philadelphia: Westminster, 1962), 228.

23 Sinclair Ferguson, *Deserted by God?* (Grand Rapids, MI: Baker, 1993), 37.

24 Rowland E. Prothero, *The Psalms in Human Life* (1903; repr., Vestavia Hills, AL: Solid Ground Christian Books, n.d.), 10.

31:3; Ex. 3:12; Deut. 31:23; Josh. 1:5; etc.). It is in the context of danger that David says, "I will fear no evil, / for you are with me." God, his shepherd, is his protector.

The likening of God to a shepherd fits the early years of David who was called from following a literal flock of sheep to leading the flock of Israel (cf. Ps. 78:70–72), and his psalm shapes the paradigm for all of Israel to view life. The outstanding theme is that of divine providence, specifically God's wise and concerned guidance, care, provision, and protection for his people. He "leads" his people through safe paths, and he does so "for his [own] name's sake" (23:3). Not because it is deserved or demanded but for his own glory he cares for his favored people and ensures their safety. One lost sheep would tarnish his reputation as a faithful shepherd, and for the sake of his own honor he tends and keeps his sheep. Moreover, the "paths" through which he leads his sheep are those that are right. Here the imagery gives way more explicitly to the spiritual reality it intends to convey—the Lord always does right for his people.

So in this first scene (23:1–4) David celebrates God's provision (23:1), his renewal (23:2), and his protection (23:3–4).

Then in 23:5 the scene and imagery change. Rather than returning to a rough and ready sheepfold, the psalmist returns to a festive banquet in a sheik's tent. The point is the same—God's rich provision, refreshing renewal, satisfaction, excessive abundance, and protection. But the imagery is heightened. Green grass is good, but this banquet is better. This wealthy host prepares a table rich with provision, a table so abundantly laden with food and drink that the cup brims over (this corresponding to the lush, green pastures for the sheep). So mighty is his host that the psalmist peacefully enjoys all this in the very presence of his enemies (corresponding to the shepherd's protection of the sheep through the dark ravine, 23:4). With enemies looking in, helpless against him, the psalmist enjoys a veritable banquet under the Lord's protection. And just as the shepherd provides his sheep with refreshing waters (23:2), the Lord (the sheik) now anoints the psalmist's head with oil. The pouring of olive oil on the guest's head connotes the wealth, generosity, and care of the host to promote the refreshment, joy, and healing of his weary and wounded guest.

It is good to be a sheep in lush pasture. It is better to be a guest in a wealthy sheik's tent. But "guest" connotes something temporary. So the scene is heightened further. Better than a sheep in the pasture or a guest in the wealthy sheik's tent is to be present with the Lord in the temple. So "I will return to dwell in the house of the LORD for endless days" (authors' translation). The psalmist is convinced that this care will be his forever (23:6). Here the metaphors are dropped to give way to the reality. "Dwelling in the house of Jehovah does not mean frequenting his sanctuary, but being a member of his household . . . enjoying his protection, holding communion with him, and subsisting on his bounty."[25] God himself is David's satisfaction, joy, and protection. Here in the Lord's presence David finds himself as the object of pursuit—chased, hunted by divine "goodness and unfailing love" (NLT). God's "goodness" is the sum of all his benevolences. When Moses requests to see the glory of God, the Lord replies, "I will make all my goodness pass before you" (Ex. 33:19–20) and proclaims that he is "merciful and gracious, slow to anger, and abounding in steadfast love and faithfulness (Ex. 34:5–6). This is the reality to which David's imagery points us.

The changing imagery is not the only shift David makes in this psalm. There is a shift in audience also. In 23:1–3 the psalmist is addressing the congregation about the shepherd, and he affirms that under this shepherd's care, he lacks nothing. Then in 23:5, in the tent, he is talking directly to God: "You prepare a table before me." He is not talking to others about God but to God himself. The shift is so smooth we scarcely notice it. This is so because, as we shall see, the shift of addressee is a janus, a transition, for the shift was already made in the first scene: "I will fear no evil, / for you are with me; / Your rod and your staff, they comfort me" (23:4). But then in 23:6 David shifts again and addresses the congregation, and here he interprets the imagery of the preceding

25 Joseph Addison Alexander, *The Psalms Translated and Explained* (Edinburgh: John Greig and Son, 1864), 109.

verses. This poetry is brilliantly conceived. The shifts are subtle yet wonderfully effective.

### Reflections

Our purpose in examining Psalm 23 at this point in the book was to highlight its poetic imagery. Here the metaphor of the Lord as shepherd expands throughout the psalm. And the escalating parallelism of shepherd to sheik is vivid also, as well as the corresponding scenes of pasture to tent and finally to temple. This is a psalm of trust. Psalms of lament characteristically include a section in which the psalmist expresses confidence in God despite the danger. This psalm is given simply to express that trust in rich pastoral imagery.

Beyond the poetic imagery we should also keep in mind what we have learned regarding the royal orientation of the Psalter. Psalm 23 is a Davidic psalm, the testimony of the anointed king to God's faithful care. As such it points us to Christ. He also learned to live under his Father's shepherding care. He knows the path in which to lead us, his flock, because once he walked that path himself ahead of us.[26] He thus became "the great shepherd of the sheep" (Heb. 13:20), the "good shepherd" who protects his sheep at all costs, laying down his life for them (John 10:11). "To enter fully into the peace of [Psalm] 23, the pilgrim must first make the daunting journey through 22, through the place where the lonely representative suffers to the uttermost" for the benefit of all.[27] It is by his sufferings and death that our shepherd provides us the rich pasture of eternal life (John 10:1–31) such that not even death can bring us ultimate harm (Rom. 8:28–39). In him "we lack nothing" (Ps. 23:1; cf. Eph. 1:3).

26 W. Graham Scroggie, *The Psalms* (1948; repr., Revell, 1978), 147.

27 John Eaton, *The Psalms: A Historical and Spiritual Commentary with an Introduction and New Translation* (New York: Continuum, 2005), 124.

7

# Form Criticism and Psalm Forms

*"To invoke, to give grateful praise, and to praise"*

THROUGHOUT HISTORY students of Scripture have recognized that there are different types of psalms—penitential psalms, royal psalms, lament psalms, praise psalms, and so on. But it was Hermann Gunkel (1862–1932) who first provided a careful analysis of these different psalms and categorized their types. He dated many of them to the first temple, but not to David. Although there is much to criticize in Gunkel's dated work, his study still proves fruitful in identifying specific forms of psalms and in their interpretation. Recall that our goal in this book is to "get behind" the psalms and, as far as we are able, to enter the mind of the psalmist himself to uncover his preunderstandings for composing a psalm. Here we learn that among his methods were various standard "forms" in the biblical world for religious poetry. These forms were not slavishly followed, but it is abundantly evident that the psalmists recognized and regularly put them to use.

Gunkel's famous work is best understood against the larger background of Old Testament studies at the time, so we will sketch out this academic backdrop first.

## The Literary Analytical Approach: Julius Wellhausen

You may wonder why so much of contemporary academic scholarship denies the Davidic authorship of the Psalms. The answer is found in the critical approach advanced most influentially by the German scholar Julius Wellhausen (1844–1918), whose work left the traditional authorship of virtually the entire Old Testament in doubt, including the superscripts of the Psalms.

The mark of modernist thought is a trust of human reason, and along with that is a distrust of any claim of revelation or divine authority. Human reason stands above any presumed divinely revealed text. Skepticism with regard to the Bible is the starting point for academic elites. Also they presume what is known as the principle of analogy—that nothing happened in the past that does not happen in the present.[1] This rules out, for example, a virgin birth and the resurrection of the dead. Another principle in their system is coherence—everything has a natural, scientific explanation. These presuppositions—skepticism, analogy, and coherence—form a systematic practical atheism that rules out divine revelation and miraculous divine interventions from the outset; such notions are regarded as mythic and folkloristic. This is a simplified, but not at all an overly simplistic, summary characterization of contemporary, mainstream academia.

Wellhausen's skepticism and denial of Mosaic authorship of the Pentateuch has strongly influenced biblical academia. His magnum opus, *Prolegomena zur Geschichte Israels* (*Prolegomena to the History of Israel*) toppled confidence in the Bible's own claims to its authorship. Wellhausen focused on dating the sources of the Pentateuch, which earlier students of the Bible had discerned. They noted that in some cases God is referred to as Yahweh—that he dubbed a J document (German doesn't have a "Y" but a "J"). Then there are cases where Elohim is used—this they identified with the "E" document, which is much like

1 Bruce K. Waltke, *An Old Testament Theology: An Exegetical, Canonical, and Thematic Approach* (Grand Rapids, MI: Zondervan, 2007), 54, 74.

"J," and "P" (priestly) documents. These documents have other criteria. The P document includes priestly material such as Leviticus. And they determined that Deuteronomy differs sufficiently to distinguish it as a separate source—the "D" document. Thus, Wellhausen postulated the J, E, D, and P documents.

Wellhausen's unique work was his dating of these documents. The pivot was "D," which had been dated to Josiah's repair of the temple (ca. 622 BC). The Bible recounts that workers found the Book of the Law, "D," in the temple (see 2 Kings 22). It seemed incredible that this important document could have been lost in the temple under the control of the priest, so Wellhausen assumed that it must have been a forgery written to justify Josiah's reformation. Having this pivot in place and tracing themes common to the four documents, such as the central sanctuary, Wellhausen dated "J" as the earliest, "E" next, and "P" to postexilic times.

Wellhausen's theory achieved an academic consensus that turned the Bible on its head. Anyone who rejected the theory was barred by many publishers and from academic posts. What the church had thought was early, from the time of Moses (traditionally ca. 1400 BC), was now dated centuries later. All the "priestly" material in Exodus and Leviticus that was thought to be Mosaic law was now dated to about the time of Ezra, a millennium after Moses. The net effect of all this is that the Bible's own claims to its authorship were no longer regarded trustworthy.

Building on all this, academics similarly concluded that the superscripts of the psalms could not be trusted and were in fact historically wrong. Many critics assume the Psalms reflect a date much later than David in the history of religion. For them, the spirituality of the psalms rendered them very late. The Davidic dominance of the Psalms, according to the academic consensus at the turn of the twentieth century, was mistaken. In fact, some critics allege that all the Bible's claims of authorship should be assumed wrong until its claims are verified by archaeology. These "minimalists," as they are called, even deny David ever existed.

## Evaluation

Historical criticism, including its skepticism, pervades academia and has had a predictably destructive effect on biblical studies and on the church itself. But one factor that has shattered this "scientific" consensus about the date of the psalms was the 1928 discovery of a corpus of texts at Ugarit (Ras Shamra), an ancient site in Syria opposite the northern tip of Cyprus. Written in the thirteenth and twelfth centuries BC, these texts were published in 1940 and reveal much about the Canaanite religion of Baal at the time, with its temples and worship of Baal, and about its literature. What is significant for the dating of the Psalms is that these texts from centuries before David show a striking resemblance to the Davidic psalms. The Ugaritic texts have similar poetry and vocabulary to the Davidic and other psalms. Indeed, these ancient texts show that the psalmists were familiar with the myths of the surrounding religions and even allude to them (e.g., Ps. 29), just as Milton alluded to the myths of the Greco-Roman world to enrich his poetry and to polemicize against the pagan religions.[2] Hence, the basic foundations of the critical approach were discredited. The Psalms could no longer be assumed to be late; there is solid scientific evidence that the Psalms could be by David. Some psalms, of course, such as 137, must be dated to the Babylonian exile, and others, such as 107, may be late also. And we must distinguish between the dating of individual psalms and of the collection as a whole. The book of Psalms consists mostly of psalms composed by David; the book of Psalms in its final form was compiled in the postexilic period.

## Form Criticism and Psalm Types

The dismissal of the Bible's claims to its authorship presents a challenge to the biblical student. An accredited method of interpretation determines the meaning of words within a given psalm according to its historical context. So

2 See the excellent excursus on mythopoeic imagery in Mark D. Futato, *Interpreting the Psalms: An Exegetical Handbook*, Handbooks for Old Testament Exegesis (Grand Rapids, MI: Kregel, 2007), 53–55. See also the excellent article by Robert B. Chisholm Jr., "Suppressing Myth: Yahweh and the Sea in the Praise Psalms," in *The Psalms: Language for All Seasons of the Soul*, ed. Andrew J. Schmutzer and David Howard Jr. (Chicago: Moody Publishers, 2013), 75–84.

if we do away with David, just what is the historical context of the Psalms? Who are the "enemies" that play a prominent role in many psalms?

Academia seeks to reconstruct a psalm's historical background by "form criticism." This approach entails first identifying the psalm's "form" (*Gattung*) and then deciding its "setting in life" (*Sitz im Leben*), the setting in which that form originated, was used, and circulated. Hymns, for example, would have been used at the temple, and proverbs in the marketplace. Establishing a precise setting in life is highly subjective and has proven of little value for the dating of the Psalms. Nevertheless, a broad consensus has been reached about their forms, and this is due to the work of Gunkel. Gunkel significantly advanced the understanding of the forms of psalms in his *An Introduction to the Book of Psalms: The Genres of the Religious Lyric of Israel*, edited by his student Joachim Begrich and published posthumously in 1933. It is a massive work, typically German in extensive detail, very precise and scientific, and was finally translated into English in 1998.

Gunkel dismissed the superscripts of the Psalms as unhistorical, but he thought many of the Psalms were composed during the first temple, albeit not by David. More importantly, by his exhaustive and rigorous study he classified the psalms into basic types by their common mood (e.g., joyful praise or sorrowful complaint), vocabulary, motifs (i.e., their patterns or structure, "forms"), and subject matter. He also documented from earlier research of others that these forms also existed in psalmody from Mesopotamia and Egypt (the Ugaritic texts had not yet been published in 1933). Archaeologists had helpfully uncovered these texts in the eighteenth and nineteenth centuries. There has long been a recognition that various psalms were given to meet God's people in every situation of their walk with God—there are psalms reflecting anguish, protest, praise, repentance, and so on. The strength of Gunkel's work is that he established this analysis on an objective level, identifying recognizable psalm forms.

Having the lens to recognize these psalm forms significantly helps the Bible student understand the various structures of a given psalm and, thus, the psalm itself. Commentators before Gunkel were often perplexed by the organization of some psalms, often by their seeming lack of structure. Today the formerly perplexing organization of these psalms often can be understood by their form. Form criticism is an extremely valuable tool in interpreting the psalms, not for dating them.

Gunkel identified several dominant types:[3]

- *Psalms of praise, or hymns* (8; 19; 29; 33; 65; 67; 68; 96; 98; 100; 103; 104; 105; 111; 113; 114; 117; 135; 136; 145–150); In addition to these are the related "Zion songs" (46; 48; 76; 84; 87; 121; 122; cf. 137:3), the comparable "enthronement songs" (47; 93; 97; 99), and the "thanksgiving songs of Israel" (124; 129).
- *Royal psalms* (2; 18; 20; 21; 45; 72; 101; 110; 132; 144:1–11; cf. 89:47–52)
- *Communal complaint songs* (e.g., 44)
- *Individual complaint songs* (e.g., 3)[4]
- *Thanksgiving songs* (both individual (e.g., 116) or community (e.g., 75)

He wrongly identified some psalms as "enthronement psalms." We will discuss these in chapter 12. They are better classified as hymns. Gunkel also classified minor types, such as "the pilgrimage songs."

Gunkel identified ten psalms as royal because these psalms mention the king. There is the famous Psalm 2, "I have set my king on Zion, / my holy hill." Psalm 18 celebrates the king's victories. Psalm 20 is a prayer for the king as he goes out to battle. In Psalm 21 the king returns vic-

3 Hermann Gunkel, *Introduction to the Psalms: The Genres of the Religious Lyric of Israel*, completed by Joachim Begrich, trans. James D. Nogalski, (Macon, GA: Mercer University Press, 1998).

4 The individual and/or complaint psalms are 3; 4; 5; 6; 7; 9; 10; 12; 13; 16; 17; 20; 22; 25; 26; 28; 31; 35; 38; 39; 40:13–17; 41; 42–43; 44; 51; 54; 55; 56; 57; 58; 59; 60; 61; 64; 68; 69; 70; 71; 74; 79; 80; 83; 85; 86; 88; 90; 94; 102; 108; 109; 119; 120; 130; 137; 139:19–24; 140; 141; 142; 143; 144.

torious from battle. Psalm 45 is the marriage of the king and his bride. Psalm 72 is by or for Solomon and about the king. Psalm 101 is more difficult from this viewpoint but is thought to be a mirror for princes, expressing what the leadership should be like. Psalm 110 is a coronation liturgy, the most famous and often echoed in the New Testament. Psalm 132 mentions David bringing up the ark of the covenant. And Psalm 144 again mentions the king. As we have indicated in chapter 4, this classification can be confusing because many complaint psalms and grateful praise ("thanksgiving") psalms pertain to the king also. Gunkel's list of royal psalms must be expanded. But Gunkel's identification of royal psalms was an important first step.

Claus Westermann helpfully defined "thanksgiving songs" not as psalms saying "thank you" to God but as giving grateful praise (תּוֹדָה, *todah*) to God in the congregation for answering prayer.[5] Thus, "songs of grateful praise" are to be distinguished from hymns. Hymns celebrate God generally. They talk about God as Creator and as the champion in Israel's history. Psalms of grateful praise are the opposite of lament or complaint: whereas lament or complaint psalms mourn, say, persecution, psalms of grateful praise celebrate God's deliverance in answer to prayer and offer thanks to him for it.

## Evaluation

What conclusion should we draw regarding Gunkel's work? On the one hand, his dismissal of the superscripts is unfortunate. On the other hand, his rigorous identification of forms of psalms interprets the inspired Chronicler's account that David appointed the Levites to sing three kinds of psalms: "Then he appointed some of the Levites as ministers before the ark of the Lord, to invoke, to thank [better, "give grateful praise"], and to praise the Lord, the God of Israel" (1 Chron 16:4). These are the three of several dominant types identified by Gunkel:

5 Claus Westermann, *Praise and Lament in the Book of Psalms* (Atlanta: John Knox, 1981), 27–28.

- to invoke (petition), an almost universal motif of the lament/complaint psalms
- to give grateful praise
- to praise (i.e., "the hymn")

We must take note here, however, of a difference in translation of 1 Chronicles 16:4 between the ESV and the NIV. Instead of "to invoke" (ESV), the NIV has "to extol." According to the NIV, there are three kinds of praise psalms rather than psalms of petition, grateful praise, and hymns. The Hebrew word here (הַזְכִּיר) in the hiphil connotes "cause to remember," reminding God, as it were, of need, and hence, petition. This word appears in the superscripts of Psalms 38 and 70, and in both instances the NIV translates it as "petition." This confirms the ESV translation of 1 Chronicles 16:4. The three types of psalms identified by the Chronicler are petition, grateful praise (praise to God for what he has done), and praise (praise to God as Creator and Lord of salvation history). Moreover, four of Gunkel's types of psalms should be reduced to three because his distinction between the lament of the individual and of the community disappears when one understands that both are mostly about the king. The individual king cannot be sharply separated from community laments/petitions. Gunkel's failure to understand the extensive royal interpretation of the Psalter led him to a needless division of these.

We should also reckon with other minor types of psalms besides these royal psalms, such as the "songs of Zion" (e.g., Ps. 48 and "Songs of Ascents"; see p. 103), songs of trust (e.g., 23), didactic psalms (e.g., 49), and prophetic (i.e., "preaching") psalms (e.g., 50).

Furthermore, it is important to note that these categories are not always distinct but are sometimes mixed. Psalm 89, for example, is both hymn and complaint. Psalm 95 is both hymn and prophecy. Psalm 139 appears at first to be a hymn of praise celebrating God's attributes, but it fits the motifs of a petition psalm. The motif of confidence is so dominant in some complaint psalms, including Psalm 139, that they seem to function as a song of trust. Not all the psalms fit neatly into these types, and the interpreter must resist the temptation to squeeze them into preconceived categories. One cannot compile a conclusive list of the one hundred and fifty psalms in discrete categories.[6] We are left to content ourselves with a broad understanding of psalm types.

In the following chapters, we will take up the study of these various types of psalms and identify their forms and characteristics.

6 Although, see Bernhard W. Anderson, *Out of the Depths: The Psalms Speak for Us Today*, 3rd ed. (Louisville: Westminster John Knox, 2000), 219–24, and our above listing of the psalms with Gunkel's dominant types.

# 8

# Praise Psalms

*"Oh come, let us sing to the LORD."*

GOD IS "ENTHRONED on the praises of Israel" (Ps. 22:3). This admittedly ambiguous declaration captures the spirit of our next category of psalms: the praise psalm. These psalms are referred to variously as "psalms of descriptive praise," "psalms of general praise," or "hymns." These are often favorites of God's people because they express praise for God's greatness, his great works in creation and redemptive history, and especially his "steadfast love." In these psalms God ignites the psalmist's heart to rejoice in him as Creator and Redeemer. As such, these psalms offer both theology and reasons for praise; in so doing, their words of praise become God's word to us and, in turn, our songs of praise to him as well.

Hymns of praise are often marked by their opening words, such as "praise," "play [a musical instrument]," "sing," and so on. More helpfully, they are marked by their motifs and structure.

## Motifs and Structure

Gunkel observed certain components and a standard structure that identify these psalms as a distinct category.[1] Hymns have these observable elements:

1 Hermann Gunkel, *Introduction to the Psalms: The Genres of the Religious Lyric of Israel*, completed by Joachim Begrich; trans. James Nogalski (Macon, GA: Mercer University Press, 1998), chap 2.

- introduction: call to praise
- main body: cause or reason for praise
- conclusion: (often) renewed call to praise

These standard elements are referred to as "motifs," standard and repeated patterns. For example, a cross on the top of a building traditionally identifies that building as a Roman Catholic church, whereas a steeple identifies the building as a Protestant church. So also a Torah marks the Jewish synagogue. These are motifs. So also the motifs of a praise psalm are the call to praise, the cause or reason for praise, and (often) the renewed call to praise. Admittedly, to analyze a psalm like this can seem tedious, like a botanist analyzing the makeup of a flower rather than just enjoying its beauty. But in the end the work of a botanist enhances our appreciation of the flower. So also an understanding of the makeup of the psalm enables us not only to identify its classification but to appreciate it more fully. Not all praise psalms are structured in just this way; as we will see, many praise psalms are recognizable as such only by theme. But this form is common to many.

In the "call to praise" the psalmist summons the people of God to "praise the LORD" (e.g., 113:1). This call to praise serves as a match to ignite the flame of worship. The cause for praise is often introduced with the word "for" or "who." This provides the fuel for praise. What follows specifies and itemizes aspects of God's praiseworthiness and offers reasons why he is to be praised. This is in large part where we learn theology from the Psalms, particularly in the themes that we will survey below. Finally, the conclusion often calls the people of God to give praise once again, now for the reasons the psalmist has just highlighted.

**Psalm 117** serves as a crisp example. It has only two verses, but it includes all three elements of the hymn:

Call to praise:

1 Praise the LORD, all nations!
    Extol him, all peoples!

Cause for praise:

2 For great is his steadfast love toward us,
and the faithfulness of the LORD endures forever.

Renewed call to praise:

Praise the LORD!

Notice the psalm begins with a call to praise (117:1) that all nations and peoples are to give to the Lord. Why? For what reason? "For great is his steadfast love toward us, / and the faithfulness of the LORD endures forever." This is the main body and essence of the psalm, the cause or reason for praise. Then in conclusion the psalmist renews his call to praise: "Praise the LORD!" In sum, the Gentile world is called upon to worship Israel's God because he can be counted on to keep his promises.

**Psalm 98** provides another example:

Call to praise:

1 Oh sing to the LORD a new song.

Cause for praise:

for he has done marvelous things!
His right hand and his holy arm
have worked salvation for him.
2 The LORD has made known his salvation;
he has revealed his righteousness in the sight of the nations.
3 He has remembered his steadfast love and faithfulness
to the house of Israel.
All the ends of the earth have seen
the salvation of our God.

Call to praise:

4 Make a joyful noise to the LORD, all the earth;
break forth into joyous song and sing praises!
5 Sing praises to the Lord with the lyre,
with the lyre and the sound of melody!
6 With trumpets and the sound of the horn
make a joyful noise before the King, the LORD!
7 Let the sea roar, and all that fills it;
the world and those who dwell in it!
8 Let the rivers clap their hands;
let the hills sing for joy together
9 before the LORD,

Cause for praise:

for he comes
to judge the earth.
He will judge the world with righteousness,
and the peoples with equity.

Here the call and cause for praise are repeated. Psalm 98:1a calls Israel to praise, and 98:1b–3 gives the reason. Then 98:4–6 calls the nations to praise with all instruments. Next, 98:7–8 calls all creation to praise. And finally, 98:9 again gives reason.

**Psalm 96** provides another example, and again the elements of a praise psalm are repeated:

Call to praise:

1 Oh sing to the LORD a new song;
sing to the LORD, all the earth!
2 Sing to the LORD, bless his name;
tell of his salvation from day to day.

3 Declare his glory among the nations,
his marvelous works among all the peoples!

Cause for praise:

4 For great is the LORD, and greatly to be praised;
he is to be feared above all gods.
5 For all the gods of the peoples are worthless idols,
but the LORD made the heavens.
6 Splendor and majesty are before him;
strength and beauty are in his sanctuary.

Second call to praise:

7 Ascribe to the LORD, O families of the peoples,
ascribe to the LORD glory and strength!
8 Ascribe to the LORD the glory due his name;
bring an offering, and come into his courts!
9 Worship the LORD in the splendor of holiness;
tremble before him, all the earth!

Second cause for praise:

10 Say among the nations, "The LORD reigns!
Yes, the world is established; it shall never be moved;
he will judge the peoples with equity."

Third call to praise

11 Let the heavens be glad, and let the earth rejoice;
let the sea roar, and all that fills it;
12 let the field exult, and everything in it!
Then shall all the trees of the forest sing for joy

Third cause for praise

13 before the LORD, for he comes,
for he comes to judge the earth.
He will judge the world in righteousness,
and the peoples in his faithfulness.

The repetition of the two motifs divides the psalm into three stanzas.

**Psalm 103** follows this form also, although here the cause for praise is lengthier:

Call to praise (here the psalmist addresses himself!):

1 Bless the LORD, O my soul,
and all that is within me,
bless his holy name!
2 Bless the LORD, O my soul,
and forget not all his benefits,

Cause for praise (here the cause for praise is introduced by "who"):

3 who forgives all your iniquity,
who heals all your diseases,
4 who redeems your life from the pit,
who crowns you with steadfast love and mercy,
5 who satisfies you with good
so that your youth is renewed like the eagle's.
6 The LORD works righteousness
and justice for all who are oppressed.

Renewed call to praise:

20 Bless the LORD, O you his angels,
you mighty ones who do his word,

obeying the voice of his word!
21 Bless the LORD, all his hosts,
his ministers, who do his will!
22 Bless the LORD, all his works,
in all places of his dominion.
Bless the LORD, O my soul!

**Psalm 150** alters the form slightly:

Call to praise:

1 Praise the LORD!
Praise God in his sanctuary;
praise him in his mighty heavens!

Cause for praise:

2 Praise him for his mighty deeds;
praise him according to his excellent greatness!

Call to praise (specifying the means of praise):

3 Praise him with trumpet sound;
praise him with lute and harp!
4 Praise him with tambourine and dance;
praise him with strings and pipe!
5 Praise him with sounding cymbals;
praise him with loud clashing cymbals!
6 Let everything that has breath praise the LORD!

Renewed call to praise:

Praise the Lord!

Let us now consider these components individually.

### The Introduction: Call to Praise

Here are more examples of the call to praise found in these psalms:

1 Oh come, let us sing to the LORD;
let us make a joyful noise to the rock of our salvation!
2 Let us come into his presence with thanksgiving;
Let us make a joyful noise to him with songs of praise! . . .
6 Oh come, let us worship and bow down;
let us kneel before the LORD, our Maker! (95:1–2, 6)

1 Oh sing to the LORD a new song! (98:1)

1 Make a joyful noise to the LORD, all the earth!
2 Serve the LORD with gladness!
Come into his presence with singing! (100:1–2)

1 Bless the Lord, O my soul, and all that is within me,
bless his holy name! (103:1)

1 Praise the Lord!
Praise, O servants of the LORD,
praise the name of the LORD! (113:1)

Note that the call to praise is a *command*. Praise is obligatory. In Psalm 95 (see below), the Lord barred Israel from the promised land because they refused to praise him in adversity. Even in lament psalms the poet offers praise, except in Psalm 88.

Nevertheless, as we have seen, Psalm 1 is a gatekeeper to the Psalter. God wants praise from the those who delight in his word, not from the disobedient.

Psalm 50, a prophetic and not a praise psalm, makes this point emphatically. It is a Psalm of Asaph, who though a priest is also a prophet

(2 Chron. 29:30). Using Asaph's voice God (see Ps. 50:1) calls the people of Israel to genuine, not merely ritualistic, worship—sacrifices offered by people whose heart and life are offered to God:

14 Offer to God a sacrifice of thanksgiving,
and perform your vows to the Most High,
15 and call upon me in the day of trouble;
I will deliver you, and you shall glorify me. (50:14–15)

But he will not accept the sacrifices of the wicked (50:9). Instead he accuses them:

16 But to the wicked God says:
"What right have you to recite my statutes
or take my covenant on your lips?
17 For you hate discipline,
and you cast my words behind you.
18 If you see a thief, you are pleased with him,
and you keep company with adulterers.
19 You give your mouth free rein for evil,
and your tongue frames deceit.
20 You sit and speak against your brother;
you slander your own mother's son.
21 These things you have done, and I have been silent;
you thought that I was one like yourself.
But now I rebuke you and lay the charge before you."

He draws the psalm to conclusion with a warning and a promise:

22 "Mark this, then, you who forget God,
lest I tear you apart, and there be none to deliver!
23 The one who offers thanksgiving as his sacrifice glorifies me;
to one who orders his way rightly I will show the salvation
of God!" (50:16–23)

The point is that God wants worship, but not apart from godliness (cf. Ex. 24–25). To sing his praise while rebelling against him with a life given to sin is a stench to him. It is an offense. The role of the didactic psalms is to direct God's people to the faithful living he requires.

Moreover, praise is to be offered with enthusiasm. This is a frequent emphasis in the praise psalms. Lukewarmness would be entirely inappropriate in the praise of this God. Leupold remarks that tepid or half-hearted praise "defeats its own purpose."[2] God deserves our fervency in praise, wholeheartedness and enthusiasm, not formality; hence, the terminology of joy, rejoicing, and exultation is characteristic of these calls to praise:

> 1 Sing aloud to God our strength;
> shout for joy to the God of Jacob!
> 2 Raise a song; sound the tambourine,
> the sweet lyre with the harp.
> 3 Blow the trumpet at the new moon,
> at the full moon, on our feast day. (Ps. 81:1–3)

Repeatedly, even characteristically, the psalmists call us to enthusiastic praise like a cheerleader at a football game.

C. S. Lewis was troubled by this. God calls us to praise him with vigor. Is that narcissistic? Is God insecure? Does he need us to tell him how great he is? It's an honest and fair question. But after reflection on the question Lewis determined that it is only right and fitting for us to praise the Lord:

> What do we mean when we say that a picture is admirable? . . . The sense in which the picture "deserves" or "demands" admiration is . . . this; that admiration is the correct, adequate or appropriate, response to it, that, if paid, admiration will not be "thrown away," and if we do not admire we shall be stupid, insensible, and great losers.

2 H. C. Leupold, *Exposition of the Psalms* (Grand Rapids, MI: Baker, 1969), 676.

His point is obvious. If you don't admire something that is truly admirable, you are the loser, and you are not really participating fully in all the beauty. And so next Lewis moves from the demand to admire objects in art and nature to the demand to praise God:

> He is the Object to admire which (or, if you like, to appreciate which) is simply to be awake, to have entered the real world; not to appreciate which is to have lost the greatest experience, and in the end to have lost all. The incomplete and crippled lives of those who are tone-deaf, have never been in love, never known true friendship, never cared for a good book, never enjoyed the feel of the morning air on their cheeks . . . are faint images of it."[3]

Lewis's point is important, and we will benefit from appreciating his insight. It is right, admirable, and fitting to praise the Lord. He is the one who is truly admirable and worthy of praise, and our expression of praise is necessary to complete our admiration of him.

It is to be expected, then, that the psalmist is not content to give praise to God himself, alone, although he is resolved to do that (e.g., 103:1–2). Nor is it enough for the temple choirs to sing his praise, although they were appointed to do that—Asaph (Pss. 50; 73–83) and the sons of Korah (Pss. 42; 44–49; 84; 85; 87; 88) appear to represent Levitical guilds. Nor was it enough that Israel should sing God's praise, although the congregation was to join the singing also. The Psalms call the entire nation to praise. But even this is not enough. God is over all. The whole world must sing his praise, and the call for universal praise pervades the Psalter as well:[4]

> 1 Make a joyful noise to the Lord, all the earth! (100:1)

> 1 Shout for joy to God, all the earth;
> 2 sing the glory of his name;

3 C. S. Lewis, *Reflections on the Psalms* (1958; repr., Orlando: Harcourt Brace Jovanovich, 1986), 92–93.

4 Gunkel provides extensive data here. Gunkel, *Introduction to the Psalms*, 24–25.

give to him glorious praise!
3 Say to God, "How awesome are your deeds!
So great is your power that your enemies come cringing to you.
4 All the earth worships you
and sings praises to you;
they sing praises to your name." (66:1–4)

All of creation owes him praise; it is the duty of all people everywhere. Isaac Watts captures this in his renderings of the Psalms for singing in English. Frequently, his paraphrases call the nations to "pay" their praise to the Lord God of Israel. Here is his rendering of Psalm 100:

Enter his gates with songs of joy,
With praises to his courts repair.
And make it your divine employ
To *pay* your thanks and honors there.[5]

The language of "pay" is entirely warranted. God is deserving of our praise, and we owe it to him. And yet the thinking goes deeper. Rendering willing praise to Israel's God implies conversion. These calls for universal praise are reflective of God's global saving purpose (Gen. 12:1–3). Gentiles are called to praise the God of Israel also, and it will be their joy through Christ to give it. The Psalter is in this sense a missionary hymnbook, calling the nations to praise the God of heaven, which they will do through the saving mission of Christ.

In connection with enthusiasm, he wants praise to be accompanied by music:

1 Oh come, let us sing to the Lord;
let us make a joyful noise to the rock of our salvation!

5 Robert Goodacre, ed., *The Psalms and Hymns of the Late Isaac Watts* (London: n.p., 1821), 247; emphasis added.

2 Let us come into his presence with thanksgiving;
let us make a joyful noise to him with songs of praise!
(95:1–2)

We will say more about the call to praise and music in our exposition of Psalms 33 and 100.

We note here that these calls to praise imply a leader. In the ancient Near East the king was responsible for the nation's worship, and this was certainly the case with David (1 Chron. 15–16), as it was with Hezekiah also (2 Chron. 29:30). So we might envision David summoning the people to the worship of the Lord together. In some cases this leader may be "the choirmaster" who is mentioned in many psalms.

Many of the psalms seem to imply multiple singers. Asaph and the sons of Korah represent temple choirs. So we might imagine—and this involves only a bit of conjecture on our part—that the leader calls to worship. He may be the lead singer.[6] And then the various voices of the psalms may respond, the Levitical choirs and possibly the larger assembly. Psalms with multiple voices and psalms with recurring refrains may well have been sung antiphonally—voices singing back and forth to each other. Instruments were called into service also: wind instruments, stringed instruments, and percussion. In any case, the call to praise marks the start of this part of the public worship.

## The Main Body: Cause for Praise

In the main body of the praise psalm attention turns from a call to praise to the reason or cause for praise. Here the focus is on God—his attributes, works, gifts, kingdom, power, glory, and so on. But essentially they praise him as Creator and Redeemer. Here our attention is directed to God himself, and, thinking theologically, we are reminded just why he is to be praised.

It is significant that when the Israelites express theology, they do so primarily in praise. Their theology is not merely academic or theoretical.

6 John H. Eaton, *Meditating on the Psalms* (Louisville: Westminster John Knox, 2004), 4.

It is certainly not dry discourse or mere scientific analysis. Theology and all thoughts of God's greatness demand praise, enthusiastic praise. Hence, the hymn or praise psalm. So in the Psalter we very appropriately learn theology as worship. The context is enthusiastic praise.

The main body of the hymns, the cause for praise, is usually introduced by "for" or "who," and what follows highlights various aspects of God's praiseworthiness. They praise him as Creator and Redeemer, reflecting on the innumerable aspects of those themes. The number of specific reasons is nearly endless as the majesty and the particular works and attributes of God are brought into view. His greatness, his kingdom rule, his justice, and especially his faithful covenant love are common. Many hymns offer praise to God for choosing Israel as his people to establish his kingdom on the earth (Pss. 66; 100; 111; 114; 149). We cannot develop an entire theology of the Psalms here, but we can highlight the major themes. As you read the Psalms, you will want to watch for key words that are often repeated:

- words describing God's character:
  - steadfast love
  - truth
  - faithfulness
  - compassion
  - love
  - right / righteousness / justice
  - good / goodness
- words describing God's gifts or works:
  - peace
  - justice
  - salvation / delivers
  - God as Maker, Redeemer, Ruler, Judge

*God as Creator and Sustainer* is a prominent theme in the Psalms. Basic to the Psalter's understanding of who God is, is the recognition that he is Creator and Preserver of all things. He not only created all that is but also sustains everything that is, and all of creation is utterly dependent upon him. If he were to withdraw his hand, all would cease to exist. Alexander von Humboldt, like other scientists, was famous in his day for recognizing the unity of everything, but he praised nature, not the Creator and Unifier of earth's ecology. The psalmists praise the Lord who gives life and sustains life, who causes light and darkness, day and night, the seasons, the weather, the quaking of the earth—it is all his doing.[7] Psalm 104 provides an outstanding example of this. God even designed the food chain:

21 The young lions roar for their prey,
seeking their food from God. (104:21)

24 O Lord, how manifold are your works!
In wisdom have you made them all. (104:24)

27 These all look to you,
to give them their food in due season.
28 When you give it to them, they gather it up;
When you open your hand, they are filled with good things.
29 When you hide your face, they are dismayed;
When you take away their breath, they die
and return to their dust. (104:27–29)

If God is Creator and Sustainer of all, then he is also *Ruler* of all. He rules over all creation and over all humanity. The hymns often describe God as the author of both life and death, of blessing and judgment (cf. 75:8; 107:33–43; 117:1–2; 146:5–9; 147:6). He is Lord over history—the God of the exodus, the God who dwells with his people Israel and rules over all to the establishing of his universal and eternal kingdom (69; 36; 86:9; 102:14–23; 147:2). This notion is unique in ancient literature: the pagan myths know nothing of a God who

7 Gunkel, *Introduction to the Psalms*, 51.

presides over history, leading it to final judgment and eternal peace. But the notion of God as Ruler is but an extension of the theme of God as Creator. It also coincides with the Davidic kingship theme that we will consider in chapter 12.

God is King over all, but not despotic. He rules *sovereignly* with *grace* and *favor*, and with *justice* (11:5–7; 33:5; 66:7; 89:15; 92:10–15; 97:2, 10; 98:9; 99:4; 103:6). God's "steadfast love and faithfulness" (חֶסֶד וֶאֱמֶת)[8] are prominent themes in the Psalms, growing largely from God's self-revelation to Moses in Exodus 34:6: "The LORD passed before him and proclaimed, 'The LORD, the LORD, a God merciful and gracious, slow to anger, and abounding in steadfast love and faithfulness.'" God's "steadfast love" was the theme of the first hymn of the temple (1 Chron. 16; see esp. 16:34, 41), and it is a particularly pronounced theme throughout the Psalter (cf. Pss. 51:1; 106:1; 107:1–2; 136). This familiar word is commonly used of God's covenant love for his people, and we will run into it often. It connotes a "committedness" and loyalty on God's part to his people, as well as his affection for them and his compassion toward them. Hence, "steadfast love" or "unfailing love" are common translations. The word also denotes a relationship in which one partner is in a strong position and the other weak, in need, and helpless. The stronger one steps in and meets that need out of love, not begrudgingly. But whereas human love and kindness may be capricious, God's love can be counted on. So love and faithfulness are often combined. His love and fidelity are so much greater than that of mankind that the psalmist speaks of them often. The great God who rules over all is a God who rules in steadfast love over those whom he chose to establish his kingdom.

*God's attributes* are continuously on display in the Psalter. God is eternal (90:1–4), holy (99:5), awesome (96:4), majestic (96:6), and exalted over all (97:9). He is powerful beyond measure (115:3), infinite in knowledge (147:5), and incomparably wonderful (139:14). In a word, the Lord God is incomparable:

8 These important words are often paired together: 25:10; 26:3; 40:10-11; 57:3, 10; 61:7; 69:13; 85:10; 86:15; 88:11; 89:2, 14, 24, 33; 92:2; 98:3; 100:5; 103:8; 108:4; 115:1; 117:2; 138:2; 145:8; cf. Ex. 34:6; John 1:14.

19 Your righteousness, O God,
reaches the high heavens.
You who have done great things,
O God, who is like you? (71:19)

10 All my bones shall say,
"O LORD, who is like you,
delivering the poor
from him who is too strong for him,
the poor and needy from him who robs him?" (35:10)

4 For great is the LORD, and greatly to be praised;
he is to be feared above all gods. (96:4; cf. 95:3; 97:9; 135:5)

13 Your way, O God, is holy.
What god is great like our God? (77:13)

8 There is none like you among the gods, O Lord,
nor are there any works like yours. (86:8)

6 For who in the skies can be compared to the LORD?
Who among the heavenly beings is like the LORD . . . ? (89:6)

In power, holiness, wisdom, and grace, this God is incomparable.

To accent these truths about Israel's God in contrast to their pagan neighbors, the psalmists at times *make use of ancient Near Eastern myths*. It is widely recognized that the Old Testament writers at times employ a "polemic theology." That is, they make reference or allude to pagan myths and mythical ideals in order to show, by contrast, the greatness of the true God, the God of Israel.[9] This is perhaps best known with regard to the creation account in Genesis 1, with its echoes

9 See, for example, John Currid, *Against the Gods: The Polemical Theology of the Old Testament* (Wheaton, IL: Crossway, 2013). Cf. Ps. 77:13; 86:8; 89:6; 95:3; 96:4–5; 97:7–9; 115:2–9; 135:5.

of the Babylonian Enuma Elish. The psalmists make allusions to these pagan myths also. This is similar to what John Milton and other English poets have done in making reference to Zeus or Jupiter. They do not in fact acknowledge the actual existence of these false gods; it is a graphic poetic method of conveying the greatness of the true God. The Hebrew poets felt secure in making reference to these pagan myths also and for the same reason—in addition to enriching their poetry, it is a polemic. "It wasn't Baal who did this, and it wasn't Marduk. It was the Lord our God" is the idea.

In the Ugaritic texts (a collection of tablets found at Ras Shamra in North Syria and dating from about the fourteenth century BC) the creator god in view is Baal. Baal is the god of storm and lightning who battles against Yam (Sea, the symbol of chaos) or against Mot (Death). Other gods of chaos in these myths are Rahab (Proud Boaster) and Leviathan (Serpent). These are names unfamiliar to most English readers, but they appear in the Psalms. These mythological allusions occur only in poetry to add vividness and color to the poem. They also function as a polemic against the pagan gods. Take Psalm 74:12–17 as an example:

> 12 Yet God my King is from of old,
> working salvation in the midst of the earth.
> 13 You divided the sea by your might;
> you broke the heads of the sea monsters on the waters.
> 14 You crushed the heads of Leviathan;
> you gave him as food for the creatures of the wilderness.
> 15 You split open springs and brooks;
> you dried up ever-flowing streams.
> 16 Yours is the day, yours also the night;
> you have established the heavenly lights and the sun.
> 17 You have fixed all the boundaries of the earth;
> you have made summer and winter.

Notice that the scene is that of a battle, a battle in which God breaks the heads of the sea monsters. It is the God of Israel, the true God, who defeated the forces of chaos. All this is poetic imagery. The psalmist has not embraced the myths, but he makes use of them to portray the greatness of God with vivid, recognizable scenes.

In Psalm 29 the psalmist presumably adopts and adapts a hymn to Baal, the god of storm. Directing attention instead to the Lord it functions also as a kind of polemic, for it is the Lord God, not Baal, who rules the storm:

> 1 Ascribe to the LORD, O heavenly beings,
> ascribe to the LORD glory and strength.
> 2 Ascribe to the LORD the glory due his name;
> worship the LORD in the splendor of holiness.
> 3 The voice of the LORD is over the waters;
> the God of glory thunders, the LORD, over many waters.
> 4 The voice of the LORD is powerful;
> the voice of the LORD is full of majesty.
> 5 The voice of the LORD breaks the cedars;
> the LORD breaks the cedars of Lebanon.
> 6 He makes Lebanon to skip like a calf,
> and Sirion like a young wild ox.
> 7 The voice of the Lord flashes forth flames of fire.
> 8 The voice of the LORD shakes the wilderness;
> the LORD shakes the wilderness of Kadesh.
> 9 The voice of the LORD makes the deer give birth and strips the forests bare,
> and in his temple all cry, "Glory!"
> 10 The LORD sits enthroned over the flood;
> the LORD sits enthroned as king forever.
> 11 May the LORD give strength to his people!
> May the LORD bless his people with peace!

Note that 29:3–4 speak figuratively of thunders over the Mediterranean as "the voice of the LORD." Then notice where the storm is going: Lebanon, the center of Baal worship. So the psalmist portrays a storm, the mighty power of God, coming off the sea with crashing thunder and flashing lightning, which then makes the nations of Lebanon and Syria skip or leap like a frightened young animal and that shakes the desert east of the Lebanese mountains and smashes their famously great cedars (29:5–8). That which represents what is mighty and majestic, the Lord crushes and brings to nothing. When the storm dies down, the Lord remains enthroned as King over all. Robert Chisholm surveys these references to the pagan myths in the Psalms and concludes that these psalms proclaim God's kingship over all, even hostile forces, and serve as encouragement to the people of God who live under his care.[10] These psalms, then, continue the praise of God's majesty and sovereign rule.

Another common theme of the Psalter is the *songs of Zion* (cf. 137:1–3), psalms that extol Jerusalem, the holy city. Psalms 46, 48, 76, 84, 87, 121, and 122 are prominent examples. Mount Zion is a hill in Jerusalem, the city of David, and the location of Israel's temple. "Zion" signifies not only Jerusalem itself but also "a complex cluster of interlocking themes" such as the temple and presence of God, Israel as the covenant people of God, the Davidic kingship and its accompanying prospect of Messiah (cf. 2:6), the Lord's kingship, and the world center from which divine justice will be dispensed.[11] Because of God's presence Zion is a "holy hill" (2:6), "the joy of all the earth" (48:2), and symbolizes strength, stability, and even invincibility for the people of God (cf. 46; 125:1).

Ugaritic texts have proved of great value to an understanding of Zion. In the Ugaritic texts, Baal dwells on "Zaphon," referred to as a "holy place," "mountain of my heritage," "chosen spot," "hill of victory." It was considered a cosmic center, universal in scope, and the place where decrees are issued. This kind of imagery is reflected (by contrast) often in the Psalms:

10 Robert B. Chisholm Jr., "Suppressing Myth: Yahweh and the Sea in the Praise Psalms," in *The Psalms: Language for All Seasons of the Soul*, ed. Andrew J. Schmutzer and David Howard Jr. (Chicago: Moody Publishers, 2013), chap. 5.

11 Leeland Ryken et al., eds., *Dictionary of Biblical Imagery* (Downers Grove, IL: InterVarsity Press, 1998), 980.

> 1 Great is the LORD and greatly to be praised
>     in the city of our God!
> His holy mountain, 2 beautiful in elevation,
>     is the joy of all the earth,
> Mount Zion, in the far north,
>     the city of the great King. (48:1–2)

Songs of Zion, among which are the Songs of Ascents, often exult in the prospect of standing and remaining in Zion (cf. 122). Psalm 84, for example, exults throughout in the thought of remaining in the temple precincts (see 84:1–2, 10). The psalmist even envies the birds who nest in its shelter (84:3) and the priests who serve there daily (84:4). It is in Zion that Israel's strength is found (84:5).

All of these are common themes in the praise psalms.

### The Conclusion

The conclusions of the praise psalms frequently take the form of the introduction. Often this is not a mere repeat but an expansion of the initial call to praise, and sometimes the psalmist will confess that there is so much more that should be said:

> 17 How precious to me are your thoughts, O God!
>     How vast is the sum of them!
> 18 If I would count them, they are more than the sand.
>     I awake, and I am still with you. (139:17–18)

And in what Gunkel calls the "contribution formula," the psalmist lays his poetic creation before the Lord, expressing hopes that his words are pleasing to him:

> 14 Let the words of my mouth and the meditation of my heart
>     be acceptable in your sight,
>     O LORD, my rock and my redeemer. (19:14)

34 May my meditation be pleasing to him,
for I rejoice in the LORD. (104:34)

Now we will examine a few more samples of praise psalms.

---

## PSALM 33

Psalm 33 follows the standard form of hymns or praise psalms, and so it serves well as our first example in this category.

33:1–3: Call to praise:

1 Shout for joy in the LORD, O you righteous!
Praise befits the upright.
2 Give thanks to the LORD with the lyre;
make melody to him with the harp of ten strings!
3 Sing to him a new song;
play skillfully on the strings, with loud shouts.

33:4–19: Cause for praise:

4 For the word of the LORD is upright,
and all his work is done in faithfulness.
5 He loves righteousness and justice;
the earth is full of the steadfast love of the LORD.
6 By the word of the LORD the heavens were made,
and by the breath of his mouth all their host.
7 He gathers the waters of the sea as a heap;
he puts the deeps in storehouses.
8 Let all the earth fear the LORD;
let all the inhabitants of the world stand in awe of him!
9 For he spoke, and it came to be;

he commanded, and it stood firm.
10 The LORD brings the counsel of the nations to nothing;
he frustrates the plans of the peoples.
11 The counsel of the LORD stands forever,
the plans of his heart to all generations.
12 Blessed is the nation whose God is the LORD,
the people whom he has chosen as his heritage!
13 The LORD looks down from heaven;
he sees all the children of man;
14 from where he sits enthroned he looks out
on all the inhabitants of the earth,
15 he who fashions the hearts of them all
and observes all their deeds.
16 The king is not saved by his great army;
a warrior is not delivered by his great strength.
17 The war horse is a false hope for salvation,
and by its great might it cannot rescue.
18 Behold, the eye of the LORD is on those who fear him,
on those who hope in his steadfast love,
19 that he may deliver their soul from death
and keep them alive in famine.

33:20–22: Conclusion or final reflection:

20 Our soul waits for the LORD;
he is our help and our shield.
21 For our heart is glad in him,
because we trust in his holy name.
22 Let your steadfast love, O LORD, be upon us,
even as we hope in you.

**Survey Exposition**

Apart from the introductory Psalms 1 and 2, Psalm 33 is the lone psalm in the first book of the Psalter (Pss. 3–41) that has no superscript designating David as its author.[12] The Septuagint includes the "of David" superscript, and the inclusion of this psalm in book 1 may indicate that the editors held it as Davidic. Judging from its contents some have referred the psalm to the time of Hezekiah and the defeat of the Assyrian army, but that, of course, is much later. The repetition of 32:11 in 33:1 may further reflect the editors' assumption of its Davidic origin; it likely explains the placement of these two psalms together, although their respective themes are quite different. Psalm 32 is an individual song of grateful praise for God's forgiveness. Psalm 33 is a hymn that calls the righteous to praise God for his dependability in consummating his program of salvation. Here his powerful word and works and his moral attributes already displayed in creation and history give assurance that his kingdom will be established in the earth.

In 33:1–3 the psalmist issues a call to praise, addressing the people, as usual, not the Lord himself:

> 1 Shout for joy in the Lord, O you righteous!
> Praise befits the upright.
> 2 Give thanks to the Lord with the lyre;
> make melody to him with the harp of ten strings!
> 3 Sing to him a new song;
> play skillfully on the strings, with loud shouts.

The first verse tells us *who* should praise: the "righteous." God detests praise offered from the unclean and the unrighteous (cf. Isa. 1:10–18; Amos 5:20–23), but he is eager for those who are "right" before him to offer their praise. We who are in a right standing with God through the blood of Jesus Christ and transformed by the indwelling of his Spirit may offer our praise to God with joy and with confidence that he delights in it. Such praise is appropriate. It "befits the upright" (Ps. 33:1b). The sense here is that "there is no exercise in

12 Psalm 10 lacks this superscript also, but Psalms 9–10 were originally one.

which they can be better employed."[13] It is the proper adornment of the righteous and that which distinguishes us as his people. The Anglican liturgy rightly says: "It is right to give him thanks and praise."[14] If we are robed in the white righteousness of Christ, then our songs of praise are the appropriate jewelry. There is nothing more befitting or suitable for us who are righteous in Christ than to have a song of praise on our lips. We should not think lightly of our praises: God calls us to it, and he delights in it.

Next, 33:1–3 tell us *how* and *what kind* of praise we should render to God. It is befitting that our praise be marked by "joy" (33:1a) and thoughtful acknowledgment of what God has done (33:2). The thanksgiving in view is that of testimony, acknowledging God's goodness to us. Joy and thanksgiving belong together. Befitting praise is also marked by singing and musical instruments (33:2–3) directed to God, as even a cursory reading through the Psalter reveals (cf. Ps. 150). The psalmist also specifies that God's praise ought to be rendered "skillfully" (33:3). God is a God of order and beauty, and he is deserving of our finest musical praise. This should not be performance to entertain the congregation, but praise offered "to the LORD" (33:2). Nor should we sing halfheartedly but joyfully and with enthusiasm—with "shouts" of joy and our affections and emotion fully engaged (33:3). Halfhearted praise is unworthy of him. "Nothing affords a surer test of the reality of worship than a worshipper's joy in it."[15]

And finally, our praise ought to be that of a "new song." The "old" song was the song of the exodus (Ex. 15). But God has done more for us since then, so there must be a new song to express new praise. Our singing in praise ought to reflect God's works throughout redemptive history. There is ground here for Isaac Watts's then-revolutionary idea to author new "hymns of human composure" as well as his "imitating"

13 John Calvin, *Commentary on the Book of Psalms*, trans James Anderson, vol. 1 (1845; repr., Grand Rapids, MI: Baker, 2003), 538.

14 Anglican Church in North America, *The Book of Common Prayer* (2019) (Huntington Beach, CA: Anglican Liturgy Press, 2019), 115.

15 Alexander MacLaren, *The Psalms*, vol. 3 (New York: A. C. Armstrong and Son, 1903), 27–28.

the Psalms to reflect their fulfillment in Christ.[16] Praise must be up to date. The saints in heaven surrounding the newly enthroned Christ did just this!

> 9 And they sang a new song, saying,
>
> "Worthy are you to take the scroll
> and to open its seals,
> for you were slain, and by your blood you ransomed people
> for God
> from every tribe and language and people and nation,
> 10 and you have made them a kingdom and priests to our God,
> and they shall reign on the earth." (Rev. 5:9–10; cf. 14:3)

So also the final triumph of Christ will be marked by a joyful singing of "the song of Moses" resung to reflect our Lord's recent accomplishments (Rev. 15:3–4).

This emphasis on singing and musical instruments along with the call to praise all reflect a temple setting and liturgical use of the psalm. "The scene is a noisy, joyous occasion with musicians, singers, and worshipers joining together in raucous praise."[17] Eaton suggests that the "new song" and the themes of the Lord's rule over the nations indicate the "lively scene" of celebration at one of Israel's leading festivals.[18] As we saw in chapter 5, we should expect to come across many indications of public worship in the Psalms.

In 33:4–19 the psalmist gives the cause or reason for praise. This section serves a teaching function and a reminder that Israel's praise is not empty formality but well-grounded in God's attributes and actions, his character and his works. As customary, this section is marked off

16 Watts's "Jesus Shall Reign" (Ps. 72) and "Joy to the World" (Ps. 98) are perhaps the best-known examples.

17 Gerald H. Wilson, *Psalms Volume 1*, The NIV Application Commentary (Grand Rapids, MI: Zondervan, 2002), 556.

18 John Eaton, *The Psalms: A Historical and Spiritual Commentary with an Introduction and New Translation* (New York: Continuum, 2005), 151.

by the explanatory conjunction "for," now rehearsing the ground of praise. Why should we give God such enthusiastic praise? Psalm 33:4–5 provides the answer in crisp summary:

> 4 For the word of the LORD is upright,
> and all his work is done in faithfulness.
> 5 He loves righteousness and justice;
> the earth is full of the steadfast love of the LORD.

That is, there are two causes for praise:

1. His greatness in his word and work (33:4)
2. His righteousness, justice, and steadfast love (33:5)

In 33:6–12, the psalmist develops and elaborates the summary statement of 33:4—God's greatness in his word in creation (33:6–9) and of his works in history (33:10–12).

> 6 By the word of the LORD the heavens were made,
> and by the breath of his mouth all their host.
> 7 He gathers the waters of the sea as a heap;
> he puts the deeps in storehouses.
> 8 Let all the earth fear the LORD;
> let all the inhabitants of the world stand in awe of him!
> 9 For he spoke, and it came to be;
> he commanded, and it stood firm.

To demonstrate the "uprightness" and dependability of God's word the psalmist here poetically expounds Genesis 1 and its affirmation that all of creation was brought into existence by the mere spoken word of God. It is a staggering thought that ought to evoke reverence and awe (Ps. 33:8). The entire universe with all its intricacies and harmony came into being by the effortless power of divine fiat. Surely, then, the word and promises of such a God can be trusted (cf. Phil. 1:6).

We may be assured also that the saving purposes of such a God will be fulfilled. He is Lord not of creation only but of history also:

10 The LORD brings the counsel of the nations to nothing;
he frustrates the plans of the peoples.
11 The counsel of the LORD stands forever,
the plans of his heart to all generations.
12 Blessed is the nation whose God is the LORD,
the people whom he has chosen as his heritage!
13 The LORD looks down from heaven;
he sees all the children of man;
14 from where he sits enthroned he looks out
on all the inhabitants of the earth,
15 he who fashions the hearts of them all
and observes all their deeds.
16 The king is not saved by his great army;
a warrior is not delivered by his great strength.
17 The war horse is a false hope for salvation,
and by its great might it cannot rescue.
18 Behold, the eye of the LORD is on those who fear him,
on those who hope in his steadfast love,
19 that he may deliver their soul from death
and keep them alive in famine.

Here the psalmist finds cause for praise in the works of God in history: the establishing of his kingdom. The nations have their "counsel" and "plans" (33:10), but the Lord God has "counsel" and "plans" that trump theirs (33:11). His plans will stand forever, and theirs will be brought to nothing (cf. Is. 45:22–25), and God's chosen nation will be blessed (33:12). The nation of Israel is in view in the old dispensation, but in the canonical context the nation is the church (1 Pet. 2:9). The psalm expands the blessedness of his nation. "He loves righteousness and justice" (Ps. 33:5) has prospective overtones: what he loves he will accomplish. God has set out to establish his kingdom in the earth, a kingdom marked by his moral attributes. This sense of anticipation is also reflected in the "hope" of those who wait for his salvation (33:16–19), as well as in the faithful waiting of God's people for God to act (33:20–22). Israel is in view, yes (33:12), and the Old Testament narratives tell us of many such deliverances. But particularly given Israel's eventual failure, the psalm necessarily looks beyond.

The anticipatory hints in this psalm, along with other psalms with related themes, and the entire biblical canon all lead us to expect more. Israel itself is but an earthly "type" of God's eternal kingdom. The world today is marked by rebellious rage (2:1), and when God's image bearers fail to reflect his word and his moral attributes in their actions, it is an offense to him (cf. Prov. 11:1). But the Lord "loves righteousness and justice" and will see to it that these are established in his creation. This psalm, then, anticipates the inbreaking of God's kingdom in its fullness. The kingdom is inaugurated now in Christ and realized in degree by his church, and this psalm implicitly looks ahead to the day when God's moral attributes will be reflected throughout the earth (cf. Isa. 11:9; Hab. 2:14)—the day when his will is done on earth as in heaven (Matt. 6:10).

This psalmist rejoices in God's hand in human history. God sees all people with searching discernment (Ps. 33:13–15) and saves, not the self-confident (33:16–17) but those who look trustingly to him (33:18–19; cf. Matt. 18:3; 19:14). And in all this he shows that the earth is full of his steadfast love. Again, the establishing of his kingdom is in view. Throughout history, kings and nations have thought themselves eternal, undefeatable, but they have all come and gone—Egypt, Assyria, Babylon, Medo-Persia, Greece, Rome, the Third Reich. And many have given themselves to stamping out the people of God. They have all come to nothing (Ps. 33:10), and together they testify to the coming fullness of God's kingdom. Despite the opposition it has seen all through the centuries, God's kingdom remains, and his people thrive in faith all over the earth. "The eye of the Lord is on those who fear him, / on those who hope in his steadfast love" (33:18). "The world is passing away, . . . but whoever does the will of God abides forever" (1 John 2:17). God's church will never be extinguished from the earth

(Matt. 16:18), and his kingdom will be brought to consummation (Ps. 33:11–12), not by human military might (33:16–17) but by God's own intervention. Here is cause for joyful praise.

Finally, in 33:20–22, the psalmist brings his psalm to a conclusion. This time his conclusion is not a renewed call to praise but an expression of confidence in God:

> 20 Our soul waits for the LORD;
> he is our help and our shield.
> 21 For our heart is glad in him,
> because we trust in his holy name.
> 22 Let your steadfast love, O LORD, be upon us,
> even as we hope in you.

The psalmist's trust is displayed in his waiting on God (33:20), his rejoicing in God (33:21), and his dependence upon God (33:22). The psalm begins with praise and concludes, fittingly, with an expression of trust, a patient trust that calls us also to wait for God to bring about his saving purposes in full. God's kingdom will yet be established in the earth (33:4–5), a kingdom characterized by uprightness, justice, righteousness, and his steadfast love. This remains the "blessed hope" of the church (Titus 2:13). We wait faithfully with expectant hope for Christ, at whose appearing God's kingdom will be realized in its fullness (2 Tim. 4:1; Rev. 11:15). "Blessed" indeed "is the nation whose God is the LORD, / the people whom he has chosen as his heritage" (33:12)!

We may outline Psalm 33 as follows:

I. Call for praise (33:1–3)
   A. Call to rejoice (33:1)
   B. Call for instruments (33:2)
   C. Call for new song (33:3)
II. Cause for praise (33:4–19)
   A. Summary (33:4–5)
      1. God's greatness: His dependability (33:4)

2. God's grace: His justice and loyal love (33:5)

B. Specifics: God's dependability (33:6–12)

1. Demonstrated in creation (33:6–9)
2. Demonstrated in history (33:10–12)

C. Specifics: God's justice and loyal love (33:13–19)

1. He sees all people (33:13–15)
2. He does not save the self-confident (33:16–17)
3. He saves those who trust in Him (33:18–19)

III. Conclusion: Demonstration of faith (33:20–22)

A. In waiting (33:20)
B. In rejoicing (33:21)
C. In petitioning (33:22)

## PSALM 100

A Psalm for giving thanks.

1 Make a joyful noise to the LORD, all the earth!
2 Serve the LORD with gladness!
Come into his presence with singing!
3 Know that the LORD, he is God!
It is he who made us, and we are his;
we are his people, and the sheep of his pasture.
4 Enter his gates with thanksgiving,
and his courts with praise!
Give thanks to him;
bless his name!
5 For the LORD is good;
his steadfast love endures forever,
and his faithfulness to all generations.

This psalm is one of the best-known psalms in English Christian hymnody. Isaac Watts's famous translation and his paraphrase have been very popular, particularly as adapted by John Wesley's "Before Jehovah's Awful Throne":

Before Jehovah's awful throne,
ye nations, bow with sacred joy;
know that the Lord is God alone;
he can create, and he destroy.

His sovereign power, without our aid,
made us of clay, and formed us then;
and, when like wandering sheep we strayed,
he brought us to his fold again.

We'll crowd thy gates with thankful songs,
high as the heavens our voices raise;
and earth, with her ten thousand tongues,
shall fill thy courts with sounding praise.

Wide as the world is thy command,
vast as eternity thy love;
Firm as a rock thy truth must stand,
When rolling years shall cease to move.[19]

The most famous English hymn rendering of this psalm is "All People That on Earth Do Dwell." The tune is named after the psalm—"Old 100th"—and comes to us from the Genevan Psalter. The words are from William Kethe (1561), a friend of John Knox and fellow exile in Geneva. It has been published in countless Christian hymnals and sung enthusiastically by Christians all over the English-speaking world.

All people that on earth do dwell,
Sing to the Lord with cheerful voice.
Him serve with fear, His praise forth tell;
Come ye before Him and rejoice.

19 Isaac Watts, "Before Jehovah's Awful Throne," Hymnary.org (website), accessed October 12, 2022, https://hymnary.org/.

The Lord, ye know, is God indeed;
Without our aid He did us make;
We are His folk, He doth us feed,
And for His sheep He doth us take.

O enter then His gates with praise;
Approach with joy His courts unto;
Praise, laud, and bless His Name always,
For it is seemly so to do.

For why? the Lord our God is good;
His mercy is for ever sure;
His truth at all times firmly stood,
And shall from age to age endure.[20]

Within the Psalter this psalm serves as the "doxology" of Psalms 95–99, psalms that proclaim God's sovereign reign over all his creation. David Howard established their unity beyond reasonable doubt.[21] Psalm 100 does not include the expression "The Lord reigns" that is common to these so-called enthronement psalms, but it has strong verbal and conceptual connections to them.[22] And its call to the nations to come before the Lord and worship continues their theme of his universal kingship and forms a fitting doxology.

## Form and Structure

The superscript of Psalm 100 identifies it as "a psalm for giving grateful praise." This term (תּוֹדָה) is used here as a general term for grateful praise; it is not used in the technical sense given it in form

20 William Kethe, "All People That on Earth Do Dwell," Christian Music and Hymns (website), accessed October 12, 2022, https://christianmusicandhymns.com/.

21 David M. Howard Jr., *The Structure of Psalms 93–100*, Biblical and Judaic Studies 5 (Winona Lake, IN: Eisenbrauns, 1997).

22 Compare 100:1 with 98:4; 100:1, 4 with 95:2; 100:1–2 with 95:1–2; 100:2 with 97:7; 100:2a, 4a with 95:6a; 100:3 with 95:6–7 and 97:6–7; 100:4 with 99:3; and 100:5 with 98:3.

criticism.[23] Its structure is that of a hymn (call to praise, cause for praise), but it does have an additional element, as we will see. And its subject matter is God's attributes and his creation of Israel, not an individual deliverance. So this psalm from a form-critical point of view is a hymn, a psalm of descriptive praise, not a psalm of declarative praise:

- call to praise (100:1–2)
- intercalation (100:3)
- renewed call and cause to praise (100:4–5)[24]

Throughout, it rivets our attention to the Lord by mentioning him in sixteen of about forty words.[25] The psalmist gives seven imperatives total: the first three are a call to praise (100:1–2), and the last three are a call to praise (100:4), with one imperative in between (100:3). The structure directs attention, then, to this center imperative: "Know that the LORD, he is God!" This is not a call to or cause for praise but a command to recognize certain truths about God. We will see the significance of this in the exposition below.

## Survey Exposition[26]

### *Call to Praise (100:1–2)*

1 Make a joyful noise to the LORD, all the earth!
2 Serve the LORD with gladness!
Come into his presence with singing!

"Shout" better represents the Hebrew than "make a joyful noise" (100:1), and in the Old Testament it frequently carries connotations of strong emotion, such as a shout of victory or the shout

23 See chap. 10, "Individual Songs of Grateful Praise."
24 Ps. 100:4–5 is a single sentence in the Hebrew.
25 Yahweh (4x), name (1x), pronoun (11x).
26 See also Bruce K. Waltke and James M .Houston, *The Psalms as Christian Praise: A Historical Commentary* (Grand Rapids, MI: Eerdmans, 2019), chap. 11.

that accompanies a trumpet blast sounding alarm (cf. Josh. 6:10, 16; 1 Sam. 17:52; Amos 1:14; Isa. 42:13; Jer. 50:15). Associated with "rejoicing" (Ps. 100:2) it indicates a kind of cheering, as when the home team scores a goal. This is no lament psalm and no funeral dirge. The psalmist calls us to give an exuberant shout to the Lord with grateful praise. It is worth noticing that the superscript identifies this is a "psalm"—a song accompanied with musical instruments, designed, it seems, to maximize the emotive effect. Musical instrumentation is an aid to attach truth to emotions, and that is its purpose here. All this together—the shouting, the singing, the musical instruments, the call for gladness—highlights the psalm as one of exuberant celebration, a song to be sung with excitement. This is joyful, celebratory confession of God's goodness set to music to be sung with enthusiasm.

Remarkably, the psalm calls not just Israel but "all the earth" (100:1) to enter God's presence (100:2; i.e., the temple; cf. 100:4) in worship. "All the earth" by metonymy indicates the earth's inhabitants—all the nations are invited to give joyful praise to Israel's God. The psalmist commands even Gentiles to join in the praise of God. On one level, he calls them to worship God because he is deserving of praise from all his creatures. Yet on another level this command to universal praise ties into the important biblical theme of God's universal saving purpose. God did not choose Israel in order to exclude other peoples but so that through Israel he could *include* all others (cf. Gen.12:1–3; Isa. 2:2–4; Mic. 4:1–4). The nations are called to come before God "with gladness" and "with singing" (Ps. 100:2) and in the safety of belonging to him. The command has redemptive implications. In this sense the Psalter is a missionary hymnbook, calling upon all people to know, love, and serve the Lord God of Israel for their own good and for his praise (cf. 2:11–12). The psalm, then, is prospective and looks beyond Israel's temple in Jerusalem to this messianic age of gospel advance in which the worship of God is not place restricted (John 4:20–21), a time when under the great commission God's people go into all the world, calling everyone to rejoice in God through his Son. The psalm is further prospective of a time when "the earth shall be full of the knowledge of the LORD / as the waters cover the sea" (Isa. 11:9; cf. Hab. 2:14). The corporate worship of the temple was—and our corporate praise today ought to be—marked by a sense of anticipation of the fullness of earth's praise.

Psalm 100:2 calls the earth to "serve" the Lord. To serve God indicates not only a recognition of God as God but a submission to him as master, rendering obedient service to him. But in the context of the Psalter this word also connotes temple worship, serving God (not other gods) with sacrifice, praise, and testimony. In our context today it would signify serving God in the work of prayer, laboring for the church and for the gospel. In brief, "serve the LORD" signifies devoted loyalty to him, and this, the psalmist says, is the duty of all people everywhere.

Moreover, it is appropriate that this service to the Lord be rendered "with gladness"—not halfhearted and not with inward joy only, but with rejoicing and shouts of joy. This word "gladness" indicates "rejoicing," even with excitement. Outward expression of joy is in view—a hand-clapping, foot-stomping, leaping-up-and-down-with-dance kind of joy.[27] Lifeless, formal ritual will not do. Worship of this God calls for exuberance. "Come before him with joyful shout" (100:2b, authors' translation).

### *Intercalation: Know That the Lord Is God and That Israel Is His People (100:3)*

An intercalation is an insertion of one literary unit into another. It constitutes a brief interruption in thought to make a related point. Psalm 100:3 interrupts the call to praise to state an implied condition for praise. It functions also as the pivot of the psalm, framed on either side by couplets. Here the psalmist calls the nations to know two things: that the Lord alone is God and that Israel is his chosen people.

27 Cf. 19:8; 104:15; 105:3.

3 Know that the LORD, he is God!
It is he who made us, and we are his;
we are his people, and the sheep of his pasture.

As we indicated above, 100:1–4 is structured to draw attention to 100:3. They consist of a series of seven commands. The first three (100:1–2) call the world to come before God in worship. The final three (100:4) do the same. It is a call to praise. The command of 100:3, however, is of a different order. It is not a call to praise but a command to recognize two fundamental truths. In this sense, it does not "fit" with the other six commands. It is an intercalation, as if to say before continuing with the call to praise, "Before you enter you must acknowledge ("know") that the God of Abraham, Isaac, and Jacob, the God of the Bible and the God of Israel, is God over all. There is no religious pluralism here. The confession that "the Lord, he is God" is an exclusive one that "dethrones and nullifies every other claimant."[28] Only thus may any "enter his gates" in worship (100:4). Praise apart from this exclusive recognition of him is unacceptable.

Would-be worshipers must also acknowledge Israel as God's people. Israel is the "us" and the "we" in view (100:3). It is Israel that God has made uniquely his own (cf. Isa. 29:23; 43:1). In one sense all the nations belong to God, for he is the Creator and sovereign Ruler over all, but Israel belongs to him in a unique sense (e.g., Amos 3:2). He has made us for himself and has formed Israel for his own praise (Isa. 43:21). The psalmist uses the language of creation. Just as God made the world by his spoken word (Gen. 1), so also he made Israel by his call of Abraham and by the exodus. It was a work of God alone, entirely of his grace and his power. And now the psalmist sees Israel as serving a mediatorial function, serving as "a kingdom of priests" (Ex. 19:6): through Israel the nations hear and learn of God and his saving power and grace. So also the church today is sent by God to proclaim the good news about Christ (Rom. 10:6–17; cf. 1 Thess. 2:13).

28 Walter Brueggemann, "Psalm 100," *Interpretation* 39 (January 1985): 66.

The church as an army of ambassadors for the Lord Jesus continues to say to the world, "Know this!"

*Renewed Call to Praise and Cause for Praise (100:4–5)*

Call to praise (100:4):

> 4 Enter his gates with thanksgiving,
> and his courts with praise!
> Give thanks to him;
> bless his name!

Now that the peoples of the earth have been instructed in their confession, they are invited to enter the sanctuary and join Israel in giving God their song and sacrifice of grateful praise, the reason or cause for which is highlighted in 100:5:

> 5 For the LORD is good;
> his steadfast love endures forever,
> and his faithfulness to all generations.

As already noted, God's "goodness" is the sum of all his benevolences (see p. 161). When Moses requests to see the glory of God, the Lord replies, "I will make all my goodness pass before you" (Ex. 33:19–20), whereupon he proclaims that he is "merciful and gracious, slow to anger, and abounding in steadfast love and faithfulness" (Ex. 34:6). God's "goodness" in the Old Testament often introduces a list of his attributes. God is "good" in character as well as actions, and his goodness is evident in that he has made us his own people (100:3). His goodness is manifested also in his "steadfast love." This is an attribute of God celebrated throughout the psalms (see Pss. 16:1; 106:1; 107:1; 118:1, 29; 136; cf. Ezra 3:11; 1 Chron. 16:34; 2 Chron. 5:13; 7:3; Jer. 33:11). This word is commonly used of God's covenant love for his people. It connotes both "loving kindness" and a faithful committedness; the translation "steadfast love" or "unfailing love" conveys both ideas. "Steadfast love" in the Old Testament also connotes a relationship in which the stronger partner comes mercifully to the aid of the weaker, even helpless, partner—not out of duress or mere obligation but from a heart of unfailing love (see Gen. 47:29; Ruth 3:10). Thus God is to Israel. And so when the psalmist affirms that God's steadfast love "endures forever," it is somewhat redundant, for "enduring" is bound up in the very meaning of "steadfast love." But the psalmist desires to press this great truth. God's steadfast love—like the Lord himself—is eternal (see Pss. 90:2; 92:8; 102:12). His "faithfulness" or reliability is likewise without end—"throughout all generations." He is trustworthy always. God is and acts always as he has pledged. "As our fathers found him faithful, so will our sons, and their seed forever."[29] His promises remain always firm.

Israel's call to the Gentiles to praise their God and their election as his people makes sense in the light of God's covenant and trustworthy promise to Abraham (Gen. 12:3), and behind the psalmist's call for the whole earth to render praise to the Lord God lies the anticipation that one day they indeed will (cf. Isa. 11:9; 66:22–23; Hab. 2:14). This is the church's task under the Great Commission. For over two millennia, the church has testified to the world, "Know that Jesus Christ is God's Son, our Savior, and that there is salvation in no other name" (see Acts 4:12). In Jesus Christ today people from all over the world come together to form God's temple (Eph. 3:6), and through him we have access to the heavenly sanctuary where we offer our sacrifice of praise to the triune God:

> 22 For as the new heavens and the new earth
>     that I make
> shall remain before me, says the LORD,
>     so shall your offspring and your name remain.
> 23 From new moon to new moon,
>     and from Sabbath to Sabbath,

29 C. H. Spurgeon, *The Treasury of David*, vol. 4 (New York: Marshall Brothers, 1883), 399.

> all flesh shall come to worship before me,
> declares the LORD (Isa. 66:22–23).

> 9 After this I looked, and behold, a great multitude that no one could number, from every nation, from all tribes and peoples and languages, standing before the throne and before the Lamb, clothed in white robes, with palm branches in their hands, 10 and crying out with a loud voice, "Salvation belongs to our God who sits on the throne, and to the Lamb!" 11 And all the angels were standing around the throne and around the elders and the four living creatures, and they fell on their faces before the throne and worshiped God (Rev. 7:9–11).

## PSALM 8

A Psalm of David.

1 O LORD, our Lord,
how majestic is your name in all the earth!
You have set your glory above the heavens.
2 Out of the mouth of babies and infants,
you have established strength because of your foes,
to still the enemy and the avenger.
3 When I look at your heavens, the work of your fingers,
the moon and the stars, which you have set in place,
4 what is man that you are mindful of him,
and the son of man that you care for him?
5 Yet you have made him a little lower than the heavenly beings
and crowned him with glory and honor.
6 You have given him dominion over the works of your hands;
you have put all things under his feet,
7 all sheep and oxen,
and also the beasts of the field,
8 the birds of the heavens, and the fish of the sea,
whatever passes along the paths of the seas.

9 O LORD, our Lord,
how majestic is your name in all the earth!
To the Choirmaster

**Overview**

The final editors of the Psalter evidently placed Psalm 8, a praise psalm, between Psalms 7 and 9 for their common theme to praise God's name (a surrogate for God himself that makes him accessible):

- "I will give to the LORD the thanks due to his righteousness, / and I will sing praise to the name of the LORD, the Most High" (7:17).
- "LORD, our Lord, / how majestic is your name in all the earth" (8:1).
- "LORD, our Lord, / how majestic is your name in all the earth" (8:9).
- "I will sing praise to your name, O Most High" (9:2).

Psalm 8 is the first praise psalm in the Psalter. Psalm 1 tells us that the Psalter is for those who delight in the law of the Lord. Psalm 2 is a coronation liturgy and introduces us to the main character of the Psalms, the king. These first two psalms are introduction, as we have seen. Psalms 3–7 are lament psalms, as are Psalms 9–10. Psalm 11 is a song of thanksgiving. In Psalm 8 we come for the first time to a psalm of praise.

The specific focus of its praise, however, is unique. Praise psalms celebrate God as majestic Creator of the universe and as the sovereign and just Ruler of history. These twin themes are prominent in Psalm 8, but with a more narrowly focused point. The moon and the stars that he put in place reflect his glory as Creator and Ruler (8:1). And this glory in the created order he has, in measure, extended to his people to rule over his enemies (8:2–8). God's glory is displayed both in his creative works and in the rule he has delegated to humanity. The psalm begins and ends with the same expression of praise, forming an *inclusio*: "LORD, our Lord, / how majestic is your name in all the earth!" (8:1a, 9).

Note that this praise psalm differs from our standard form: instead of the usual call to praise, we have a declaration of praise. That is, rather than calling all the earth to praise, all the earth is giving praise. This is the posture of the psalm and its theme.

First, David speaks of the creation, the order of creation, and the splendor of God in creation (8:1). Then he moves to the order of history, the order of redemption, and how God eliminates evil from the earth. He extols the splendor of God in the creation and the splendor of God in history and in the elimination of his enemies (8:2). In 8:3, he speaks again of the glory of God in creation and then in 8:4–5 of the glory of mankind who rules over it all. In 8:6–8 he addresses these same themes in reverse order and then concludes with the expression of praise with which he began (8:1, 9). The psalm is framed to draw attention to its major theme of praise to God—"LORD, our Lord" (יְהוָה אֲדֹנֵינוּ, *Yahweh adonenu*, 8:1, 9), the great Creator of all things. But the pivot (8:4–5) draws attention to his specific point of praise—the dignity given to "mere mortals" (אֱנוֹשׁ, 8:4a, authors' translation), just "common human beings" (בֶן־אָדָם, 8:4b, authors' translation) in giving them rule over it all. The psalm, then, has a touch of irony: Give praise to the God who gave such glory to humanity!

## Survey Exposition[30]

David's praise centers on Yahweh Adonai: "O LORD, our Lord, / how majestic is your name in all the earth!" (8:1, 9). His "name" ("I am") identifies him as the eternal, self-existing God to whom nothing can be compared (Ex. 3:14–16). He is the Creator and sovereign Ruler of all the earth who made Israel his own (Ps. 100:3), and here David (with Israel) praises him for it and submits to him accordingly ("our Lord") as his servant. Whatever glory God has given humanity, even the king

30 See also Bruce K. Waltke and James M. Houston, *The Psalms as Christian Worship: A Historical Commentary* (Grand Rapids, MI: Eerdmans, 2010), chap. 8.

is yet his servant. In 8:1–2 David portrays the whole people of God praising him ("our Lord"), but in the second stanza he narrows the language to the first person singular and speaks for himself: "When I look" (8:3)."Majestic" (8:1, 9) signifies someone or something that commands respect through the excellence of power. This God displays majesty "in all the earth" and in the heavens (8:1, 3). This word is used to express his dominion over the Red Sea and the Egyptian army (Ex. 1:10), the storm and sea (Job 37:4; Ps. 93:4), and all his enemies (Ps. 45:4). The sense here is that of God's exceeding power to defeat his enemies (8:2) and bring everything under the feet of his people to rule (8:4–8). God's "name" is "majestic . . . in all the earth."

Psalm 8:1b praises God's "splendor" (NASB) in created order: "You who have set your splendor upon the heavens" (authors' translation). The preposition "upon" (עַל) can mean "above" (ESV, NASB, KJV), but in 8:3 David in parallel specifies his point of reference—the created heavenly bodies—so God's splendor "upon" the heavens seems more suitable; his point is that God's splendor is observable. The vastness of the planetary systems and of the galaxies are in view, in comparison to which the mortal seems infinitesimally small and insignificant (8:3–4).

Psalm 8:2 advances the theme of God's splendor, but now with reference to human affairs:

> Out of the mouth of babies and infants,
> you have established strength because of your foes,
> to still [eliminate] the enemy and the avenger.

The enemies in view are God's enemies, and eliminating them is the cause of God's kingdom in the world (cf. Gen. 3:15). Here David employs multiple figures of speech to depict God's advance against evil. It is from the mouth of children and nursing infants that he lays the foundation of strength. Mouth in the context of the Psalter almost certainly indicates praise. Nursing infants cannot give petitions or praise, so again we have poetic imagery—a metaphor for God's people who in themselves are, like children, helpless. "The context suggests that these 'babes' are the weak and humble worshippers, whose inadequate singing of God's glory is yet used by him to still the avenger."[31] God will establish his kingdom and defeat his enemies by means of these "babies" and "infants" who sing his praise.

At his triumphal entry Jesus cited this verse (Matt. 21:16) and likened the praises of little children to the praises of all his people who in their helplessness depend on him in faith for rescue (cf. Matt. 18:3; 19:14).[32] These are the ones through whom God will overthrow his enemies.

Similarly, "man" (אֱנוֹשׁ, Ps. 8:4) signifies man in his weakness, and "son of man" (בֶן־אָדָם) refers to human beings generically—this in contrast to the "majestic" sovereign. So again, there is irony. God eliminates his enemies by means of weak, helpless humanity (cf. 1 Cor. 1:25–29) who worship him. "The enemies of God, blinded by their proud rebellion, do not see His glory, but they are confounded by [metaphorical] children and infants."[33] The proclamation of God's name throughout the world is the duty and privilege of his people—indeed, their very reason for being. It is our marching orders still today (Matt. 28:18–19) to proclaim in Jesus the name of the triune God and call the nations to submit to him.

In Psalm 8:3–4 David contemplates the difference between God and man:

> 3 When I look at your heavens, the work of your fingers,
> the moon and the stars, which you have set in place,
> 4 what is man that you are mindful of him,
> and the son of man that you care for him?

In 8:3 David continues to marvel at God's greatness as displayed in creation. The heavens are "your heavens" because they are "the work of your fingers." He is their Maker, and so they are his. "There is no

31 Eaton, *The Psalms*, 81.

32 Benjamin B. Warfield, *Selected Shorter Writings of Benjamin B. Warfield*, 2 vols., ed. John E. Meeter (Nutley, NJ: Presbyterian and Reformed, 1973), 2:231–32.

33 John Stott, *Favorite Psalms* (Chicago: Moody Press, 1988), 10.

pantheism here."[34] Indeed, the contrast between the great God of transcendent otherness who made all things, and "man" or "mere mortal" (v. 4), is staggering, and David's contemplation of the heavens reminds him of it. Weiser's comment captures the sense here well:

> When man gazes up at the illimitable expanse of the heavens studded with stars, the difference between God and man is revealed in all its magnitude, and the whole contradictory quality of that difference is made manifest. The finite is confronted with the infinite, the transient with the eternal, the perpetual sorrows and anxieties of man, who constantly goes astray, with the peace, steadiness and order manifested by the heavenly bodies which run their prescribed course. All these thoughts are implied in the question, "What is man?"[35]

More narrowly, David exults in the fact that this God of heavenly splendor has stooped to concern himself with weak humanity so as to endow it with a nobility unparalleled in all the created order:

5 Yet you have made him a little lower than the heavenly beings
and crowned him with glory and honor.
6 You have given him dominion over the works of your hands;
you have put all things under his feet,
7 all sheep and oxen,
and also the beasts of the field,
8 the birds of the heavens, and the fish of the sea,
whatever passes along the paths of the seas.

"Heavenly beings" (8:5) is *elohim*—God or gods. The Septuagint (and Heb. 2:7, following it) renders this "angels," who seem to be in view.

34 James L. Mays, *Psalms*, Interpretation: A Bible Commentary for Teaching and Preaching (Louisville: John Knox, 1994), 65.

35 Artur Weiser, *The Psalms: A Commentary*, The Old Testament Library (Philadelphia: Westminster, 1962), 143.

"You made him lack a trifle from heavenly beings" (Ps. 8:5, authors' translation) and gave him dominion over all the created order (8:6), creatures of both the land (8:7) and the water and the sky (8:8). Here David reflects on the creation of man in the image of God and the mandate of Genesis 1:26–28, giving it something of a devotional exposition. God manifests his royal splendor in the heavens, but on earth he mediates his royal splendor through his image bearers. "You have put all things under his feet" (Ps. 8:6). The famous western ballad observes:

How often at night when the heavens are bright
With the light from the glittering stars
Have I stood here amazed and asked as I gazed
If their glory exceeds that of ours.[36]

The psalmist answers, "It does not." As vast and incomprehensible as the heavens are, and though the mortal seems in contrast to them so fleeting, small, and insignificant, human beings have a higher dignity as God's vice-regents over creation and in the eschaton will endure after the present heavens and earth will be destroyed.

David was surely aware of ancient Near Eastern cosmogonies that unanimously depict mankind as created as slaves of the gods.[37] Informed by God himself (Gen. 1:26–28), David is persuaded otherwise. Nor will it do to explain humanity merely in evolutionary terms: created in God's image, mankind is set apart from the created order uniquely as ruler. "If one were to imagine a scale of 1 to 10 with living creatures such as beasts as 1 and God as 10, then, so high is the writer's estimation of humanity, he should have to put him at 8 or 9. It is God, and not animals, who is man's closest relative."[38] The theme of the psalm is

36 "Home on the Range," Scout Songs (website), accessed September 12, 2022, https://www.scoutsongs.com/. The popular song is based on the poem "Oh, Give Me a Home on The Range" (1873), by Brewster Higley VI.

37 Richard J. Clifford, *Psalms 1–72*, Abington Old Testament Commentaries (Nashville: Abingdon, 2002), 70.

38 Elmer A. Martens, *God's Design: A Focus on Old Testament Theology*, 3rd ed. (North Richland Hills, TX: BIPAL Press, 1998), 202–3.

mankind as God's chief self-revelation and representative on earth.[39] God made humankind like himself and delegates his rule accordingly. "Man is a king, and not a king without territory; the world around, with the works of creative wisdom which fill it, is his kingdom."[40] Such is the royal dignity God has given to "mere mortals," and this is the focus of David's praise to God. Calvin aptly comments,

> The prophet, therefore, speaking interrogatively, abases their condition, intimating that God's wonderful goodness is displayed the more brightly in that so glorious a Creator, whose majesty shines resplendently in the heavens, graciously condescends to adorn a creature so miserable and vile as man is with the greatest glory, and to enrich him with numberless blessings.[41]

The dominion envisioned is God's kingdom established in the earth through the mediating rule of mankind. The ascription of the psalm to David shows that "our" (8:1, 9) refers to the king and the nation he represents. David is zealous to see God's universal rule established in the earth through his people (cf. Matt. 6:10). But in a fallen world the exercise of this God-given dominion will not come without struggle. Subduing all things "under his feet" (Ps. 8:6) implies resistance. They rule over "the [wild] beasts of the field," as well as over the domesticated "sheep and oxen." Moreover, this dominion entails more than physical dominion—rule over the animals (8:7–8). It entails dominion over the spiritual realm also (Gen. 3:15), rule over God's enemies (Ps. 8:2). This is where Adam failed (Gen. 3), and all humanity after him has failed also. "We do not yet see everything in subjection to him" (Heb. 2:8). Satan presently regards himself "the ruler of this world" (John 12:31; cf. 2 Cor. 4:4; 1 John 5:19), and for the kingdom of God to be established

39 A. F. Kirkpatrick, *The Book of Psalms: Book I* (Cambridge: Cambridge University Press, 1892), 35.

40 C. F. Keil and F. Delitzsch, *Commentary on the Old Testament*, vol. 5 (Peabody, MA: Hendrickson, 1996), 94.

41 Calvin, *Psalms*, vol. 1, 100.

he must be defeated (Gen. 3:15). The creation mandate itself (Gen. 1:28) suggests that the goal of history will not be realized until humanity's assigned role to rule over creation is realized. And so, as Hebrews 2 informs us, the eternal Son of God *stooped* to our exalted status so that as our new representative head he may succeed where Adam failed:

> [5] For it was not to angels that God subjected the world to come, of
> which we are speaking. [6] It has been testified somewhere,
>
> "What is man, that you are mindful of him,
> or the son of man, that you care for him?
> 7 You made him for a little while lower than the angels;
> you have crowned him with glory and honor,
> 8 putting everything in subjection under his feet."
>
> Now in putting everything in subjection to him, he left nothing outside his control. At present, we do not yet see everything in
> subjection to him. [9] But we see him who for a little while was made
> lower than the angels, namely Jesus, crowned with glory and honor because of the suffering of death, so that by the grace of God he might taste death for everyone.
>
> [10] For it was fitting that he, for whom and by whom all things exist, in bringing many sons to glory, should make the founder of their salvation perfect through suffering. . . .
>
> [14] Since therefore the children share in flesh and blood, he himself likewise partook of the same things, that through death he might
> destroy the one who has the power of death, that is, the devil, [15] and
> deliver all those who through fear of death were subject to lifelong slavery. (Heb. 2:5–10, 14–15)

In his incarnation God the Son condescended to become one of us in order to accomplish our redemption and, as our representative, to restore human dominion over all things, including death and Satan himself. Having accomplished his redeeming work he ascended to

God's right hand where he is enthroned as universal king with "all things under his feet" (Eph. 1:20–22). At last, in his glorious return the Lord Jesus will bring his rule to consummation:

> [22] For as in Adam all die, so also in Christ shall all be made alive. [23] But each in his own order: Christ the firstfruits, then at his coming those who belong to Christ. [24] Then comes the end, when he delivers the kingdom to God the Father after destroying every rule and every authority and power. [25] For he must reign until he has put all his enemies under his feet. (1 Cor. 15:22–25)

This psalm is not in praise of God as Creator only but also of God at work in the historical process, establishing his kingdom in the earth through Christ. Humanity's rule over God's enemies and all creation will yet be achieved through the mediatorial work of the incarnate Son of God. "It has been said that this Psalm might be called 'Genesis 1 turned into a prayer'; but it is more truly 'the Genesis 1 of the new Earth.' It corresponds to Isaiah 11:6, 7, in the scene it exhibits."[42]

Psalm 8:9 concludes the psalm with a restatement of the theme: "O Lord, our Lord, / how majestic is your name in all the earth!" This is David's theme. God is majestic in creation and in redemption. And yet the bulk of the psalm exults in the dignity given to mankind: How does this theme serve the larger theme of God's greatness? The answer is in 8:2: this great God triumphs over his enemies by means of helpless infants, men and women who from their helplessness look to him and sing his praise.

The vision of Psalm 8 encompasses the whole drama of human history from the creation to the consummation. Psalm 8 may be likened to a play:

- playwright and director: the triune God
- prologue: praise to the triune God

42 Andrew Bonar, *Christ and His Church in the Book of Psalms* (London: James Nisbet, 1859), 28.

- cast: God, his people, and his enemies
- plot: the struggle for universal dominion
- protagonist: the (weak) people of God
- antagonist: Satan and the world
- hero of the play: Jesus
- epilogue: praise to the triune God

A mere mortal in an incomprehensible cosmos,
Created to make the name of the Triune God majestic in all the earth
By praising him as creator and covenant keeper
and subduing the earth in his name.

## PSALM 81

Of Asaph.
1 Sing aloud to God our strength;
shout for joy to the God of Jacob!
2 Raise a song; sound the tambourine,
the sweet lyre with the harp.
3 Blow the trumpet at the new moon,
at the full moon, on our feast day.
4 For it is a statute for Israel,
a rule of the God of Jacob.
5 He made it a decree in Joseph
when he went out over the land of Egypt.
I hear a language I had not known:
6 "I relieved your shoulder of the burden;
your hands were freed from the basket.
7 In distress you called, and I delivered you;
I answered you in the secret place of thunder;
I tested you at the waters of Meribah. *Selah*
8 Hear, O my people, while I admonish you!
O Israel, if you would but listen to me!

9 There shall be no strange god among you;
you shall not bow down to a foreign god.
10 I am the Lord your God,
who brought you up out of the land of Egypt.
Open your mouth wide, and I will fill it.
11 "But my people did not listen to my voice;
Israel would not submit to me.
12 So I gave them over to their stubborn hearts,
to follow their own counsels.
13 Oh, that my people would listen to me,
that Israel would walk in my ways!
14 I would soon subdue their enemies
and turn my hand against their foes.
15 Those who hate the Lord would cringe toward him,
and their fate would last forever.
16 But he would feed you with the finest of the wheat,
and with honey from the rock I would satisfy you."

We select Psalm 81 at this point to highlight its exceptional form. Recall that we have said that the psalmists are not bound to particular forms, and they frequently make adjustments and even mix or combine psalm forms to suit the purpose at hand. We have seen that Psalm 8, though a praise psalm, does not have the usual "call to praise" but instead a declaration of praise. Psalm 81 has another exception to the usual praise form. It has the standard components of the hymn or praise psalm, but it differs in that it adds an additional prose section in the second half—a homily or, more precisely, a didactic psalm. Psalm 81:1–7 is a praise psalm, and 81:8–16 is a homily or prophetic oracle:

- praise psalm
  - 81:1–3: call to praise
  - 81:4: cause for praise
- 81:6–16: homily/prophetic oracle

- 81:5–7: janus (transition) and prologue to the first commandment
- 81:8–16: admonition to hear the first commandment, and reflection

Asaph was both a poet and a prophet, and here his psalm reflects both functions. He marks off these sections with the common signals for each:

- "Sing aloud" (81:1), the call to praise
- "For" (81:4), the cause for praise
- "He made it a decree" (81:5–7) introduces the prophetic address and transitions to the admonition
- "Hear, O my people" (81:8) begins the admonition

The *call to praise* (81:1–3) is a familiar one in the Psalter, summoning the people of God to loud, enthusiastic praise, and that with the accompaniment of musical instruments, including the tambourine and the ram's horn ("trumpet"). The scene is that of joyful celebration at one of Israel's feasts (81:3).

The *reason* or *cause for praise* (81:4) is that God made it a rule to do so (81:4). He delivered Israel from Egypt and provided for them in the wilderness. God had made Israel a free people.

In the *homily* section (81:8–16), the psalmist admonishes the people to remain faithful in the worship of God (81:8–10). He then reminds them of their historic failure in this regard (81:11–12). And then he concludes with a renewed invitation to hear (81:13–16), pleading with the people to faithfulness and reminding them of the blessedness of it.

More fully, we could outline the psalm like this:

81:1–4: Praise psalm
  81:1–3: Call to praise
  81:4: Cause for praise
81:6–16: Homily/prophetic oracle
  81:5–7: Janus and prologue to the first commandment

81:8–16: Admonition to hear the first commandment, and reflection
- 81:8–10: Admonition to hear the first commandment
- 81:11–12: Accusation and punishment
- 81:13–16: Renewed invitation

Recognizing psalm forms is helpful to our interpretive task. Recognizing the exceptions and alternatives is helpful also. Psalm 95 presents us with a similar case.

## PSALM 95

1 Oh come, let us sing to the LORD;
let us make a joyful noise to the rock of our salvation!
2 Let us come into his presence with thanksgiving;
let us make a joyful noise to him with songs of praise!
3 For the LORD is a great God,
and a great King above all gods.
4 In his hand are the depths of the earth;
the heights of the mountains are his also.
5 The sea is his, for he made it,
and his hands formed the dry land.
6 Oh come, let us worship and bow down;
let us kneel before the LORD, our Maker!
7 For he is our God,
and we are the people of his pasture,
and the sheep of his hand.
Today, if you hear his voice,
8 do not harden your hearts, as at Meribah,
as on the day at Massah in the wilderness,
9 when your fathers put me to the test
and put me to the proof, though they had seen my work.
10 For forty years I loathed that generation
and said, "They are a people who go astray in their heart,

and they have not known my ways."
11 Therefore I swore in my wrath,
"They shall not enter my rest."

**Survey Exposition**[43]

Psalm 95 has the standard components of a praise psalm, but it differs from the usual form in two ways. First, there is repetition of the call to praise and the cause for praise. Also, the second half of the psalm is a related homily, as we saw in Psalm 81, resembling a didactic psalm. The entire psalm is structured as follows:

- praise psalm (95:1–7a)
    - call to praise (95:1–2)
    - cause or reason for praise (95:3–5)
    - call to praise (95:6)
    - cause or reason for praise (95:7a)
- didactic psalm or homily (95:7b–11)

In our exposition of Psalm 100, we noted that Psalm 100 is the climatic doxology of psalms celebrating "the LORD reigns." The praise of Psalm 95:1–6 matches Psalm 100, both in structure and content. Both frame a center line pertaining to knowing that the Lord is God and that Israel is his people by couplets summoning people to praise the Lord. But whereas Psalm 95 calls Israel to praise the Lord, Psalm 100 calls the Gentiles; and whereas Psalm 95 assumes Israel knows that the Lord is God and that Israel is his people, Psalm 100 commands the Gentiles to make that same confession of faith.

First, in 95:1–2, we have the *call to praise*:

1 Oh come, let us sing to the LORD;
let us make a joyful noise to the rock of our salvation!

43 See also Bruce K. Waltke and James M. Houston, *Psalms as Christian Praise: A Historical Commentary* (Grand Rapids, MI: Eerdmans, 2019), chap. 13.

2 Let us come into his presence with thanksgiving;
let us make a joyful noise to him with songs of praise!

Here the worship leader summons Israel ("us") to joyful praise. "Come" implies a call to make their way to the temple ("his presence") with heart and tongue tuned to praise. The commands "let us sing" (95:1a) and "make a joyful noise" (95:1b, 2) both connote a shout or loud cry. Loud, joyful praise is the idea. This is a note frequently sounded in the Psalter—halfhearted praise is unworthy of God. The specific praise in view is that of "thanksgiving" (95:2a, or "acknowledgment," see chapter 10) and singing of "songs of praise with musical accompaniment" (see 95:2b, זָמִיר; cf. 2 Sam. 23:1).

Why? What is the *reason* or *cause* for such enthusiastic praise? Psalm 95:3–5 explains:

3 For the Lord is a great God,
and a great King above all gods.
4 In his hand are the depths of the earth;
the heights of the mountains are his also.
5 The sea is his, for he made it,
and his hands formed the dry land.

The Lord God is worthy of such praise simply because of his exalted status. He is transcendent, above all rulers and above all the created realm. All that exists "outside" of him exists by his own hand. He is the Creator. Notice again the parallels: 95:3b explains 95:3a with respect to all other spiritual rulers and all false gods. The parallelism is broadly synonymous but not exact; there is a clarification. The parallels in 95:4 and 95:5 employ merisms: 95:4 looks on the vertical axis (everything from the depths of the earth to the mountaintops is in his firm grasp), whereas 95:5 measures on the horizontal axis (everything in the seas and on the dry land is of his making also). This God, the Creator, is "the Lord" (95:1a), the God of Israel. Worship ought to be cheerful, for Israel's God is none other than the Creator of all things. He is therefore the great refuge for his people, "the rock of our salvation" (95:1b).

Then in 95:6 we have another *call to praise*:

> 6 Oh come, let us worship and bow down;
> let us kneel before the LORD, our Maker!

Here "come" means "enter," and the call is not to sing but to "bow down." So this call to praise (95:6) broadly parallels that of 95:1–2, but the mood and specific commands are different. The initial call to praise invited the faithful to come to the temple; this call invites them into temple courtyards. And here they are not called to sing but to do obeisance, to bow before their Creator in awe and deep admiration. The mood changes from that of raucous joy to silent reverence.

Why? What is the *cause* or *reason* for such worship? Psalm 95:7a explains explicitly what the previous verses implied:

> 7 For he is our God,
> and we are the people of his pasture,
> and the sheep of his hand.

Not only is the Lord God the Creator of the world; he is the Creator of Israel herself, as a nation ("we"). He has made them his own covenant people. Here the thought is not that of creation specifically but of redemptive history and God's redemptive work. Praise is due this God because he is the Creator—creaturely praise is due him. But beyond that, praise is due him for his gracious redeeming work. The psalmist combines the related themes of God as Creator and God as Lord of history.

Next, rather than the usual conclusion with a renewed call to praise, 95:7b begins the second half of the psalm with a prophetic warning. Until now in this psalm Asaph has taken the role of a priest, calling the people to worship. Here he takes the role of the prophet and exhorts the people. Note the shift from the first person ("let us sing . . . / let us make joyful noise . . . / let us come . . . / let us worship and bow down . . . / let us kneel," 95:1, 2, 6) to the second person ("you," 95:7b). In the first half of the psalm, the psalmist positions himself entirely with the worshiping community, Israel, but now he faces them, as it were, and issues a stern exhortation to trust in the Lord and maintain faithful worship so that they may enter his rest:

> Today, if you hear his voice,
> 8 do not harden your hearts, as at Meribah,
> as on the day at Massah in the wilderness,
> 9 when your fathers put me to the test
> and put me to the proof, though they had seen my work.
> 10 For forty years I loathed that generation
> and said, "They are a people who go astray in their heart,
> and they have not known my ways."
> 11 Therefore I swore in my wrath,
> "They shall not enter my rest."

So these two sections of the psalm are rather evenly divided. Here God warns feckless Israel not to neglect their worship of him. Here the mood changes radically. Rather than a worship leader, we have a prophet. Instead of a call to worship, we have prophetic exhortation. Rather than a call to joyful singing, we have a warning against unfaithfulness. Instead of "us" and "we," it is "you."

The prophet begins with an introductory exhortation and warning:

> Today, if you hear his voice,
> 8 do not harden your hearts, as at Meribah,
> as on the day at Massah in the wilderness. (95:7b–8)

This psalm was apparently composed in time of drought, hence the references to Meribah and Massah in the first year of the exodus (Ex. 17:2–7) and in the fortieth (Num. 14:22). This new generation of Israel is warned not to be rebellious as was the first. That generation hardened their heart (Ps. 95:8) and failed to trust him, though they had seen his work. Instead of trusting God on the basis of his many preceding miracles in Egypt, at the Red Sea, and in the wilderness, they forgot his miracles and refused to trust him when they lacked water at Meribah. In each new crisis, instead of remembering God's track record they demanded another miracle to prove that he was faithful and with them. As a result, God loathed that generation: they did not know his ways. So he did not allow that generation to enter the promised land and "rest" (95:10–11). So the psalmist warns the people of his day ("today," 95:7b) to learn from their ancestors' mistake and remain trusting and faithful in spite of the crisis. We could paraphrase his thought in this way: "Even today, in this difficult time of drought, you must remember the Lord's past faithfulness and trust and worship him as he deserves."

The psalmist faults Israel for lack of trust "though they had seen my work" (95:9). They had reason for trust, but they were faithless, and this is why God loathed them. The New Testament warns us similarly. The Lord's Supper is given to remind us of God's work in Christ. We must remember this always and in every crisis remain trusting. "Name it and claim it" theology like ancient Israel demands a new miracle for each new crisis, but this is not the way of faith that pleases God.

Hebrews 3:7–4:11 takes up Psalm 95 and applies it just this way to the church in crisis. The writer addresses believing Jews who, because of difficulty, are tempted to turn away from Christ and back to the Mosaic system of worship. Directing their attention to Psalm 95, he reasons that because the psalmist—more than four centuries after Joshua—still called Israel to God's rest ("today"), the rest that Joshua provided did not exhaust the promise. God's rest "remains for some to enter it" (Heb. 4:6). The promised land that Israel failed to enter represents the place of ultimate rest that is found only in union with Christ by faith—both now (Matt. 11:25–12:8) and in its fullness in the age to come. The writer of Hebrews calls upon the professing covenant community not to harden their hearts in unbelief against the living God but to hold fast to Christ lest they miss God's rest.

**Review**

The first section consists in a call to praise (Ps. 95:1–2, 6) and a cause for praise (95:3–5, 7), and the second consists in a warning not to neglect praise (95:8–9) and a threat of consequent judgment (95:10–11). Or we may say more simply that 95:1–7a forms the worship section of the psalm and 95:7b–11 the warning section. The flow of thought through the psalm, then, is as follows:

- Give joyful praise to the Lord (95:1–2).
- Why? Because he is the sovereign Creator (95:3–5).
- Come, bow before him (95:6).
- Why? Because we are his (95:7a).
- Corresponding warning (95:7b–11):
  - Do not harden yourself against him (95:7b–9).
  - Why? Because he will be wrathful, and you will not enter his rest (95:10–11).

# 9

# Petition-Lament Psalms

*"Hear me, O God, and deliver me!"*

IN THIS CHAPTER we come to the third type of psalm identified by the inspired writer in 1 Chronicles 16:4—the lament or petition psalm. Various terms are used to describe them. In some of these psalms the term "lament" fits best; the psalmist is simply lamenting his situation, as in the book of Lamentations. At other times the tone is more of a protest—the psalmist is innocent and protesting the injustice that his enemies inflict on him—and so "complaint" may be more precise. Or they may be called "petition" because this motif is so prominent in these psalms. Further distinctions may be made. Some of these lament psalms are community oriented,[1] reflecting a time when the entire nation is experiencing difficulty. Some are individual laments,[2] with, say, sickness (Pss. 6; 31; 38; 39; 41; 88; 102), although the "sickness" is often metaphorical; persecution (3; 9; 10; 35; 52; 55; 56; 57; 62; 69; 70; 86; 109; 120; 139; 140; 141; 143); military crisis (12; 44; 58; 60; 74; 79; 80; 83; 90; 137); or injustice (7;

1 Pss. 12; 44; 58; 60; 74; 79; 80; 83; 85; 89:38–51; 90; 94; 123; 126; 129; 137.

2 Pss. 3; 4; 5; 6; 7; 9; 10; 13; 14 (= 53); 17; 22; 25; 26; 27:7–14; 28; 31; 35; 36; 38; 39; 40:12–17 (= 70); 42; 43; 51; 52; 54; 55; 56; 57; 59; 61; 63; 64; 69; 70 (= 40:13–17); 71; 86; 88; 89:38–51; 102; 109; 120; 130; 139; 140; 141; 142; 143.

17; 26; 27) in view.[3] Some of the laments combine both corporate and individual lament. This is so because the king is in view; he is the "I" of the psalm, and he represents the people, "we." Some of these psalms lament the psalmist's sin and thus are penitential psalms.[4] And some of these psalms lament an enemy and call for retribution; these are imprecatory psalms, which we will examine separately. All of these are a form of the psalms of petition, and various terminology may be deemed specifically appropriate in given psalms.

We should recall here that the poetry of the psalms is marked by imagery and figurative language, so it is difficult at times to discern the exact point of reference in the laments.

**Petition-Lament and Praise**

Claus Westermann, mentioned earlier, has influentially pointed out that praise and lament are the two contrasting ways of addressing God. On one level, of course, his point is obvious, and the contrasting perspective is helpful. Yet it is important to note that the petition psalms, even the laments, are always doxological. With the complaint is always praise (except Ps. 88) and never a loss of confidence in God. In the main, this is the difference between Job and the psalmist. Both protest strongly about injustice, but Job has no praise until the very end of the story.

Psalm 88 is the "black sheep" of the psalter, with no praise offered, and it stands out as the exception. Yet, despite unrelenting affliction and unanswered prayer, Heman, the author, does not lose hope in the God of Israel. In the honor roll of the faithful, he stands higher than even Job and Qoheleth. Unlike Job, this hero of faith does not question God's goodness (cf. Job 9:22–24; 10:1) or, unlike Qoheleth, question the value of his life (Eccles. 4:2–3). Against all the contrary evidence to God's goodness, the Lord is his God and remains his hope

3 See Bruce K. Waltke, "Psalms," in *New International Dictionary of Old Testament Theology and Exegesis*, ed. Willem A. VanGemeren, 5 vols. (Grand Rapids, MI: Zondervan, 1997), 4:1104.

4 Pss. 6; 32; 38; 51; 102; 130; 143.

for salvation (Ps. 88:1). He persists in prayer: constantly (88:1), daily (88:9), and yet this one more time (88:13). His hope and prayer are as insistent as his afflictions.

### Lament and Faith

We may wonder how lament or complaint can coexist with faith, so it is worth recalling well that over a third of the Psalms are laments. This observation by itself informs us that lament and faith are not incompatible. Certainly, it is sinful to complain in unbelief, but lament need not be untrusting of God's providential care. R. W. L. Moberly rightly comments: "The experience of anguish and puzzlement in the life of faith is not a sign of deficient faith, something to be outgrown or put behind one, but is intrinsic to the very nature of faith."[5]

The reality is that the righteous suffer in various ways, and God does not always give us what we ask for in prayer—and this, often, while the unrighteous prosper. We may be sure that in the end righteousness will triumph, but in this fallen age, that is not always evident. God is sovereign in his dispensing of grace. Moreover, it would not be for our spiritual profit if God were always to reward virtue immediately. If he always rewarded virtue immediately, it would destroy us spiritually. We would use God. He would be to us like the genie in Aladdin's lamp. We would not worship him for who he is but simply for our own self-gratification. Instead of our being his servants, he would become our servant. We would use God. And so he delays answer to our prayers so we are not destroyed by confounding morality and true faith with pleasure.

In Deuteronomy 8 Moses emphasized this very point to the people of Israel:

> [1] The whole commandment that I command you today you shall be careful to do, that you may live and multiply, and go in and possess

5 R. W. L. Moberly, "Lament," in VanGemeren, *New International Dictionary of Old Testament Theology and Exegesis*, 4:879; cf. Moberly, *Old Testament Theology: Reading the Hebrew Bible as Christian Scripture* (Grand Rapids, MI: Baker Academic, 2013), 231, 240.

> the land that the Lord swore to give to your fathers. [2] And you shall remember the whole way that the Lord your God has led you these forty years in the wilderness, that he might humble you, testing you to know what was in your heart, whether you would keep his commandments or not. [3] And he humbled you and let you hunger and fed you with manna, which you did not know, nor did your fathers know, that he might make you know that man does not live by bread alone, but man lives by every word that comes from the mouth of the Lord. (Deut. 8:1–3)

God does not always give immediate deliverance from trials. And as a result, we learn to glory not only in our justification but also in our sufferings, "knowing that suffering produces endurance, and endurance produces character, and character produces hope" (Rom. 5:3–4). Moreover, Jesus himself experienced suffering also. "He learned obedience through what he suffered" (Heb. 5:8). So we also learn obedience and trust through the crises of trial and unanswered prayer—we learn to depend upon God. This is at the heart of these lament psalms. We know this because the psalmist never laments without praise. There is always that expression of confidence. In the context of praise, lament and even protest can be an important function of faith.

### The Psalmist's Enemies

The lament or complaint is commonly in reference to the psalmist's experience of suffering, the absence of God (or worse yet, his misunderstood anger),[6] and the enemy. Of the sixty lament psalms, most mention an enemy. Just who are the enemies the psalmist faces? The psalmist may speak of enemies in military terms, as on a battlefield. He may speak of being hunted like an animal, or he

6 For an excellent reflection on God's absence and/or anger, see Allen P. Ross, "The 'Thou' Sections of Laments; The Bold and Earnest Prayers of the Psalmists," in *The Psalms: Language for All Seasons of the Soul*, ed. Andrew J. Schmutzer and David Howard Jr. (Chicago: Moody Publishers, 2013), 135–50.

may describe the enemy as an animal who seeks to devour him. He also describes them in moral terms—they are arrogant, evil, violent, deceitful, crooked, lying, and so on. Their ways, thoughts, and words are wicked. And he often describes them also as enemies of God. Taken together this language points most obviously to the enemies of God, his kingdom, his king, and his people. The "war" is a spiritual one as well as personal (Eph. 6:10–12). In David's case, the enemy and his "arrow" or "sword" in view is often literal; and as David's enemies they are enemies of God who appointed him. The Psalter is a royal hymnbook, and its laments concern the welfare of God's kingdom. The lament psalms are for glory of God and the healing and preservation of his kingdom—therapeutic effects are secondary.

### Form

The petition psalms have distinct elements. The order is not always fixed, but the elements are normally discernible. The initial mark of a petition or lament psalm is usually the opening direct address "O LORD," or the equivalent. The following components are usually present also, and normally in this order:

**Direct Address with Introductory Petition:** Here the psalmist in his extremity turns to God, his covenant Lord, commonly asking God to hear the petition that follows.

**Lament/Complaint:** Here the psalmist describes his lamentable situation (enemies, persecution, danger, false accusation, fear of death, sins, etc.).

**Confidence:** Here the psalmist asserts his confidence in God despite the desperation. He will often appeal to God's attributes, his covenant relationship, his past actions, or even the psalmist's own innocence—protesting the injustice of the adversity.

**Petition:** Here the psalmist seeks to move God to act—to hear, to be favorable, to punish the enemy (and gives the reason why).

**Conclusion/Praise:** Laments regularly conclude with praise or a vow to praise, what the psalmist will say or do after his prayer is answered. Or the psalmist may burst forth in immediate praise, so certain is he that God will hear and answer.

**Psalm 54**, an individual lament, provides a good first example:

**Address** (with introductory petition):

1 O God, save me by your name,
and vindicate me by your might.
2 O God, hear my prayer;
give ear to the words of my mouth.

**Lament** or **complaint**:

3 For strangers have risen against me;
ruthless men seek my life;
they do not set God before themselves. *Selah*

**Confidence**:

4 Behold, God is my helper;
the Lord is the upholder of my life.

**Petition**:

5 He will return the evil to my enemies;
in your faithfulness put an end to them.

**Praise**:

6 With a freewill offering I will sacrifice to you;
I will give thanks to your name, O LORD, for it is good.

7 For he has delivered me from every trouble,
and my eye has looked in triumph on my enemies.

This pattern is common to both individual and community laments. It may not hold in every case, but usually petition psalms consist of these five elements. Here again we follow Gunkel's famous research.[7]

The **address** summons God. It is among the first words of the psalm. It is usually abrupt and often includes a preliminary cry for help and a brief portrayal of the psalmist in his approach to God. Consider the address of Psalm 5:

1 Give ear to my words, O LORD;
consider my groaning.
2 Give attention to the sound of my cry, my King and my God,
for to you do I pray. (5:1–2)

"O LORD," "O God," or "O Shepherd of Israel" are common addresses that mark the petition/lament psalm. This address is essential to identifying the lament psalm.

The **complaint** commonly has three elements: the suffering of the psalmist, the absence of God, and the too-powerful enemy. All three occur in Psalm 69:2–4:

*Personal suffering*:

2 I sink in deep mire,
where there is no foothold;
I have come into deep waters,
and the flood sweeps over me.

7 Hermann Gunkel, *Introduction to the Psalms: The Genres of the Religious Lyric of Israel*, completed by Joachim Begrich; trans. James Nogalski (Macon, GA: Mercer University Press, 1998), chaps. 4 and 6.

*God's absence*:

3 I am weary with my crying out [to God];
my throat is parched.
My eyes grow dim
with waiting for my God.

*Foes too powerful*:

4 More in number than the hairs of my head
are those who hate me without cause;
mighty are those who would destroy me,
those who attack me with lies.

The cry "how long" is often heard (e.g., 4:2).

The **petition** is the heart of the complaint psalms, a plea for deliverance. This is the goal of the lament. These petitions customarily begin with a general prayer for God to "hear" (17:1), "rise up" (94:2), "awake" (7:6), or "look" (80:14), and the plea itself is for God to intervene on the psalmist's behalf. The language may at times be strong with regard to the enemy, but the hope is that God will have "compassion" (79:8), "remember" (74:2), "help" (109:26), "deliver" (6:4), take up the psalmist's case and execute justice (7:9), and bring vindication (26:1). Often the psalmist is tormented with the question "Why?" (22:1), and the related inquiry is, "How long?" (6:3).

In his plea for deliverance the psalmist regularly offers a rationale. Often his appeal is grounded in divine attributes—God's righteousness and justice (5:8), grace (51:1), and steadfast love (6:4). The psalmist's confidence rests in God (119:42). When the psalmist proclaims his "innocence," as he does in Psalm 26, he is not being self-righteous like the Pharisees (see Luke 18:9–14). Rather, to pray with confidence in God's justice, he needs a clear conscience. Elsewhere the psalmist says, "If I had harbored sin in my heart, the Lord would not have listened" (Ps. 66:18 NET). To assure himself of a right standing with God, David says, "Who can discern his errors? / Declare me innocent from hidden faults" (19:12). So he calls on God to examine him and bring vindication (26:2; 139:23).

Moreover, when suffering is deserved, God may use enemies to chastise his guilty people, but Israel has not wronged them, and so their oppression is unjust and the just God will punish the oppressor:

> 5 Woe to Assyria, the rod of my anger;
> the staff in their hands is my fury!
> 6 Against a godless nation I send him. . . .
> 7 But he does not so intend,
> and his heart does not so think;
> but it is in his heart to destroy,
> and to cut off nations not a few;
> 8 for he says:
> "Are not my commanders all kings? . . ."
>
> 12 When the Lord has finished all his work on Mount Zion and on Jerusalem, he will punish the speech of the arrogant heart of the king of Assyria and the boastful look in his eyes. (Isa. 10:5–8, 12)

So the psalmist's plea for help is grounded in his trust in God's justice.

The **confidence** section expresses the reason or ground of the psalmist's trusting petition. With a variety of expressions the psalmist affirms that God is his refuge, hope, and help. This section is often introduced by "but you," and it is consistently God-centered. God's character and attributes (Ps. 25:8), his power (3:3), his covenantal relationship ("My God," 7:1, 3), his past performances (63:7), his justice and his steadfast love, all attributes lead the psalmist to trust him fully in trial. The Lord has heard his people in the past (22:4–5, 9–11), and so he trusts he will again (38:15). The psalmist knows he is the king appointed by God, he knows who God is, and he knows how God has proven faithful in the past (3:4–6). He also knows that God has no pleasure in the wicked (5:4–6). And all this gives him confidence that God will come to his aid yet again.

The **conclusion** may be a final expression of lament (120:5–7), but often it is a wish that the psalmist will be part of a witness to the entire world for what the Lord has done. There may also be a vow (54:6–7; 56:12) or a reaffirmation of certain faith that God will indeed help (6:9–10; 13:5–6).

With slight variations all sixty of the petition-lament psalms demonstrate this basic form. Learning to watch for these elements will aid us considerably in our interpretation. Moreover, we learn from these models how to pray. The psalmist goes to God in prayer (address); he states his need (lament/complaint); he makes his request (petition), often reasoning with God for it; he expresses his trust (confidence); and he vows still to praise. This is remarkably similar to the apostle Paul's instruction in Philippians 4:6: "Do not be anxious about anything, but in everything by prayer and supplication with thanksgiving let your requests be made known to God."

Next we will sample several petition-lament psalms in order to get acquainted with this psalm form.

---

## PSALM 5

**Address** with introductory **petitions**:

1 Give ear to my words, O LORD;
consider my groaning.
2 Give attention to the sound of my cry,
my King and my God,
for to you do I pray.
3 O LORD, in the morning you hear my voice;
in the morning I prepare a sacrifice for you and watch.

**Confidence** with **lament:**

4 For you are not a God who delights in wickedness;
evil may not dwell with you.
5 The boastful shall not stand before your eyes;
you hate all evildoers.
6 You destroy those who speak lies;
the LORD abhors the bloodthirsty and deceitful man.

**Petition** with **confidence** for salvation:

7 But I, through the abundance of your steadfast love,
will enter your house.
I will bow down toward your holy temple
in the fear of you.
8 Lead me, O LORD, in your righteousness
because of my enemies;
make your way straight before me.

**Petition** with **confidence** in judgment:

9 For there is no truth in their mouth;
their inmost self is destruction;
their throat is an open grave;
they flatter with their tongue.
10 Make them bear their guilt, O God;
let them fall by their own counsels;
because of the abundance of their transgressions cast them out,
for they have rebelled against you.

Public **praise** by the righteous:

11 But let all who take refuge in you rejoice;
let them ever sing for joy,

and spread your protection over them,
that those who love your name may exult in you.
12 For you bless the righteous, O Lord;
you cover him with favor as with a shield.

## PSALM 13

Superscript:

A Psalm of David

In 13:1, we have the **direct address**:

1 How long, O Lord?

Then 13:1–2 express David's threefold **complaint**:

1 How long, O Lord? Will you forget me forever?
How long will you hide your face from me?
2 How long must I take counsel in my soul
and have sorrow in my heart all the day?
How long shall my enemy be exalted over me?

It seems that God is doing nothing while David's soul is in turmoil and his enemies boast over him.

Then in 13:3–4, David offers his **petition**:

3 Consider and answer me, O Lord my God;
light up my eyes, lest I sleep the sleep of death,
4 lest my enemy say, "I have prevailed over him,"
lest my foes rejoice because I am shaken.

In the three "lest" clauses of 13:3–4, David reasons that his is a moral cause. His motivations are for God and his kingdom.

In 13:5, he expresses his **confidence**:

5 But I have trusted in your steadfast love;
my heart shall rejoice in your salvation.

Finally, in 13:6, David **vows to praise** as though the answer has already come:

6 I will sing to the LORD,
because he has dealt bountifully with me.

## PSALM 38

Superscript:

A Psalm of David, for the memorial offering.

**Direct address:**

1 O LORD, rebuke me not in your anger,
nor discipline me in your wrath!

**Lament:**

2 For your arrows have sunk into me,
and your hand has come down on me.
3 There is no soundness in my flesh
because of your indignation;
there is no health in my bones
because of my sin.
4 For my iniquities have gone over my head;
like a heavy burden, they are too heavy for me.
5 My wounds stink and fester
because of my foolishness,

6 I am utterly bowed down and prostrate;
all the day I go about mourning.
7 For my sides are filled with burning,
and there is no soundness in my flesh.
8 I am feeble and crushed;
I groan because of the tumult of my heart.

**Confidence**:

9 O Lord, all my longing is before you;
my sighing is not hidden from you.

**Lament**:

10 My heart throbs; my strength fails me,
and the light of my eyes—it also has gone from me.
11 My friends and companions stand aloof from my plague,
and my nearest kin stand far off.
12 Those who seek my life lay their snares;
those who seek my hurt speak of ruin
and meditate treachery all day long.
13 But I am like a deaf man; I do not hear,
like a mute man who does not open his mouth.
14 I have become like a man who does not hear,
and in whose mouth are no rebukes.

**Confidence**:

15 But for you, O Lord, do I wait;
it is you, O Lord my God, who will answer.

**Lament**:

16 For I said, "Only let them not rejoice over me,
who boast against me when my foot slips!"
17 For I am ready to fall,
and my pain is ever before me.
18 I confess my iniquity;
I am sorry for my sin.
19 But my foes are vigorous, they are mighty,
and many are those who hate me wrongfully.
20 Those who render me evil for good
accuse me because I follow after good.

**Petition** (with hint of **praise**):

21 Do not forsake me, O LORD!
O my God, be not far from me!
22 Make haste to help me,
O Lord, my salvation!

Postscript:

To the choirmaster: to Jeduthun.

## PSALM 58

Superscript:

A Miktam of David.

**Lament** (in the form of a prophetic accusation against mankind):

1 Do you indeed decree what is right, you gods?
Do you judge the children of man uprightly?

2 No, in your hearts you devise wrongs;
your hands deal out violence on earth.

3 The wicked are estranged from the womb;
they go astray from birth, speaking lies.
4 They have venom like the venom of a serpent,
like the deaf adder that stops its ear,
5 so that it does not hear the voice of charmers
or of the cunning enchanter.

**Address** and **petition**:

6 O God, break the teeth in their mouths;
tear out the fangs of the young lions, O LORD!
7 Let them vanish like water that runs away;
when he aims his arrows, let them be blunted.
8 Let them be like the snail that dissolves into slime,
like the stillborn child who never sees the sun.

**Confidence** or confession of trust:

9 Sooner than your pots can feel the heat of thorns,
whether green or ablaze, may he sweep them away!

**Praise**:

10 The righteous will rejoice when he sees the vengeance;
he will bathe his feet in the blood of the wicked.
11 Mankind will say, Surely there is a reward for the righteous;
surely there is a God who judges on earth."

Postscript:

To the choirmaster.

## PSALM 102

Superscript:

A Prayer of one afflicted, when he is faint and pours out his complaint before the LORD.

Direct **address** with introductory **petition**:

1 Hear my prayer, O LORD;
let my cry come to you!
2 Do not hide your face from me
in the day of my distress!
Incline your ear to me;
answer me speedily in the day when I call!

**Lament**:

3 For my days pass away like smoke,
and my bones burn like a furnace.
4 My heart is struck down like grass and has withered;
I forget to eat my bread.
5 Because of my loud groaning
my bones cling to my flesh.
6 I am like a desert owl of the wilderness,
like an owl of the waste places;
7 I lie awake;
I am like a lonely sparrow on the housetop.
8 All the day my enemies taunt me;
those who deride me use my name for a curse.
9 For I eat ashes like bread
and mingle tears with my drink,
10 because of your indignation and anger;
for you have taken me up and thrown me down.

11 My days are like an evening shadow;
I wither away like grass.

**Confidence** or confession of trust:

12 But you, O Lord, are enthroned forever;
you are remembered throughout all generations.
13 You will arise and have pity on Zion;
it is the time to favor her;
the appointed time has come.
14 For your servants hold her stones dear
and have pity on her dust.
15 Nations will fear the name of the Lord,
and all the kings of the earth will fear your glory.
16 For the Lord builds up Zion;
he appears in his glory;
17 he regards the prayer of the destitute
and does not despise their prayer.
18 Let this be recorded for a generation to come,
so that a people yet to be created may praise the Lord:
19 that he looked down from his holy height;
from heaven the Lord looked at the earth,
20 to hear the groans of the prisoners,
to set free those who were doomed to die,
21 that they may declare in Zion the name of the Lord,
and in Jerusalem his praise,
22 when peoples gather together,
and kingdoms, to worship the Lord.
23 He has broken my strength in midcourse;
he has shortened my days.

**Petition:**

24 "O my God," I say, "take me not away
in the midst of my days—
you whose years endure
throughout all generations!"

**Confidence:**

25 Of old you laid the foundation of the earth,
and the heavens are the work of your hands.
26 They will perish, but you will remain;
they will all wear out like a garment.
You will change them like a robe, and they will pass away,
27 but you are the same, and your years have no end.
28 The children of your servants shall dwell secure;
their offspring shall be established before you.

## PSALM 142

The superscript places the psalm in David's flight from Saul "in the cave." The cave of Engedi is probably in view (1 Sam. 24). Here David laments that his life is in peril, and he will petition God for deliverance.

Superscript:

A Maskil of David, when he was in the cave. A Prayer.

In 142:1–2 David **addresses** God with an introductory expression of his plea:

1 With my voice I cry out to the LORD;
with my voice I plead for mercy to the LORD.

2 I pour out my complaint before him;
  I tell my trouble before him.

In 142:3–4 David express his **lament**:

3 When my spirit faints within me,
  you know my way!
In the path where I walk
  they have hidden a trap for me.
4 Look to the right and see:
  there is none who takes notice of me;
no refuge remains to me;
  no one cares for my soul.

Psalm 142:3 gives us a sense of David's desperation—he is overwhelmed to the point of fainting. It is a crisis moment; he has nowhere to turn, no one to help him, and no apparent escape. The "trap" (cave) has sprung, and like a bird in a snare, he is facing death. This seems to him to be the end.

But then in 142:5 David expresses his **confidence**:

5 I cry to you, O Lord;
  I say, "You are my refuge,
  my portion in the land of the living."

Here David describes God with two metaphors. God is his "refuge," the safe place where he can flee to for protection. God is also his "portion." This is the vocabulary of the conquest and the allotment of land to each tribe for all to earn their livelihood. So God is both David's protector and his sustaining power, that upon which he can depend for provision and life. David's confidence rests in God alone.

Then in 142:6–7a David makes his threefold **petition** to God:

6 Attend to my cry,
for I am brought very low!
Deliver me from my persecutors,
for they are too strong for me!
7 Bring me out of prison,

In the remainder of 142:7 David expresses his **vow of praise**:

that I may give thanks to your name!
The righteous will surround me,
for you will deal bountifully with me.

## PSALM 27

Psalm 27 presents an interesting case study in that the form is mixed. Here David begins with such a robust expression of confidence that it appears to be a psalm of trust. But beginning with 27:7 the form of the lament psalm becomes clear.

In 27:1–6 David expresses his **confidence**:

Of David.
1 The LORD is my light and my salvation;
whom shall I fear?
The LORD is the stronghold of my life;
of whom shall I be afraid?
2 When evildoers assail me
to eat up my flesh,
my adversaries and foes,
it is they who stumble and fall.
3 Though an army encamp against me,
my heart shall not fear;
though war arise against me,
yet I will be confident.
4 One thing have I asked of the LORD,

that will I seek after:
that I may dwell in the house of the LORD
all the days of my life,
to gaze upon the beauty of the LORD
and to inquire in his temple.
5 For he will hide me in his shelter
in the day of trouble;
he will conceal me under the cover of his tent;
he will lift me high upon a rock.
6 And now my head shall be lifted up
above my enemies all around me,
and I will offer in his tent
sacrifices with shouts of joy;
I will sing and make melody to the LORD.

Then in 27:7–12 we have the **petitions**:

7 Hear, O LORD, when I cry aloud;
be gracious to me and answer me!
8 You have said, "Seek my face."
My heart says to you,
"Your face, LORD, do I seek."
9 Hide not your face from me.
Turn not your servant away in anger,
O you who have been my help.
Cast me not off; forsake me not,
O God of my salvation!
10 [Though my father and mother forsake me,
the LORD will receive me (NIV)][8]
11 Teach me your way, O LORD,

8 So also NAB, CJB, CSB, NLT. The ESV translates according to the usual meaning of the Hebrew, the others the less usual. We choose this because the notion that Jesse forsook David does not fit the book of Samuel, and the notion that David's mother forsook him contradicts Psalm 116:16, the only reference to her.

and lead me on a level path
because of my enemies.
12 Give me not up to the will of my adversaries;
for false witnesses have risen against me,
and they breathe out violence.

Then he closes with an expression of **confidence**:

13 I believe that I shall look upon the goodness of the LORD
in the land of the living!
14 Wait for the LORD;
be strong, and let your heart take courage;
wait for the LORD!

## PSALMS 42–43

These two psalms appear to have originally been one, as evidenced by the lack of superscript in Psalm 43 and the repeated "Why are you cast down, O my soul" in every fifth verse (42:5, 11; 43:5), not counting the center line (42:8). Also, these two psalms together have the common components of the lament psalm. The petition section was probably separated in ancient times for liturgical purposes, as happened in Psalm 40:13–17 (= Ps. 70).

**Address** and **lament**:

1 As a deer pants for flowing streams,
so pants my soul for you, O God.
2 My soul thirsts for God,
for the living God.
When shall I come and appear before God?
3 My tears have been my food
day and night,
while they say to me all the day long,

"Where is your God?"
4 These things I remember,
as I pour out my soul:
how I would go with the throng
and lead them in procession to the house of God
with glad shouts and songs of praise,
a multitude keeping festival.

**Confidence**:

5 Why are you cast down, O my soul,
and why are you in turmoil within me?
Hope in God; for I shall again praise him,
my salvation 6 and my God.

**Lament**:

My soul is cast down within me;
therefore I remember you
from the land of Jordan and of Hermon,
from Mount Mizar.
7 Deep calls to deep
at the roar of your waterfalls;
all your breakers and your waves
have gone over me.

Center line—**praise**:

8 By day the LORD commands his steadfast love,
and at night his song is with me,
a prayer to the God of my life.

**Lament:**

9 I say to God, my rock:
"Why have you forgotten me?
Why do I go mourning
because of the oppression of the enemy?"
10 As with a deadly wound in my bones,
my adversaries taunt me,
while they say to me all the day long,
"Where is your God?"

**Confidence:**

11 Why are you cast down, O my soul,
and why are you in turmoil within me?
Hope in God; for I shall again praise him,
my salvation and my God.

**Petition:**

43:1 Vindicate me, O God, and defend my cause
against an ungodly people,
from the deceitful and unjust man
deliver me!
2 For you are the God in whom I take refuge;
why have you rejected me?
Why do I go about mourning
because of the oppression of the enemy?
3 Send out your light and your truth;
let them lead me;
let them bring me to your holy hill
and to your dwelling!

**Vow to Praise:**

4 Then I will go to the altar of God,
to God my exceeding joy,
and I will praise you with the lyre,
O God, my God.

**Confidence:**

5 Why are you cast down, O my soul,
and why are you in turmoil within me?
Hope in God; for I shall again praise him,
my salvation and my God.

## PSALM 69

Of David.

1 Save me, O God!
For the waters have come up to my neck.
2 I sink in deep mire,
where there is no foothold;
I have come into deep waters,
and the flood sweeps over me.
3 I am weary with my crying out;
my throat is parched.
My eyes grow dim
with waiting for my God.
4 More in number than the hairs of my head
are those who hate me without cause;
mighty are those who would destroy me,
those who attack me with lies.
What I did not steal
must I now restore?

5 O God, you know my folly;
the wrongs I have done are not hidden from you.
6 Let not those who hope in you be put to shame through me,
O Lord God of hosts;
let not those who seek you be brought to dishonor through me,
O God of Israel.
7 For it is for your sake that I have borne reproach,
that dishonor has covered my face.
8 I have become a stranger to my brothers,
an alien to my mother's sons.
9 For zeal for your house has consumed me,
and the reproaches of those who reproach you have fallen on me.
10 When I wept and humbled my soul with fasting,
it became my reproach.
11 When I made sackcloth my clothing,
I became a byword to them.
12 I am the talk of those who sit in the gate,
and the drunkards make songs about me.
13 But as for me, my prayer is to you, O Lord.
At an acceptable time, O God,
in the abundance of your steadfast love answer me in your saving faithfulness.
14 Deliver me
from sinking in the mire;
let me be delivered from my enemies
and from the deep waters.
15 Let not the flood sweep over me,
or the deep swallow me up,
or the pit close its mouth over me.
16 Answer me, O Lord, for your steadfast love is good;
according to your abundant mercy, turn to me.
17 Hide not your face from your servant,
for I am in distress; make haste to answer me.

18 Draw near to my soul, redeem me;
ransom me because of my enemies!
19 You know my reproach,
and my shame and my dishonor;
my foes are all known to you.
20 Reproaches have broken my heart,
so that I am in despair.
I looked for pity, but there was none,
and for comforters, but I found none.
21 They gave me poison for food,
and for my thirst they gave me sour wine to drink.
22 Let their own table before them become a snare;
and when they are at peace, let it become a trap.
23 Let their eyes be darkened, so that they cannot see,
and make their loins tremble continually.
24 Pour out your indignation upon them,
and let your burning anger overtake them.
25 May their camp be a desolation;
let no one dwell in their tents.
26 For they persecute him whom you have struck down,
and they recount the pain of those you have wounded.
27 Add to them punishment upon punishment;
may they have no acquittal from you.
28 Let them be blotted out of the book of the living;
let them not be enrolled among the righteous.
29 But I am afflicted and in pain;
let your salvation, O God, set me on high!
30 I will praise the name of God with a song;
I will magnify him with thanksgiving.
31 This will please the LORD more than an ox
or a bull with horns and hoofs.
32 When the humble see it they will be glad;
you who seek God, let your hearts revive.
33 For the LORD hears the needy

and does not despise his own people who are prisoners.
34 Let heaven and earth praise him,
the seas and everything that moves in them.
35 For God will save Zion
and build up the cities of Judah,
and people shall dwell there and possess it;
36 the offspring of his servants shall inherit it,
and those who love his name shall dwell in it.
To the choirmaster.

Broadly, we might divide this psalm into two parts:

69:1–29: prayer
69:30–36: praise

But the standard components of a lament are present:

69:1a: direct address and introductory petition
69:1b–12: lament
69:13–29: petition
- 69:13–18: plea for deliverance
- 69:19–29: imprecation or plea to avenge

69:30–36: praise
- 69:30–33: the king's praise
- 69:34–36: universal praise

## PSALM 6

A Psalm of David.
1 O Lord, rebuke me not in your anger,
nor discipline me in your wrath.
2 Be gracious to me, O Lord, for I am languishing;
heal me, O Lord, for my bones are troubled.
3 My soul also is greatly troubled.

But you, O LORD—how long?
4 Turn, O LORD, deliver my life;
save me for the sake of your steadfast love.
5 For in death there is no remembrance of you;
in Sheol who will give you praise?
6 I am weary with my moaning;
every night I flood my bed with tears;
I drench my couch with my weeping.
7 My eye wastes away because of grief;
it grows weak because of all my foes.
8 Depart from me, all you workers of evil,
for the LORD has heard the sound of my weeping.
9 The LORD has heard my plea;
the LORD accepts my prayer.
10 All my enemies shall be ashamed and greatly troubled;
they shall turn back and be put to shame in a moment.

**Overview and Message**

The components of a petition psalm here are easily discernable:

- direct address (6:1a)
- petition and lament (6:1–5)
    - seven petitions
- lament (6:6–7)
- confidence (6:8–10)
    - (implicit praise)

We may outline the psalm as follows:

6:1–5: stanza 1: petitions
  6:1–3: strophe 1: four petitions for healing
  6:4–5: strophe 2: three petitions for salvation
6:6–10: stanza 2: basis of petitions
  6:6–7: strophe 3: lament because of foes

6:8–10: strophe 4: confidence—God has heard and will deliver

In this psalm David laments a severe illness that seems as though it may result in his death (6:1–6); this, in turn, seems to embolden his enemies (6:7–10). Swooning into death and terrified that his ungodly enemies will exploit his death so that they will triumph over the faithful, the anointed king petitions the Lord to heal and save him. By faith he routs his enemies—"Get away from me"—and fortifies the faithful, assuring them that evildoers will be put to shame. Psalm 6 is an exemplary prayer of how the faithful, even on the brink of the grave, triumph by faith over evildoers and death. By six cogent theological reflections the anointed king moves the Lord to act on his behalf:

- God has disciplined him so long and so severely that the blows of his chastening rod have become a fatal sword thrust; and so he swoons in grief (6:1, 3).
- God displays his glory by his grace and unfailing love to his covenant partner (6:2).
- God will promote his glory and praise by rescuing his chosen king from the grave (6:4–5).
- David's bed-drenching tears display his extreme suffering (6:6–7).
- His malicious and malignant enemies taunt him that he is under God's curse, justifying their reason to reject him as their king (6:8–9).
- God's heaping shame on the fleeing foe will fortify the faith of the faithful (6:10). The thought is unthinkable that the Lord . . .
  - would not show his compassion to his anointed,
  - would not save him,
  - would obscure his glory,
  - would be insensitive David's tears,
  - would vindicate the wicked in their rejection of God's king,
  - and would destroy his faithful people.

**Literary Context**

This is the psalm in brief. We want to pause here to point out that although each psalm stands on its own, each psalm has a larger literary context also. In a later chapter we will seek to analyze the collection of the Psalter as a whole, but note here some evidence of editorial work in the arrangement of Psalms 1–6:

Psalm 1: blessed person—loves Torah
Psalm 2: commissions king to pray
Psalms 3–6: royal petitions for protection from enemies
  Psalm 3: many make war against king
  Psalm 4: leaders are apostates
  Psalm 5: treacherous liars subvert king
  Psalm 6: opportunistic traitors

Notice further the various situations reflected in David's petitions:

Psalm 3: war—son is the enemy
Psalm 4: drought—the cabinet is disloyal
Psalm 5: slander—bloody and deceitful rebels
Psalm 6: severe sickness—close to death

Still further, notice the alternating day-night pattern in these psalms:

Psalm 3: morning prayer (6:5)
Psalm 4: evening prayer (6:8)
Psalm 5: morning prayer (6:3)
Psalm 6: evening prayer (6:6)

Finally, notice the escalation of troubles in the evening prayers:

Psalm 4: highborn men (cabinet) losing confidence in king
Psalm 6: evildoers celebrate king's imminent death

Psalm 4: prayer before sleep
Psalm 6: doleful appeals every night

These kinds of observations evidence careful editorial work and often shed light on a given psalm under consideration. Literary context is often an enlightening factor in interpretation.

## PSALM 44

### A PSALM OF COMMUNITY LAMENT

A Maskil of the Sons of Korah.

1 O God, we have heard with our ears,
our fathers have told us,
what deeds you performed in their days,
in the days of old:
2 you with your own hand drove out the nations,
but them you planted;
you afflicted the peoples,
but them you set free;
3 for not by their own sword did they win the land,
nor did their own arm save them,
but your right hand and your arm,
and the light of your face,
for you delighted in them.
4 You are my King, O God;
ordain salvation for Jacob!
5 Through you we push down our foes;
through your name we tread down those who rise up against us.
6 For not in my bow do I trust,
nor can my sword save me.
7 But you have saved us from our foes
and have put to shame those who hate us.

8 In God we have boasted continually,
and we will give thanks to your name forever. *Selah*
9 But you have rejected us and disgraced us
and have not gone out with our armies.
10 You have made us turn back from the foe,
and those who hate us have gotten spoil.
11 You have made us like sheep for slaughter
and have scattered us among the nations.
12 You have sold your people for a trifle,
demanding no high price for them.
13 You have made us the taunt of our neighbors,
the derision and scorn of those around us.
14 You have made us a byword among the nations,
a laughingstock among the peoples.
15 All day long my disgrace is before me,
and shame has covered my face
16 at the sound of the taunter and reviler,
at the sight of the enemy and the avenger.
17 All this has come upon us,
though we have not forgotten you,
and we have not been false to your covenant.
18 Our heart has not turned back,
nor have our steps departed from your way;
19 yet you have broken us in the place of jackals
and covered us with the shadow of death.
20 If we had forgotten the name of our God
or spread out our hands to a foreign god,
21 would not God discover this?
For he knows the secrets of the heart.
22 Yet for your sake we are killed all the day long;
we are regarded as sheep to be slaughtered.
23 Awake! Why are you sleeping, O Lord?
Rouse yourself! Do not reject us forever!
24 Why do you hide your face?

Why do you forget our affliction and oppression?
25 For our soul is bowed down to the dust;
our belly clings to the ground.
26 Rise up; come to our help!
Redeem us for the sake of your steadfast love!
To the choirmaster: according to the Lilies.

**Introductory Observations**

The superscript tells us that this psalm was written by the sons of Korah. The sons of Korah were a priestly family who played an important role in temple worship. These valiant adherents of God's chosen king both guarded the temple (1 Chron. 26:19) and led in temple music that accompanied the Mosaic ritual (2 Chron. 20:19).

The psalm places its complaint in the mouth of the afflicted king and his people or army. As such it is uniquely related to Psalm 60, which also laments an otherwise unknown national defeat during David's reign. It is a community lament. We might call it "A Prayer for the Martyrs." These psalms give us a point of reference, a theology that will hold us on course. Suffering is in view, but not just any kind of suffering. Specifically, it is undeserved suffering that is in view, suffering that comes in the pursuit of faithfulness. This is often the most difficult kind of suffering. Some of the lament psalms may have deserved suffering in view, such as Psalm 51, where David pleads for relief from his suffering with guilt. But here the suffering is undeserved. The people had been faithful to the Lord and his covenant and therefore would have expected victory (cf. Deut. 28). No law has been violated, and, in fact, it is because of righteousness that they suffer, as Psalm 44:22 makes plain: "Yet for your sake we are killed all the day long; / we are regarded as sheep to be slaughtered." The suffering is not for doing what is evil but for doing what is good and right, and it is a protest, not merely a lament.

So this psalm for martyrs gives us truths to live by when we suffer unjustly. Note that at the end of the psalm the situation is not yet resolved—there has been no answer to prayer. But the psalmist has not lost faith.

Psalm 44 is rather elaborate and carefully structured on multiple levels.[9] Here we will note its components, which are standard of a lament psalm:

- direct address (44:1)
- confidence and praise (44:1–8)
- complaint (44:9–16)
- protest (44:17–22)
- petition (44:23–26)

The psalm also seems to be structured by verb tense:

- the past prosperity of Israel (44:1–8)
- the present adversity of Israel (44:9–22)
- the cry for future divine help (44:23–26)

The word "maskil" means "making prudent," but the significance of this term for the psalms that are so designated is not clear. It would seem that every psalm in the Psalter is for "making prudent." There are some words in the psalms whose meaning or precise significance is lost to us, and "maskil" is one of them, just as "Selah."

This maskil psalm reminds us that God's blessings are not automatic, a reality that remains in this dispensation (cf. Rom. 8:35–37). Yet the psalm inspires praise for and confidence in God's sublimities in the face of irrational adversity. It is preserved in Scripture to give martyrs the theology they need to continue to struggle for God's name even in death. The reason why martyrs suffer may be unknown, but the reasons for sustaining their faith can be learned from each stanza of this psalm.

**Survey Exposition**[10]

Stanza 1 (Ps. 44:1–8) teaches us the value of Scripture and history. Here from the days of the monarchy the psalmist looks to God's past deal-

9 See Bruce K. Waltke, James M. Houston, and Erika Moore, *The Psalms as Christian Lament: A Historical Commentary* (Grand Rapids, MI: Eerdmans, 2014), 187–90.

10 See also Waltke, Houston, and Moore, *Psalms as Christian Lament*, chap. 8.

ings with his people. Specifically, the exploits of Joshua, many centuries earlier, are in view. The time of grace for the Canaanites had ended. Judgment had come, and God had replaced them with his own people:

> 2 with your hand you drove out nations
> to plant them in [the land],
> you crushed peoples
> to make room for them. (CJB)

Note the parallels: from "drove out" to "crushed," a reprise of Joshua 1–12); and from "to plant" to "to make room," a reprise of Joshua 13–19. In broad sweep he recalls the events of the days of Joshua and states that it was not, in fact, Joshua's sword that accomplished so much but God himself through working wonders. In the psalmist's day their ears had heard of these things. Their "fathers [had] told" them how God had provided for his people Israel (44:1). Faithful parents had passed these accounts of God's work along to their children for generations. We still do the same today. The people of God have been finding confidence in God through the historical narratives of the Old Testament for centuries. This is how they were intended to be used (cf. Heb. 11), and this especially so for us who have received the full revelation of the greater Joshua who has come. This psalmist had been the recipient of such faithful teaching, and he draws confidence from it amid difficulty, as we do still today.

In 44:4–6 the psalmist applies these historical lessons to his own situation:

> 4 You are my King, O God;
> ordain salvation for Jacob!
> 5 Through you we push down our foes;
> through your name we tread down those who rise up against us.
> 6 For not in my bow do I trust,
> nor can my sword save me.

But we should notice the change of pronoun in 44:6. In 44:5 it is "we," but in 44:6 it is "I." Who is this "I"? The most plausible answer is the king. The psalmist has put this plea in the mouth of the king who leads the army. "I trust not in our weapons of war but in you!" The king is pleading to God on behalf of his people and his army. So we have a royal psalm in which the king and nation express praise and confidence in the Lord.

We might pause here to note that many of the Psalms are historically oriented—"psalms of narrative praise" they are sometimes called. This type of psalm has taken a prominent place in Israel's history, reaching back at least to Exodus 15 and Deuteronomy 32, narrating God's "mighty works" in Israel's earlier days. Some recount God's works during the times of the patriarchs (Ps. 105) or the exodus (106) or even the time of David (78), and some reach back to creation itself (135). Psalm 136 recounts God's works in wide panoramic view from creation onward. And many psalms, like Psalm 44, recount God's works for his people in previous generations briefly and in just broad brush.

This historical orientation of the Psalms reflects the nature of Israel's faith as historically grounded. Its theology was rooted in divine activity within history on behalf of his chosen people, a people with whom he had entered covenant relationship and therefore had done many wonderful works for them. Usually the focus is on God's saving activity, his deliverance of, and his provision for Israel. These historical realities demonstrated God's faithfulness, trustworthiness, and his steadfast love for Israel. Reciting history, then, was not only praise but also faith-stimulating encouragement. God is not remotely absent—he intervenes in history on behalf of his people and in keeping with his ancient promises. More to the point, his past actions stand as a witness and pledge of his continued love for Israel and his continued dependability.

This is the thinking that underlies 44:1–8. God is trustworthy, and he has demonstrated his faithfulness to his people throughout Israel's past history.

Present circumstances seem to belie it, however. Beginning in 44:9 we learn that the king and his army have gone down into humiliating defeat, and this is the cause for the king's complaint. Here he confesses that his strength is in the Lord, and later in the psalm he will protest that he has fought faithfully. He has fought by faith. He and his people have not turned from the Lord—they have been true to him and have trusted him. Yet they have gone down in defeat, and this is what they find so perplexing (44:9–16). This is the complaint. God does not seem to have upheld his end of the relationship. They have fought in faith for his sake (44:22), yet they have been defeated. And with a sustained rhythm and repetition of "you" introducing 44:9–13, the psalmist blames God for Israel's defeat and humiliation. His complaint is not merely that God has allowed other nations to desolate Israel, but rather that God himself has actively sought to defeat them. Psalm 44:9–10 describes their plight in literal terms:

9 But you have rejected us and disgraced us
and have not gone out with our armies.
10 You have made us turn back from the foe,
and those who hate us have gotten spoil.

So the psalmist sees a stark contrast. Whereas God previously favored the fathers and gave victory, he has now "rejected" and abandoned Israel, subjecting them to humiliation. For earlier generations he routed and plundered the enemy; now it is Israel that is routed. Psalm 44:11–12 describes their devastation in metaphorical terms:

11 You have made us like sheep for slaughter
and have scattered us among the nations.
12 You have sold your people for a trifle,
demanding no high price for them.

The dead soldiers are depicted as defenseless sheep being butchered and the survivors as sent into exile. God has "sold" them for a mere pittance—

it cost the enemy almost nothing in terms of their army's own loss of life. So the psalmist is complaining, "We lost our army, and we got nothing from the fight. We didn't kill them. They killed us. They came out flourishing, and we were plundered." Health, wealth, and prosperity gospel this is not.

Then 44:13–16 describes the king's and the nation's shame that came as a result of their defeat:

13 You have made us the taunt of our neighbors,
the derision and scorn of those around us.
14 You have made us a byword among the nations,
a laughingstock among the peoples.
15 All day long my disgrace is before me,
and shame has covered my face
16 at the sound of the taunter and reviler,
at the sight of the enemy and the avenger.

Then 44:17 begins the psalmist's protest:

17 All this has come upon us,
though we have not forgotten you,
and we have not been false to your covenant.
18 Our heart has not turned back,
nor have our steps departed from your way;
19 yet you have broken us in the place of jackals
and covered us with the shadow of death.
20 If we had forgotten the name of our God
or spread out our hands to a foreign god,
21 would not God discover this?
For he knows the secrets of the heart.
22 Yet for your sake we are killed all the day long;
we are regarded as sheep to be slaughtered.

The psalmist protests that they have been faithful and have kept the covenant. They have lived in obedience to God's law. They have not turned to false gods or idols. Israel had "not forgotten . . . / not been false . . . / not turned back . . . / [not] departed" or looked to false gods for help (44:17, 18, 20). In fact, they had gone to battle for God's own sake (44:22). And yet God had "broken" them (44:19) and had seemingly not noticed their faithfulness (44:22). The protest, very simply, is that this suffering is undeserved, as God himself knows. To be perplexed is not abnormal or wrong (cf. 2 Cor 4:8–11). Loss of faith, however, is wrong.

So we should note that the psalmist has not lost faith. His very lament assumes a covenant relationship with God that continues. Yes, he is perplexed. Yet throughout this complaint the psalmist presupposes two great truths about God that serve to sustain his faith. The first is that God is sovereign. The psalmist has no doubt that God was directing the entire situation or that their defeat could be traced in some way back to him—"*You* have crushed us" is the sense. The psalmist recognizes that God rules and that in his ruling he has reasons for all he does, even if he does not let us in on those reasons (cf. Ps. 44:24, "Why? . . . Why?"). This is vital for martyrs and all sufferers—that we know that God rules over all our affairs. And it is here that the psalmist finds confidence and ground for trust and praise. So while stanza 1 teaches us the value of Scripture and history, stanzas 2 and 3 (44:9–16, 17–22) teach us that God remains sovereign over all things.

Stanza 4 (44:23–26) petitions God to "wake up" from his indifference and "rise up" to his people's aid.

> 23 Awake! Why are you sleeping, O Lord?
> Rouse yourself! Do not reject us forever!
> 24 Why do you hide your face?
> Why do you forget our affliction and oppression?
> 25 For our soul is bowed down to the dust;
> our belly clings to the ground.
> 26 Rise up; come to our help!
> Redeem us for the sake of your steadfast love!

In his plea the psalmist provides a model of rugged faith. The basis of his plea is God's "steadfast love" (44:26), and here we find the second great truth that sustains the psalmist. Given God's covenantal commitment to his people, surely this defeat will not be the final word. The Lord will yet help. Like a child receiving a painful injection at the doctor's office, not understanding the reason for it, he just clings to his father or mother in loving trust, so the psalmist clings to Lord in the knowledge of his unfailing love. And by this he is emboldened to bring his petition. "Awake! Why are you sleeping, O Lord? / Rouse yourself! Do not reject us forever!" (44:23). It seems to the psalmist as though God has fallen asleep. "Our soul is bowed down to the dust" (44:25) in utter defeat and humiliation when it ought to be the serpent who is in the dust. "Rise up and help us; / rescue us because of your unfailing love" (44:26 NIV).

The psalm ends here, with the problem unresolved and the psalmist still pleading with God to help. The psalm leaves us where we are sometimes left, feeling as though the end has come. Help has not come, but we trust it yet will.

Psalm 44:22 affirms that Israel had suffered "for [the LORD's] sake," but it does not elaborate. But as Kidner perceptively remarks, "It implies the revolutionary thought that suffering may be a battle-scar rather than a punishment; the price of loyalty in a world which is at war with God."[11]

When the psalmist completes his psalm he hands it "to the choirmaster" (ESV) or "for the director of music" (NIV) for us all to sing. His psalm is in the canon of Scripture because God eventually answered him. And we sing with him, and with the apostle Paul (Rom. 8:35–37), suffering yet trusting and with eager anticipation for final vindication.

Defeated though righteous—this is what our Lord Jesus experienced on the cross. He was abandoned, rejected, and utterly humiliated. And yet he died trusting his Father that final help would yet come. This is a "royal" psalm, a psalm about the king and his army who have gone

11 Derek Kidner, *Psalms 1–72* (London: Inter-Varsity Press, 1973), 187.

down in defeat. And in that respect this king foreshadows the greater King who went down in defeat also. But, of course, that was Friday.

Today, righteous sufferers recall the history of God's power and faithfulness in redemptive history also, particularly the climactic defeat of sin in the death of Jesus, his vindication in resurrection, his present kingly reign, and his promised return.

## PSALM 51

### A PSALM OF INDIVIDUAL PENITENTIAL LAMENT

One subcategory of lament psalms is the penitential lament, psalms that make confession of and lament sin. The lament form remains, only the subject matter is not personal adversity but moral failure; the "enemy" in view is the psalmist's own sin and guilt. Here David cannot protest his innocence but rather confesses his guilt; hence, the petition is for God's forgiveness. Invariably, in a penitential psalm the psalmist is in distress borne out of a consciousness of sin, and he longs and hopes that the God of mercy will intervene in grace. There are seven of these "penitential psalms": Psalms 6, 32, 38, 51, 102, 130, and 143. Here we examine the most famous of them.

A Psalm of David, when Nathan the prophet went to him, after he had gone in to Bathsheba.

1 Have mercy on me, O God,
according to your steadfast love;
according to your abundant mercy
blot out my transgressions.
2 Wash me thoroughly from my iniquity,
and cleanse me from my sin!
3 For I know my transgressions,
and my sin is ever before me.
4 Against you, you only, have I sinned
and done what is evil in your sight,
so that you may be justified in your words

and blameless in your judgment.
5 Behold, I was brought forth in iniquity,
and in sin did my mother conceive me.
6 Behold, you delight in truth in the inward being,
and you teach me wisdom in the secret heart.
7 Purge me with hyssop, and I shall be clean;
wash me, and I shall be whiter than snow.
8 Let me hear joy and gladness;
let the bones that you have broken rejoice.
9 Hide your face from my sins,
and blot out all my iniquities.
10 Create in me a clean heart, O God,
and renew a right spirit within me.
11 Cast me not away from your presence,
and take not your Holy Spirit from me.
12 Restore to me the joy of your salvation,
and uphold me with a willing spirit.
13 Then I will teach transgressors your ways,
and sinners will return to you.
14 Deliver me from bloodguiltiness, O God,
O God of my salvation,
and my tongue will sing aloud of your righteousness.
15 O Lord, open my lips,
and my mouth will declare your praise.
16 For you will not delight in sacrifice, or I would give it;
you will not be pleased with a burnt offering.
17 The sacrifices of God are a broken spirit;
a broken and contrite heart, O God, you will not despise.
18 Do good to Zion in your good pleasure;
build up the walls of Jerusalem;
19 then will you delight in right sacrifices,
in burnt offerings and whole burnt offerings;
then bulls will be offered on your altar.

To the choirmaster.

## Setting

Psalm 51 is another of the fourteen psalms that identifies its historical situation in the superscript: this psalm was written in the aftermath of David's sin against Bathsheba and her husband Uriah. It is another lament-petition psalm, but it differs from Psalm 3 in one very important respect: in Psalm 3 David's suffering, though in a broad sense the consequences of his own failures, was undeserved. In cases of undeserved suffering the lamenting psalmist may even ground his appeal for help in his own innocence. But in Psalm 51 David's trial is of his own making—he was guilty of heinous sins. And so the petition is for forgiveness: it is a penitential lament, and his plea for help is grounded only in God's mercy.

In Jewish tradition this psalm was appropriately sung in conjunction with the sounding of the ram's horn on the Day of Atonement. In some Christian traditions this psalm has been routinely read on Ash Wednesday. In this psalm David models genuine repentance, and so, given our continual sin, this is a psalm that all God's people should know well.

According to the superscript, if we are to understand the psalm, we must review that chapter of David's life recorded for us in 2 Samuel 11–12. There are sins of passion, committed suddenly in the heat of the moment, and there are calculated sins, sins carefully planned and carried out. David's adultery with Bathsheba may have been a sin of passion, but his murder of Uriah was cold and calculated and carried out over a two-week period; it was premeditated murder. And as we saw in connection with Psalm 3, this complex of sins would haunt David for the rest of his life.

The account of David's sin begins with a notice that it was the time of year "when kings go out to battle" (2 Sam. 11:1), so it seems David should have been out with his troops. And remaining home, from his palace roof he sees Bathsheba bathing, and he lusts for her. Perhaps she could have been more careful, but the biblical writer lays the blame on David who had her brought to him; David also blames himself, not her. This adulterous affair resulted in a pregnancy, and when Bathsheba notified David of it, he launched a plan to cover it up.

Uriah was a Hittite, a Gentile, who had converted to Israel's God and now was a loyal soldier in David's army—one of thirty great warriors, in fact, whom David celebrates. He was away to battle with Joab, so David had him brought home under the guise of seeking a report from him concerning the war. The plan was to make it appear that the child to be born to Bathsheba was from her husband. But principled as he was, Uriah refused the comforts of home while his brothers were away to battle, and he did not return home to his wife but slept instead at the palace. David made him drunk, but still he would not go home to his wife.

So David sends Uriah back to the front with a message for Joab—a death sentence for Uriah—to put Uriah up in the front of the attack and press against the city (Rabbah Ammon), and then pull back from Uriah so that he will be slain. And what appears to be a tragedy of war is David's calculated murder of a loyal soldier. It was the sword of the Ammonites that killed him, but it was David's murder. Still, the plan worked, and when Bathsheba's time of mourning was over, David made her his wife. He thought his sin was successfully hidden. The baby was born, a boy, and David was spared from scandal.

"But the thing that David had done displeased the LORD" (2 Sam. 11:27), and so next in the narrative (2 Sam. 12) we read that God sends his prophet Nathan to confront David and expose his sin. Nathan tells him a parable of a rich man who abused a poor man and stole his only sheep. David was enraged over it and demanded that justice be served. But then Nathan told him that he, David, was the man—that he had defied God and rejected his word in his sins of adultery and murder:

> Why have you despised the word of the LORD, to do what is evil in his sight? You have struck down Uriah the Hittite with the sword and have taken his wife to be your wife and have killed him with the sword of the Ammonites. (2 Sam. 12:9)

The prophet's indictment is that David had "despised the word of the LORD," and it would seem that specifically he had two or three passages of the Torah in mind. First, Numbers 35:16, which assigns the death penalty for premeditated murder. The second is Leviticus 20:10 (cf. Deut. 22:22), which assigns the death penalty to both the man and the woman involved in the adulterous affair. Both of David's sins were capital offenses.

In response to the prophet's confrontation, as the superscript implies, David owns up to everything. He does not, like Adam before him, blame his wife, or, like King Jeroboam after him, rebel (1 Kings 13:4). His immediate response is, "I have sinned against the LORD" (2 Sam. 12:13). He takes full responsibility, and he humbles himself, broken before the Lord. He is guilty, and he knows it. He is under sentence of death, and it is too late to change it. He cannot go back and undo what is done.

It may be good at this point to address the question of how a man guilty of such sins could be "a man after [God's] heart" (1 Sam. 13:14; cf. 16:7). Can such a sinner be a saint? The problem is more apparent than real. David was indeed capable of great sins. But flawed and inconsistent as it was, his heart was for God. He reveals his heart at the return of the ark to Jerusalem (2 Sam. 6:5, 14; 1 Chron. 15–16; Ps. 132:1–5) and in his affection for the place of God's presence (Ps. 27:4). We see his zeal for God in his eagerness to build a temple for him (2 Sam. 7; cf. Ps. 69:9). We see his heart for God in his praise psalms and even in his laments, which are consistently doxological. And we see his heart even here in his prompt and frank confession. David was a deeply flawed man, and there is evidence of it beyond the specific sins in view here. God's work in him was not yet complete. But in the larger picture it is equally evident that his heart followed God's heart. And here it is with broken heart that he humbles himself before the Lord, repents fully, and acknowledges that his only hope is mercy. By his parable of the rich man taking the poor's man lamb, Nathan brought out David's true nature: a zeal for justice and, having seen his awful sin, he confessed he was guilty. In that confession, he handed his life over to God to kill him according to his law, or to forgive him according to his grace.

As we will see in connection with the imprecatory psalms, God offers the penitent escape from the judgment of the law. "Whoever conceals his transgressions will not prosper, / but he who confesses and forsakes them will obtain mercy" (Prov. 28:13). Confessing and forsaking sin is what David does in Psalm 51. Offering no excuses he confesses his sin and renounces it. So Nathan responds, "The LORD also has put away your sin; you shall not die" (2 Sam. 12:13). And David finds full forgiveness. There are life consequences to his sin that will haunt him, but God has forgiven him; he will not be put to death. In fact, the forgiveness is so great that out of his marriage to Bathsheba would come another son, Solomon, who was called Jedidiah—"beloved by God"—and through whom the Messiah would come. Where David's sin abounded, God's grace abounded more.

This is the setting David recalls for us as we read his psalm.

### Survey Exposition[12]

We should also keep in mind what we have learned about the structure of petition psalms. Psalm 51 adapts this form to his lament of sin and includes these elements:

- superscript
- direct address and introductory petition (51:1–2)
- lament: confession of sin (51:3–6)
- petition for salvation (51:7–12)
- thanksgiving (praise) and postlude (51:13–19)
- postscript

The **direct address** is first: "O God" (51:1). And in this case it is combined with an **introductory petition**:

12 See also Bruce K. Waltke and James M. Houston, *Psalms as Christian Worship: A Historical Commentary* (Grand Rapids, MI: Eerdmans, 2010), chap. 14; also Bruce K. Waltke, "Atonement in Psalm 51," in *The Dance between God and Humanity: Reading the Bible Today as the People of God* (Grand Rapids, MI: Eerdmans, 2013), 203–11.

1 Have mercy on me, O God,
  according to your steadfast love;
according to your abundant mercy
  blot out my transgressions.
2 Wash me thoroughly from my iniquity,
  and cleanse me from my sin!

The superscript identifies the occasion of this psalm as not just his sin with Bathsheba but first the confrontation of Nathan (2 Sam. 12:1–15). David's response to the prophet was immediate confession (2 Sam. 12:13, "I have sinned!"), of which this psalm gives fuller account.

One striking feature of this introductory petition is David's vocabulary for sin: transgression (פֶּשַׁע), iniquity (עָוֹן), and sin (חַטָּאת). These are the primary terms for sin in the Old Testament. Each connotes a deviation from a standard. "Transgression" implies rebellion. "Iniquity" connotes perversion, a twisting out of order, and entails the notion of guilt. And "sin" implies a missing the mark or standard. At the outset David comes clean and without reservation confesses his unqualified guilt.

Another striking feature of this introductory petition is David's focus on three attributes of God that display his glory: his mercy (חָנַן), his unfailing love (חֶסֶד), and his compassion (רַחֲמִים). It appears David is making use of Exodus 34:6–7, where, after Moses asks to see God's glory, God proclaims his name:

> [6] The Lord passed before him and proclaimed, "The Lord, the Lord, a God merciful and gracious, slow to anger, and abounding in steadfast love and faithfulness, [7] keeping steadfast love for thousands, forgiving iniquity and transgression and sin.

David's initial plea for forgiveness is grounded in the gracious character and ways of God. He cannot in this case protest his innocence. His only hope is that the Lord is compassionate, a God who takes pity on frail, sinful people, and a God whose love is utterly devoted, covenantally, to his people's good.

The third feature of this introductory petition is David's specific requests. Again, there are three: "blot out . . . wash . . . cleanse." First, he pleads for forensic pardon, legal forgiveness: "blot out my transgressions." The Old Testament has about fifty ways of expressing forgiveness. There are proper terms, like "forgiveness," and there are figurative expressions, like "casting sins into the sea," or "removing them as far as east is from west." Here David asks God to "blot out" his transgressions—to wipe the slate clean, as it were, erase them, delete them. But David does not plead for legal forgiveness only; he also asks for moral cleansing. His sin has made him unclean, and so he asks, "Wash me." That is, "Launder me," "De-sin me!" Third, he asks God to "cleanse" him, to purify him and befit him for temple worship. This is what God does for his people. In 1 Corinthians 6:9–10, for example, the apostle Paul makes a list of different kinds of sinners: unrighteous, sexually immoral, idolaters, adulterers, men who practice homosexuality, thieves, the greedy, drunkards, revilers, swindlers. But then he adds, "And such were some of you. But you were washed, you were sanctified, you were justified in the name of the Lord Jesus Christ and by the Spirit of our God" (1 Cor. 6:11). In Christ Jesus we receive both pardon and cleansing, and in him we are made pure and acceptable in worship.

After the address and introductory petition we have the **lament** (Ps. 51:3–6), here a lament over sin with confession:

3 For I know my transgressions,
and my sin is ever before me.
4 Against you, you only, have I sinned
and done what is evil in your sight,
so that you may be justified in your words
and blameless in your judgment.
5 Behold, I was brought forth in iniquity,
and in sin did my mother conceive me.
6 Behold, you delight in truth in the inward being,
and you teach me wisdom in the secret heart.

David's lament has two areas of focus. First, he confesses his sinful behavior, his overt acts of transgression (51:3–4). And in doing so, he takes full responsibility, as the personal pronouns indicate: "my transgressions . . . / my sin . . . / have I sinned / and done evil." That is to say, "I am guilty. It's all on me." There is no holding back. God is right to judge him (51:4). And adding "my sin is ever before me" (51:3), he seems to indicate that his sins continue to haunt him, and now he asks God to take away the memory of them.

David's remark in 51:4 shows his spiritual insight: "against you, you only, have I sinned / and done what is evil in your sight." He had sinned against God only? To be sure, David had sinned against Bathsheba, against Uriah, against Joab, against his army—against all Israel. And yet his vocabulary—"transgressions," "iniquity," "sin"—reminds him that his actions were above all else a violation of God's law. It was not just human standards but God's moral demands that were transgressed. And what concerned David above all else was not whether the people of Israel—Bathsheba, Ahithophel, Uriah, his family, Joab, or others—forgave him. What mattered was that God would forgive him.

But in his confession David goes deeper than just his sinful actions. He probes and considers just why he sinned so terribly. And he finds the answer in his own moral impotence:

> 5 Behold, I was brought forth in iniquity,
> and in sin did my mother conceive me.
> 6 Behold, you delight in truth in the inward being,
> and you teach me wisdom in the secret heart.

The only sufficient explanation for his extreme sins is his deep sinfulness. David's sins can be explained only in terms of his own morally twisted heart, and so he confesses himself to be the root problem. From his birth onward—no, from his very conception—his moral state was sinful. This is the contradiction of human nature. Made in the image of God, we know right from wrong. And we learn responsibility from God's word. But there is a struggle—in our heart, we find a distinct drive to sin. And so David confesses his original sin, that *he* is the root cause of his sins. No excuses may be found.

We should take note here of the thoroughness of David's repentance. We may wonder if "repentance of original sin" is necessary. Indeed, scoffers have asked this in ridicule, and some may be tempted to find in original sin an excuse for certain behavior. But not David. If repentance is not merely sorrow but a renunciation of all sin with corresponding change of life direction, and if "original sin" entails not merely Adam's first transgression but our own inherent depravity and aversion to God, then apart from a recognition and abhorrence of our iniquitous hearts, any "repentance" is altogether inadequate. David probes deeply, beneath his sinful actions, and finds the root cause in his own sinful heart, and when he sees it, he deplores it, and he takes sides with God against himself.

All this shapes his **petition** in 51:7–12, which he expresses in a series of imperatives:

> 7 Purge me with hyssop, and I shall be clean;
> wash me, and I shall be whiter than snow.
> 8 Let me hear joy and gladness;
> let the bones that you have broken rejoice.
> 9 Hide your face from my sins,
> and blot out all my iniquities.
> 10 Create in me a clean heart, O God,
> and renew a right spirit within me.
> 11 Cast me not away from your presence,
> and take not your Holy Spirit from me.
> 12 Restore to me the joy of your salvation,
> and uphold me with a willing spirit.

These twelve petitions correspond to his twofold confession of his sins and of his sinfulness. In 51:7–9 David asks God for forgiveness of his sins, and here his overt acts of sin are in view. Hyssop (51:7) was a bushy plant used on two occasions. When a person came into contact with a carcass, he would go to the priest who then would dip a hyssop branch into blood and water and sprinkle him with both. Here "hyssop" stands in metonymy for the atoning blood which it ritually applied. In that symbolic act of ritual cleansing, the person was transferred from the realm of death, into the realm of life. According to the book of Hebrews this all anticipates the cleansing blood of Christ (Heb. 9:13–14). In a similar way the hyssop was also used in the ritual cleansing of a person who had been healed of leprosy. So in Psalm 51:7 David appeals to the sacrificial system for ritual cleansing.

Psalm 51:9 employs two metaphors for forgiveness, while 51:8 pleads for the desperately needed word and assurance of pardon. "Let me hear joy and gladness" (51:8) is a figurative expression—we cannot hear gladness or any emotional state. The idea is that David desires to hear that which would produce joy and gladness: the word of forgiveness from God spoken by the prophet (2 Sam. 12:13). The affliction of soul David sensed because of his sin was devastatingly poignant, and he finds, correspondingly, that there can be no joy to compare with that of appeased remorse and forgiveness.

In Psalm 51:10–12 David, with his original sin and moral impotence in mind, asks for spiritual renewal. If we are born sinful, what is needed is deep moral renewal—a "clean heart" and a "right spirit." David recognizes this need and confesses it. He needs moral enablement—a new spirit—and he highlights this need in the second line of each of these verses:

51:10b: "renew a right spirit within me."
51:11b: "take not your Holy Spirit from me."
51:12b: "uphold me with a willing spirit."

David was the anointed king, enabled by the Holy Spirit. He had seen how Saul, his predecessor, could not function as king when God took his Spirit from him. And so in 51:11 he acknowledges his dependence upon the Spirit of God and asks that he not be taken away as he was from Saul.

Next, in 51:13–17 David offers **praise**:

13 Then I will teach transgressors your ways,
and sinners will return to you.
14 Deliver me from bloodguiltiness, O God,
O God of my salvation,
and my tongue will sing aloud of your righteousness.
15 O Lord, open my lips,
and my mouth will declare your praise.
16 For you will not delight in sacrifice, or I would give it;
you will not be pleased with a burnt offering.
17 The sacrifices of God are a broken spirit;
a broken and contrite heart, O God, you will not despise.

As we have seen, petition psalms routinely include an expression of trust at this point, but in this case, David cannot presume on God's forgiveness. Instead, he anticipates his praise with the petition, "Then I will teach transgressors your ways" (51:13). The "ways" of God are his mercy, unfailing love, and compassion to which David appealed in 51:1—the actions of God in grace toward sinners. David's plea here, and implicit vow, is that he may declare God's ill-deserved kindness and compassion to others from his own experience of forgiveness, as a result of which others "will return" to God in repentance also. Likewise in 51:14–15 he vows that in forgiveness he will "sing aloud" and "declare" God's praise.

Some have assumed that in 51:16–17 David rejects the sacrificial system of Moses, but this misses David's point. At this point in a lament the psalmist will typically include an expression of grateful praise accompanied with a thank (acknowledgment) offering, as we will see in the next chapter. Here in 51:13–15 David anticipates such words of praise, and in 51:16–17 he anticipates his sacrifice. But given the circumstances of this lament (i.e., his sins, a pregnant mistress, her dead husband), such celebratory activity is inappropriate. "You do not delight in [such a] sacrifice, or I would bring it. . . . / My sacrifice, O God, is a broken spirit" (NIV). David is not rejecting the sacrificial system or his own need of it; indeed, in 51:7 and 51:19 he affirms it.

David's words conform with Leviticus 5:1–6 and Numbers 5:5–10, which call for confession of sin before sacrifice.[13]

Finally, in the closing verses we have the characteristic **conclusion** and **wish**:

> 18 Do good to Zion in your good pleasure;
> build up the walls of Jerusalem;
> 19 then will you delight in right sacrifices,
> in burnt offerings and whole burnt offerings;
> then bulls will be offered on your altar.

David has sinned, he has repented before the Lord, and in mercy God has forgiven him. But David wishes for more—that God's blessing would not be withdrawn from the kingdom because of his sin. If the king is restored, he pleads, then restore the kingdom also (51:18). And then God will again be pleased with whole burnt offerings (51:19). The kingdom can be right again because the king himself is right.

David's cleansing was so thorough and his forgiveness so great that out of his adultery sprang Solomon, the most richly blessed of all kings, and through him, though David did not see it in his lifetime, came the King of kings.

It is significant that after writing this psalm, David delivers it "to the choirmaster" for the congregation to sing. Such lament over sin is appropriate for us all. So also is his plea for mercy and forgiveness. The atoning blood applied by the hyssop (51:7) echoes the substitutionary sacrifice of the Passover lamb (Ex. 12:22) and points forward to Christ—who took the adulterer's and murderer's sins to himself (Isa. 53:6; Rom. 4:25; 2 Cor. 5:21)—and to his sacrifice (cf. John 19:29) that alone satisfies for sin (Rom. 3:25) and secures forgiveness (Eph. 1:7; 1 John 1:7). The many metaphors David employs to describe God's forgiveness—"blot out . . . / wash . . . / cleanse . . . / hide your face . . . / deliver," etc.—all find their reality in Christ. The "new heart" for which David pled is precisely

13 Waltke, *Dance between God and Humanity*, 211.

what is promised in the new covenant (Jer. 31:31–34; Ezek. 36:26; 2 Cor. 5:17). And it is the very essence of the Christian gospel that bestows the unsurpassed joy of the sinner's acceptance in bold assurance that in Jesus Christ God has been appeased and our sins justly forgiven.

## PSALM 22

A Psalm of David.

1 My God, my God, why have you forsaken me?
Why are you so far from saving me, from the words of my groaning?
2 O my God, I cry by day, but you do not answer,
and by night, but I find no rest.
3 Yet you are holy,
enthroned on the praises of Israel.
4 In you our fathers trusted;
they trusted, and you delivered them.
5 To you they cried and were rescued;
in you they trusted and were not put to shame.
6 But I am a worm and not a man,
scorned by mankind and despised by the people.
7 All who see me mock me;
they make mouths at me; they wag their heads;
8 "He trusts in the Lord; let him deliver him;
let him rescue him, for he delights in him!"
9 Yet you are he who took me from the womb;
you made me trust you at my mother's breasts.
10 On you was I cast from my birth,
and from my mother's womb you have been my God.
11 Be not far from me,
for trouble is near,
and there is none to help.
12 Many bulls encompass me;
strong bulls of Bashan surround me;

13 they open wide their mouths at me,
like a ravening and roaring lion.
14 I am poured out like water,
and all my bones are out of joint;
my heart is like wax;
it is melted within my breast;
15 my strength is dried up like a potsherd,
and my tongue sticks to my jaws;
you lay me in the dust of death.
16 For dogs encompass me;
a company of evildoers encircles me;
they have pierced my hands and feet—
17 I can count all my bones—
they stare and gloat over me;
18 they divide my garments among them,
and for my clothing they cast lots.
19 But you, O Lord, do not be far off!
O you my help, come quickly to my aid!
20 Deliver my soul from the sword,
my precious life from the power of the dog!
21 Save me from the mouth of the lion!
You have rescued me from the horns of the wild oxen!
22 I will tell of your name to my brothers;
in the midst of the congregation I will praise you:
23 You who fear the Lord, praise him!
All you offspring of Jacob, glorify him,
and stand in awe of him, all you offspring of Israel!
24 For he has not despised or abhorred
the affliction of the afflicted,
and he has not hidden his face from him,
but has heard, when he cried to him.
25 From you comes my praise in the great congregation;
my vows I will perform before those who fear him.
26 The afflicted shall eat and be satisfied;

those who seek him shall praise the LORD!
May your hearts live forever!
27 All the ends of the earth shall remember
and turn to the LORD,
and all the families of the nations
shall worship before you.
28 For kingship belongs to the LORD,
and he rules over the nations.
29 All the prosperous of the earth eat and worship;
before him shall bow all who go down to the dust,
even the one who could not keep himself alive.
30 Posterity shall serve him;
it shall be told of the Lord to the coming generation;
31 they shall come and proclaim his righteousness to a people yet unborn,
that he has done it.

## Introductory Considerations

In this section of the book we are examining lament psalms with some specific samples. Psalm 3 is the first lament. Psalm 51 is a distinctive kind of lament, a penitential lament. Psalm 22 is distinctive also in that it is both an individual lament and a distinct type of messianic psalm. Here David's experience of *abandonment* foreshadows that of Christ, who took the words of this psalm on his own lips in his crucifixion (Ps. 22:1; Matt. 27:46). The Gospel writers, especially Matthew and John, frequently allude to this psalm in their accounts of Christ's passion:

- the cry of abandonment (Ps. 22:1; Matt. 27:46; Mark 15:34)
- the mocking of his enemies (Ps. 22:7–8; Matt. 27:43; Luke 23:35)
- the agony of his stretched bones (Ps. 22:14)
- the parching thirst (Ps. 22:15; John 19:28–29)
- the digging holes into his hands and feet (Ps. 22:16; John 20:27)
- the gloating of the crowds (Ps. 22:17; Matt 27:39–40)

- the casting lots for his garments (Ps. 22:18; Matt. 27:35; Mark 15:24; John 19:23–24)

So also Psalm 22:22 is placed on the lips of Jesus in Hebrews 2:11–13. No psalm is alluded to more frequently in the Gospels than this one. This psalm functions "typically" in its David-Christ foreshadowings. But the psalm is more than that. It is prophetic, for David's language at times far transcends his own experience and corresponds directly to that of Jesus. David, after all, was not just a "type" of Christ but also an inspired prophet who spoke of him (Matt. 22:41–43; Luke 24:44; Acts. 2:30–31). Franz Delitzsch's designation of Psalm 22 as typical-prophetic is appropriate,[14] and Kidner remarks accordingly:

> The language of the psalm defies a naturalistic explanation; the best account is in the terms used by Peter concerning another psalm of David: "Being therefore a prophet . . . he foresaw and spoke of . . . the Christ" (Acts 2:30f).[15]

Jesus's cry of abandonment, then, must not be misunderstood in terms of despair. Jesus went to his cross with a sense of determination (Luke 9:51), intending by his death to fulfill the prophetic word (Matt. 26:53–56; Mark 10:32–33; Luke 24:27, 44), as his citation of this psalm in Matthew's narrative makes plain (Matt. 27:39–46). Yet this psalm may well reflect in the background David's own lament and sense of divine abandonment, and as such it serves all the church in her following Christ in the way of the cross.

### Survey Exposition[16]

The introductory cry, "My God, why have you forsaken me?" expresses a complaint, but in the rest of the psalm the tone is lament, not complaint. In any case, the motifs of a petition psalm are obvious:

14 C. F. Keil and F. Delitzsch, *Commentary on the Old Testament*, vol. 5 (Peabody, MA: Hendrickson, 1996), 193–94.

15 Kidner, *Psalms 1–72*, 122.

16 See also Waltke and Houston, *Psalms as Christian Worship*, chap. 12.

- direct address (22:1a, 19a)
- lament and confidence (22:1–10)
    - lament (22:1b–2, 6–8, 11b–18)
    - confidence (22:3–5, 9–10)
- lament and petition (22:11–21)
    - transition (22:11)
    - lament (22:12–18)
    - petition (22:19–21)
- praise (22:22–31).

We may outline this more simply:

22:1–10: lament combined with confidence and praise
  22:1–5: forsaken by God and God's faithfulness to ancestors
  22:6–10: forsaken by mankind and God's faithfulness to psalmist
22:11: transition verse (janus) that continues the lament yet begins the petition that will follow
22:12–21: lament and petition
  22:12–18: lament
  22:19–21: petition
22:22–31: praise
  22:22–26: in the present generation of God's people
  22:27–31: in future generations of God's people

Although the elements of a lament psalm are not entirely separated, the psalmist artfully constructs his psalm with extensive symmetry. The psalm falls into three stanzas of ten verses each, plus a transition verse (22:11). Each stanza consists of two strophes; stanza 1 consists of alternating parallels; and stanzas 1 and 3 balance exactly, each with two strophes of five verses each. Beyond this, parts of the psalm alternate almost rhythmically between lament and confidence, and between "But I . . . Yet you." As Kidner observes, 22:1–21 is

> marked by a throbbing alternation of "I/me"-sections, of increasing length (verses 1–2, 6–8, 12–18), with "Thou"-sections of increasing urgency and immediacy (verses 3–5, 9–11, 19–21). The pattern will change at verse 22 from this alternation to a rapidly expanding circle of praise and vision.[17]

The psalmist's situation may seem desperate, but he is able to compose the psalm with great skill. He laments and has cause to lament. And he is passionate. But his emotions have not left him out of control.

*Stanza 1 (22:1–10)*

In the first stanza David laments that he is forsaken by God (22:1–5) and the people (22:6–10). The God who has forsaken him is the very God who appointed him as king and promised him so much. Despite David's suffering, God remains silent and does not answer the king's prayers (22:1–2). David's circumstances are dire, yet for all his pleading "day and night," there is no response from heaven. God appears to have forsaken him. In his *A Grief Observed*, C. S. Lewis employs the extended metaphor of a supplicant knocking desperately on the door of heaven only to be shut out and refused.[18] This was David's experience, and this was the experience of our Lord (Matt. 27:46).

"But you" (Ps. 22:3) marks the typical turn from complaint to confidence. In 22:3–5 David finds confidence in God's past faithfulness to the fathers. They trusted him, he was "enthroned on their praises," and he brought them to safety. Yet David's enemies despise him and mock his God-forsaken condition (22:6–8). Still not losing his confidence, he is bolstered by God's past faithfulness even to David himself (22:9–10). From infancy he has trusted God, and God has cared for him. His situation is dire, but he has not lost all hope. Though he laments, he does not do so without faith, and his lament will end in praise. This is doxological lament, and that is what sanctifies it.

17 Kidner, *Psalms 1–72*, 123.

18 C. S. Lewis, *A Grief Observed* (New York: Harper One, 1961).

*Stanza 2 (22:11–21)*

Psalm 22:11 transitions from the first to the second stanza, expressing both lament and the petition that will follow. "Be not far from me, / for trouble is near, / and there is none to help." In 22:12–18 David expresses lament over persecution by prominent and powerful people, and then in 22:19–21 he expresses his petition. His lament first describes his enemies as animals—as bulls (22:12) and as lions (22:13)—the powerful. Then he describes his own condition and experience (22:14–15). Then he again describes his enemies as animals, this time scavenging and dangerous dogs (22:16). And then again he describes his own condition and experience (22:17–18). The picture he draws is that of weakness and helplessness before the overwhelming strength of a vicious and determined enemy.

In 22:19–21, David finally expresses his petition, but it is a petition woven together with lament, resuming his depiction of his enemies as wild animals. He asks God to reverse his situation and with the same imagery he used previously, only in reverse order. His petition is that God will not delay (22:19) and save him from death (22:20–21).

*Stanza 3 (22:22–31)*

The opening of the closing stanza could not stand in sharper contrast to the opening of the first—from the cry of abandonment to a celebration of "the good life in God's presence as the 'seed' serves the Lord."[19] David's shift to praise (22:22) is as sudden and dramatic as a resurrection from the dead. He offers both words of praise (22:22–24) and a sacrifice of praise (22:25–26), and his extended note of exulting praise marks the entire final stanza. After lament for abandonment and ruthless persecution, he now rejoices in triumph from death and the prospect of universal dominion. First, he addresses the Lord with words of his own resolve: "I will tell of your name to my brothers; / in the midst of the congregation I will praise you" (22:22). Then he calls

19 James M. Hamilton Jr., *Psalms*, vol. 1, Evangelical Biblical Theology Commentary (Bellingham, WA: Lexham, 2021), 278.

the whole covenant people to praise the Lord (22:22–27). There is a noticeable escalation here as David's testimony of praise for salvation from death expands in both space and time—from brothers (22:22) to all the offspring of Jacob (22:23) to all the nations who tell the praise throughout all generations (22:27–31). The deliverance God gives will result in God's praise from everywhere forever.

Typical of lament psalms, David concludes with an expression of wish—a wish for all peoples of all generations to worship the Lord, the God of Israel. The psalm's essential message is summarized in this final stanza. God delivered the psalmist from death at the hands of the wicked. In spite of God's awful delay, he answers prayer and upholds ultimate justice. And that saving act will bring all people in space and time to worship the Lord.

**The Bigger Picture**

The features and structure of this lament psalm are clearly discernible—the lament, the expressions of confidence, the petition, and the praise. It seems to have been written in the context of great suffering. And on this level it serves as a model of faithful suffering. He takes his suffering to the Lord in prayer. He takes hope from God's past faithfulness to his people and to David himself. He pleads for deliverance. And even before deliverance comes he vows to give God praise. We learn from David how to suffer—and lament—faithfully.

And yet David's point of reference is not always immediately clear. The language seems metaphorical, but the metaphors have no obvious point of reference in David's own experience. To our knowledge, David's physical condition was never so marred as Psalm 22:14–15 and 22:17 describe—bones out of joint, body disfigured, heart failing, tongue sticking to his jaws, and in the very pains of death. Nor were his hands and feet ever pierced (22:16). And no one ever cast lots for his clothing (22:18). Even if we grant hyperbole, David's language goes well beyond his own experience. Yet all of this—the casting of lots for the garments (22:18), the parching thirst (22:15), the agony of disjointed bones (22:14), the digging of holes into the hands and feet (22:16), and the mocking by enemies (22:8)—describes exactly the scene of a Roman crucifixion, a form of execution unknown to David.

As we noted above, David was a prophet, and not until our Lord's crucifixion would this psalm be fully understood. As it turns out, the suffering described here involves little hyperbole and metaphor; rather, it prophetically describes in exact terms the experience of the Lord Jesus Christ:

> And those who passed by derided him, wagging their heads and saying, "You who would destroy the temple and rebuild it in three days, save yourself! If you are the Son of God, come down from the cross." So also the chief priests, with the scribes and elders, mocked him, saying, "He saved others; he cannot save himself. He is the King of Israel; let him come down now from the cross, and we will believe in him. He trusts in God; let God deliver him now, if he desires him. For he said, 'I am the Son of God.'" And the robbers who were crucified with him also reviled him in the same way.
>
> Now from the sixth hour there was darkness over all the land until the ninth hour. And about the ninth hour Jesus cried out with a loud voice, saying, "Eli, Eli, lema sabachthani?" that is, "My God, my God, why have you forsaken me?" (Matt. 27:39–46)

Our Lord's cry of abandonment can be explained only in terms of his voluntary sin-bearing death as the substitute for his people, for he was innocent. His suffering was in place of his people. He was abandoned by God because he bore our curse (Gal. 3:13). His weakness before the Jewish and Roman authorities was no surprise to him, as he himself signals for us in his citation of Psalm 22 and as Matthew's narrative confirms. It was the fulfillment of the prophetic word. Moreover, the call for vengeance on his enemies, so typical of the lament psalms, is absent here. This was the hour for which the Lord Jesus had come, the hour that David described so precisely some ten centuries in advance.

So also with David's concluding praise. His words, "I will tell of your name to my brothers; / in the midst of the congregation I will praise you" (Ps. 22:22), echo in the words of the resurrected Christ: "Do not be afraid; go and tell my brothers to go to Galilee, and there they will see me" (Matt. 28:10). It would seem that this psalm was on our Lord's mind still. And the (resurrection) deliverance that God brought him resulted in God's praise from all the nations forever (Ps. 22:27–31). David's call for all peoples universally for all generations to praise the Lord is precisely the defining mission of this age (Matt. 28:18–19). Psalm 22 is not merely a sample of Davidic typology; it is prophecy.

Some years ago, I (Bruce) was vacationing with my wife in Victoria, Canada. At the inn where we stayed, there was a picture on the wall, showing a blacksmith's armory, and a blacksmith stood in front; his hearth and bellows were in the back. There was also a shiny new canon in the front that he had just made, and a messenger was reading to him. Evidently the news being read to him was not good because in the painting the blacksmith's face was marked by a gasping astonishment. So I asked the proprietress if she would tell us the story behind the picture. She told us that the picture captures the moment when the message came that the Duke of Wellington had been defeated.

In 1815 the Duke of Wellington led his army against the French army of Napoleon Bonaparte—the famous battle of Waterloo. After the battle, they wanted to inform the people of England of the victory. In those days they communicated at such a distance by semaphore with lights. The signals could be seen across the English channel from Calais, France, to Dover, England. Those in Dover would see the message and then send messengers throughout the island to carry the news. As it happened, the message received at Dover after the battle of Waterloo was "Wellington defeated." Then a fog set in, so that was all the people in Dover saw: "Wellington defeated." The people in Dover who read the message were dismayed, of course, and this was the moment captured in the painting. It was not until the fog lifted that the full message appeared. It did not say, "Wellington defeated." It said, "Wellington defeated the enemy."

That is the message of Psalm 22. It tells us of the cross—"Christ defeated." But then comes Sunday, and the full message reads,

"Christ defeated the enemy." And today the word goes out to the world: "Christ is risen!" And that changes everything.

## PSALM 90

### A PSALM OF COMMUNITY LAMENT

A Prayer of Moses, the man of God.

1 Lord, you have been our dwelling place
in all generations.
2 Before the mountains were brought forth,
or ever you had formed the earth and the world,
from everlasting to everlasting
you are God.
3 You return man to dust
and say, "Return, O children of man!"
4 For a thousand years in your sight
are but as yesterday when it is past,
or as a watch in the night.
5 You sweep them away as with a flood; they are like a dream,
like grass that is renewed in the morning:
6 in the morning it flourishes and is renewed;
in the evening it fades and withers.
7 For we are brought to an end by your anger;
by your wrath we are dismayed.
8 You have set our iniquities before you,
our secret sins in the light of your presence.
9 For all our days pass away under your wrath;
we bring our years to an end like a sigh.
10 The years of our life are seventy,
or even by reason of strength eighty;
yet their span is but toil and trouble;
they are soon gone, and we fly away.
11 Who considers the power of your anger,

and your wrath according to the fear of you?
12 So teach us to number our days
that we may get a heart of wisdom.
13 Return, O Lord! How long?
Have pity on your servants!
14 Satisfy us in the morning with your steadfast love,
that we may rejoice and be glad all our days.
15 Make us glad for as many days as you have afflicted us,
and for as many years as we have seen evil.
16 Let your work be shown to your servants,
and your glorious power to their children.
17 Let the favor of the Lord our God be upon us,
and establish the work of our hands upon us;
yes, establish the work of our hands!

This psalm is the lone psalm of Moses in the Psalter, and many have noted verbal similarities to Deuteronomy 32–33, Moses's "song" and his final blessing to Israel. Moses was the great intercessor for the nation, and his psalm stands strategically here at the beginning of book 4, following the lament over the seeming collapse of the Davidic covenant at the end of book 3 (Psalm 89). The superscript identifies Moses as "the man of God," a designation of a revered prophet—in this case, the most highly revered prophet of the Old Testament. This is his "prayer," recorded for the people of God.

Psalm 90 appears to have been written toward the end of Israel's forty-year sojourn in the wilderness. Perhaps the events of Numbers 20 lie in the background—the death of Moses's sister, Miriam, and his brother, Aaron. In this psalm, Moses laments death as God's punishment on all mankind and on Israel in particular. Israel failed to trust God at Kadesh Barnea, and as a result, the entire adult generation failed also to see the promised land (Num. 14:29). They all died off in that harsh wilderness-cemetery, a land of scorpions and venomous snakes. For forty years, multiple deaths must have marked the daily life of the fledgling nation. This gloomy backdrop is reflected in the dark tone and "minor key" of this psalm.

Psalm 90 is one of the better-known psalms, made more familiar by Isaac Watts's paraphrase of it in his hymn "O God Our Help in Ages Past," widely regarded as one of the finest in the English language. All that concerns the psalmist here is set against the greatness of the eternal God. The psalm's expression of humble trust in God is such that its lament, though so desperate, is more than answered by it.

This psalm has the standard form we have come to expect in a lament:

- direct address (90:1a): "Lord!"
- confidence (90:1–2): "our dwelling place"
- lament (90:3–12): God's harsh discipline of humankind and of sinful Israel
- petitions and wishes with praise (90:13–17)

**Moses's Confidence (90:1–2)**

1 Lord, you have been our dwelling place
  in all generations.
2 Before the mountains were brought forth,
  or ever you had formed the earth and the world,
  from everlasting to everlasting you are God.

Addressing God as "Lord" (*Adonai*) Moses positions himself as his servant (cf. 90:13, 16), and referring to him as "our dwelling place," he recalls God's covenant with Abraham but more recently the exodus from Egypt and the covenant relationship God entered with Israel at Sinai. More particularly, with "Lord, you have been our dwelling place," Moses graphically confesses his humble trust in God's care and provision even through such a gloomy era. It is an affirmation of confidence. The Lord remains Israel's God and only help. The psalm's lament is couched from the outset in the context of praise and trust. However deep their sin and desperate their plight, the Lord remains their refuge. And he is this for "all generations"—since Abraham and after Moses, from before creation and "to everlasting" he is the eternal, self-existing God.

**Lament (90:3–12): God's Harsh Discipline of Humankind and of Sinful Israel**

3 You return man to dust
and say, "Return, O children of man!"
4 For a thousand years in your sight
are but as yesterday when it is past,
or as a watch in the night.
5 You sweep them away as with a flood; they are like a dream,
like grass that is renewed in the morning:
6 in the morning it flourishes and is renewed;
in the evening it fades and withers.
7 For we are brought to an end by your anger;
by your wrath we are dismayed.
8 You have set our iniquities before you,
our secret sins in the light of your presence.
9 For all our days pass away under your wrath;
we bring our years to an end like a sigh.
10 The years of our life are seventy,
or even by reason of strength eighty;
yet their span is but toil and trouble;
they are soon gone, and we fly away.
11 Who considers the power of your anger,
and your wrath according to the fear of you?
12 So teach us to number our days
that we may get a heart of wisdom.

Moses's lament is of death (90:3). For the eternal God any length of time is nothing (90:4); by contrast, the time of man's life on earth is brief and then passes away (90:5–6)—like a dream that in the morning is forgotten (90:5a) and like grass that flourishes in the morning and fades in the evening (90:5b–6). The contrast makes the momentary brevity of human life seem insignificant. Moreover, it is God himself who brings man's life to an end, and he does so as an act of judgment

(Ps. 90:3, 5a, 7–9; cf. Gen. 3:19). This is the case with respect to humanity itself (Ps. 90:3–6), and it has been the case vividly experienced in Israel throughout its time in the wilderness ("we," 90:7–10). In brief, as Moses summarizes in 90:10, the span of human life is short—seventy, maybe eighty years[20]—and marked by toil (cf. Eccles. 1:2, 5). Then, like a puff of smoke, life's little day has been spent and cannot be recovered. Humanity and Israel herself, as the past forty years have so vividly reminded them, languishes under a divine curse that renders all our proud accomplishments futile.

Moses's lament is a sobering but realistic perspective. We all, small and great, have this in common: we die. We are "a mist that appears for a little time and then vanishes" (James 4:14). And yet, blind as the human heart is, few consider it (Ps. 90:11). We spend our lives wandering in the desert of trivialities, and we take little time to consider that we are "soon gone" (90:10) or that we live under the curse of a just God (90:11). We all die, but we seldom consider why. Our hearts are such that we suppress considerations of eternal significance. And we do not consider that it is only "if the Lord wills, we will live and do this or that" (James 4:15).

No one knows the vehemence of God's wrath against sin (90:11). And so the man of God prays, "Teach us to number our days that we may know this wrath, and in that way we may get a heart of wisdom"—by counting our days we realize how brief and few they are compared to the eternity they could have been without sin (90:1–3).[21] On the positive side, counting up the sum total of our days makes us also consider the significance and value of each day. Sobered, Moses asks first "not for the end of the crisis, but for knowledge or insight into the crisis."[22] What

20 Both Moses (Deut. 34:7) and Aaron (Num. 33:39) lived considerably longer, as did Joshua (Josh. 14:10) and Caleb (Josh. 14:10). But the biblical writers indicate that these are exceptional cases. The longevity of these four great men of the exodus-wilderness generation, which merits biblical notices, actually proves the psalm's rule for the majority of Israel.

21 For this translation and interpretation, see Bruce K. Waltke and James M. Houston, *Psalms as Christian Praise: A Historical Commentary* (Grand Rapids, MI: Eerdmans, 2019), 48–50.

22 Frank-Lothar Hossfeld and Erich Zenger, *Psalms 2: A Commentary on Psalms 51–100*, trans. Linda M. Maloney, Hermeneia (Minneapolis: Fortress , 2005), 418.

he desires is "a lesson not in elementary arithmetic but in life-changing theology."[23] He wishes to be wise, and he has learned that we can be wise only as we realize that "the wages of sin is death" (Rom. 6:23). He has connected human mortality to divine wrath—we die because of sin and judgment. And this makes sin infinitely serious.

Note here that Psalm 90:11–12 concludes the lament section of the psalm and transitions to the petitions of 90:13–17. In 90:3–10 Moses laments God's harsh judgment on humanity and on Israel. Then in 90:11 Moses laments the lack of fear of God, which is foundational to wisdom (cf. Prov. 9:10), and in 90:12 shows us the very way to wisdom. This transition alters the standard form of a lament psalm by adding a brief theology of wisdom. The book of Ecclesiastes, with its "all is vanity" theme, expounds this theme at length.

**Petitions and Wishes with Praise (90:13–17)**

13 Return, O LORD! How long?
Have pity on your servants!
14 Satisfy us in the morning with your steadfast love,
that we may rejoice and be glad all our days.
15 Make us glad for as many days as you have afflicted us,
and for as many years as we have seen evil.
16 Let your work be shown to your servants,
and your glorious power to their children.
17 Let the favor of the Lord our God be upon us,
and establish the work of our hands upon us;
yes, establish the work of our hands!

Moses has expressed his confidence in the care of the eternal God (90:1–2), and so turning from his lament (90:3–10) and his plea for wisdom (90:11–12), he offers petitions for the repentant and wise people. Addressing God by name, his covenant Lord (90:13), Moses

23 Michael Wilcock, *The Message of Psalm 73–150: Songs for the People of God* (Downers Grove, IL: InterVarsity Press, 2001), 77.

pleads for him to take pity on his people (90:13), to bring them to rejoice in his unfailing love (90:14–15), to allow them and their children to experience his splendor in his saving deeds (90:16–17), and to establish their work and give them lives of value (90:17). With the boldness of humble faith, he asks God to compensate their sufferings in proportion to their suffering. The psalmist, then, concludes on a note of confidence with which he began, no longer lamenting the harshness of God's punishment but anticipating his favor and blessing.[24]

"The time had not yet come when the hope of personal immortality could be appealed to as the consolation of sorrow and the consecration of effort (1 Cor. 15:58),"[25] but the thought of resurrection and eternal life "is here in embryo."[26] They ask to be delivered from the sleep of death and mention the morning of the new age without mentioning the night; yet they speak of their future years as "for as many days as you have afflicted us" (Ps. 90:15), and their hope is for their descendants. In the new dispensation their embryonic desire would come to fruition in a way immeasurably greater than they could ask or imagine.

The ultimate answer to Moses's prayer was born finally in the advent of Jesus Christ, who rose as the firstfruits from the dead; it continues to be fulfilled in this day, and it will reach consummation in his glorious return.

### Final Reflections on Lament Psalms

Before we leave these psalms of lament we should note again the dominance of this genre in the Psalter, an observation that rings true to life. The world is a fallen one. It is broken and marked by suffering of all kinds, injustice and failure also. The book of Job is given to this problem, as is Jeremiah's extended lament (Lamentations). About one-third of

24 Cf. Allen P. Ross, *Commentary on the Psalms: 90–150*, vol. 3, Kregel Exegetical Library (Grand Rapids, MI: Kregel, 2016), 39–40.

25 A. F. Kirkpatrick, *The Book of Psalms: Books IV and V* (Cambridge: The University Press, 1912), 553.

26 J. J. Stewart Perowne, *The Book of Psalms*, vol. 2, 4th rev. ed. (1878; repr., Grand Rapids, MI: Zondervan), 161.

the Psalms or portions of psalms are given to this also, and they remind us that pain is the frequent experience of God's people.

Sometimes our lament demands accompanying repentance, but not always—some suffering is undeserved. In either case, these psalms teach us to take the concern to God and lay open our hearts before him. The psalmists do not think on a philosophical level only—"Such is life in a cursed world!" "All things happen for a reason!" "All this is for my good and God's glory!" The pain is very personal, and it is on this level they take it before the Lord. We may learn to do likewise. As Scripture these psalms are God's word to us, but they are also prayers—our words to him. And taking our laments to God with open hearts we keep our sufferings in Godward perspective. These same psalms teach us to keep our hope fixed on him. They teach us to honor him in our suffering by maintaining trust and expressing his praise even through tears, for he is always deserving of both. There is never a time when God is not deserving of our trust and our praise. These "complaints" are made in the context of faith and praise and of God's steadfast covenant love. To complain otherwise would be inappropriate.

Note also, finally, that in our treatment of these lament psalms we have related them to Christ—in fact, too briefly. We have emphasized that our Lord is the subject and leading character of the Psalter, and we need not doubt that in his earthly life he found these psalms to express his own lament. In the penitential psalms he who was without sin, yet was baptized with sinners, represents us. "In the days of his flesh, Jesus offered up prayers and supplications, with loud cries and tears, to him who was able to save him from death, and he was heard because of his reverence" (Heb. 5:7). He too "learned obedience through what he suffered" (Heb. 5:8). And in his dying hours he found David's lament of Psalm 22 to be his own (Matt. 27:46; cf. 26:39). He was the righteous sufferer. Without doubt he also sang the "confidence" sections of these psalms, and the psalms of trust that we will see in a later chapter (cf. Acts 2:25–26). But the laments are his also, and these foreshadow an important aspect of our Lord's work. The royal orientation of the Psalter and our obligation to interpret the Psalms in light of the full biblical canon does not stop short of the lament psalms.

---

## IMPRECATORY PSALMS

### "SLAY THE WICKED, O GOD!"

As we have noted, there are about sixty petition-lament psalms (see p. 64). These psalms normally petition God for deliverance from life-threatening situations. Many of these go beyond the positive of deliverance and ask God to punish the enemy. These are the imprecatory psalms. "Imprecatory" psalm is actually a misnomer. An imprecation is a calling down of a curse on an enemy, and that is not what these psalms do. They are certainly not prayers for revenge. Rather, these psalms are prayers that God will avenge the psalmist for the wrong being done by an enemy by justly punishing the violator. Psalms that are commonly referred to as imprecatory include 35, 55, 59, 69, 79, 83, 109, 137, and 139.[27] Certain of these Psalms seem particularly harsh. Psalm 69:28, for example, asks, "Let them be blotted out of the book of the living; / let them not be enrolled among the righteous." Psalm 137 is a well-known example:

1 By the waters of Babylon,
  there we sat down and wept,
  when we remembered Zion.
2 On the willows there
  we hung up our lyres.
3 For there our captors
  required of us songs,
 and our tormentors, mirth, saying,

27 Others include 5, 7, 9, 16, 25, 28, 31, 35, 38, 52, 55, 56, 59, 63, 64, 69, 79, 86, 109, 139, 140, 143.

"Sing us one of the songs of Zion!"
4 How shall we sing the LORD's song
in a foreign land?
5 If I forget you, O Jerusalem,
let my right hand forget its skill!
6 Let my tongue stick to the roof of my mouth,
if I do not remember you,
if I do not set Jerusalem
above my highest joy!
7 Remember, O LORD, against the Edomites
the day of Jerusalem,
how they said, "Lay it bare, lay it bare,
down to its foundations!"
8 O daughter of Babylon, doomed to be destroyed,
blessed shall he be who repays you
with what you have done to us!
9 Blessed shall he be who takes your little ones
and dashes them against the rock!

We may outline this psalm as follows:

I. Lament for Destruction of Zion: 1–3
II. Resolve to Remember Zion: 4—6
III. Imprecations against Zion's Enemies: 7—9

As for the petition that entails bashing babies (137:9), it should be noted that the exiles are asking for strict justice: repay the Babylonians for what they had done to us (137:8). In warfare neither women nor children were spared (cf. 1 Kings 8:24; Isa. 13:16, Hos. 10:14; 13:16). That was so because a family thought of itself as a solidarity, not as a group of separate individuals. The family is like the father, as seeds are to plants. Women and children alike of Israel's enemies hated God's chosen people (cf. Judg. 5:28–30; 2 Kings 2:23–24). Family solidarity was also true of Israel. For this reason, Israel stoned to death the entire family of sinful Achan (Josh. 7).

## The Problem of the Imprecatory Psalms

In light of Jesus's teachings in Matthew 5:39–42 and 5:43–48, these kinds of psalms can be puzzling to the Christian, and various proposals have been offered for understanding them from a Christian point of view. At one end of the spectrum, some have just declared these psalms to be unchristian and that they have no relevance to the Christian. C. S. Lewis and others held various forms of this view. But this would seem to disregard the doctrine of inspiration altogether: the teaching of these psalms is sound doctrine (2 Tim. 3:16). There is no indication in these psalms themselves that the cries for punishment were displeasing to the Lord. In fact, they were intended for public worship ("to the choirmaster"). Nor are such calls for judgment unique to the Psalter. Moses prayed that God would scatter their enemies (Num. 10:35), and prayers of judgment are not uncommon in the prophets (cf. Jer. 11:18–19; 15:15–16; 17:18–19; 18:19–20; 20:11–12). C. John Collins points out that the New Testament writers "portray themselves as heirs of the OT ethics (cf. Matt. 22:34–40)" and in fact pronounce some curses of their own (e.g., 1 Cor. 16:22; Gal. 1:8–9).[28] On one occasion the apostle Paul miraculously brought down the curse himself, blinding an opponent of their work (Acts 13:9–11). The New Testament writers cite imprecatory psalms approvingly (compare Acts 1:20 and Rom. 11:9, 10 with Pss. 69:22–28 and 109:6–15), record prayers for divine judgment (2 Tim. 4:14), and speak of severe treatment of certain enemies (see Acts 8:20; 13:10–11; 23:3; 1 Cor. 5:5; 2 Tim. 4:14; Rev. 6:10; 16:17–20; 19:11–19). In fact, even the martyred saints in heaven pray for punishment of their persecutors:

> When he opened the fifth seal, I saw under the altar the souls of those who had been slain for the word of God and for the witness they had borne. They cried out with a loud voice, "O Sovereign Lord, holy and true, how long before you will judge and avenge our blood on those who dwell on the earth?" (Rev. 6:9–10)

28 C. John Collins, "Introduction to the Psalms," in *ESV Study Bible* (Wheaton, IL: Crossway, 2008), 938.

The imprecatory psalms simply cannot be dismissed—they are still being prayed today in heaven.

Yet it is clear that the church should not make direct use of these psalms simply "as is." Jesus's commands to turn the other cheek (Matt. 5:39–42) and "love your neighbor" (Matt. 5:43–48) indicate that some qualification is needed. Jesus prayed for those crucifying him: "Father, forgive them, for they know not what they do" (Luke 23:34). And Stephen, the first martyr after Jesus sent the empowering of the Spirit, prayed, "Lord, do not hold this sin against them" (Acts 7:60). These martyrs exemplify that we should yearn for the salvation of our enemies, not for their punishment. Nevertheless, the unrepentant will be punished when the Lord Jesus will be revealed from heaven (2 Thess. 1:5–10).

The question of the Christian use of the imprecatory psalms is complex, and the answer must be nuanced accordingly.

### Toward a Christian Understanding[29]

How, then, should the Christian understand and make use of the imprecatory psalms today? Some have understood these not as prayers but as prophecies—not "May God punish them" but "God will punish them." This appears to provide a convenient escape from the dilemma, but it lacks exegetical warrant. The Hebrew verb form can often be an imperfect, which commonly signifies the future tense ("He will *x*"). But it can also be a jussive, a volitional form expressing command or entreaty ("May he *x*"). Some forms, however, are distinctly and unambiguously jussive and must be translated as volitional, not indicative. And so the unclear, ambiguous verb forms in these psalms should be interpreted consistently with the clear and unambiguous forms.

There is, however, an eschatological aspect to these psalms that we should not miss. Throughout the Psalter the king represents and anticipates the King, David's greater son. The king's victories typify the

29 See Bruce K. Waltke, *An Old Testament Theology: An Exegetical, Canonical, and Thematic Approach* (Grand Rapids, MI: Zondervan, 2007), 878–80; Waltke and Houston, *Psalms as Christian Worship*, 95–98; Waltke, "Psalms," in VanGemeren, *New International Dictionary of Old Testament Theology and Exegesis*, 4:1106–07.

Messiah's ultimate victory, as we have seen in Psalm 92 and as we will see in chapter 12 (cf. Gen. 3:15; Pss. 2; 110; Rev. 19). The psalmist's outlook is not purely eschatological—he prays for the destruction of his own enemies. But within the Psalter as a whole, and within the larger canonical perspective, the eschatological perspective is evident. Greg Beale cites John's reference to Psalm 137:8–9 in Revelation 18:6 and argues that they serve as types of God's eschatological judgment of the world.[30] His case gains further strength in noting that words from Psalm 69, one of the harshest of the imprecatory psalms, are found in John 15:25 on the lips of Christ (cf. Rom. 15:3). Jonathan Edwards treated the imprecatory psalms somewhat similarly.[31] This eschatological dimension may not fully answer our present question as to the church's use of these psalms today, but it is surely part of the answer.

Moreover, the psalmist frequently reflects his enemies' extremely violent intents when he describes them metaphorically as wild animals (Pss. 35:17; 59:6, 14–15), as "bloodthirsty" (59:2) men who gnash at him with their teeth (35:16). And David depicts his enemies as coming after him with painful military weapons. The "imprecatory" prayers aim for strict justice—"Do to them as they have done to us" is the gist. They ask the Lord to be as just as he expected Israel's judges to be:

> 17 He loved to curse; let curses come upon him!
> He did not delight in blessing; may it be far from him!
> 18 He clothed himself with cursing as his coat;
> may it soak into his body like water,
> like oil into his bones! (109:17–18)

As Hassell Bullock points out, this "eye-for-an-eye and tooth-for-a-tooth ethic" was one level of the Mosaic code.[32] Moreover, the psalmist

30 G. K. Beale, *The Morality of God in the Old Testament*, Christian Answers to Hard Questions (Philadelphia: Westminster Seminary Press; Phillipsburg, NJ: P&R, 2013), 19–21.

31 David P. Barshinger, "Spite or Spirit? Jonathan Edwards on the Imprecatory Language of the Psalms," *Westminster Theological Journal* 77 (2015), 53–69.

32 C. Hassell Bullock, *Encountering the Book of Psalms: A Literary and Theological Introduction*, Encountering Biblical Studies (Grand Rapids, MI: Baker Academic, 2001), 236.

views himself as innocent, undeserving of his enemies' hatred and pursuit. These prayers for justice are grounded in a recognition of right and wrong, and they plead for God to uphold what is right and destroy what is wrong—and this, often, in order to terminate further threat. Yet we would do well to recall that this is poetry, not prose, and that in poetry some imprecatory language may be intentional hyperbole,[33] excessive language that leaves the precise fulfillment to God.

We would also do well to read these psalms "sympathetically." That is, first, we should recognize the psalmist's piety. There is no indication that the inspired writer was out of line in writing these psalms. Additionally, we should consider the psalmist's position and experience as he writes, perhaps especially so as we recognize that he is the king. He is severely oppressed, and that unjustly, and his very life is under continual attack. Rory Prest writes,

> Most commentators read the Psalms from the comfortable perspective of security and economic affluence. Few have experienced the agony of utterly unprovoked, naked aggression and gross exploitation. It is questionable whether such a detached discussion on responding to enemies would take place in the face of people with manifestly evil intentions.[34]

More importantly, the king's enemies are in fact God's enemies. David's concern is not merely personal. Zion was the place of God's saving presence on the earth (9:11; 76:2; 87:1–3; 132:13), and Israel was a nation whose king was the Lord. The success of the king's enemies reflects their success against the Lord God who appointed that king and promised to establish him. Thus, the psalmist's passion is not mere nationalism but zeal for the kingdom of God whose rule is love of God and others. His motive is theocratic, not self-centered. His zeal is for God—his name and reputation, his kingdom, and his people:

33 Chalmers Martin, "Imprecations in the Psalms," *Princeton Theological Review* 1 no. 4 (1903): 548.

34 Rory Prest, "Enemies in the Psalms" (unpublished paper, Regent College, 1980), 8.

12 Return sevenfold into the lap of our neighbors
the taunts with which they have taunted you, O Lord! (79:12)

26 Let them be put to shame and disappointed altogether
who rejoice at my calamity!
Let them be clothed with shame and dishonor
who magnify themselves against me!
27 Let those who delight in my righteousness
shout for joy and be glad
and say evermore,
"Great is the LORD,
who delights in the welfare of his servant!"
28 Then my tongue shall tell of your righteousness
and of your praise all the day long. (35:26–28)

19 Oh that you would slay the wicked, O God!
O men of blood, depart from me!
20 They speak against you with malicious intent;
your enemies take your name in vain.
21 Do I not hate those who hate you, O LORD?
And do I not loathe those who rise up against you?
22 I hate them with complete hatred;
I count them my enemies (139:19–22).

Seeking to capture the spirit of Psalm 139:21 ("Do I not hate those who hate you, O LORD?) Spurgeon connects it with 1 Corinthians 16:22 and comments:

> He was a good hater, for he hated only those who hated good. Of this hatred he is not ashamed, but he sets it forth as a virtue to which he would have the Lord bear testimony. To love all men with benevolence is our duty; but to love any wicked man with complacency would be a crime. To hate a man for his own sake, or for any evil done to us, would be wrong; but to hate a man because he is the foe of all

goodness and the enemy of all righteousness, is nothing more nor less than an obligation. The more we love God the more indignant shall we grow with those who refuse him their affection. "If any man love not the Lord Jesus Christ let him be Anathema. Maranatha."[35]

Yet there is an "evangelistic" connotation involved. The psalmist prays that by God's action against the wicked all the world will see that Israel's God is supreme and just:

16 Fill their faces with shame,
that they may seek your name, O Lord.
17 Let them be put to shame and dismayed forever;
let them perish in disgrace,
18 *that they may know* that you alone,
whose name is the Lord,
are the Most High over all the earth. (83:16–18)

Similarly, these prayers must also be understood in their covenantal context, where wrong against God's people is perceived as a wrong against God:[36]

7 For it is for your sake that I have borne reproach,
that dishonor has covered my face.
8 I have become a stranger to my brothers,
an alien to my mother's sons.
9 For zeal for your house has consumed me,
and the reproaches of those who reproach you have fallen on me. (69:7–9)

Further, the imprecatory prayers are prayers of faith. They call upon God to avenge gross injustice (cf. Deut. 32:25; Ps. 94:1); they do not

35 C. H. Spurgeon, *The Treasury of David*, vol. 6 (New York: Marshall Brothers, 1883), 265.
36 Chalmers Martin, "Imprecations in the Psalms," 537–53.

envision the psalmist avenging himself. Derek Kidner observes insightfully that "there have been few men more capable of generosity under personal attack than David. As he proved by his attitudes toward Saul and Absalom, to say nothing of Shimei."[37] Chalmers Martin before him remarked similarly: "Rarely has a man of equal strength of character and warmth of feeling shown himself so far from the spirit of revenge."[38] David was not a Lamech (Gen. 4:23–24). He called on God to bring about the justice he desired to see.

We must recognize further that even within the Old Testament context, exception to such condemnation was held out for those who repent. Compare, for example, Deuteronomy 7:1–2 with Joshua 2:12–14. In Deuteronomy Moses commands the Israelites to exterminate the enemy entirely and without mercy.

> "When the LORD your God brings you into the land that you are entering to take possession of it, and clears away many nations before you, the Hittites, the Girgashites, the Amorites, the Canaanites, the Perizzites, the Hivites, and the Jebusites, seven nations more numerous and mightier than you, [2] and when the LORD your God gives them over to you, and you defeat them, then you must devote them to complete destruction. You shall make no covenant with them and show no mercy to them." (Deut. 7:1–2)

And yet when they enter the land—in this case, Jericho—we find an exception in the famous passage about Rahab the harlot and her family:

> "Now then, please swear to me by the LORD that, as I have dealt kindly with you, you also will deal kindly with my father's house, and give me a sure sign [13] that you will save alive my father and mother, my brothers and sisters, and all who belong to them, and deliver our lives from death." [14] And the men said to her, "Our life for yours

37 Kidner, *Psalms 1–72*, 40–41.

38 Martin, "Imprecations in the Psalms," 542.

> even to death! If you do not tell this business of ours, then when the LORD gives us the land we will deal kindly and faithfully with you." (Josh. 2:12–14)

In this passage Rahab acknowledges Israel's God, and in such a case the Mosaic command (Deut. 7) did not have her in view. She obtained mercy. This is not nationalism. This is a spiritual war. Her protection of the spies was an expression of faith in the Lord God on her part. Her faith was no longer in Baal and the Canaanite gods. And by this faith she was brought into the covenant family (cf. Josh. 6:25). By contrast, in Joshua 7, when Achan—who was of the tribe of Judah—violated the Mosaic command and kept a Babylonian garment for himself, it cost him his life. This was not a war of plunder but a holy war, a war on behalf of righteousness. The harlot was spared; the Judean was put to death.

Jeremiah 18:7–10 is the definitive passage here:

> If at any time I declare concerning a nation or a kingdom, that I will pluck up and break down and destroy it, and if that nation, concerning which I have spoken, turns from its evil, I will relent of the disaster that I intended to do to it. And if at any time I declare concerning a nation or a kingdom that I will build and plant it, and if it does evil in my sight, not listening to my voice, then I will relent of the good that I had intended to do to it.

All of these considerations must be allowed to shape our understanding of the imprecatory psalms. Yet one additional factor would seem to have enormous bearing on the question of our use of the imprecatory psalms: a recognition of the distinction between the ethics of the church and the state. It would be a mistake to take the ethics of the Sermon on the Mount and apply it to the state—as if the state should turn the other cheek and not seek to punish evil or use the sword. The ethics of the church and the state are distinct. The ethics of the church is the cross, where you die for your enemy. The ethics of the state entails the sword to avenge wrong (Rom. 13:1–4). This is not given to the church.

But the psalmist did not work with such distinctions. Israel was a theocratic state, and David was seeking, under God, to establish an earthly kingdom, even with the sword. The kingdom of God and the kingdom of Israel were coextensive. Avenging wrong is the role of the state today, but it is not the role of the church (2 Cor. 10:4).

So in a sense, Christians wear two hats. As Christians, we pray that God will give our enemies repentance. And yet as citizens of the state, we pray that our leaders will give us protection, maintain justice, and punish wrongdoers (Rom. 13:1–4; cf. 2 Tim. 2:1–2). Vengeance belongs to the Lord, and he avenges through the state. In any case, Christians must not avenge themselves (Rom. 12:17–21). Like the psalmist we pray with kingdom focus, and our concern is for righteousness to triumph and for God to be honored by all. We pray "Thy kingdom come," holding in mind all that God's kingdom entails—gospel advance throughout this age until the climactic return of Christ, at which time Babylon will be destroyed and all the world brought to bow before him.

10

# Individual Songs of Grateful Praise

*"I cried, God heard, and he delivered!"*

INDIVIDUAL SONGS of grateful praise are also known as "declarative praise psalms," "psalms of acknowledgment," or "thanksgiving psalms." These psalms are a subset of the praise psalms, but they are individually focused. They may also be understood as a later counterpart of a lament. In a lament psalm the psalmist petitions God for some particular help; the individual psalm of grateful praise looks back to the help that was given, the prayer that was answered, and offers praise to God for it. In the lament psalms, as we have seen, the psalmist expresses trust that God will deliver; praise for that deliverance is expressed in these individual psalms of grateful praise. The king publicly petitioned God, and he publicly praised God; he did not privately say "Thank you, God."

Notice, for example, the superscript of Psalm 56, a lament psalm: "A Miktam of David, when the Philistines seized him in Gath." Psalm 34 is written in light of the same circumstances—"Of David, when he changed his behavior before Abimelech, so that he drove him out, and he went away"—only now he writes a psalm of grateful acknowledgment of the deliverance God then gave. "This poor man cried [out loud], and the LORD heard him / and saved him out of all his troubles" (34:6).

So also Psalm 51 is David's lament of his sin "after he had gone in to Bathsheba" (51:1), a penitential psalm asking God for mercy and pardon; Psalm 32 is his acknowledgment and praise to God for the forgiveness received. Other "psalms of acknowledgment" or psalms of individual grateful praise include 18, 30, 32, 34, 40:1–11, 41, 66:13–20, 92, 116, 118, and 138. These are often referred to as "psalms of thanksgiving." Hannah also provides us with a hymn of grateful praise in 1 Samuel 2:1–10, as does the prophet Jonah (2:1–9). Their public songs of grateful praise glorified God in the eyes of others.

**Background and Setting**

By way of background recall that Moses's law provided for what has traditionally been called a "thank offering" that a worshiper could offer in thanks to God.

> [11] "And this is the law of the sacrifice of peace offerings that one may offer to the Lord. [12] If he offers it for a thanksgiving, then he shall offer with the thanksgiving sacrifice unleavened loaves mixed with oil, unleavened wafers smeared with oil, and loaves of fine flour well mixed with oil. [13] With the sacrifice of his peace offerings for thanksgiving he shall bring his offering with loaves of leavened bread. [14] And from it he shall offer one loaf from each offering, as a gift to the Lord. It shall belong to the priest who throws the blood of the peace offerings. [15] And the flesh of the sacrifice of his peace offerings for thanksgiving shall be eaten on the day of his offering. He shall not leave any of it until the morning. (Lev. 7:11–15)

This offering was not required but voluntary for the expressing of praise to God for his provision or his protection from peril (cf. Jonah 2:9). In this act of worship the entire offering is given to God, and it is the one offering in which the offerer could partake. It may be a burnt offering of an animal (Lev. 1) or a grain offering (Lev. 2), but in either case the entire offering is given to God.

The term "Thanksgiving" psalm is something of a misnomer. There is in fact no word for thanksgiving in the Old Testament. That is an odd thought to us, and we have the translation "thanksgiving" and "giving thanks" in our English Bibles. But in the Hebrew Old Testament no one says thank you to God. The word is "confess" (תּוֹדָה, cf. 100:1)—to acknowledge, declare, or proclaim. Of course the idea of gratitude is in the atmosphere, but specifically the Old Testament worshiper would confess or acknowledge the favor God has shown. It was an expression of praise. And this confession is never merely private. It is a public acknowledgment—praising God by confessing his goodness to others. It was an occasion of joy in the expressing of praise to God for the blessings he had bestowed.

Individual songs of grateful praise, then, are to be understood as accompanying a communal meal. Both the offering and the song were "acknowledging" God in grateful praise. With David's institution of psalm singing in temple worship, the offering took on a musical dimension, and psalms of grateful praise were composed for these occasions. They were individually oriented but intended for community use at the temple. This ceremony features regularly in the Psalms.

## Form

Psalms of grateful praise typically follow a common form with these components:

- **Proclamation**: "I will praise the Lord." Sometimes the opening line expresses not the psalmist's intention to praise but simply the praise itself, as in 116:1, "I love the LORD."
- **Introductory summary** statement of what God has done: "for he saved me."
- **Reflection** on past need and deliverance: "I cried, he heard, he answered." Here the psalmist may echo a previous lament.
- **Praise**: "Come join with me in praise."

## Grateful Praise in the Church

The tradition of individual grateful praise continues in the church today under the new covenant. It is customary in many churches to have a congregational time given to public "testimony." In these services there is prayer and the singing of psalms and hymns and spiritual songs as individuals give public expression to what God is doing in their own lives. And often these times of "testimony" are accompanied with singing. Most frequently, and appropriately, these are testimonies of salvation. Both the testimony and the song are our "sacrifice of praise." "Through him then let us continually offer up a sacrifice of praise to God, that is, the fruit of lips that acknowledge his name" (Heb. 13:15).

Let us look at some samples of these psalms.

---

## PSALM 66:13–20

Psalm 66:1–12 is community oriented in its praise, but 66:13–20 narrows to an individual psalm of grateful praise. Notice that 66:13–15 speak of the thank offering itself, and 66:16–20 the accompanying service.

### Proclamation:

13 I will come into your house with burnt offerings;
I will perform my vows to you,
14 that which my lips uttered
and my mouth promised when I was in trouble.
15 I will offer to you burnt offerings of fattened animals,
with the smoke of the sacrifice of rams;
I will make an offering of bulls and goats. *Selah*

**Introductory summary:**

16 Come and hear, all you who fear God,
and I will tell what he has done for my soul.

**Reflection:**

17 I cried to him with my mouth,
and high praise was on my tongue.
18 If I had cherished iniquity in my heart,
the Lord would not have listened.
19 But truly God has listened;
he has attended to the voice of my prayer.

**Praise:**

20 Blessed be God,
because he has not rejected my prayer
or removed his steadfast love from me!

## PSALM 30

**Proclamation:**

1 I will extol you, O Lord, for you have drawn me up
and have not let my foes rejoice over me.

**Summary statement:**

2 O Lord my God, I cried to you for help,
and you have healed me.
3 O Lord, you have brought up my soul from Sheol;
you restored me to life from among those who go down to the pit.

The saints are called to **praise** the Lord with him:

4 Sing praises to the Lord, O you his saints,
and give thanks to his holy name.
5 For his anger is but for a moment,
and his favor is for a lifetime.
Weeping may tarry for the night,
but joy comes with the morning.

**Reflection** on deliverance:

6 As for me, I said in my prosperity,
"I shall never be moved."
7 By your favor, O Lord,
you made my mountain stand strong;
you hid your face;
I was dismayed.
8 To you, O Lord, I cry,
and to the Lord I plead for mercy:
9 "What profit is there in my death,
if I go down to the pit?
Will the dust praise you?
Will it tell of your faithfulness?
10 Hear, O Lord, and be merciful to me!
O Lord, be my helper!"

**Praise**:

11 You have turned for me my mourning into dancing;
you have loosed my sackcloth
and clothed me with gladness,
12 that my glory may sing your praise and not be silent.
O Lord my God, I will give thanks to you forever!

## PSALM 34:1–11

Of David, when he changed his behavior before Abimelech, so that he drove him out, and he went away.

1 I will bless the LORD at all times;
his praise shall continually be in my mouth.
2 My soul makes its boast in the LORD;
let the humble hear and be glad.
3 Oh, magnify the LORD with me,
and let us exalt his name together!
4 I sought the LORD, and he answered me
and delivered me from all my fears.
5 Those who look to him are radiant,
and their faces shall never be ashamed.
6 This poor man cried, and the LORD heard him
and saved him out of all his troubles.
7 The angel of the LORD encamps
around those who fear him, and delivers them.
8 Oh, taste and see that the LORD is good!
Blessed is the man who takes refuge in him!
9 Oh, fear the LORD, you his saints,
for those who fear him have no lack!
10 The young lions suffer want and hunger;
but those who seek the LORD lack no good thing.
11 Come, O children, listen to me;
I will teach you the fear of the LORD.

As we noted above, the superscript to Psalm 34 links it to Psalm 56. Psalm 34 is a psalm of grateful praise acknowledging God's answer to the lament and petition of Psalm 56. The form of the psalm is that of an acknowledgment psalm:

34:1–3 is a proclamation to praise God
34:4 gives the summary statement

34:5–6 looks back to the time of need and reports God's deliverance.

34:7–11 expresses praise and begins a homily that expands in 34:12–22. As such, these verses resemble a wisdom psalm.

## JONAH 2

We have another example of a song of grateful praise from the prophet Jonah.

1 Then Jonah prayed to the LORD his God from the belly of the
fish, [superscript] 2 saying,
"I called out to the LORD, out of my distress,
and he answered me;
out of the belly of Sheol I cried,
and you heard my voice.
3 For you cast me into the deep,
into the heart of the seas,
and the flood surrounded me;
all your waves and your billows
passed over me.
4 Then I said, 'I am driven away
from your sight;
yet I shall again look
upon your holy temple.'
5 The waters closed in over me to take my life;
the deep surrounded me;
weeds were wrapped about my head
6 at the roots of the mountains.
I went down to the land
whose bars closed upon me forever;
yet you brought up my life from the pit,
O LORD my God.
7 When my life was fainting away,

I remembered the LORD,
and my prayer came to you,
into your holy temple.
8 Those who pay regard to vain idols
forsake their hope of steadfast love.
9 But I with the voice of thanksgiving
will sacrifice to you;
what I have vowed I will pay.
Salvation belongs to the LORD!"

In Jonah's psalm there is no "proclamation"; instead, he begins with a summary (2:2): "I was as good as dead" is the sense. Then in 2:3–7 he looks back to his time of need (2:3–6a, the sea) and reports his deliverance (2:6b–7). Then in 2:8–9 he gives praise with a brief homily. He has made a vow, now he goes to the temple to offer sacrifice, paying his vow, and declares to all that "salvation belongs to the LORD!" (2:9). This form is rather typical of the psalms of grateful praise.

## PSALM 116

1 I love the LORD, because he has heard
my voice and my pleas for mercy.
2 Because he inclined his ear to me,
therefore I will call on him as long as I live.
3 The snares of death encompassed me;
the pangs of Sheol laid hold on me;
I suffered distress and anguish.
4 Then I called on the name of the LORD:
"O LORD, I pray, deliver my soul!"
5 Gracious is the LORD, and righteous;
our God is merciful.
6 The LORD preserves the simple;
when I was brought low, he saved me.

7 Return, O my soul, to your rest;
for the LORD has dealt bountifully with you.
8 For you have delivered my soul from death,
my eyes from tears,
my feet from stumbling;
9 I will walk before the LORD
in the land of the living.
10 I believed, even when I spoke:
"I am greatly afflicted";
11 I said in my alarm,
"All mankind are liars."
12 What shall I render to the LORD
for all his benefits to me?
13 I will lift up the cup of salvation
and call on the name of the LORD,
14 I will pay my vows to the LORD
in the presence of all his people.
15 Precious in the sight of the LORD
is the death of his saints.
16 O LORD, I am your servant;
I am your servant, the son of your maidservant.
You have loosed my bonds.
17 I will offer to you the sacrifice of thanksgiving
and call on the name of the LORD.
18 I will pay my vows to the LORD
in the presence of all his people,
19 in the courts of the house of the LORD,
in your midst, O Jerusalem
Praise the LORD!

Note again the form:

116:1–2 combines the proclamation and summary statement and produces a resolve to praise the Lord. And 116:2b might better be rendered, "therefore I will proclaim (i.e., praise) him as long as I live."

116:3–11 looks back to the time of need (116:3) and cry for help (116:4), and reports and reflects on God's deliverance (116:5–11).

116:12–19 offers praise in word and sacrifice.

This psalm reflects clearly the typical circumstances and public ceremony associated with the individual songs of grateful praise. The psalmist had faced a time of great need—evidently a near-death experience (116:3). In his distress he cried out to God for help (116:4) and vowed that upon deliverance he would give him praise (116:14). This was not "bargaining" with God but a sincere pledge of devotion. Nor was this vow to praise to be fulfilled merely in private but in a public ceremony of praise, involving a meal (116:12–14) and sacrifice (116:17–19) at the LORD's house. The "cup of salvation" (116:14) was a standard part of the ceremony. But this is not ceremony only: fulfilling his vow, the psalmist pledges in praise of devotion to give himself afresh to God's service (116:16)

The significance of this "cup of blessing" is ratcheted up considerably in the New Testament as a reminder of our Lord's death (1 Cor. 10:16), in response to which we give ourselves wholly to him (Rom. 12:1–2; 2 Cor. 5:14–15).

## PSALM 32

A Maskil of David.

1 Blessed is the one whose transgression is forgiven,
whose sin is covered.
2 Blessed is the man against whom the LORD counts no iniquity,
and in whose spirit there is no deceit.
3 For when I kept silent, my bones wasted away
through my groaning all day long.
4 For day and night your hand was heavy upon me;
my strength was dried up as by the heat of summer. *Selah*
5 I acknowledged my sin to you,

and I did not cover my iniquity;
I said, "I will confess my transgressions to the Lord,"
and you forgave the iniquity of my sin. *Selah*
6 Therefore let everyone who is godly
offer prayer to you at a time when you may be found;
surely in the rush of great waters,
they shall not reach him.
7 You are a hiding place for me;
you preserve me from trouble;
you surround me with shouts of deliverance. *Selah*
8 I will instruct you and teach you in the way you should go;
I will counsel you with my eye upon you.
9 Be not like a horse or a mule, without understanding,
which must be curbed with bit and bridle,
or it will not stay near you.
10 Many are the sorrows of the wicked,
but steadfast love surrounds the one who trusts in the Lord.
11 Be glad in the Lord, and rejoice, O righteous,
and shout for joy, all you upright in heart!

In this psalm of grateful praise, David answers his lament of Psalm 51. Both pertain to his sin against Uriah and Bathsheba but from contrasting perspectives. In Psalm 51, David expresses his repentance and petition for forgiveness; in Psalm 32 he expresses his joy in the realization of that forgiveness freely granted.

We should note that this psalm is often referred to as a penitential psalm because here David reflects on the agony of his unconfessed sin (32:3–4). But unlike Psalm 51 he makes no petition for forgiveness. Nor does he make confession. He only reflects on the confession made previously. This psalm is also referred to as a wisdom psalm. The designation of this psalm as a "maskil" may support this categorization, and its beatitudes (32:1–2) and parable (32:9) and proverb (32:10) may also. But this psalm has the characteristics of an acknowledgment psalm: it looks back on a situation of distress, reports deliverance, expresses trust, and calls for praise. Yet it lacks the introductory resolve to praise, the reference to a thank offering of words and sacrifice, and the conclusion that returns to the theme and wording of the introduction. In truth, this psalm is unique in that it is all three—an individual song of grateful praise, a penitential psalm, and a wisdom psalm.

Though the expected form that we have seen for other individual songs of grateful praise does not stand out as clearly in this psalm, the flow of thought is very similar:

In 32:1–2 David exclaims the blessedness of forgiven sin.
In 32:3–4 he reflects on the anguish of heart he felt under conviction for his sin.
In 32:5 he recounts his repentance (cf. Ps. 51) and God's forgiveness.
In 32:6–7 he reflects on the grace he has experienced, commending it to others (32:6) and addressing God in grateful praise (32:7).
In 32:8–9 he reflects on the lesson learned, here citing (in summary) words from God to him.
In 32:10 he testifies again to the blessedness of forgiveness and of God's steadfast love.
In 32:11 he offers a call to praise.

In Romans 4:7–8 the apostle Paul cites David's opening lines from this psalm, clarifying in light of gospel revelation how forgiveness is obtained. Rather than imputing our sins to us, God imputes our sins to Christ and Christ's righteousness to us. Here, in Christ, the joy of free forgiveness is firmly secured. This psalm teaches us that free justification in Christ is foundational to blessedness and joy.

## PSALM 40

A Psalm of David.
1 I waited patiently for the LORD;
he inclined to me and heard my cry.

2 He drew me up from the pit of destruction,
out of the miry bog,
and set my feet upon a rock,
making my steps secure.
3 He put a new song in my mouth,
a song of praise to our God.
Many will see and fear,
and put their trust in the Lord.
4 Blessed is the man who makes
the Lord his trust,
who does not turn to the proud,
to those who go astray after a lie!
5 You have multiplied, O Lord my God,
your wondrous deeds and your thoughts toward us;
none can compare with you!
I will proclaim and tell of them,
yet they are more than can be told.
6 In sacrifice and offering you have not delighted,
but you have given me an open ear.
Burnt offering and sin offering
you have not required.
7 Then I said, "Behold, I have come;
in the scroll of the book it is written of me:
8 I delight to do your will, O my God;
your law is within my heart."
9 I have told the glad news of deliverance
in the great congregation;
behold, I have not restrained my lips,
as you know, O Lord.
10 I have not hidden your deliverance within my heart;
I have spoken of your faithfulness and your salvation;
I have not concealed your steadfast love and your faithfulness
from the great congregation.
11 As for you, O Lord, you will not restrain

your mercy from me;
your steadfast love and your faithfulness will
ever preserve me!
12 For evils have encompassed me
beyond number;
my iniquities have overtaken me,
and I cannot see;
they are more than the hairs of my head;
my heart fails me.
13 Be pleased, O LORD, to deliver me!
O LORD, make haste to help me!
14 Let those be put to shame and disappointed altogether
who seek to snatch away my life;
let those be turned back and brought to dishonor
who delight in my hurt!
15 Let those be appalled because of their shame
who say to me, "Aha, Aha!"
16 But may all who seek you
rejoice and be glad in you;
may those who love your salvation
say continually, "Great is the LORD!"
17 As for me, I am poor and needy,
but the Lord takes thought for me.
You are my help and my deliverer;
do not delay, O my God!
To the choirmaster

We have noted that exact classification of psalms is sometimes difficult, and exhaustive definitive lists of the psalms according to psalm type are almost impossible to come by. One reason for this is that some of the psalms combine these standard psalm forms. We have seen that Psalms 81 and 95 are "combination" psalms, combining a praise psalm and prophetic psalm together. Similarly, Psalm 40 combines the two forms of thanksgiving (acknowledgment) and lament. This is a psalm of praise and petition.

Notice that in 40:1–4 David addresses the congregation; he talks *about* God to the people, giving a report of God's deliverance in David's time of need. This is a "new song" (40:3) of praise reflecting God's recent kindness to him. Thus, 40:4 is a kind of homily counseling the people, in essence, "I have seen and experienced God's goodness, and you will too if you trust in him." Then in 40:5–8 he speaks *to* God and offers words (40:5) and sacrifice (40:6–8) of praise in reporting God's kindness to him. All this reflects the standard components of an individual song of grateful praise (acknowledgment psalm).

Notice, however, that 40:11 is an expression of confidence. Then 40:12 expresses lament. Then 40:13 begins a petition. And 40:16–17 expresses hope of praise and confidence. These are all the components of a lament psalm.

This psalm, then, combines two psalm types: it begins with a psalm of acknowledgment and ends with lament. Psalm 40:1–8 is an acknowledgment psalm, moving from report of deliverance to praise. Then 40:9–12 transitions to 40:13, which begins petition. So we may outline the psalm as follows:

- Psalm of acknowledgment or grateful praise (40:1–8)
  - Addressed to the congregation (40:1–4)
  - Addressed to God (40:5–8)
- Transition (40:9–12)
  - Affirmation of David's praise (40:9–10)
  - Affirmation of God's faithfulness (40:11–12)
- Psalm of petition/lament (40:13–17)
  - Petition for deliverance (40:13–15)
  - Hope of praise (40:16)
  - Concluding petition and affirmation of trust (40:17)

**David's Testimony of Deliverance (40:1–4)**

1 I waited patiently for the LORD;
he inclined to me and heard my cry.
2 He drew me up from the pit of destruction,

out of the miry bog,
and set my feet upon a rock,
making my steps secure.
3 He put a new song in my mouth,
a song of praise to our God.
Many will see and fear,
and put their trust in the LORD.
4 Blessed is the man who makes
the LORD his trust,
who does not turn to the proud,
to those who go astray after a lie!

In 40:1–4 David addresses the congregation with praise for God's merciful deliverance. He does not identify the event or specify any details. "My cry" and the figurative "pit of destruction . . . miry bog" (40:1–2), however, inform us that the circumstances were severe, likely life-threatening. Perhaps he is reflecting on his days fleeing from King Saul. In any case, the deliverance was great—God set him on a massive "rock" (40:2) where his footing was secure. This experience gave David new cause for praise, and the singing of a "new song" testifying of God's great deliverance (40:3a). He intends by his testimony of deliverance to encourage others to trust God also (40:3b). Convinced that God is always faithful to his people, David concludes this opening section by pronouncing the blessedness of all who trust in God and who do not turn aside to false supports (40:4).

**David's Pledge of Praise (40:5–8)**

In 40:5–8, David turns from the congregation to address God himself:

5 You have multiplied, O LORD my God,
your wondrous deeds and your thoughts toward us;
none can compare with you!
I will proclaim and tell of them,
yet they are more than can be told.

6 In sacrifice and offering you have not delighted,
but you have given me an open ear.
Burnt offering and sin offering
you have not required.
7 Then I said, "Behold, I have come;
in the scroll of the book it is written of me:
8 I delight to do your will, O my God;
your law is within my heart."

Here David both pledges to proclaim God's faithfulness to the congregation (40:5) and offers himself in continual service to God (40:6) as prescribed for him in the law (40:7, "scroll of the book").

Psalm 40:6–8 requires further explanation. As we have seen, psalms of grateful praise are ordinarily accompanied by a thank offering. But in this case there will be no sacrifice and no communal meal celebrating the deliverance. Instead, David pledges to give himself to God. The Hebrew of 40:6 reads, "My ear you have dug"—God bored out his ear, as it were. This figure of speech (metonymy) connotes that God gave David ears to hear God. The ear itself is figurative also, a synecdoche in which a part of the body represents the whole. If God has your ear, he has *you*, your whole body. The Septuagint translators rightly understood this figure of speech, and so they rendered it interpretively, "A body you have prepared for me." The parallel, then, is antithetical: "You don't want a sacrifice or meal offering—you want me!" The thought is akin to Romans 12:1–2. So in glad appreciation for God's goodness to him, David offers himself wholly to God.

But the language of Psalm 40:6–8 goes further. This life offered to God replaces not only a "sacrifice and [meal] offering," the usual thank offerings, but also the "burnt offering and sin offering." This language seems excessive, for David's life at its best could never constitute a sin offering. So it seems here the purview expands. Indeed, the writer of Hebrews places this psalm on the lips of Jesus who alone could offer his life to God as a sin offering.

4 For it is impossible for the blood of bulls and goats to take away sins.
5 Consequently, when Christ came into the world, he said,

> "Sacrifices and offerings you have not desired,
> but a body have you prepared for me;
> 6 in burnt offerings and sin offerings
> you have taken no pleasure.
> 7 Then I said, 'Behold, I have come to do your will, O God,
> as it is written of me in the scroll of the book.'"

8 When he said above, "You have neither desired nor taken pleasure
in sacrifices and offerings and burnt offerings and sin offerings"
(these are offered according to the law), 9 then he added, "Behold,
I have come to do your will." He does away with the first in order to
establish the second. (Heb. 10:4–9)

Inspired by God, the writer of Hebrews interprets Psalm 40 as the prayer of Jesus.[1] David's giving of himself to God anticipates Christ's giving of himself in sacrifice. David's example of giving himself in service to God is a model for us all, but specifically it represents our Lord. Psalm 40 is a psalm of grateful praise that climaxes in David's giving of himself to God, and in this the psalm intentionally looks ahead to the one who would give himself to God in ultimate sense as sin offering.

### David's Affirmations (40:9–12)

> 9 I have told the glad news of deliverance
> in the great congregation;
> behold, I have not restrained my lips,
> as you know, O Lord.
> 10 I have not hidden your deliverance within my heart;

1 Note that "my sins" in 40:12 would be better rendered "the sins committed against me"; cf. Gen. 16:5, "my violence" = "violence done to me."

I have spoken of your faithfulness and your salvation;
I have not concealed your steadfast love and your faithfulness
from the great congregation.
11 As for you, O Lord, you will not restrain
your mercy from me;
your steadfast love and your faithfulness
will ever preserve me!
12 For evils have encompassed me
beyond number;
my iniquities have overtaken me,
and I cannot see;
they are more than the hairs of my head;
my heart fails me.

Here we see why a grateful praise song precedes the lament. David can be counted on to give God the glory he deserves. In these verses David affirms that he has proclaimed God's faithfulness to the congregation (40:9–10). He pledged to give praise, and he has done so. But just as he has "not restrained" his lips from praise (40:9–10), so also he affirms that God will "not restrain" further mercies from him (40:11) now in this yet another distress (40:12). In 40:12 David laments the insuperable opposition he faces. "My iniquities" here would be better rendered, "the iniquities done against me" (cf. Gen. 16:5, "my violence" = "violence done to me"). Again, David does not identify this event in his life precisely, but in view are those who "seek to snatch away my life" (Ps. 40:14). And with this briefly stated lament he moves next to his petition.

**David's Plea for Deliverance (40:13–17)**

David concludes his psalm with a petition, first for his own deliverance (40:13–15):

13 Be pleased, O Lord, to deliver me!
O Lord, make haste to help me!

14 Let those be put to shame and disappointed altogether
who seek to snatch away my life;
let those be turned back and brought to dishonor
who delight in my hurt!
15 Let those be appalled because of their shame
who say to me, "Aha, Aha!"

Then, as a note of confidence, he expresses hope that he and all who trust in the Lord will proclaim his praise:

16 But may all who seek you
rejoice and be glad in you;
may those who love your salvation
say continually, "Great is the LORD!"

Finally, David concludes his psalm with a plea and an affirmation of his continued trust:

17 As for me, I am poor and needy,
but the Lord takes thought for me.
You are my help and my deliverer;
do not delay, O my God!

This petition section was later cherry-picked for liturgical use, as can be seen in Psalm 70 of book 2.

The overall logic of the psalm is simple: After a consideration of God's answer to prayer (40:1–10), David highlights a new need (40:11–12) and petitions God accordingly (40:13–17). He moves from the experience and testimony of deliverance to a new need and petition. The psalm brings together two psalm forms. And again this serves as a model of instruction for our own prayers in dependence on God.

## PSALM 92

A Psalm. A Song for the Sabbath.

1 It is good to give thanks to the LORD,
to sing praises to your name, O Most High;
2 to declare your steadfast love in the morning,
and your faithfulness by night,
3 to the music of the lute and the harp,
to the melody of the lyre.
4 For you, O LORD, have made me glad by your work;
at the works of your hands I sing for joy.
5 How great are your works, O LORD!
Your thoughts are very deep!
6 The stupid man cannot know;
the fool cannot understand this:
7 that though the wicked sprout like grass
and all evildoers flourish,
they are doomed to destruction forever;

8 but you, O LORD, are on high forever.

9 For behold, your enemies, O LORD,
for behold, your enemies shall perish;
all evildoers shall be scattered.
10 But you have exalted my horn like that of the wild ox;
you have poured over me fresh oil.
11 My eyes have seen the downfall of my enemies;
my ears have heard the doom of my evil assailants.
12 The righteous flourish like the palm tree
and grow like a cedar in Lebanon.
13 They are planted in the house of the LORD;
they flourish in the courts of our God.
14 They still bear fruit in old age;
they are ever full of sap and green,

15 to declare that the Lord is upright;
he is my rock, and there is no unrighteousness in him.

**Introduction**

In the aftermath of God's work on his behalf, the psalmist composes his song of grateful praise (92:1). In the final arrangement of the Psalter it serves to complement the strong affirmation of trust in Psalm 91. The superscript identifies this as a psalm written for use on "the Sabbath day," though this may be a later editorial addition. This notation along with 92:3 and 92:13 indicate that the setting is the temple. The psalmist's mention of the enemy attack (92:9) and his "exalted . . . horn" (92:10) indicate that the king, perhaps David himself, is the speaker. In 92:1a he addresses the congregation, and in 92:1b he addresses God. Then in 92:13, he positions himself among the people of God to sing with them in the temple in conjunction with his sacrifice.

The precise connotations of the psalm's use "for the Sabbath" are uncertain. According to the Mishnah, the Levitical choir in the second temple chanted a psalm each day of the week. On Sunday they sang Psalm 24; on Monday, Psalm 48; on Tuesday, Psalm 82; on Wednesday, Psalm 94; on Thursday, Psalm 81; on Friday, Psalm 93; and on the Sabbath, Psalm 92. So in the Second Temple period, the temple singers would sing this psalm on the Sabbath, and there would be a lamb offered in sacrifice of the burnt offering (Num. 28:9, 1). There is no reason to assume that this was not the practice during the first temple period also. In any case, Psalm 92 is a song the people of God have sung for many centuries. It is almost without question that Jesus and his disciples sang it, as have believers ever since.

The figures of speech in this psalm are vivid. For example, the wicked flourish like grass (Ps. 92:7), but the righteous like palm trees and the cedars of Lebanon (92:12). The contrast is imaginative and vivid. The grass grows quickly and quickly dies, but the palm tree and the cedars of Lebanon grow tall and seem to live forever. The figurative language and the terseness of it call for reflection. They are like snapshots, a slideshow, not like prose or a motion picture, and the reader must consider how these differing verses and stanzas are related to one another.

**Survey Exposition**[2]

The psalm has the common components of an individual song of grateful praise:

- proclamation (92:1–3)
- summary statement with reflection (92:4–8)
- report of deliverance (92:9–11)
- reflection (92:12–14)
- praise (92:15)

However, it may be more precise to understand Psalm 92 is a mixture of a hymn and of an individual song of grateful praise:

- 92:1–8: hymn or praise psalm
  - call to praise (92:1–3)
  - cause or reason for praise (92:4–8)
- 92:9–15: individual song of grateful praise
  - report of deliverance (92:9– 11)
  - reflection (92:12–14)
  - praise (92:15)

The key to the psalm is in the center: "But you, O LORD, are on high forever" (92:8, reflecting "O Most High," 92:1). This verse climaxes the first stanza, which highlights the prosperity of the wicked, and it establishes the theme of the second, which speaks of God's ultimate triumph over them. So it is a janus or transition verse. Overall, the psalm is structured chiastically so as to draw attention to 92:8. The significance of this we will see as we go along. Before going into a

2 See also Bruce K. Waltke and James M. Houston, *The Psalms as Christian Praise: A Historical Commentary* (Grand Rapids, MI: Eerdmans, 2019), chap. 4.

more detailed exposition, here is the content and structure of the psalm at a glance:

A. The king praises the Lord (92:1–4)
  B. Praise for God's great work and profound thoughts (92:5–6)
    C. All evildoers eliminated (92:7)
      X. The Lord is on high forever (92:8)
    C.′ All evildoers perish (92:9)
  B.′ King rejoices in victory (92:10–11)
A.′ The righteous and the king praise the Lord (92:12–15)[3]

First, the leader speaks to the congregation: "It is good to give grateful praise to the Lord" (92:1, authors' translation). Instead of a call to praise, he makes a declaration that it is good to praise. Then he proclaims God's attributes of unfailing love and reliability (92:2) and praises him specifically for his work (92:4), which the psalmist specifies in 92:10–11 in terms of God's victory when under enemy attack. Then in 92:12–15 he reasons from this particular triumph of God to the universal truth that when the wicked prosper, it is part of God's plan that will lead to their extermination, to God's universal victory over evil, and to the universal prosperity of the righteous.

This psalm seems to have two introductions: a hymn (92:1–3) and a grateful praise (92:4). Psalm 92:1–3 differs from the typical praise form in that instead of a call to praise, the psalmist simply asserts, "It is good to praise." But typical of the hymns, these verses celebrate God's unfailing love and reliability. The individual song (92:9–15) is typical in its praise for God's acts in history on behalf of the king. Spurgeon cites Aquinas, who helpfully summarizes, "We thank God for His benefits and praise Him for His perfections."[4]

3 See Waltke and Houston, *Psalms as Christian Praise*, 103.

4 C. H. Spurgeon, *The Treasury of David*, vol. 6 (New York: Marshall Brothers, 1883), 269. Spurgeon cites Aquinas's *Fillicius*.

## Stanza 1 (92:1–8)

### *A Call to Praise (92:1–3)*

The psalm begins with a series of imperatives (92:1–3). The opening line declares, "It is good to give grateful praise to the LORD [I AM]." The second line is the parallel: "to sing praises to your name [which is, I AM], O Most High." The congregational setting is apparent. In liturgy, the leader addresses the congregation (92:1–3) and then addresses God also, by his name (92:4–5).

Psalm 92:1–2 calls the people of God to give praise for his "steadfast love" and "faithfulness," a common theme in the Psalter. This praise is to be ceaseless, both morning and night (92:2). And it deserves to be accompanied by musical instruments (92:3). This praise is all-deserved, and it is "good" (92:1) to render it always.

### *Cause or Reason for Praise (92:4–8)*

The Lord is worthy of continual praise because his "steadfast love" and "faithfulness" have been manifested to the psalmist in great works on his behalf (92:4–5). Still more to the point, these works reflect God's purposes in history, and his "thoughts," which are profound and "deep" (Ps. 92:5; cf. Rom. 11:33–36), are worthy of reflection and praise.

"Only through the relationship with God is man enabled to recognize ultimate truth and reality; without that relationship he lapses into a deceptive illusion"[5] (cf. Ps. 111:10); thus, fools are unable to grasp these thoughts (92:6). The wicked are unable to grasp that though they may prosper for a time, they will at last be eliminated (92:7). "Unspiritual men fail to perceive that the prosperity of the wicked is but the prelude to their ruin,"[6] that they are being set up for destruction (cf. Rom. 9:17). They do not understand that the Lord is "on high forever" (Ps. 92:8) and reigns even over their wickedness and rebellion.

5 Artur Weiser, *The Psalms: A Commentary*, The Old Testament Library (Philadelphia: Westminster, 1962), 615.

6 A. F. Kirkpatrick, *The Book of Psalms: Books IV and V* (Cambridge: Cambridge University Press, 1912), 559.

### Stanza 2 (92:9–15)

Psalm 92:8 is the center line of the psalm and a janus: "But you, O LORD, are on high forever." This is both the climax of the first stanza (92:1–7) and the subject of the second (92:9–15) where the thought is developed: God's enemies may sprout and grow quickly like the grass, but their time will be short. God will destroy them (92:7). The Lord rules on high forever (92:8), and he will dispose of his enemies by means of his king (92:9–11). This stanza begins where the first stanza ends—with the extermination of the wicked (92:9–11), a precursor of the eschaton. In 92:11 the psalmist gives his narrative recounting God's saving acts: "my eyes gazed in triumph at those who tried to ambush me" (authors' translation[7]). Then in his reflections in 92:12–15 he extrapolates from this experience to a universal truth. Like the authors of Psalms 37, 49, 73 (didactic psalms), this psalmist gives serious thought to the prosperity of the wicked, but unlike them he resolves the problem of theodicy from considerations of his personal salvation. The king is an earwitness and eyewitness that, in the end, the righteous triumph over the wicked.

So in his psalm of praise the psalmist draws a stark contrast between the wicked and the righteous (cf. Ps. 1). The wicked may flourish like grass (92:7a), but they will surely come to destruction (92:7b, 9, 11). By contrast, the righteous will flourish like palm trees and the great cedars of Lebanon (92:12), and they will praise God in his presence forever (92:13–15). Specifically, they will give praise that he is "upright" and without "unrighteousness" (92:15). The wicked may prosper for now, but ultimately God will be shown to be just.

The psalm is about God, as the center line of the psalm (92:8) makes clear. God is transcendent over all, both in space and in time. "On high," as Tate explains, "refers to the realm where Yahweh lives and works and from whence he sends forth his power and help for those in need, or against those whom he punishes (e.g., Ps 18:17; // 2 Sam 22:17; 93:4; 102:20; 144:7; Isa 32:15; 33:5; 57:15; 58:4)."[8] He is the exalted one who

7 See Waltke and Houston, *Psalms as Christian Praise*, 100.

8 Marvin E. Tate, *Psalms 51–100*, Word Biblical Commentary 20 (Dallas: Word, 1990), 467.

rules over all that is. This is crucial to understanding the psalm. Elsewhere it is the king who eliminates the enemy, but here the psalmist is careful to clarify that it is God who destroys the enemy by means of the king. Behind the king is the purpose of the God who is over all (cf. Pss. 2, 110).

Note again that the first stanza concludes with a purpose clause explaining the divine intention behind the short-term flourishing of the unrighteous (i.e., their extermination, 92:7b), and the second stanza concludes with a purpose clause also, now explaining the divine intention behind the long-term flourishing of the righteous (i.e., their praise of God, 92:15).

> 9 For behold, your enemies, O LORD,
> for behold, your enemies shall perish;
> all evildoers shall be scattered.

> 15 to declare that the LORD is upright.

These are God's "deep thoughts" (92:5) that the psalmist extols: the wicked flourish for a time but only for their ultimate destruction; the righteous will flourish forever to declare God's praise (cf. Rom. 9:22–23). With its focus on the king's destruction of God's enemies the outlook of the psalm takes an eschatological turn (Ps. 92:12–15). The king's triumph over his enemies with God's help foreshadows the kingdom of God and Christ's ultimate triumph over death, Satan, and all evil.

Ancient Jewish interpreters also understood it eschatologically. The Targum on 92:8 reads, "But you are high and supreme in this age, O LORD, and you are high and supreme in the age to come."[9] And Mishnah Tamid 7:4 comments on "for the Sabbath": "A psalm for the future, for the day that is completely Shabbat [tranquil] for

9 Targum, Ps. 92:9, The Newsletter for Targum and Cognate Studies (website), accessed October 12, 2022, http://targum.info/pss/ps4.htm.

all eternity."[10] The New Testament writers see this trajectory also and in specific connection to the Lord Jesus Christ.

**Final Reflections**

The psalm is eschatological in its outlook. It anticipates the final and complete destruction of the wicked and the eternal praise of the righteous in the presence of God, the eternal temple of the new heaven and new earth. The mention of the palm trees and the cedars of Lebanon growing together likewise has eschatological perspective, for these two very different kinds of trees do not grow together any more than wolves and lambs dwell together (Isa. 11:6–8).[11] Palm trees grow in low and hot environments, cedars in high and cold. Psalm 92 therefore ties into an outlook that is pervasive in Scripture—the new creation. Most of the stories of the Bible, including the exodus and the gospel itself, represent the final triumph of the righteous over the temporary prosperity of the wicked. This theme is especially prominent in biblical prophecy—in Daniel 7, for example, where the raging nations prosper but only for a time until they fall in judgment. The book of Revelation is given in large part to demonstrate dramatically the eventual fall of the kingdom of this world to Christ (e.g., Rev. 11:15). Worldly kingdoms, from that of Sargon of Akkad to the Third Reich of Hitler, have all passed away, but God's kingdom endures forever. "The Lord knows the way of the righteous, / but the way of the wicked will perish" (Ps. 1:6).

One (not altogether unique) contribution Psalm 92 makes to this larger theme is that the wicked are unable to grasp their inevitable ruin (92:6–7). The blindness of natural man is a common biblical theme, but here it is applied specifically to their eventual ruin (cf. Ps. 73:9–11; Prov. 9:18). Created in God's image, they have within them a sense of right and wrong and of justice. Indeed, "though they know God's righteous decree that those who practice such things

10 Mishnah Tamid 7, Sefaria (website), accessed October 12, 2022, https://www.sefaria.org/texts.

11 We owe this observation to Professor Warren Gage, in personal conversation.

deserve to die, they not only do them but give approval to those who practice them" (Rom. 1:32). Yet this knowledge is suppressed (Rom. 1:18), and warnings—such as that of the psalmist here—go unheeded until it is too late.

11

# Songs of Trust

*"The Lord is my rock!"*

SONGS OF TRUST ARE JUST THAT: psalms that express a settled confidence in the Lord for his goodness and continuing care. This note of trust in God dominates throughout the Psalter, and we have seen that one component of the petition-lament psalm is this expression of confidence. But some of the psalms develop this theme in a more prominent way, and as such these "psalms of confidence" are often among the favorites of the people of God—such as Psalm 23, which we have already examined. Other examples of these psalms of trust include Psalms 11, 16 (but begins with a petition), 27:1–6, 62, 63, 91, 121, 125, and 131.

These songs of trust are a derivative of the lament psalm in that they typically reflect a context of trouble or concern of some kind, only it is the expression of trust that dominates. These troubles are not usually identified specifically—"my enemies," for example, suffices for Psalm 23. Whatever trouble there is lies in the background. Psalms of trust do not lament (Ps. 63 may be an exception) or make petition. Nor do they yet express the grateful praise of the individual songs of this genre. With trouble in the background they express a firm trust in the Lord's faithful care. These songs of trust are almost all oriented to the psalmist himself (e.g., 23), although the psalmist may represent the community. Psalm 125 pertains to the community. Generally, some specific threat of death gives rise to these expressions of confidence, and despite these external threats, a sense of peace dominates (e.g., 131:2). Tremper Longman observes that these psalms are often marked by striking metaphors that graphically portray God as the one in whom the psalmist may safely trust: God as refuge (11:1; 16:1), shepherd (23:1), light (27:1), rock (62:2), and help (121:2).[1]

The individual songs of trust open with a declaration of trust, as Psalm 125: "Those who trust in the LORD are like Mount Zion." Hassell Bullock notes other common motifs:[2]

- An **interior lament**, which in these psalms is usually only in the background but occasions this expression of trust.
- An **invitation to trust** calls others to put their trust in the Lord along with the psalmist.
- The **basis of trust** specifies something about God that renders him trustworthy—for example, God's character, his majesty, his covenant love, his power in creation, or his past deliverances.

These components appear in any order, and not all are present in every psalm in this category. Nevertheless, it is helpful to note them. Psalm 23 is the best-known song of trust. We have already commented on it (see p. 156 for its figures of speech that inform its structure), so we will not touch upon it again here. Here we will look first at Psalm 131.

---

1 Tremper Longman III, *How to Read the Psalms*, How to Read Series (Downers Grove, IL: InterVarsity Press, 1988), 31.

2 C. Hassell Bullock, *Encountering the Book of Psalms: A Literary and Theological Introduction*, Encountering Biblical Studies (Grand Rapids, MI: Baker Academic, 2001), 168–70.

## PSALM 131

Superscript:

A Song of Ascents. Of David.

**The king's declaration of trust and interior lament:**

1 O LORD, my heart is not lifted up;
my eyes are not raised too high;
I do not occupy myself with things
too great and too marvelous [better: *difficult*] for me.
2 But I have calmed and quieted my soul,
like a weaned child with its mother;
like a weaned child is my soul within me.

**The king's invitation to Israel to trust:**

3 O Israel, hope in the LORD
from this time forth and forevermore.

Here David humbles himself before the Lord in simple trust. Some crisis lies in the background, but he does not identify it. Nor will he be so proud as to demand explanations (131:1). Rather, he calms himself (131:2) and gives Israel hope that that God will intervene and save her (131:3).

## PSALM 62

Psalm 62, another psalm of David, serves as another example of a song of trust.

**Declaration of trust:**

1 For God alone my soul waits in silence;
from him comes my salvation.
2 He alone is my rock and my salvation,
my fortress; I shall not be greatly shaken.

**Interior or background lament:**

3 How long will all of you attack a man
to batter him,
like a leaning wall, a tottering fence?
4 They only plan to thrust him down from his high position.
They take pleasure in falsehood.
They bless with their mouths,
but inwardly they curse. *Selah*

**Further affirmation of trust:**

5 For God alone, O my soul, wait in silence,
for my hope is from him.
6 He only is my rock and my salvation,
my fortress; I shall not be shaken.
7 On God rests my salvation and my glory;
my mighty rock, my refuge is God.

**Invitation to trust:**

8 Trust in him at all times, O people;
pour out your heart before him;
God is a refuge for us. *Selah*
9 Those of low estate are but a breath;
those of high estate are a delusion;
in the balances they go up;
they are together lighter than a breath.
10 Put no trust in extortion;

set no vain hopes on robbery;
if riches increase, set not your heart on them.

**Basis of trust:**

11 Once God has spoken;
twice have I heard this:
that power belongs to God,
12 and that to you, O Lord, belongs steadfast love.
For you will render to a man
according to his work.

## PSALM 91

1 He who dwells in the shelter of the Most High
will abide in the shadow of the Almighty.
2 I will say to the LORD, "My refuge and my fortress,
my God, in whom I trust."
3 For he will deliver you from the snare of the fowler
and from the deadly pestilence.
4 He will cover you with his pinions,
and under his wings you will find refuge;
his faithfulness is a shield and buckler.
5 You will not fear the terror of the night,
nor the arrow that flies by day,
6 nor the pestilence that stalks in darkness,
nor the destruction that wastes at noonday.
7 A thousand may fall at your side,
ten thousand at your right hand,
but it will not come near you.
8 You will only look with your eyes
and see the recompense of the wicked.
9 Because you have made the LORD your dwelling place—
the Most High, who is my refuge—

10 no evil shall be allowed to befall you,
no plague come near your tent.
11 For he will command his angels concerning you
to guard you in all your ways.
12 On their hands they will bear you up,
lest you strike your foot against a stone.
13 You will tread on the lion and the adder;
the young lion and the serpent you will trample underfoot.
14 "Because he holds fast to me in love, I will deliver him;
I will protect him, because he knows my name.
15 When he calls to me, I will answer him;
I will be with him in trouble;
I will rescue him and honor him.
16 With long life I will satisfy him
and show him my salvation."

### The Voices of Psalm 91

The first challenge in interpreting this psalm is the identification of the pronouns and the voices who speak.

In 91:1–2 we have "I" speaking—the voice of the one confessing to God his faith in him:

2 I will say to the Lord, "My refuge and my fortress,
my God, in whom I trust."

The "I," the speaker, is presumably the psalmist. The Hebrew text has no superscript identifying the author, but the Septuagint does, naming David—as does the Targum. As we have mentioned, the Septuagint superscripts in book 4 appear reliable (cf. Heb. 4:7 of Ps. 95). Moreover, the rest of the psalm is addressed to him as the one whom God protects in battle, presumably a king. So the "I" is probably King David, the "protomessianic" king—that is to say that he represents the ideal king in his loins.

In 91:3–13 another voice speaks, a voice who assures the previous speaker of God's deliverance and protection. Here the "I" (91:2) becomes the "you" to whom someone else is speaking.

> 3 He will deliver you from the snare of the fowler
> and from the deadly pestilence.

The reprise of 91:2 in 91:9 makes this identification explicit:

> 9 Because you have made the LORD your dwelling place—
> the Most High, who is my refuge.

The speaker of 91:3–13 is unidentified, probably a prophet or a priest.

Then in Psalm 91:14–16 there is another "I" who assures "him" of security, exaltation, fullness of life. This is obviously the Lord God, the one who delivers and protects this one who takes refuge in him:

> 14 Because he holds fast to me in love, I will deliver him;
> I will protect him, because he knows my name.
> 15 When he calls to me, I will answer him;
> I will be with him in trouble;
> I will rescue him and honor him.
> 16 With long life I will satisfy him.

The psalm includes several voices, and to understand the psalm we must discern who is being represented by these pronouns or voices. The third voice is God, who speaks in 91:14–16. The "I" of 91:1–2 is the "you" of 91:3–13—the one who takes refuge in God and who is given assurance, therefore, of God's protection. And the speaker who gives this assurance in 91:3–13 is not identified, but he must be a prophet or a priest, for he speaks authoritatively for God.[3]

3 The attenuation from prophetic speech to divine speech occurs commonly in prophetic literature. (e.g., Mic. 1:2–5, 6–7, 8–14, 15–16).

So we have these three persons in view:

1. The "I" who is speaking (91:1–2)
2. The prophet or priest who is speaking to him (91:3–13)
3. God, who talks about him (91:14–16)

We are left, then, to discern the identity of the first speaker, who is also the subject of the entire psalm. It is common to read this psalm as though it refers to the faithful generally, any godly Israelite. Others have suggested that it refers to a traveler facing threats, or perhaps those on a pilgrimage to a festival, or that the dialogue here is between a worshiper and a priest. But none of these suggestions adequately takes into account the military language that characterizes the psalm, the promise that he will see his enemies in defeat (91:7–8), or the assurance that he will be kept around the clock safe from every danger. This is not a promise that God has given to "Mr. Everyman," or even to faithful Israel (cf. Ps. 44; Matt. 23:35, 37; Rom. 8:36; Heb. 11:35–40). It would seem that a Davidic king is in view, the "I" who takes refuge in God's protection. In Psalm 91:5–7 he is one who is surrounded by thick arrows flying around him (91:5), who has an innumerable enemy hosts slain at his right hand (91:7), and who in every battle sees victory (91:8). It is not surprising that the Targum understands this as David speaking to Solomon.

But does this psalm describe Solomon? Note that this king is untouchable, invincible, and sees only triumph. God gives him around-the-clock protection and every success in battle. He will trample lions and snakes (91:13) in ultimate triumph. This is not true of just any Davidic king. The king of Psalm 44, for example, laments that he went down in defeat, and God's people throughout history have been martyred (cf. Rom. 8:36). This king, however, cannot be defeated. It appears that in his assured invincibility, this king anticipates the greater Davidic King to come, the Lord Jesus Christ whose final triumph over the nations is everywhere assured (cf. Ps. 2). Even throughout his earthly life he was invulnerable until when in his own time he laid down his life. "I lay down my life that I may take it up again. No one takes it from me, but I lay it down of my own accord. I have authority to lay it down, and I have authority to take it up again" (John 10:17–18). Not Herod, not the storm at sea, not the leper's contagious disease, not the Jewish authorities—no one could take his life from him until he would lay it down of himself. And when he returns to bring his kingdom to its culmination, he is promised complete success also.

We find hints of this interpretation in the New Testament. On the mount of temptation Satan recognizes Psalm 91:11–12 as referring to Christ (Matt. 4:5–6; Luke 4:9–11), and Jesus does not refute him on that basis but allows the reference to stand. And in Luke 10:19 Jesus confers the protection of Psalm 91:13 on the seventy-two messengers to the towns where he himself was about to go, implying that the verse refers first to him: "Behold, I have given you authority to tread on serpents and scorpions, and over all the power of the enemy, and nothing shall hurt you."

So we have identified the three voices in the psalm:

1. The messianic King who asserts his faith (91:1–2)
2. The prophet who assures him of God's protection (91:3–13)
3. And the Lord God himself who speaks of the king and promises his protection and certain success (91:14–16)

## Survey Exposition[4]

First we have the king's confession of faith in the Lord God:

1 He who dwells in the shelter of the Most High
will abide in the shadow of the Almighty.
2 I will say to the Lord, "My refuge and my fortress,
my God, in whom I trust."

4 See Waltke and Houston, *Psalms as Christian Praise*, chap. 3. See also the excellent exegesis of Psalm 91 in Andrew J. Schmutzer, "Psalm 91: Refuge, Protection, and Their Use in the New Testament," in *The Psalms: Language for All Seasons of the Soul*, ed. Andrew J. Schmutzer and David Howard Jr. (Chicago: Moody Publishers, 2013), chap. 6.

In his confession of faith the king uses four divine names or titles. "God" (אֱלֹהִים) is the Creator's title that draws attention to his universal power. "Lord" (יהוה) is his covenant name to Israel, highlighting his aseity. "The Most High" (עֶלְיוֹן) highlights his universal rule and supremacy over all things, the title of God "which cuts every threat down to size."[5] The precise meaning of "the Almighty" (שַׁדַּי) is not entirely clear, but it at least entails the idea of "almighty," so this translation is the best we can do.

"The secret place" is a place of intimate fellowship, a poetic reference (metonymy) to the temple. It is the place of the presence of God where only the righteous are allowed. "The shadow of the Almighty" is the place of protection (cf. 17:8). Put simply, the king dwells safely in the sanctuary.

Psalm 91:2 records the content of the king's faith that he confesses: "I will say to the Lord, '[he is] my refuge and my fortress / my God, in whom I trust'" (91:2). The connotation is that the psalmist "says" this habitually—"It is my custom to say." That is, the king declares his faith publicly and as a matter of course. "Refuge and fortress" refers to a citadel on a cliff that is impregnable.[6] This is the psalmist's sense of security in the safekeeping of the Most High, Almighty God. This is a song of trust.

Then the prophet speaks (91:3–13), and his speech has two cycles: 91:3–8 and 91:9–13. In 91:9 the prophet reprises the words of the king from 91:2, and as such it functions as a transition between the two halves of his speech:

91:3–8: promises of assurance to the king
91:9: reprise of the king's faith
91:10–13: more promises to the king

So the psalm as a whole functions antiphonally, proceeding from the words of the king, to the words of the prophet, then back to the

5 Derek Kidner, *Psalms 73–150* (London: Inter-Varsity Press, 1975), 364.

6 The Hebrew for "fortress" is מְצוּדָה, *metsuda*, the term now well known from the famous stronghold Masada.

words of the king again (in the prophets reprise), then the words of the prophet, and then climactically God himself speaks:

91:1–2: the king's confession of faith
91:3–8: the prophet's assurance to the king
91:9: reprise of the king's faith
91:10–13: more promises to the king
91:14–16: God himself speaks with assurance or promises to the king.

The prophet speaks to encourage the king with promises of safety and success—assurances that our king is invulnerable and that he will triumph. Israel's covenant Lord—the Most High, the Almighty, God—hides this king in his protective care both day and night (91:5). Psalm 91:3–8 is composed of a couplet assuring the king that God will deliver him and protect him (91:3–4), and of a quatrain (two couplets) pertaining to battlefield perils: human weapons and nature's plague (91:5–6) and the king's triumph through the plague (91:7–8). The perils alternate as several merisms. In 91:5–6 the perils are by humans (91:5) and by God through nature (91:6). In 91:5 they come at night and by day—that is, both hidden and open. In 91:6 the perils come in the darkness and at noon, both open and hidden. Through it all the king will be safe.

Some speculate that the perils in view are demons or sunstroke, but those interpretations have no solid foundation in this text. Goldingay comments, "The military language reflects the king's literal position as commander in chief; reference to epidemic and to his tent may link with that."[7] He also notes, "There is no explicit indication of this reference [demons], and it would be unique in the OT, which makes hardly any reference to demons."[8] The gifted poet of Psalm 91 discerns and reports the telling details of the battle to represent the whole: terror

7 John Goldingay, *Psalms*, vol. 3, *Psalms 90–150* (Grand Rapids, MI: Baker Academic, 2008), 39.

8 Goldingay, *Psalms*, vol. 3, 45.

at night, arrows that fly by day, and an unscathed king gazing at the tens of thousands of soldiers around him, felled by a plague that accompanies battle.

A "trap" or "snare" (91:3) conceals its deadly danger so to take its victim suddenly and by surprise (cf. Eccles. 9:12). This may be a reference to death or to secret plots of the enemy (Ps. 91:8), but here too the king is promised safety.

The "pestilence" or "plague" (91:3, 6) likely refers to the bubonic plague, which is associated with war elsewhere. The Angel of the Lord killed 185,000 in the Assyrian army in 701 BC, probably through a bubonic plague (2 Kings 19:35). The Greek historian Herodotus, writing his history in the fourth century BC, heard an Egyptian story about Sennacherib's campaign that also ascribed the Assyrian withdrawal from Jerusalem to a miracle.[9] The presence of mice in his account suggests that a bubonic plague destroyed the Assyrian army because rat fleas are the usual carriers of the disease. So also the Lord's ark of the covenant probably inflicted a bubonic plague on the Philistines, for their apotropaic devices of tumors and rats are connected with a bubonic plague (1 Sam. 6:5). A bubonic plague was a most serious threat that God leveled against Israel (Lev. 26:25; Num. 14:12). This plague "stalks in darkness" (Ps. 91:6a) as one soldier after another dies, and "rushes at noon" (91:6b, authors' translation[10]) as it now reaches epidemic proportions. As a result the army falls all around, as with the Assyrian army in the days of Hezekiah. Psalm 91:7–8 elaborates upon the plague rather than weapons, presumably because it is an act of God and not the king's army. The king is not said to use his sword, yet the entire army of the enemy lies in waste at his right

9 "So when presently king Sanacharib came against Egypt, with a great force of Arabians and Assyrians . . . during the night were overrun by a horde of field mice that gnawed quivers and plows and the handles of shields, with the result that many were killed fleeing unarmed the next day." Herodotus, *The Histories*, ed. A. D. Godley, 2.141.2, 5, Perseus Digital Library (website), https://www.perseus.tufts.edu/hopper/. Mice are a Greek symbol of pestilence; it is Apollo Smintheus (the mouse god) who sends and then ends the plague in Homer, *Iliad*, 1.39.

10 Waltke and Houston, *Psalms as Christian Praise*, 65n15.

hand as he gazes on it. Close as he is to it, the plague destroys others but not the king.

The king is assured that God will cover him "with his pinions" (91:4; cf. 91:9), which evokes the image of a mother bird protecting her brood by spreading her wings over them (cf. Ruth 2:12). This imagery is unique to the Old Testament and in the ancient Near East and quite possibly finds its origins in the Jerusalem temple, where God resides above the wings of the cherubim over the ark (Ex. 25:20; 1 Kings 8:6–7). The figurative reference to the temple in Psalm 91:1 supports this interpretation (cf. 91:11–12).

The second cycle of the prophet's speech (91:9–13) reprises the king's faith (91:9) and assures him further of divine (91:10) and angelic (91:11–13) protection. God's angels will protect him in all his ways (91:11), prevent his foot from stumbling (91:12), and give him victory over his foes (91:13). The serpent and lion symbolize Israel's political and historical enemies and the spiritual powers that inspire and empower them (cf. Gen. 3:16; Isa. 51:9–10, 34; Ezek. 29:3; 32:2; Luke 10:19; Rom. 16:20). Their defeat by the Messiah finds their echo in Revelation 12 and anticipates the climactic event of Revelation 19. The Messiah will trample them under his feet as Jehu's horse trampled Jezebel's corpse (2 Kings 9:30–37).

In the final stanza (91:14–16), God himself speaks:

14 Because he holds fast to me in love, I will deliver him;
I will protect him, because he knows my name.
15 When he calls to me, I will answer him;
I will be with him in trouble;
I will rescue him and honor him.
16 With long life I will satisfy him
and show him my salvation.

"Because he holds fast to me" indicates the king's loving fidelity to God. This expression is used of a man fancying a woman (Gen. 34:8; Deut. 21:11) and of the Lord's attraction to Israel (Deut. 7:7).

"Beauty is in the eye of the beholder" is famous because it rings true to a universal human experience: people have different ideas of what beauty is. The spiritual purity of the king enables him to see what is truly beautiful, the transcendental and absolute beauty of God himself, and he clings to it. In response, God gives the king rescue, triumph, and endless joy.

God sometimes responds to the faithful with assurance that their prayer is answered (cf. Pss. 12:5; 46:10; 60:6; 75:2; 81:6; 95:8). Here God gives assurance to the king by talking about him, not to him. This psalm is for us, but it is not in its first point of reference about us. It concerns the great King, the Lord Jesus Christ, and it assures us of his endless rule and ultimate triumph over evil. And in his triumph we will have a part. Salvation from evil, including its elimination, consummates God's purpose on history (cf. 50:23). Christ has already conquered death, and at the end of history the Lord Jesus will prove victorious over every enemy: "For he must reign until he has put all his enemies under his feet. The last enemy to be destroyed is death" (1 Cor. 15:25–26). This psalm assures us that our Lord Jesus Christ, presently exalted to the right hand of God, will bring God's kingdom to its final, culminating purpose. He will succeed against all enemies and will never meet with defeat.

## PSALM 139

A Psalm of David.

1 O Lord, you have searched me and known me!
2 You know when I sit down and when I rise up;
you discern my thoughts from afar.
3 You search out my path and my lying down
and are acquainted with all my ways.
4 Even before a word is on my tongue,
behold, O Lord, you know it altogether.
5 You hem me in, behind and before,
and lay your hand upon me.

6 Such knowledge is too wonderful for me;
it is high; I cannot attain it.
7 Where shall I go from your Spirit?
Or where shall I flee from your presence?
8 If I ascend to heaven, you are there!
If I make my bed in Sheol, you are there!
9 If I take the wings of the morning
and dwell in the uttermost parts of the sea,
10 even there your hand shall lead me,
and your right hand shall hold me.
11 If I say, "Surely the darkness shall cover me,
and the light about me be night,"
12 even the darkness is not dark to you;
the night is bright as the day,
for darkness is as light with you.
13 For you formed my inward parts;
you knitted me together in my mother's womb.
14 I praise you, for I am fearfully and wonderfully made.
Wonderful are your works;
my soul knows it very well.
15 My frame was not hidden from you,
when I was being made in secret,
intricately woven in the depths of the earth.
16 Your eyes saw my unformed substance;
in your book were written, every one of them,
the days that were formed for me,
when as yet there was none of them.
17 How precious to me are your thoughts, O God!
How vast is the sum of them!
18 If I would count them, they are more than the sand.
I awake, and I am still with you.
19 Oh that you would slay the wicked, O God!
O men of blood, depart from me!
20 They speak against you with malicious intent;

your enemies take your name in vain.
21 Do I not hate those who hate you, O Lord?
And do I not loathe those who rise up against you?
22 I hate them with complete hatred;
I count them my enemies.
23 Search me, O God, and know my heart!
Try me and know my thoughts!
24 And see if there be any grievous way in me,
and lead me in the way everlasting!
To the choirmaster.

**Introductory Considerations**

Psalm 139 is among the greatest of the Psalms, and for many of God's people it has been a favorite. It so extensively expresses confidence in God (139:1–18) that we treat it here as a song of trust. But it ends with a petition and a situation where the psalmist is in crisis (139:19–24), so it is properly a petition-lament psalm, the confidence section of which is unusually prominent:

- confidence (139:1–12)
- praise (139:13–18)
- lament (139:19–22)
- petition (139:23–24)

Two factors date this psalm as preexilic:

- David is the author (superscript).
- He wrote the psalm to be sung in temple worship (subscript).

Yet the editors of the psalter placed this psalm in book 5, a collection of psalms generally reflecting the postexilic community living under Persian imperialism and opposition by neighboring states. Israel hoped for a Messiah, an ideal David to come, and until then David's psalms served as models on how to live as exiles.

## Survey Exposition[11]

The psalm broadly has two sections: meditations or reflections on God's greatness (139:1–18) and petition or lament (139:19–24). More narrowly, the psalm consists of four stanzas composed symmetrically, each stanza consisting of six verses.

In 139:1–18 David gives us three stanzas of meditation on the "omnis" of God—his omniscience (139:1–6), his omnipresence (139:7–12), and his omnificence (139:13–18). In the latter part of 139:18 David says, "I awake," which segues into the final stanza (139:19–24). So David moves from meditation (139:1–18) to petition (139:19–24). The second half of 139:18, then, seems to connote that David, having contemplated the greatness of God, awakes to the realities of his world and makes petition accordingly. Once again David is hounded by enemies (139:19), but once again he remains in full control of his rationality and his emotions, able to compose brilliant and deeply reflective poetry.

Throughout the first three stanzas of the psalm David exults in the greatness of God. His reflections on these divine attributes is not purely theoretical but intensely personal: God knows *me*; God is with *me*; God made *me*. And it is with all this in mind that he finally expresses his lament and petition in the final stanza, a lament and petition still intensely personal yet uncharacteristic of other lament psalms.

### *Stanza 1: God Knows Me*

In the first stanza (139:1–6) David exults in God's omniscience—God knows him. "Searched" here metaphorically connotes scrutinizing, a thorough examination. He knows David's thoughts and even his intentions. It is impossible for us truly to know the hearts and minds of another person; it is nearly impossible to know our own hearts objectively. But David marvels that God knows him to his core. That is, God knows who we truly are. Then David develops this by the use

11 See also Bruce K. Waltke and James M. Houston, *The Psalms as Christian Worship: A Historical Commentary* (Grand Rapids, MI: Eerdmans, 2010), chap. 16. Waltke is heavily indebted to Harriet Lovitt, "A Critical and Exegetical Study of Psalm 139" (UMI Dissertation Series, 1964).

of merisms (139:2–3)—my rising and reclining, my walking and lying down. God knows "all my ways" (139:3) to the depth of my being all day and all night long, publicly and privately. "From afar" (139:2b) may be understood either spatially or temporally. Donald Glenn thinks the temporal sense is in view because David's focus here is not on God's transcendence but on the thoroughness of his knowledge.[12] God discerns our thoughts ahead of our thinking them. Even at the point of verbalizing our thoughts, God already knows them (139:4). That is, God knows the future, all events before they happen (cf. Isa. 40:13–14; 41:21–29; 42:8–9; 43:8–13; 44:6–8; 46:8–10). He knows our thoughts, our speech, and our ways before we think, speak, or act. There is nothing about us that is unknown to God. God's knowledge is beyond all human comprehension (Ps. 139:5–6; cf. 147:5). Psalm 139:6 is a plain affirmation of the incomprehensibility of God. Our awareness of this divine attribute can have a confining effect (139:5). But despite the restrictive sense expressed in 139:5, David seems to celebrate God's omniscience and find it a source of comfort, and on the basis of this awareness he humbly offers himself to the Lord for moral appraisal (139:23–24).

### *Stanza 2: God Is with Me*

In the second stanza (139:7–12) David exults in God's omnipresence—God is with him. David's awareness of God's omniscience leaves him with a sense that he lives under divine rule, and so he considers next the universality of this divine presence from which there is no possibility of escape. He imagines this on the vertical axis (139:8) and on the horizontal axis (139:9–10):

> 8 If I ascend to heaven, you are there!
> If I make my bed in Sheol, you are there!
> 9 If I take the wings of the morning

12 Donald G. Glenn, "An Exegetical and Theological Exposition of Psalm 139," in *Tradition and Testament: Essays in Honor of Charles Lee Feinberg*, ed. John S. Feinberg and Paul D. Feinberg (Chicago: Moody Press, 1981), 172.

and dwell in the uttermost parts of the sea,
10 even there your hand shall lead me,
and your right hand shall hold me.

Then he considers it from yet another angle—darkness. Darkness in poetry regularly symbolizes death, danger, fear, chaos. In the darkness you stumble or may be robbed. But darkness makes no difference to God—he sees in the darkness as he sees in the light. In brief, there is no place where God is not. We cannot run quickly ahead of him to find a place to hide, for he is already there, wherever we may be. Not just God's omniscience but contemplation of his omnipresence also is both staggering to the mind and potentially threatening. And yet again, these thoughts of God seem for David to be a source of comfort, for he revels in them.

*Stanza 3: God Made Me*

In the third stanza (139:13–18) David exults in God's omnificence—God made him. This stanza is offered as validation of the previous two: "for[13] you gave birth" (139:13, authors' translation). David is looking to the ultimate cause of his existence. The sense is "I say God knows me thoroughly and is always with me because he made me from the time of my conception in the darkness of my mother's womb (139:15). Darkness is not dark to God."

The first part of 139:13 translates literally, "For you gave birth to my kidneys," but this makes for poor poetry in English.[14] Nor does it convey the intended sense. "Inward parts" reads better to our ears but leaves the emphasis on the physical body only. "Kidneys" is the term often used to refer to our basic emotional structure, much like our figurative use of the word "heart" in English. David is referring to the entire person as the creative work of God's meticulous care: "For you formed my

13 Stanza three is introduced with the logical כִּי, "because."

14 The King James translators rendered the Hebrew word (קָנָה) as "you possessed" and then rendered "reins" instead of "kidneys." "Reins" is French for kidneys, but their decision preserved the poetic sound.

inward parts; / you knitted me together in my mother's womb" (v. 13). "You made me who I am, inside and out" is the idea. In 139:14 David marvels at this work of God. Indeed, David marvels further that God made more than his physical and emotional being—he charted the entire course of his life also, from his embryonic formation onward, each day for his own purposes (139:16). God's knowledge of David is thorough and complete, for he wrote the script for his entire life. These thoughts are awesome and yet countless (139:17–18).

Contemplation of God's "omnis" and his creative work staggers the human mind and leaves us humbled in adoration. Again, David's reflections on the greatness and perfections of God are not merely theoretical but personal and worshipful. As confining as this awareness of God's thorough knowledge of him may seem—for who could escape the God who formed my entire being and foreordained the whole course of my life?—he takes up such thoughts eagerly and finds them praiseworthy (139:14), "precious" (139:17–18), and useful for his own encouragement. As Delitzsch remarks, "He falls asleep over the pondering upon them, wearied out; and when he wakes up, he is still with God, i.e., still ever absorbed in the contemplation of the Unsearchable One, which even the sleep of fatigue could not entirely interrupt."[15]

### *Stanza 4: God, My Enemies, and Me*

In the final stanza David turns from these extended reflections on God to address his own situation. We should note that at the end of the third stanza, David says, "I awake, and I am still with you" (139:18), revealing this (God's presence with him) has been on his mind throughout the psalm. Thus, 139:18 serves as a janus as he transitions to "the real world" of the wicked that surround him. Here he expresses his desire for God's help and the removal of his enemies. And he inquires as to his own loyalty to God. "I am on God's side, and I hate the wicked who hate him; indeed, I hate them with a seething hatred." David "does not

15 C. F. Keil and F. Delitzsch, *Commentary on the Old Testament*, vol. 5 (Peabody, MA: Hendrickson, 1996), 813.

occupy a neutral position" with regard to God's enemies but lines up with God against them.[16] In this he exemplifies the virtue of righteous indignation. His prayer in 139:19–22 is that God's kingdom would be established and his will done on earth as it is in heaven (Matt. 6:20). The greatness of this God demands that all his enemies be eliminated.

But if God knows us as thoroughly as David describes in the previous stanzas, David's concern turns to himself also. So in 139:23–24 he pauses, and in genuine worship he wonders whether he is truly allied with God (cf. John 21:17; Acts 17:24–31). So instead of attempting to flee or hide, he calls on God to lay bare his heart—to search him to determine if there is any waywardness in him. He does not resist but rather welcomes God's all-seeing investigation. He wants to be certain that he is indeed on God's side. "As I hate the wicked in their way, so would I hate every wicked way in myself."[17] And should God find any offensive "way" in him, David asks God to direct his path to faithfulness: "lead me in the way everlasting."

This petition, then, is not typical of the petition-lament psalms but differs in at least three ways. First, David does not ask for deliverance but merely wishes that bloodthirsty blasphemers be eliminated. Second, he does not protest innocence or confess sin but seeks the integrity of loyalty to God. And third, he asks for intimacy—that God would test the mettle of his integrity against his own misgivings (139:23–24) and lead him in the way everlasting. Throughout this psalm, and still here in its conclusion, David considers God's attributes not by way of theological abstraction but in terms of personal application and devotion. This is what made David the king he was.

Finally, David hands off his psalm "to the choirmaster," extending its message to all God's covenant people. With him we confess today that Christ, the Creator of all things, knows what is in the heart, that he is always present with us, that his enablement in our own spiritual warfare is essential, and that we love him supremely and want more

16 C. H. Spurgeon, *The Treasury of David*, vol. 6 (New York: Marshall Brothers, 1883), 265.
17 Spurgeon, *Treasury of David*, vol. 6, 266.

than anything else to remain loyal to him always. And like David, we, God's people today, although we are zealous for him, confess our own conflicted hearts and plead with God to keep us faithful to him.

> Keep us, Lord, oh, keep us cleaving
> To Thyself and still believing,
> Till the hour of our receiving
> Promised Joys with Thee!
>
> Then we shall be where we would be,
> Then we shall be what we should be;
> Things that are not now, nor could be,
> Soon shall be our own![18]

18 Thomas Kelly, "Praise the Savior, Ye Who Know Him" (1806), Timeless Truths (website), accessed September 13, 2022, https://library.timelesstruths.org/.

12

# Messianic Psalms

*"May all kings fall down before him!"*

WE HAVE IT ON THE AUTHORITY of the Lord Jesus himself that the Psalms speak of him (Luke 24:44; cf. Matt. 21:42; 22:41–45), and the New Testament writers repeatedly affirm the same (e.g., John 19:24; Acts 2:22–31, 33–36; Heb. 1:5, 8–9, 13; 2:6–8). In fact, of the New Testament's 283 direct citations of the Old Testament 116 (41 percent) are from the Psalter, overwhelmingly in reference to Christ. Jesus himself cited or alluded to the Psalms more than 50 times, again, overwhelmingly with reference to himself. Table 12.1 below is selective, but it demonstrates that the New Testament writers understood the Psalms as pointing to Christ in his life and character, his passion, and his glory.

Amyraut's famous counsel, that when we read of the Davidic king in the Psalms we must look with one eye to the historical kings and the other eye to the Messiah whom they represent, is well grounded. Indeed, if Jesus and the New Testament writers are our guide, we are not reading the Psalms rightly if we do not read the Psalms with an eye toward the Messiah. It is these considerations that shape the goal of this chapter. Here we will survey the larger background to this Messianic expectation and then suggest some ways in which the Psalter contributes to it.[1]

Table 12.1 Christ and the Psalms in the New Testament[2]

| Psalms | Topic | New Testament |
|---|---|---|
| | CHRIST'S PASSION | |
| 6:3 | "My soul is troubled" | John 12:27 |
| 22:1 | "Why have you forsaken me?" | Matt. 27:46 |
| 22:18 | "Divided my garments" | John 19:24* |
| 31:5 | "Into your hands I commit" | Luke 23:46 |
| 34:20 | "not one of his bones will be broken" | John 19:36* |
| 35:19 | "hated me without a cause" | John 15:25* |
| 40:6–8 | "a body . . . prepared for me" | Heb. 10:5–10* |
| 41:9 | "lifted his heel against me" | John 13:18 |
| 42:5 | "my soul is very sorrowful" | Matt. 26:38 |
| 69:21 | "sour wine . . . to drink" | Matt. 27:34, 48 |
| 109:25 | "wagging their heads" | Matt. 27:39 |
| 2:2 | "against his Anointed" | Acts 4:25–26 |
| | CHRIST'S FERVOR | |
| 69:9 | "zeal for your house" | John 2:17* |
| | CHRIST'S AUTHORITATIVE TEACHING | |
| 78:2 | "I will open my mouth" | Matt. 13:35* |
| 37:11 | "the meek shall inherit the earth" | Matt. 5:5 |
| 48:2 | "Jerusalem . . . city of the great King" | Matt. 5:35 |

1 See also Bruce K. Waltke, *An Old Testament Theology: An Exegetical, Canonical, and Thematic Approach* (Grand Rapids, MI: Zondervan, 2007), 887–993.

2 Scriptures marked with an asterisk are citations from the Psalms; the unmarked are allusions to it.

*(Table 12.1 continued)*

| Psalms | Topic | New Testament |
|---|---|---|
| 78:24 | "bread from heaven" | John 6:31–32* |
| 82:6 | "you are gods" | John 10:34* |
| | CHRIST'S GLORY | |
| 8:4–5 | Humiliation and glory | Heb.2:5–10*; 1 Cor. 15:27* |
| 2:7 | My Son | Acts 4:25–26*; Heb. 1:5*; 5:5* |
| 45:6–7 | Throne forever | Heb. 1:8–9* |
| 110:1 | David's Lord | Matt. 22:44* |
| 118:22–23 | Rejected stone as capstone | Matt. 21:42* |

## Messiah and Messianism

The word *messiah* (מָשִׁיחַ) derives from a word that means "to paint, smear, sprinkle, or daub"—or, in a ritual sense, "to anoint" (מָשַׁח; cf. Ps. 45:7; 89:20). *Messiah* means "anointed" or "anointed one" (cf. 2:2) and reflects the ritual by which the king was officially appointed (cf. 1 Sam. 16:13; 2 Sam. 2:4, 7; 5:3). As we saw in reference to Psalm 2, anointing with sacred oil by the prophet was necessary to qualify and equip the king for his office. It served to consecrate him as God's property and place him under his protection (105:15). "The anointed one" (Messiah) came to refer to the ideal King who would introduce the new age, ushering in the kingdom of God that would extend over the whole world (cf. Isa. 61:1–3). *Messianism*, then, pertains to the expectation and realization of this ideal king at the end of the age. The Messiah is the promised King—promised by the Lord in covenant with David. He is the ideal King—both gifted and faithful. And he will rule universally in righteousness and peace at the end of the age.

## The Messianic Hope in the Old Testament

The origins of this messianic hope appear already in the garden of Eden. Mankind was created as God's vice-regents to extend his rule over all the earth (Gen. 1:26–28). Adam did not rule faithfully over the garden and surrendered to Satan (Gen. 3). In the aftermath, God promised a champion of the woman's seed who would reestablish God's rule and bring Satan to utter defeat (3:14–15), though at some cost to himself (3:15). That is, this champion will establish God's kingdom through suffering.

The remainder of the Genesis narrative is given in large part to identifying that promised seed of the woman who will be victorious over Satan, tracking it through Seth (4:25), Shem (9:26–27), preeminently Abraham (12:1–3; 22:17–18), then Isaac (Gen. 26:1–5; cf. Rom. 9:7), and Jacob (Gen. 27:28–29; 28:3–4, 12–15; 35:9–12). And of Jacob's twelve sons it is Judah who will hold the kingly scepter (49:8–12). The Old Testament narrative does not narrow the promise further until it is given to David, of the tribe of Judah (1 Chron. 28:4). The prophet Samuel anointed him (1 Sam. 16:1–13), and God entered into a covenant with him, promising that his house and his throne (i.e., his dynasty) would be established forever. This event marks a watershed moment in the outworking of God's purpose:

> 1 Now when the king lived in his house and the Lord had given him
> rest from all his surrounding enemies, 2 the king said to Nathan the
> prophet, "See now, I dwell in a house of cedar, but the ark of God
> dwells in a tent." 3 And Nathan said to the king, "Go, do all that is in
> your heart, for the Lord is with you." 4
>
> But that same night the word of the Lord came to Nathan, 5 "Go and
> tell my servant David, 'Thus says the Lord: Would you build me a house
> to dwell in? 6 I have not lived in a house since the day I brought up the
> people of Israel from Egypt to this day, but I have been moving about
> in a tent for my dwelling. 7 In all places where I have moved with all the
> people of Israel, did I speak a word with any of the judges of Israel, whom
> I commanded to shepherd my people Israel, saying, "Why have you not
> built me a house of cedar?"' 8 Now, therefore, thus you shall say to my
> servant David, 'Thus says the Lord of hosts, I took you from the pasture,
> from following the sheep, that you should be prince over my people
> Israel. 9 And I have been with you wherever you went and have cut off
> all your enemies from before you. And I will make for you a great name,

like the name of the great ones of the earth. [10] And I will appoint a place for my people Israel and will plant them, so that they may dwell in their own place and be disturbed no more. And violent men shall afflict them no more, as formerly, [11] from the time that I appointed judges over my people Israel. And I will give you rest from all your enemies. Moreover, the LORD declares to you that the LORD will make you a house. [12] When your days are fulfilled and you lie down with your fathers, I will raise up your offspring after you, who shall come from your body, and I will establish his kingdom. [13] He shall build a house for my name, and I will establish the throne of his kingdom forever. [14] I will be to him a father, and he shall be to me a son. When he commits iniquity, I will discipline him with the rod of men, with the stripes of the sons of men, [15] but my steadfast love will not depart from him, as I took it from Saul, whom I put away from before you. [16] And your house and your kingdom shall be made sure forever before me. Your throne shall be established forever.'" [17] In accordance with all these words, and in accordance with all this vision, Nathan spoke to David. (2 Sam. 7:1–17; cf. 1 Chron. 17:1–14)

Several elements of this promise are significant in light of our developing theme:

- God promises that he will establish the throne of David: a Davidic son will reign on his throne (2 Sam. 7:12).
- This dynasty will be "for my [God's] name" (7:13a). In light of 7:13b (eternal reign) and later revelation, this seems to imply that the Davidic king will preside in God's kingdom. That is to say, God will administrate his rule through this Davidic king.
- This reign and kingdom will be eternal (7:13b).
- God will be a "father" to this Davidic king, and the king will be God's "son" (7:14). This language of the king as God's "son" is significant in the developing theme (e.g., Ps. 2:7), as we will see. With reference to Jesus, "Son of God" is freighted with implications of deity also (cf. John 5:18), but it is a messianic title (cf. John 1:49).

- A degree of tension is built into the promise in that it is conditioned on obedience (2 Sam. 7:14), and thus the kingly line is nearly snuffed out altogether as a result of the successive failures of Israel's unfaithful kings. Yet David is assured that the promise will not ultimately be revoked as it was from Saul (2 Sam. 7:15–16; see Ps. 89). He will have a son whose rule and kingdom will never end. That is, the divine promise directs us to look for a faithful, ideal Davidic son.
- This promise could be read to imply that David's throne will continue and prosper via an endless succession of descendants, but the sustained singular references ("he," "his," "him," son") point ultimately to a Davidic king who will reign forever. The New Testament writers refer this to the resurrected Lord Jesus Christ (e.g., Heb. 7).
- Finally, it is worth noting that in 1 Chronicles 28:4 David himself connects this promise to the Judah prophecy in Genesis 49:10. Judah's scepter has been passed along to David and his greater son.

The messianic hope, then, grows significantly from this covenant that God enters with David. The Psalms present the ideal messianic King in terms of joyful hope, as we will see. The anticipation of the rise of the Davidic King looms large in the prophets also, and they unpack the promise in significant ways:

> 1 "Woe to the shepherds who destroy and scatter the sheep of my
> pasture!" declares the LORD. 2 Therefore thus says the LORD, the
> God of Israel, concerning the shepherds who care for my people:
> "You have scattered my flock and have driven them away, and you
> have not attended to them. Behold, I will attend to you for your
> evil deeds, declares the LORD. 3 Then I will gather the remnant of
> my flock out of all the countries where I have driven them, and I
> will bring them back to their fold, and they shall be fruitful and
> multiply. 4 I will set shepherds over them who will care for them,

and they shall fear no more, nor be dismayed, neither shall any be
missing, declares the LORD.
[5] "Behold, the days are coming, declares the LORD, when I will
raise up for David a righteous Branch, and he shall reign as king
and deal wisely, and shall execute justice and righteousness in the
land. [6] In his days Judah will be saved, and Israel will dwell securely.
And this is the name by which he will be called: 'The LORD is our
righteousness.'" (Jer. 23:1–6)

[20] "Therefore, thus says the Lord GOD to them: Behold, I, I myself
will judge between the fat sheep and the lean sheep. [21] Because you
push with side and shoulder, and thrust at all the weak with your
horns, till you have scattered them abroad, [22] I will rescue my flock;
they shall no longer be a prey. And I will judge between sheep and
sheep. [23] And I will set up over them one shepherd, my servant David,
and he shall feed them: he shall feed them and be their shepherd. [24]
And I, the LORD, will be their God, and my servant David shall be
prince among them. I am the LORD; I have spoken." (Ezek. 34:20–24;
cf. 37:15–28)

The well-known "Christmas prophecy" of Isaiah 9:6 likewise promises a "son" whose kingdom will be universal, eternal, and marked by peace and righteousness (see 9:1–7). Isaiah 11 prophesies that this "shoot from the stump of Jesse" (11:1) will be uniquely endowed with the Spirit of God to rule and judge in righteousness and bring transformation to the entire world. Micah prophesies that this king will come from Bethlehem (Mic. 5:2), the city of David. And Daniel 7 famously describes the kingdom of God being imposed on the raging nations of earth. This vision, undoubtedly informed by the Davidic promise, presents "one like a son of man" who rises on the clouds of heaven to stand before the Ancient of Days and receive the kingdom (7:13):

14 And to him was given dominion
    and glory and a kingdom,

that all peoples, nations, and languages
should serve him;
his dominion is an everlasting dominion,
which shall not pass away,
and his kingdom one
that shall not be destroyed. (7:14)

One feature of this prophetic hope is particularly striking. On the one hand the prophets envision a day when God himself will come and establish his kingdom. God himself will break into history, establish his rule universally, and judge the earth:

4 Say to those who have an anxious heart,
"Be strong; fear not!
Behold, your God
will come with vengeance,
with the recompense of God.
He will come and save you." (Isa. 35:4)

10 Behold, the Lord GOD comes with might,
and his arm rules for him;
behold, his reward is with him,
and his recompense before him.
11 He will tend his flock like a shepherd;
he will gather the lambs in his arms;
he will carry them in his bosom,
and gently lead those that are with young. (Isa. 40:10–11)

10 Sing and rejoice, O daughter of Zion, for behold, I come and I will dwell in your midst, declares the LORD. 11 And many nations shall join themselves to the LORD in that day, and shall be my people. And I will dwell in your midst, and you shall know that the LORD of hosts has sent me to you. (Zech. 2:10–11; cf. Jer. 31:2; Zech.14:3, 5, 9; Mal. 3:1)

The Psalms hold out this hope also:

11 Let the heavens be glad, and let the earth rejoice;
let the sea roar, and all that fills it;
12 let the field exult, and everything in it!
Then shall all the trees of the forest sing for joy
13 before the LORD, for he comes,
for he comes to judge the earth.
He will judge the world in righteousness,
and the peoples in his faithfulness. (96:11–13)

The Old Testament hope is replete with this expectation of God's personal intervention in history to establish his rule. The establishing of his kingdom is a work that God takes on himself, and he will indeed bring the whole world under his sway.

And yet, as we have seen, the hope was that it is David's son who will rule. Remarkably, in some of the prophetic passages, these two lines of prophecy—that God will rule and that David's son will rule—begin to merge. In Psalm 45, as we shall see below, David's son is addressed as "God," whose throne endures forever (45:6). And in 110 David addresses this son as his Lord (see p. 121). In Isaiah 9:6 the (Davidic) child who is born and son who is given will be called "the Mighty God, / Everlasting Father." In Daniel 7 the "one like a son of man" rides on the clouds of heaven, a distinctly divine activity (cf. Ps. 104:3; Isa. 19:1). In Jeremiah 23:5–6 God says he will raise up "for David a righteous branch" (i.e., a Davidic son) who will himself be "the LORD our righteousness." In Ezekiel 34:20–24, as we have seen, God promises to establish the Davidic king, and yet in this passage God says that he himself will be king (34:11–19). All this will, of course, resolve in the incarnation of Christ, but until then, these two tracks of prophecy, although they at times merge, remained a mystery.

This messianic hope is preserved in a prominent way in the apocalyptic literature of later Judaism as well. The intertestamental literature envisions all of history in terms of two radically differing ages: this age and the age to come. This age is marked by sin, suffering, death, and injustice. The age to come is marked by righteousness, resurrection, justice, peace, and prosperity. This present age is under the rule of Satan. The age to come will be ruled by "David," the messianic King who ushers in the kingdom of God over all the earth, bringing salvation to his people and judgment to his enemies. At the time of Maccabees (ca. 175 BC) the Jews recognized that for some time prophecy had ceased in Israel (1 Macc. 4:46; 9:27; 14:41).

### The Messianic Hope in the New Testament

This brief sketch of the messianic hope in Old Testament Judaism forms the backdrop of John the Baptist's dramatic announcement of the arrival of the kingdom of God (Matt. 3:1–3). Jesus himself announced the same (Matt. 4:17; Mark 1:14–15). In the birth of Jesus the kingdom of God breaks into history, and the King begins his work of overthrowing Satan (Matt. 12:27–29; Luke 10:18), inaugurating the new age. The New Testament itself opens with this announcement (Matt. 1:1),[3] and in a sense the New Testament in its entirety is given to expounding its significance. The narrative of Jesus's birth and infancy in Matthew has a pronounced Davidic focus. The genealogy (1:1–17) has a distinct Davidic shape, and the following narrative makes the note of *fulfillment* prominent (1:22–23; 2:15, 17–18, 23). The wise men also identify Jesus as the Davidic King (2:1–2), and Herod's advisers provide confirmation from the prophet Micah (Matt. 2:1–6; cf. Mic. 5:2). Luke's narrative stresses the same (Luke 1–2), most pointedly in the angelic announcement:

> [32] He will be great and will be called the Son of the Most High. And the Lord God will give to him the throne of his father David, [33] and he will reign over the house of Jacob forever, and of his kingdom there will be no end. (1:32–33)

3 Jesus's title "Christ" (Χριστός) is the Greek equivalent of "Messiah" ("anointed one").

John's narrative of the beginning of Jesus's public ministry drives our attention to the same (John 1:29–49), climaxing in Nathaniel's exclamation, "Rabbi, you are the Son of God! You are the King of Israel!" (1:49). Then at the end of his Gospel the apostle affirms that this recognition of Jesus as Messiah was his purpose in writing (20:31). Jesus himself laid claim to his messiahship (Luke 4:16–21; 24:27, 44; John 4:25–26; 5:29; 10:24–25), and for this claim he was held guilty of blasphemy and delivered over to the Roman authorities to be crucified (Matt. 26:63–66). And when Peter acknowledges Jesus as the Messiah, Jesus affirms that recognition as the result of divine revelation (Matt. 16:16–17). Then Jesus's passion narratives in the Gospels are marked by a cluster of reminders of this affirmation: the royal purple robe (John 19:2, 5); the crown of thorns (19:2); the reed for a kingly scepter (Matt. 27:29); Jesus's discussions with Caiaphas (Matt. 26:63–64) and Pilate (John 18:33, 37) about his kingship; the soldiers' mocking, "Hail, King of the Jews" (John 19:3); Pilate's "Behold your King" (John 19:14); the inscription over the head of Christ on his cross (Matt. 27:37); and even the centurion's confession (Matt. 27:54) all direct us to this theme. That Jesus is the long-awaited Christ would seem to be the central theme of the Gospels.

The book of Acts continues this emphasis. The apostle Peter interprets the events of Pentecost as evidence of Jesus's messianic enthronement (Acts 2:33–36). The proclamation of Jesus as messianic King marked the preaching of Stephen (7:37), Philip (8:35), and Apollos (18:28) also, and it was Paul's regular practice to press the point in the synagogues (17:2–3). And finally, too numerous to recount here, the epistles are replete with Old Testament citations connecting the messianic hope to Jesus (cf. Rom. 1:1–4; 2 Cor. 1:20; Heb. 7; Rev. 5:5).

The first promise of the Messiah (Gen. 3:15) informs us cryptically that Christ's ascent to kingship hinges on his suffering (cf. Isa. 53:11–12), and so it should not have been surprising that the Messiah would die (cf. Luke 24:44–47). The cluster of kingly reminders surrounding his passion (see above) serve to remind us that it is by his death that Jesus secures his kingdom (cf. John 12:31–33). But it is in his resurrection that his kingship is publicly declared (Rom. 1:1–4), and it is in his ascension that he is enthroned in heaven (Acts 2:33–36; Phil. 2:5–11).

The prophets of the Old Testament "searched and inquired carefully, inquiring what person or time the Spirit of Christ in them was indicating when he predicted the sufferings of Christ and the subsequent glories" (1 Pet. 1:10–11). For them the subsequent glories followed immediately. But that did not happen; they did not anticipate this gospel age. Jesus resolved the riddle in terms of "the secrets [mysteries] of the kingdom" (Matt. 13:11). The King has come, he has successfully accomplished his mediatorial work, he has achieved universal mediatorial rule (Matt. 28:18), and he has ascended to his throne (Luke 24:50–51; Acts 1:8–9). But Satan is still at work. The anticipated final judgment of God's enemies has not yet taken place, and the kingdom of God has not yet been brought to its culminating dominance in the world. At the end of the gospel age Christ will send his angels, and they will gather the weeds from the world and throw them into the fire (Matt. 13:39–43), and Christ will separate the sheep from the goats (Matt. 25). Now the kingdom is "inaugurated," the gospel of the kingdom is proclaimed accordingly (Matt. 11:1–9, 18–23; Acts 28:30–31), and by it men and women are rescued in faith from the kingdom of Satan and brought safely into the kingdom of Christ (Col. 1:13). As citizens of this kingdom we are to live faithfully unto him as we await his return. Then at last God's kingdom will be realized in its fullness (Matt. 6:10; Rev. 11:15), and Christ's universal lordship will be acknowledged by all (Phil. 2:9–11). Christ has come, and he will yet return. And in these two advents the messianic kingdom is established and the hope fulfilled.

### The Psalter and the Messianic Hope

This overview of the messianic hope both in its Old Testament anticipation and its New Testament fulfillment provides the broad biblical context for examining this hope as it is expressed in the Psalter. We have seen that the very royal orientation of the Psalter inevitably points ahead to David's greater messianic son promised to him in 2 Samuel 7:8–16 and finally realized in the Lord Jesus Christ.[4]

> Although the "I" in post-monarchic psalms (e.g., Ps. 137) refers to an anonymous leader or personifies Israel, the "I" of many pre-exilic psalms is the king; and if so, why not David?" . . . [As such] "most psalms—perhaps all the pre-exilic psalms—refer to the house of David, and if so, refer at least indirectly refer [*sic*] to Jesus Christ as member of that house.[5]

Indeed, the final editors of the Psalter seem to make this point by placing our Psalm 2 up front—a psalm of God's anointed. This link to the Old Testament messianic theme announces from the outset that the book concerns David's greater son. Let us explore this a bit further.

The Old Testament narrative directs us to look for an ideal son of David, and the Psalter presents him in just such idealistic terms. We will take **Psalm 72** as an example, a psalm that in its petition for the king describes the nature of the King's rule. The opening verses present the King as one who will rule in righteousness.

1 Give the king your justice, O God,
   and your righteousness to the royal son!
2 May he judge your people with righteousness,
   and your poor with justice!
3 Let the mountains bear prosperity for the people,
   and the hills, in righteousness!
4 May he defend the cause of the poor of the people,
   give deliverance to the children of the needy,
   and crush the oppressor!

4 See appendix 2.

5 Bruce K. Waltke, "Christ in the Psalms," in *A Hope Fulfilled: Essays in Honor of O. Palmer Robertson*, ed. Robert L. Penny (Phillipsburg, NJ: P&R, 2008), 27.

Here the psalmist offers prayer for the establishing of God's kingdom on earth. He longs for a king who will bring justice, prosperity, and peace to the world—that God's will would be done on earth as in heaven (Matt. 6:10). In 72:3 the "mountains" in view are the mountains of Jerusalem—the place of the temple, the royal court, the place where the king administrates justice. The prospect here is as of yet unrealized; not even Solomon, who in his old age abused the people, could establish such a kingdom.

Then 72:5–7 presents the king as eternal, reigning in peace and prosperity as long as the sun and moon endure:

> 5 May they fear you while the sun endures,
> and as long as the moon, throughout all generations!
> 6 May he be like rain that falls on the mown grass,
> like showers that water the earth!
> 7 In his days may the righteous flourish,
> and peace abound, till the moon be no more!

Again the prospect of a perpetual reign of a righteous king is as of yet unrealized. The king and his kingdom here are presented in their ideal that remains in hope.

In turn, 72:8–11 describes his kingdom as universal, again a hope that remains unrealized:

> 8 May he have dominion from sea to sea,
> and from the River to the ends of the earth!
> 9 May desert tribes bow down before him,
> and his enemies lick the dust!
> 10 May the kings of Tarshish and of the coastlands
> render him tribute;
> may the kings of Sheba and Seba
> bring gifts!
> 11 May all kings fall down before him,
> all nations serve him!

Psalm 72:12–14 describes the Davidic king as kind and compassionate, one who cares for and protects his subjects;

12 For he delivers the needy when he calls,
the poor and him who has no helper.
13 He has pity on the weak and the needy,
and saves the lives of the needy.
14 From oppression and violence he redeems their life,
and precious is their blood in his sight.

In 72:15–17 the psalmist prays for the exaltation and felicity of his kingdom:

15 Long may he live;
may gold of Sheba be given to him!
May prayer be made for him continually,
and blessings invoked for him all the day!
16 May there be abundance of grain in the land;
on the tops of the mountains may it wave;
may its fruit be like Lebanon;
and may people blossom in the cities
like the grass of the field!
17 May his name endure forever,
his fame continue as long as the sun!
May people be blessed in him,
all nations call him blessed!

The final verses are a doxology:

18 Blessed be the LORD, the God of Israel,
who alone does wondrous things.
19 Blessed be his glorious name forever;
may the whole earth be filled with his glory!
Amen and Amen!

Similar to familiar passages in the prophets (e.g., Isa. 9, 11), this psalm depicts the Davidic king in terms that transcend all the historic kings and look to the ideal King, the Messiah. He is righteous, faithful, and compassionate, and his kingdom is both universal and eternal in the age to come.

Other prominent "messianic" psalms include the following:

Psalm 2: the coronation of the King
Psalm 18: the King's salvation
Psalm 20: prayer for the King as he goes to battle
Psalm 21: blessing for the King
Psalm 24: the victorious King
Psalm 45: the King's wedding
Psalm 89: lament of house of David, hope for its restoration
Psalm 91: the King's protection and success
Psalm 101: guide for the ruler, his moral perfection
Psalm 110: King and priest
Psalm 144: the royal welfare

Alec Motyer helpfully summarizes the Psalter's presentation of the Messiah in brief:

> Summarizing the material offered in Psalms, the expected king would meet world-opposition (2:1–3; 110:1ff) but, as victor (45:3–5; 89:22–23) and by the activity of the Lord (2:6, 8; 21:1–13; 110:1–2), he would establish world-rule (2:8–12; 45:17; 72:8–11; 89:25; 110:5–6) based on Zion (2:6) and marked by a primary concern for morality (45:4, 6–7; 72:2-3; 101:1–8). He would rule for ever (21:4; 45:6; 72:5), in peace (72:7), prosperity (72:16) and undeviating reverence for the Lord (72:5). Pre-eminent among men (45:2, 7), he would be the friend of the poor and the enemy of the oppressor (72:2–4, 12–14). Under his rule the righteous would flourish (72:7). He would possess an everlasting name (72:17) and be the object of unending thanks (72:15). He is the recipient of the Lord's

everlasting blessing (45:2), the heir of David's covenant (89:28–37; 132:11–12) and of Melchizedek's priesthood (110:4). He belongs to the Lord (89:18), and is devoted to him (21:1, 7; 63:1–8, 11). He is his son (2:7; 89:27), seated at his right hand (110:1) and is himself divine (45:6).[6]

## Varieties of Messianic Psalms

The Lord Jesus himself taught that the Psalter speaks of him, and so we must learn to read it accordingly. But not all of the psalms speak of him *in the same way*. Here we will highlight some of the ways in which the Psalter anticipates Christ, but first it will be of help to observe the New Testament use of the Psalter.

### *The Psalter in the New Testament*

Even a brief examination of the New Testament citations of the Psalter show that Jesus and the apostles use the Psalms in a variety of ways. A psalm may be cited in defense of a theological position or to teach a given point of doctrine, as in Paul's teaching of the universal depravity of mankind (Rom. 3:11–12; cf. Ps. 14:1–3; 55:1–3). So also in Matthew 22:41–45 where Jesus cites Psalm 110:1 (even its superscript) to affirm the deity of Messiah. This usage affirms the authority of the Psalms as Scripture. Jesus's "proof texting" of Psalm 110:1, however, entails some notion of fulfillment also in that he embodies the psalm's expectation: he is both David's son and David's Lord.

Sometimes a psalm is cited to shed light on the significance of an episode in the life of Jesus. John does this for us in John 2:17 where he cites Psalm 69:9 to highlight Jesus's zeal for God's house. And in the parable of the landowner (Matt. 21:33–44) Jesus cites Psalm 118:22–23 to explain the significance of his rejection by the Jewish leaders and the eventual inclusion of the Gentiles into the kingdom. This is another kind of "fulfillment" use of the Psalms.

6 Alec Motyer, *Look to the Rock: An Old Testament Background to Our Understanding of Christ* (Grand Rapids, MI: Kregel, 1996), 31–32.

A psalm may also establish the theological confession of the church, as in the New Testament's repeated affirmation of Jesus's place at the throne of heaven (e.g., Eph. 1:20; cf. Ps. 110:1). This again is a kind of fulfillment use.

Sometimes the fulfillment idea is more obvious and direct, as in Jesus's use of Psalm 41:9 in John 13:18 to characterize his betrayal by Judas as a fulfillment of prophecy, and Peter's proclamation of the resurrection of Jesus in Acts 2:24–28 as a fulfillment of Psalm 16:8–11.

It is these "fulfillment" uses of the Psalter that concern us here.

*Anticipations of Christ in the Psalter*

To see how the Psalter speaks of Christ we must examine several representative samples. Consider the prophecy of **Psalm 110:1**:

> The LORD said to my Lord,
> "Sit at my right hand,
> until I make your enemies your footstool."

David's "Lord" must be the Messiah, and here Yahweh welcomes him to the throne of heaven. It is an enthronement scene, and the prophecy is clear: the Messiah will reign on the throne of heaven. In this case the relation between the prophecy and the fulfillment is clear and direct.

**Psalm 2** also, as we have seen, gives a direct prophecy of the Messiah's ultimate universal triumph. God has established him as King:

> 6 "As for me, I have set my King
> on Zion, my holy hill."

And the Messiah himself affirms it:

> 7 I will tell of the decree:
> the LORD said to me, "You are my Son;
> today I have begotten you."

As King he will inherit all the nations:

8 "Ask of me, and I will make the nations your heritage,
and the ends of the earth your possession."

And his enemies will be subdued:

9 "You shall break them with a rod of iron
and dash them in pieces like a potter's vessel."

Again the prophecy is forthright and clear, and the New Testament writers interpret it accordingly (e.g., Rev. 2:26–27; 19:15).

Or consider Peter's use of **Psalm 16** in Acts 2 on the day of Pentecost. As we will see, Psalm 16 is a petition psalm in which David prays for God's protection, and in 16:8–11 he expresses his confidence that God will, in fact, keep him safe:

8 I have set the LORD always before me;
because he is at my right hand, I shall not be shaken.
9 Therefore my heart is glad, and my whole being rejoices;
my flesh also dwells secure.
10 For you will not abandon my soul to Sheol,
or let your holy one see corruption.
11 You make known to me the path of life;
in your presence there is fullness of joy;
at your right hand are pleasures forevermore.

Both Peter and Paul understand David's confidence as prophetic, fulfilled in the resurrection of Jesus Christ. Peter appeals to this psalm in his famous sermon on the day of Pentecost:

[22] "Men of Israel, hear these words: Jesus of Nazareth, a man attested to you by God with mighty works and wonders and signs that God did through him in your midst, as you yourselves know—[23] this Jesus,

delivered up according to the definite plan and foreknowledge of God, you crucified and killed by the hands of lawless men. [24] God raised him up, loosing the pangs of death, because it was not possible for him to be held by it. [25] For David says concerning him,

"'I saw the Lord always before me,
for he is at my right hand that I may not be shaken;
26 therefore my heart was glad, and my tongue rejoiced;
my flesh also will dwell in hope.
27 For you will not abandon my soul to Hades,
or let your Holy One see corruption.
28 You have made known to me the paths of life;
you will make me full of gladness with your presence.'

[29] "Brothers, I may say to you with confidence about the patriarch David that he both died and was buried, and his tomb is with us to this day. [30] Being therefore a prophet, and knowing that God had sworn with an oath to him that he would set one of his descendants on his throne, [31] he foresaw and spoke about the resurrection of the Christ, that he was not abandoned to Hades, nor did his flesh see corruption. [32] This Jesus God raised up, and of that we all are witnesses." (Acts 2:22–32; cf. 13:35)

Peter finds the psalm's prophecy of Christ so clear that his Jewish audience must find it compelling, and so he presses it accordingly. His argument is simple:

- David said God would not allow his body to remain in the grave to see corruption.
- David's body in fact has remained in the grave for centuries.
- As a prophet David spoke of the Messiah, his greater son.
- Jesus's body did not see corruption: he has been raised from the dead.
- Jesus is the Messiah of whom David spoke!

The argument is indeed compelling. But notice that in its original context Psalm 16:8–11 is not so obviously "prophetic." It was an expression of David's own confidence in God's protection. And yet his language is so specific and his claim so grand that, at least after the fact, it is shown unmistakably to be a prophecy of the resurrection of Christ. The prophecy may not in its original setting be as obviously prophetic as Psalm 110:1. But the language was excessive with reference to David himself, and now in hindsight, at least, the connection to the Messiah is clear. The fulfillment is direct, but not until after the fact was it so recognized.

Now consider again **Psalm 45**:

A Maskil of the Sons of Korah; a love song.

1 My heart overflows with a pleasing theme;
I address my verses to the king;
my tongue is like the pen of a ready scribe.
2 You are the most handsome of the sons of men;
grace is poured upon your lips;
therefore God has blessed you forever.
3 Gird your sword on your thigh, O mighty one,
in your splendor and majesty!
4 In your majesty ride out victoriously
for the cause of truth and meekness and righteousness;
let your right hand teach you awesome deeds!
5 Your arrows are sharp
in the heart of the king's enemies;
the peoples fall under you.
6 Your throne, O God, is forever and ever.
The scepter of your kingdom is a scepter of uprightness;
7 you have loved righteousness and hated wickedness.
Therefore God, your God, has anointed you
with the oil of gladness beyond your companions;
8 your robes are all fragrant with myrrh and aloes and cassia.
From ivory palaces stringed instruments make you glad;

9 daughters of kings are among your ladies of honor;
at your right hand stands the queen in gold of Ophir.
10 Hear, O daughter, and consider, and incline your ear:
forget your people and your father's house,
11 and the king will desire your beauty.
Since he is your lord, bow to him.
12 The people of Tyre will seek your favor with gifts,
the richest of the people.
13 All glorious is the princess in her chamber, with robes interwoven with gold.
14 In many-colored robes she is led to the king,
with her virgin companions following behind her.
15 With joy and gladness they are led along
as they enter the palace of the king.
16 In place of your fathers shall be your sons;
you will make them princes in all the earth.
17 I will cause your name to be remembered in all generations;
therefore nations will praise you forever and ever.

The superscript of this psalm identifies it as a love song, and as the psalm progresses, it becomes obvious that it is a psalm to be sung at the king's wedding. He is dressed for the occasion, and the opening verses praise his handsomeness, grace, and valor. Later verses speak of his Gentile bride (45:10) and the sons she will bear him (45:16). The psalm has no historical superscript, so we cannot identify a specific Davidic king who is in view. The language throughout is grand, as we would expect in poetry. But the language of 45:6–7 is excessive in reference to any human king:

6 Your throne, O God, is forever and ever.
The scepter of your kingdom is a scepter of uprightness;
7 you have loved righteousness and hated wickedness.
Therefore God, your God, has anointed you
with the oil of gladness beyond your companions;

To the Christian reading with New Testament lenses, this divine-human King is quickly identified with Christ, the incarnate Son of God. And this is how the writer of the letter to the Hebrews cites it—an Old Testament "proof text" for the deity of the Messiah (Heb. 1:8–9). We cannot know how the original readers would have understood these verses, but this degree of "poetic license" must have been puzzling. But on this side of the incarnation of Christ we can see immediately that this psalm to the king is prospective of a greater King. Commentators routinely labor to identify the particular king in view in this psalm, but no such identification is given in the superscript. It is not about any particular historical king: it is about every Davidic king. And ultimately it is about the great King. And once we see this, we may suspect further that the Gentile bride in view foreshadows the church, Christ's bride. But in any case, this "prophecy" is not as immediately clear or direct as we saw in Psalm 110, at least not until after its fulfillment. It is prospective of the Messiah in a representative way: the king is a type or foreshadowing of the King.

We saw something similar to this in **Psalm 22**, where David's description of his own forsakenness (22:1) employs language that exceeds his own experience and is, in fact, exactly descriptive of Christ's crucifixion (22:14–18):

14 I am poured out like water,
    and all my bones are out of joint;
my heart is like wax;
    it is melted within my breast;
15 my strength is dried up like a potsherd,
    and my tongue sticks to my jaws;
    you lay me in the dust of death.
16 For dogs encompass me;
    a company of evildoers encircles me;
they have pierced my hands and feet—
17 I can count all my bones—
    they stare and gloat over me;

18 they divide my garments among them,
and for my clothing they cast lots.

From the vantage point of historical fulfillment, we can see clearly that David's words were prophetic, and the Gospel writers are careful to make the point (Matt. 27:35, 39, 43, 46; Luke 23:34; 27:35; John 19:24, 28; cf. Heb. 2:12). But until the fulfillment actually came, David's words would have seemed only excessive and without any specific referent, and the prospective element not so clear.

Now consider **Psalm 34:19–20**, where David celebrates God's protective care:

19 Many are the afflictions of the righteous,
but the Lord delivers him out of them all.
20 He keeps all his bones;
not one of them is broken.

The apostle John later picks up this psalm (John 19:32–36):

32 So the soldiers came and broke the legs of the first, and of the other
who had been crucified with him. 33 But when they came to Jesus and
saw that he was already dead, they did not break his legs. 34 But one of
the soldiers pierced his side with a spear, and at once there came out
blood and water. 35 He who saw it has borne witness—his testimony
is true, and he knows that he is telling the truth—that you also may
believe. 36 For these things took place that the Scripture might be
fulfilled: "Not one of his bones will be broken."

Note that in David's celebration of God's protective care John finds a "prophecy" that is fulfilled in Christ. This is obviously another kind of prophetic fulfillment—another category entirely, it would seem. The relation of Psalm 34:20 to the cross of Jesus is not immediately clear, and we might wonder what interpretive approach John used to justify his claim. The language of Psalm 34:20 is from Exodus 12:46, but neither is the Exodus passage itself obviously "prophetic"; it is merely a detail of instruction concerning the Passover meal. Yet in this psalm it seems that David, making use of other exodus imagery also, sees himself as a "type" of his promised greater son and so views his experience as prospective of Christ's. James Hamilton contends that "David's understanding of both God's promises and the patterns of earlier Scripture led him to present himself in the Psalms as a type of Christ."[7]

In **Psalm 8** David reflects on Genesis 1:26–28 and celebrates the God-given dignity of man as God's vice-regent over the world:

> 5 Yet you have made him a little lower than the heavenly beings
> and crowned him with glory and honor.
> 6 You have given him dominion over the works of your hands;
> you have put all things under his feet.

As we have seen, Hebrews 2 and 1 Corinthians 15 refer this psalm to Christ, our forerunner, who in his incarnation took our humanity to succeed for us where Adam and all humanity had failed.

Consider again **Psalm 40**. In our survey exposition of this psalm in an earlier chapter we explained that 40:5–8 points beyond David to the Lord Jesus:

> 5 You have multiplied, O Lord my God,
> your wondrous deeds and your thoughts toward us;
> none can compare with you!
> I will proclaim and tell of them,
> yet they are more than can be told.
> 6 In sacrifice and offering you have not delighted,
> but you have given me an open ear.

7 James M. Hamilton, "David's Biblical Theology and Typology in the Psalms: Authorial Intent and Patterns of the Seed of Promise," in *Reading the Psalms Theologically: Studies in Scripture and Biblical Theology*, ed. David Howard Jr. and Andrew Schmutzer (Bellingham, WA: Lexham, forthcoming 2023); Hamilton Jr., *Psalms*, vol. 1, Evangelical Biblical Theological Commentary (Bellingham, WA: Lexham Academic, 2021), 382–84.

Burnt offering and sin offering
  you have not required.
7 Then I said, "Behold, I have come;
  in the scroll of the book it is written of me:
8 I delight to do your will, O my God;
  your law is within my heart."

As we saw in our previous treatment of this psalm, the language of David's pledge to give himself wholly to God exceeds his own ability and experience. The inspired writer of Hebrews 10:4–9 places this prayer on the lips of Jesus, who alone could give his life as a sin offering. David's words are prophetic, and his giving of himself to God foreshadows Christ's giving of himself in sacrifice.

In **Psalm 69** David laments his suffering for his zeal for God, and several times in the New Testament his words are referred to Jesus. In John 15:18–25, Jesus warns his disciples about coming opposition, that the world will hate them as it hated him. He concludes the warning with a citation of David's psalm: "But the word that is written in their Law must be fulfilled: 'They hated me without a cause'" (John 15:25). His reference is to David's lament (Ps. 69:4):

4 More in number than the hairs of my head
  are those who hate me without cause;

Notice that Jesus speaks of this psalm as "fulfilled" in his own experience. That is, he understood Psalm 69 to be in some way prophetic of him. This seems to be a prophetic typology. David's experience of suffering for the cause of God pointed to the righteous suffering of Christ, and in Jesus's experience David's type was fulfilled. According to John 2, the disciples understood Psalm 69 this way also. After Jesus's cleansing of the temple John remarks, "His disciples remembered that it was written, 'Zeal for your house will consume me'" (John 2:17). This is a citation of Psalm 69:9, where David continues his lament of suffering for God's sake:

9 For zeal for your house has consumed me,
and the reproaches of those who reproach you have fallen on me.

Again David's experience is understood as foreshadowing that of Christ. In Romans 15:2–3 Paul understood Psalm 69:9 as referring to Christ also: "Let each of us please his neighbor for his good, to build him up. For Christ did not please himself, but as it is written, 'The reproaches of those who reproached you fell on me.'" As he reads the psalm he assumes it speaks of Jesus. So also in Psalm 69:21 David laments, "For my thirst they gave me sour wine to drink." When Jesus was on the cross the soldiers gave him sour wine, and John points it out as a fulfillment of David's psalm (John 19:28–29; cf. Matt. 27:34, 48). In all these examples Jesus and the apostles read Psalm 69 and assume that David prefigures his greater son.

In **Psalm 118**, the last of the "Egyptian Hallel" psalms, the king leads Israel in festive praise of God's deliverance from bondage in Egypt. The psalm, however, focuses on the king who is opposed by "all nations" (118:10) and rejected by "the builders" (118:22). In his pointed parable of the wicked tenants (Luke 20:9–19), Jesus applies this to himself:

> What then is this that is written:
>
> "The stone that the builders rejected
> has become the cornerstone"?
>
> Everyone who falls on that stone will be broken to pieces, and when it falls on anyone, it will crush him. (20:17–18)

Jesus, the stone rejected by Israel's leaders, became in rejection the very cornerstone of the kingdom. The apostle Peter, in turn, interprets this psalm accordingly (Acts 4:11; 1 Pet. 2:6–7). It is further significant that in his citation of Psalm 118 Jesus connects it with Isaiah 8:14–15 and Daniel 2:34, 44–45, passages also brimming with messianic implications. Again we see that Jesus (and his apostles) understood the king in the Psalter as foreshadowing him.

These samples could be multiplied, but our point is clear: the Psalms speak of the Messiah, but they do so in varying ways. Some are directly predictive (110:1), plainly stated, and the fulfillment direct and anticipated. Others are more indirect. "Types" are prospective also, only not as obviously predictive in their initial occurrence. But both categories are "prophetic" and anticipate later fulfillment. And in this way the distinction between royal psalms (psalms of the historical kings) and messianic psalms (psalms of the Messiah himself) is not always clear.

With the Psalms the interpretive task is somewhat mapped out for us by several factors:

- The Davidic promise (2 Sam. 7) has already set up the reader with an anticipation of David's greater son.
- We are informed up front (Ps. 2) that the Messiah is the subject of the Psalter.
- David and the Davidic kings are prominent throughout the Psalms: the "I" who speaks and the "he" and "him" who is spoken of.
- The larger trajectory of Davidic anticipation in the prophets dominates the Psalter also. The prophetic prospect of "David's" rule serves to inform the Psalms.
- The specific language of the Psalter often depicts the king and his kingdom in terms that transcend any of the historic Davidic kings.
- Jesus specifically instructed us to read the Psalms with reference to him (Luke 24:44).
- We have both Jesus and the New Testament writers to guide us with later revelation.

Finally, John Woodhouse suggests a number of interrelated concepts that are introduced in Psalm 2 and then echo throughout the Psalter, all of which foreshadow the ultimate king, the Lord Jesus Christ:

- The king's kingdom is God's kingdom.
- The king's enemies are God's enemies.
- The king trusts God's promise of triumph.
- The king is obedient to God and applies his ways to his people.
- The king shares the majesty and glory of God.
- The king is God's son.
- The king is God's servant.
- The king lives and reigns for the benefit of his people.
- The king subdues the nations and proclaims the gospel to them.[8]

In all these ways and more the Psalter points us to the Lord Jesus. We should recall also that Psalm 2 and Psalm 110, both of which seem to prophesy most directly, were originally composed as liturgy for the coronation of the Davidic kings. All of David's sons inherited the covenant God made with him (2 Sam. 7), but none of them proved up to the ideal prescribed in that covenant or described in these psalms. Thus, like all the psalms that pertain to the king (and that is most of them), these psalms depict the newly minted king as a type of Christ, the great King. The distinctiveness of these two psalms is that the king is especially idealized and points uniquely to Christ.

The royal psalms and the messianic psalms were therefore like robes put on the shoulders of the historical kings who represented the ideal. But for all of those kings, the robes were too big, and their shoulders too small, and so the royal robe slipped off of them, as it were. The robe was draped on the shoulders of each successor, and some filled the robes better than others (e.g., Hezekiah). But the ideal was just too high.[9] The shoulders of each successor, in fact, became smaller until there was no king at all. The tree of Jesse had been cut down to a mere stump, and all that was left was the robe itself, awaiting one who was

8 John Woodhouse, "Reading the Psalms as Christian Scripture," in *Stirred by a Noble Theme: The Book of Psalms in the Life of The Church*, ed. Andrew Shead (Nottingham, UK: Apollos, 2013), 57–73.

9 Bruce K. Waltke and James M. Houston, *The Psalms as Christian Worship: A Historical Commentary* (Grand Rapids, MI: Eerdmans, 2010), 107.

worthy of it. At last, the Lord Jesus Christ donned the robe, and it fits him perfectly: he lives up to its every ideal.

We might categorize at least three ways in which the Psalms find prophetic fulfillment in Christ:[10]

1. Some are prophetic in the directly predictive sense. Psalm 110 is the clear example here.
2. Some are typico-prophetic, involving the king as a "type" of the greater King to come. Psalm 22 is an example of this—David's experience is "typical" of Chris's suffering, but his vocabulary goes well beyond his own experience and speaks directly of Christ.
3. Some are more indirect and typical—indeed, so indirect that the New Testament use of them would seem to indicate that the king throughout the Psalter functions as a type of Christ, as we saw in Psalms 3 and 4. In Psalm 69, as another example, David laments his mistreatment by others. Psalm 69:6–9 is applied to Jesus in John 2:17—David's zeal for God had brought him the ill-treatment of others, and in this sense he remains a "type" of Christ. Even when David confesses his wrongdoing in Psalm 69:5 he may be a type of Christ. As Andrew Shead remarks, "He [Jesus] was baptized for sin he did not commit. He led his disciples in praying 'forgive us our sin,' and he died condemned for sins he alone was not guilty of. His whole life was representative, and in that sense David's prayers [of confession] are his as well."[11] The New Testament use of psalms such as 6:3, 31:5, 35:19, and 42:6 appear to be but "samples of a much larger corpus. It would scarcely seem too much to infer from this treatment that wherever David or the Davidic king appears in the Psalter . . . he foreshadows in some degree the Messiah."[12]

10 See also Waltke, *Old Testament Theology*, 893–95.

11 Forthcoming book by Andrew Shead, shared in personal correspondence.

12 Derek Kidner, *Psalms 1–72* (London: Inter-Varsity Press, 1973), 38.

## Enthronement Psalms

The so-called enthronement psalms present yet another way in which the Psalms anticipate Christ. These are psalms that proclaim God's sovereign or kingly reign over all his creation (47; 93; 95–99). Their characteristic exclamation is "The Lord reigns," or "the Lord is King" (יְהוָה מָלָךְ,[13] Pss. 93:1; 96:10; 97:1; 99:1; cf. 29:10; Isa. 52:7), or something similar (Pss. 47:7; 95:3; 98:6). This proclamation is addressed to the nations, calling them to confess the Lord's universal kingship. Psalm 100 is often recognized as the "doxology" of the enthronement psalms—it shares much in common with the others and is a fitting doxology for them.[14]

Gunkel restricted this group to Psalms 47, 93, 96, 97, and 99 because they contain the expression "The Lord is king." However, according to him this expression should be translated, "The Lord *has become* king" because he associates these psalms with a festival that celebrated the enthronement of Israel's king over the nations.[15] According to him these originally royal psalms of the first temple were adapted in the second temple to Yahweh as king and his future universal kingdom. In 1922 Gunkel's disciple Sigmund Mowinckel significantly modified Gunkel's view.[16] According to him these psalms proclaimed "the Lord had become king" in an annual fall festival that celebrated the entrance of Yahweh into his sanctuary. He alleged that Israel borrowed this ceremony from their neighbors who enthroned their gods annually. Moreover, Mowinckel associated a host of other psalms with this ceremony, not just those using the precise enthronement terminology. Mowinckel's theory has significantly impacted many commentators; by enthronement psalms they mean an annual festival in which "the Lord has become king"

13 The second qamets of מָלָךְ is exceptional, suggesting it was part of proclamation.

14 Compare 100:1 with 98:4; 100:1, 4 with 95:2; 100:1–2 with 95:1–2; 100:2 with 97:7; 100:2a, 4a with 95:6a; 100:3 with 95:6–7 and 97:6–7; 100:4 with 99:3; and 100:5 with 98:3. See also our brief discussion of this on p. 205.

15 Hermann Gunkel, *Introduction to the Psalms: The Genres of the Religious Lyric of Israel*, completed by Joachim Begrich; trans. James Nogalski (Macon, GA: Mercer University Press, 1998), 66.

16 Sigmund Mowinckel, *Psalmenstudien II, Das Thronbesteigungsfest Jahwäs und der Ursprung der Eschatologie* (Amsterdam: B. R. Grüner, 1922).

was proclaimed. Grammatically, the term could also be translated "the LORD has become king," but no translation has adopted it. There is no real evidence at all of such an important ceremony in the Psalter itself or in the Law and the Prophets. Of course, Mowinckel's understanding of "the LORD has become king" in an annual enthronement replaces the eternal God, who reigns universally, with a temporal god dependent on an annual enthronement ceremony. The theological difference is stark (cf. Isa. 52:7). These psalms call us not to imagine that God *has become* king but to trust the God who reigns eternally and without rival or interruption. "The proclamation 'I AM is King' dethrones all pretenders to ultimate sovereignty."[17] "Enthronement," then, is not the best designation of these psalms. "Kingship of Yahweh" psalms, as Bullock suggests, is more to the point.[18]

Aside from the precise kingship terminology, these "Kingship of Yahweh" psalms have no distinctive structure; they are hymns (praise psalms) celebrating the Lord as king over all the earth and over all gods. This conviction of the eternal, universal reign of the God of Israel informs and undergirds the entire Psalter (indeed, the entire Bible) but these psalms in a specific way. Grouped as they are at the outset of book 4 of the Psalter, this collection of psalms, beginning with Psalm 93, serves to answer the question left open at the end of book 3 (Ps. 89)—the seeming failure of the Davidic promise. They call all nations to the joyful worship of God (98:4; 100:1) and anticipate (as Gunkel rightly notes) the future reign of God over all the earth (e.g., 96:10, 13).

In this way these psalms inform our theme of the Messiah's kingship also. The Lord is the king's King (5:2; 44:4; 145:1); David serves under him. As we have already observed, God will establish his kingdom, but he will do so through the mediating rule of his chosen servant (78:70; 89:3, 20; 132:10; 143:10) and representative, the Anointed (2; 89:27), who shares his throne (110:1) as well as his name (Pss. 89:24; 118:10–12; cf. Matt. 28:19) and is himself the Creator and Ruler of all the earth. The

17 Bruce K. Waltke and James M. Houston, *The Psalms as Christian Praise: A Historical Commentary* (Grand Rapids, MI: Eerdmans, 2019), 22; see 19–22 for a fuller discussion.

18 C. Hassell Bullock, *Encountering the Book of Psalms: A Literary and Theological Introduction*, Encountering Biblical Studies (Grand Rapids, MI: Baker Academic, 2001), 188.

apostle John seems to understand Psalm 97 in this way. In Revelation 19:6 he echoes these enthronement psalms with his victory shout, "The Lord our God / the Almighty reigns," and then beginning in 19:11 he describes that reign graphically in terms of the glorious advent of Christ.[19] As we will see in chapter 15, the final editors arranged the Psalter with the messianic hope in mind, and it seems these psalms were placed accordingly.

Moreover, these psalms that proclaim the Lord's universal rule have a distinct eschatological element that is consistently associated with Messiah's reign:

> 11 Let the heavens be glad, and let the earth rejoice;
> let the sea roar, and all that fills it;
> 12 let the field exult, and everything in it!
> Then shall all the trees of the forest sing for joy
> 13 before the LORD, for he comes,
> for he comes to judge the earth
> he will judge the world in righteousness,
> and the peoples in his faithfulness. (96:11–13)

> 7 Let the sea roar, and all that fills it;
> the world and those who dwell in it!
> 8 Let the rivers clap their hands;
> let the hills sing for joy together
> 9 before the LORD, for he comes
> to judge the earth.
> He will judge the world with righteousness,
> and the peoples with equity. (98:7–9)

As we have emphasized previously, Christ reigns today over God's kingdom, and the church shares in that reign. But along with such messianic psalms as Psalm 2, whose prospect has not yet been realized, these passages look to the future for their climactic fulfillment. A future

19 See also the allusion to Psalm 98:9 in Acts 17:31.

aspect of God's kingdom is in view in which the Psalter, with all the Bible, affirms that Jesus Christ, the incarnate Son-Messiah will be judge of all. These psalms make the assuring affirmation that God's kingdom remains unchallenged, but they also direct us to think specifically in terms of the Messiah's rule in the consummation of that kingdom as the universally recognized Lord and judge (cf. Phil. 2:10–11).

In his introductory remarks to Psalm 96 Calvin provides a helpful whole-Bible perspective for all of these "Kingship of Yahweh" psalms:

> This psalm contains an exhortation to praise God, an exhortation which is directed not only to [Israel], but to all nations. We must infer from this, that it has reference to the kingdom of Christ. God's name could not be called upon in any other part of the world than Judea, until it had been revealed; and the heathen nations were at that time necessarily altogether incapacitated for any such exercise. Yet it is evident that the Holy Spirit stirred up the saints who were under the Law to celebrate the Divine praises, till the period should arrive when Christ, by the spread of the Gospel, should fill the whole earth with his glory.[20]

## PSALM 16

With each of our "approaches" to the Psalms we have examined a selected corresponding psalm. We have already examined several messianic psalms, such as Psalm 2, 22, 91, and 110, and so we have already begun to see how an understanding of the messianic hope is important for interpreting the Psalter. Here we take up Psalm 16, a psalm that features prominently in Peter's sermon on the day of Pentecost (cf. Acts 2:22–32). Paul uses this psalm also in evangelizing the Jews at Antioch in Pisidia (cf. Acts 13:32–38). For these inspired apostles this psalm plays a crucial role in understand-

20 John Calvin, *Commentary on the Book of Psalms*, trans James Anderson, vol. 4 (Grand Rapids, MI: Baker, 2003), 47.

ing the significance of the resurrection of Christ (Ps. 16:9–10). In its own setting, the psalm offers wonderful hope in the prospect of resurrection. So this psalm takes on this added significance for us today.

A Miktam of David.

1 Preserve me, O God, for in you I take refuge.
2 I say to the Lord, "You are my Lord;
I have no good apart from you."
3 As for the saints in the land, they are the excellent ones,
in whom is all my delight.
4 The sorrows of those who run after another god shall multiply;
their drink offerings of blood I will not pour out
or take their names on my lips.
5 The Lord is my chosen portion and my cup;
you hold my lot.
6 The lines have fallen for me in pleasant places;
indeed, I have a beautiful inheritance.
7 I bless the Lord who gives me counsel;
in the night also my heart instructs me.
8 I have set the Lord always before me;
because he is at my right hand, I shall not be shaken.
9 Therefore my heart is glad, and my whole being rejoices;
my flesh also dwells secure.
10 For you will not abandon my soul to Sheol,
or let your holy one see corruption.
11 You make known to me the path of life;
in your presence there is fullness of joy;
at your right hand are pleasures forevermore.

## Introductory Matters

The superscript identifies this psalm as "a *Miktam* of David." The meaning of this word *miktam* is not known, so our English versions provide no translation of the word, only a transliteration. The Septuagint translators understood it to mean "inscription."

The structure of this psalm may be analyzed as follows:

16:1–8: trust in the Lord in life
16:9–11: trust in the Lord in death

Or more fully:

I. Trust in the Lord in life (16:1–8)
  A. Petition and confession of trust (16:1)
  B. Trust proven by loyalties (16:2–4)
    1. Loyalty to the Lord (16:2)
    2. Loyalty to the saints (16:3–4)
  C. Reasons for trust (16:5–8)
    1. The Lord as inheritance (16:5–6)
    2. The Lord as protection (16:7–8)
II. Trust in the Lord in death (16:9–11)
  A. Joyful commitment of body to the grave (16:9–10)
  B. Eternal pleasure with God (16:11)

The opening petition, "Preserve me, O God," resembles that of a lament, but the psalm consists entirely in an elaboration of David's trust. Recall that psalms of trust have some life-threatening situation lying in the background. The theme of the psalm is that of trust in God who will protect in both life and death. It is not trust only that David expresses here, however, but trust coupled with deep affection.

**Survey Exposition**[21]

*Trust in the Lord in Life (16:1–8).*

David's opening plea is not for deliverance, as in a lament, but for preservation. This distinction is important for understanding the psalm. The Hebrew word rendered "preserve" (שָׁמַר) connotes an exercise of

21 See also Bruce K. Waltke and James M. Houston, *The Psalms as Christian Worship: A Historical Commentary* (Grand Rapids, MI: Eerdmans, 2010), chap 10.

care; "keep me safe" is the idea. The precise preservation for which he pleads will become clear in the closing verses of the psalm: what David wants is preservation *in death*, not from death (16:9–11). He addresses God by the name *El* (אֵל), a name that refers to God in his omnipotence and transcendence over all his creation, and it is in this great God that David says he "takes refuge." His plea is that the Creator and author of life and of all creation, including David's own body, will keep him safe in life and in death. The petition is combined with a confession of confidence—"for in you I take refuge" (16:1). David does not see himself as autonomous or master of his own fate but as one who has taken refuge in God's protective care.

In 16:2–4 David expresses his loyalty, first to the Lord in whom he has taken refuge:

> 2 I say to the LORD, "You are my Lord;
> I have no good apart from you."

"LORD" is the divine name, and acknowledging him as "my Lord" (*Adonai*), David positions himself as his servant. "I have no good apart from you" expresses complete and exclusive reliance upon God for every good thing. It is in effect James 1:17 expressed in more worshipful terms. "I say" assumes an audience: David wants the congregation to hear his affirmation of utter confidence in God and loyalty to him.

Devotion to God entails loyalty to the covenant community, which David expresses in 16:3–4:

> 3 As for the saints in the land, they are the excellent ones,
> in whom is all my delight.
> 4 The sorrows of those who run after another god shall multiply;
> their drink offerings of blood I will not pour out
> or take their names on my lips.

God's people are "saints," or "holy ones." "In the land" specifies that David is speaking in reference to his fellow Israelites (and not to angels).

These "excellent ones" (אַדִּיר) give him delight; he desires their company, and he associates himself with them. They are "noble" (NIV) or "majestic" (NASB) precisely because they belong to God and depend on him. To delight in others, those who do not share in this exclusive devotion to God (16:4), would compromise his relationship with God and with them. Nor will he worship with "those who run after another god" (16:4a). He will not so much as speak their names (16:4b). J. J. Stewart Perowne suggests 1 Samuel 26:19 as the background here, where in the wilderness of Ziph David complains, "They have driven me out this day that I should have no share in the heritage of the Lord, saying, 'Go, serve other gods.'" Though forced to hide among his pagan neighbors, he remains loyal to the Lord God, and though away from the Lord's people they remain his delight.[22] David's trust in God is pure. He is utterly devoted to the Lord with all that loyalty entails.

In 16:5–8 David further expresses his joyful confidence in God. First, he affirms that the Lord is his inheritance:

> 5 The LORD is my chosen portion and my cup;
> you hold my lot.
> 6 The lines have fallen for me in pleasant places;
> indeed, I have a beautiful inheritance.

The language of inheritance in these verses reflects the distribution of land among the tribes of Israel. Each portion was determined by the casting of lots—probably the Urim and the Thummim of the high priest. "The LORD is my portion" reflects the Levites whose portion was God himself. The "cup" metaphor (16:5) depicts the sovereign handing the king a cup to drink; that is, God determines David's portion—for life and for eternity. And so like the Levites and like Asaph (73:25), David is joyful in having God alone. The idea is that of utter and glad abandonment to God's care. Augustine comments, "Let others choose for themselves portions, earthly and temporal, to enjoy: the portion

22 J. J. Stewart Perowne, *The Book of Psalms*, vol. 1 (Andover: Warren F. Draper, 1879), 165.

of the Saints is the Lord eternal. Let others drink of deadly pleasures, the portion of My cup is the Lord."[23] Weiser comments also, "If man turns his thoughts to the providential rule of God and envisages that providential rule with gratitude and joy, he is thus taught to discern in material benefits the visible proof of the benevolence of his God."[24]

In 16:7–8 David praises God for his instruction also, the authoritative counsel by which David lives:

> 7 I bless the LORD who gives me counsel;
> in the night also my heart instructs me.
> 8 I have set the LORD always before me;
> because he is at my right hand, I shall not be shaken.

"I will bless the LORD" indicates that David desires to give the Lord a benefaction by acknowledging him as Benefactor. Here he gives God the gift of acknowledging him as the source and director of his life. "Heart" here probably refers to his conscience, which directs his will. "In the night," when he is not distracted by the world, God's counsel, his *torah*, shapes David's sense of good and evil, right and wrong. David will then keep his eye on God (16:8a), with his counsel ever before him. With God "at [his] right hand," the place of protection, David is confident that he is safe: "I will not be toppled" (16:8b, authors' translation).

*Trust in the Lord in Death (16:9–11)*

In his final stanza David draws a conclusion ("therefore") from what he has just considered and expresses his trust in God in death also:

> 9 Therefore my heart is glad, and my whole being rejoices;
> my flesh also dwells secure.
> 10 For you will not abandon my soul to Sheol,

23 Saint Augustine, *Expositions on the Book of Psalms*, vol. 8 of *Nicene and Post-Nicene Fathers*, 1st ser., ed. Philip Schaff (New York: Christian Literature, 1888), 48.

24 Artur Weiser, *The Psalms: A Commentary*, The Old Testament Library (Philadelphia: Westminster, 1962), 175.

or let your holy one see corruption.
11 You make known to me the path of life;
in your presence there is fullness of joy;
at your right hand are pleasures forevermore.

"Therefore" is inferential. "Therefore my heart is glad" (16:9). That is, because of his trust in the Lord—because of his confidence in God's protective care, because God holds his destiny, because God himself is his inheritance, because God has proven so good, because of God's marvelous providence—David's entire emotional state is affected. His heart leaps and his whole being rejoices (16:9a). Indeed, this joyful confidence remains in reference to death, even with reference to David's body: "my flesh also dwells secure" (16:9b). Here we find the point of reference in David's petition for God's (not deliverance but) safekeeping (16:1). David commits even his corpse to God in the certainty that death will not have the last word (16:10–11). David's devotion to God extends over the entirety of his existence, and he anticipates continued joy in God's presence after the grave.

With this expression of confidence in death and its accompanying plea for God's continued safekeeping, the psalm ends.

But not quite. Upon careful consideration David's language in 16:10 seems to imply much more:

10 For you will not abandon my soul to Sheol,
or let your holy one see corruption.

David claims that his body will not decay. He will be exempt from the corruption of the body, which sets in after three days (cf. John 11:38–39). As we have seen, Peter made the simple observation that David's body did, in fact, see corruption and that as a prophet he therefore spoke not of himself but of the Messiah (Acts 2:24–31). David sees himself as a "type" of his greater son in whom these words will find dramatic fulfillment. Jesus's body did not see corruption, but he was raised "the third day." That Jesus was raised from the dead has been the

Christian proclamation ever since, but that it was "the third day" is a point that received repeated emphasis (see Matt. 16:21; 17:23; 20:19; 27:64; Luke 9:22; 18:33; 24:7, 46; Acts 10:40; 1 Cor. 15:4), presumably to highlight this prophecy (as Peter does in Acts 2:24–31) that Jesus's body was not left in the grave and did not decay. In the fuller teaching of the New Testament we learn that it is our union with Christ that gives us hope of resurrection also (John 11:23–27; 1 Cor. 15:12–13, 19–23). David's prophecy of God's presence after death was fulfilled in Christ and, by extension, it will be fulfilled in David's and in our experience also. In his death our Lord canceled sin, the cause of death, and in his resurrection he brings us with him to eternal life to be enjoyed now and forever. Nevertheless, the preservation of the body in death is unique to the Messiah.

### Additional Note on "Corruption"[25]

So the crucial word in this psalm is the Hebrew word in 16:10 translated "corruption" or "decay" (שַׁחַת, *šaḥat*). The Septuagint translates this word as "decay" (διαφθορά), which the apostles accepted also (Acts 2:27, 31; 13:34–37). Probably under the influence of historical criticism, many scholars insist that the Hebrew word must mean "pit" and cannot mean "corruption." So rather than the psalmist expressing hope that his body will not see corruption, according to the critical view, he is expressing hope, merely, that he will not (in this particular crisis) die. There is no life of resurrection in view. S. R. Driver, for example, says this:

> The hope which the Psalmist expresses is thus not that he will rise again, but that he *will not die*. . . . The Psalmist does not speak explicitly of a future life (for v. ii does not refer to it at all); but he expresses the hope of superiority over death, grounded on the close personal relation in which he himself stands towards God, and which he cannot believe will be interrupted by death. . . . The Psalm is thus Messianic

25 See Waltke and Houston, *Psalms as Christian Worship*, 335–36.

> not in being a prediction of Christ's resurrection, for it is plain that the feelings and hopes expressed in it are those of the Psalmist himself, or, at most, if the plural in v. 10 be the original reading, of himself and other like-minded godly Israelites, but in expressing an ideal—a hope of superiority to death—which transcended experience, and was fully realized only by Christ.[26]

That is to say, the apostles followed the Septuagint incorrectly and were mistaken in their interpretation of the psalm. According to Driver, Psalm 16:10 is not, in fact, a prediction that Christ would not see decay. This view has had significant impact on some translations (RSV, NRSV, NAB, NJB, NET, NLT).

So the interpretation of the psalm hangs on the translation of this word, as well as its value as an apologetic for the resurrection and messiahship of Jesus, as the apostles insisted. The discussion is an important one.

The word in Hebrew is a homonym, and its many uses are indecisive as to whether it means "pit" or "corruption." If the homonym is derived from the verb that means "to sink down," then it is a feminine noun and means "pit."[27] But if it is derived from the verb that means "decay," then it is a masculine noun and means "corruption." Both nouns would be spelled the same. David Clines conflates these meanings and offers the options "pit of corruption" and "corruption."[28]

In the Hebrew language all nouns are either so-called masculine or feminine in form. In languages with this gender inflection poets personify abstract and inanimate nouns according to the gender form of that noun—e.g., "woman wisdom" for personification of the ab-

26 S. R. Driver, *Studies in the Psalms* ed. C. F. Burney (London: Hodder and Stoughton, 1915), 202, 207, 208; emphasis original.

27 Francis Brown, S. R. Driver, and Charles A. Briggs, *A Hebrew and English Lexicon of the Old Testament: With an Appendix Containing the Biblical Aramaic*, based on the lexicon of William Gesenius as translated by Edward Robinson (Oxford: At the Clarendon Press, 1907), 1001 (s.v. שַׁחַת).

28 David J. A. Clines, ed., *The Concise Dictionary of Classical Hebrew* (Sheffield: Sheffield Phoenix Press, 2009), 457 (s.v. שַׁחַת).

stract, feminine noun "wisdom." This masculine form of the homonym can be inferred from Job 17:14, for the noun *šaḥat* is personified as masculine—"If I say to [*šaḥat*], 'You are my father,' / and to the worm [feminine], 'My mother' or 'My sister'" (NIV)—pointing beyond reasonable doubt that the word (*šaḥat*) can be masculine, and if so means something like "corruption." Homonyms can be distinguished by their collocation with verbs. Here, if "pit" were in view, then we would expect "descend" or "enter," but instead we have "see," a verb of experience denoting a state, not a place. Moreover, Psalm 16:10a specifically affirms that David will not be "left" or "abandoned" (עָזַב) in Sheol, an expression that itself implies resurrection. "Corruption" (16:10b), then, is the suitable parallel. The Septuagint translators understood the word and along with other ancient versions translated this as "decay" or "corruption." So also the KJV, ASV, NIV, and ESV.[29] David understood the promise God had made, that his son would reign on his throne forever, and here he sees that promises fulfilled in the resurrected Christ.

29 For a fuller discussion, see Bruce Waltke, "The NT Interpretation of the Psalms," in *New International Dictionary of Old Testament Theology and Exegesis*, 5 vols., ed. Willem A. VanGemeren (Grand Rapids, MI: Zondervan, 1997), 4:1113–14; also Waltke and Houston, *Psalms as Christian Worship*, 323–24, 338–39.

# 13

# Didactic Psalms

*"Blessed is the man who fears the Lord!"*

## Genre of Didactic Psalms

We have seen that 1 Chronicles 16:4 indicates at least three types of psalms: psalms of petition ("to invoke"), psalms of grateful praise ("to thank"), and hymns ("to praise"). There is a fourth form of psalm that the chronicler did not mention, and that is didactic psalms, psalms of instruction, as we saw in Psalm 1. We do not know why David did not appoint the priest to sing this kind of psalms, but Psalm 49:1–4 and Psalm 73, which sound like the book of Proverbs, were composed by the sons of Korah and Asaph, respectively—the sons of Korah a Levitical guild and Asaph himself the choir leader. And David himself composed Psalm 37, a didactic psalm. So this genre of psalms was evidently recognized also.

All Scripture is profitable for teaching (2 Tim. 3:16), and Gordon J. Wenham, in his magnificent book *Psalms as Torah*, has made an important contribution to our understanding of the Psalms as a book of instruction in ethics and in piety. In a chapter titled "The Psalter as an Anthology to Be Memorized," he summarizes *Writing on the Tablets of the Heart* by David M. Carr. Carr documented that in the biblical world "literary and religious texts were memorized by the educated elite and then transmitted to the masses at public festivals to transmit the values of its culture."[1]

We have observed that Psalm 1 functions as an introduction to the Psalter by describing the kind of person who can sing praises to God—the righteous, the one who reveres and treasures God's law. Those who would give God praise must be of "clean hands and a pure heart" (24:3–4). This is a note that recurs throughout the Psalms, and those who sing God's praise are described accordingly. They are:

- the Lord's pious ones (30:5; 145:10; 149:5)
- the righteous (32:11; 33:1; 68:4; 140:14)
- upright (33:1)
- upright in heart (32:11)
- those who fear the Lord (22:24)
- those who love his name (5:12)
- those who love his salvation (40:17)
- those who seek him (22:27; 40:17; 105:3)
- those who hide themselves in him (5:12)

But by "didactic psalms" we mean psalms specifically composed for this purpose. The didactic psalm is not distinguished by form but by content: they are didactic. They are given to instruct Israel in piety and ethics, seeking to honor God in a life devoted to him in faithfulness and shaped by his revealed will. These psalms are not designed to offer praise, as such. And they are neither prayers nor laments. Their purpose is that of instruction. They are designed to instruct Israel in faithful living under God.

### Subgenres of Didactic Psalms

These psalms are sometimes called "wisdom psalms," but it is better to recognize three types of didactic psalms: Torah psalms, historical psalms, and wisdom psalms.

1 Gordon J. Wenham, *Psalms as Torah: Reading Biblical Song Ethically* (Grand Rapids, MI: Baker Academic, 2012), 56.

### *Torah Psalms*

The Torah psalms (1; 19; 119) passionately extol the Torah and its value. This subgenre of didactic psalms is distinctive by its focus on the law. Psalm 1, for example, directs the reader to meditate on the law of the Lord (1:2) and to live accordingly, taking the eternal "way" of the righteous (Ps. 1:6; Prov 8:20). It uses wisdom vocabulary (e.g., "blessed," and "scoffer") and contrasts two ways, and it may reflect a later stage in Israelite religion when "wisdom" became equated with "the law." Perowne, who wrote before the scholarly awareness of form criticism, remarked that Psalm 1 with its contrasting two ways "is little more than the expansion of a proverb."[2] Psalm 19 highlights the life-transforming effect of Torah; though a petition psalm, it praises the Torah. And in Psalm 119 the sustained attention to God's "law," his "statues," his "precepts," his "commandments," and his "rules" draws attention to the life-shaping role of his "word."

### *Historical Psalms*

The historical psalms, of which Psalms 78 and 136 are perhaps the most famous, recount Israel's history, but not for history's sake merely. They rehearse Israel's history mostly from the Exodus to the monarchy, as a vehicle of instruction and exhortation to faith and life. Wenham calls them "Narrative Law."[3] Psalm 78 aims to nerve Israel to covenant fidelity. Psalm 114, addressed to the nations and overheard by the temple congregation, explains to them the meaning of Israel's salvation history. Israel also recounts her glorious history to the nations in Psalm 66 and 105 but in a song of grateful praise. But whereas Psalm 105 praises God's faithfulness, Psalm 106 recounts Israel's covenant infidelity in the form of a lament.

### *Wisdom Psalms*

We begin this section by considering wisdom in the Old Testament and then in the Psalms in particular.

2 J. J. Stewart Perowne, *The Book of Psalms*, vol.1 (Andover: Warren F. Draper, 1879), 85.
3 Wenham, *Psalms as Torah*, 19–137.

Jeremiah 18:18 informs us indirectly of the three kinds of persons through whom God revealed his will to his people—three instruments God used. Here Jeremiah's opponents are speaking:

> 18 Then they said, "Come, let us make plots against Jeremiah, for the law shall not perish from the priest, nor counsel from the wise, nor the word from the prophet. Come, let us strike him with the tongue, and let us not pay attention to any of his words."

Notice there is the priest, the wise man, and the prophet. This verse also states the specific function of each: the priest was designated to teach the law (*torah*), the wise man or sage—whether a royal figure or an elder or the wise woman of Tekoa (2 Sam. 14:2)—gave authoritative counsel, and the prophet gave a word from God—new revelation. The priest was responsible to teach God's law so that the people would know what he required of them. The prophet would bring new revelation regarding present responsibilities and matters of justice, of covenant faithfulness, and of God's purpose for the future. And the sage would apply the law of God to the individual daily lives of the people, thus providing authoritative counsel for living successfully under God. Kidner begins his commentary on Proverbs: "There are details of character small enough to escape the mesh of the law and the broadsides of the prophets, yet decisive in personal dealings."[4]

The primary Hebrew word for wisdom (חָכְמָה) connotes skill and is used in reference to various kinds of "skilled" endeavors. This word is used to describe Bezalel's and Oholiab's "ability" or "skill" in the building of the tabernacle (Ex. 31:1–6), Hiram's work in building the temple (1 Kings 7:13–14), of governmental officials (Jer. 50:35), administrators (Deut. 1:13), and other select areas of expertise. Wisdom implies a masterful understanding or expertise in a given area. In an Old Testament context wisdom is the skill of living successfully—specifically, living

4 Derek Kidner, *Proverbs*, Tyndale Old Testament Commentaries (Downers Grove, IL: InterVarsity Press, 1964), 13.

successfully under God, living in the way of eternal life. It is the ability to navigate life according to God's revealed will, whether in the Law of Moses or in prophetic sermons or in the counsel of the inspired sage. Of his teaching Solomon says, "For the LORD gives wisdom, from his mouth come knowledge and understanding" (Prov. 2:6).

Wisdom literature teaches us to see ourselves as living in God's world and to live before him accordingly. Wisdom therefore implies righteousness, and these two concepts are somewhat interchangeable in Old Testament wisdom contexts (cf. Prov. 9:9; 23:24). To be wise is to be righteous, and to be righteous is to be wise. This skill in living successfully before God is grounded in the "fear of the LORD" (Prov. 1:7; 9:10), which entails accepting God's revelation of his will in all its various forms (Heb. 1:1–2). In Psalm 19 "the fear of the LORD" is equated with Torah. Similarly, the sage counsels, "My son, if you receive my words / . . . then you will understand the fear of the LORD" (Prov. 2:1–5). The inspired sage guides in doing what is right, just, and fair (Prov. 1:5)—loving God and our neighbors (e.g., Prov. 3:27–29). Wisdom is life-oriented, and wisdom psalms provide instruction accordingly.

The Torah provided laws that shaped Israel's faith and life. Wisdom is sometimes personified as a street preacher in the marketplace, the main street of life, calling out and offering freely the wisdom to live (e.g., Prov. 1:20–21). But the personification may not be simply poetic. As Jeremiah 18:18 indicates, the sage was evidently recognized as such by his giftedness, as in the case of Solomon (1 Kings 3:28), in ancient Israel.[5] Informed by the Torah, but never citing it, the inspired sage applied its directives to how to speak, to be money wise, to being a friend, and so on. Wisdom is behavior oriented.

The wisdom literature of the Old Testament is most prominently associated with Job, Proverbs, and Ecclesiastes. But in fact other portions of the Old Testament are "wisdom" oriented also—Song of Solomon, for example, and portions of Deuteronomy and the prophets. And several

5 See also Fred G. Zaspel, "Called in Two Directions: Proverbs 1:8-33," *Credo Magazine* (website), May 7, 2020, https://credomag.com/.

of the Psalms are of this genre also.[6] Bernhard Anderson categorizes these as wisdom psalms: 36 (mixed type), 37, 49, 73, 78 (storytelling), 112, 127, 128, and 133.[7] In wisdom psalms the psalmist takes the posture of a sage in Israel who looked at life with the vantage point of faith in the God who gave his covenants to Israel and gave counsel to the people accordingly.

Wisdom literature is commonly divided into teachings that promise prosperity (Proverbs) and reflective wisdom that grapples with the prosperity of the wicked (Job and Ecclesiastes), but both types teach the fear of the Lord. Similarly, Psalm 37 sounds very much like the book of Proverbs, but Psalm 73 like Ecclesiastes. As we have mentioned, classifications of the Psalms are not always hard and fast, and a given psalm may contain a mixture of genres. Psalm 34, for example, is a declarative praise psalm (34:1–10) but ends with an extended homily in the form of wisdom (34:11–22). And many of the psalms have "wisdom sayings" also (e.g., 33:16–18). Still, the categories are useful and often definitive.

Now, we will examine some samples.

---

## PSALM 37

1 Fret not yourself because of evildoers;
  be not envious of wrongdoers!
2 For they will soon fade like the grass
  and wither like the green herb.
3 Trust in the LORD, and do good;
  dwell in the land and befriend faithfulness.
4 Delight yourself in the LORD,

6 In *The Tree of Life: An Exploration of Biblical Wisdom Literature* (Grand Rapids, MI: Eerdmans, 1996), Roland Murphy devotes a chapter to "Echoes of Wisdom" found in the Hebrew Bible outside of Job, Proverbs, and Ecclesiastes.

7 Bernhard Anderson, *Out of the Depths: The Psalms Speak for Us Today* (Philadelphia: Westminster, 1983).

and he will give you the desires of your heart.
5 Commit your way to the LORD;
trust in him, and he will act.
6 He will bring forth your righteousness as the light,
and your justice as the noonday.
7 Be still before the LORD and wait patiently for him;
fret not yourself over the one who prospers in his way,
over the man who carries out evil devices!
8 Refrain from anger, and forsake wrath!
Fret not yourself; it tends only to evil.
9 For the evildoers shall be cut off,
but those who wait for the LORD shall inherit the land.
10 In just a little while, the wicked will be no more;
though you look carefully at his place, he will not be there.
11 But the meek shall inherit the land
and delight themselves in abundant peace.
12 The wicked plots against the righteous
and gnashes his teeth at him,
13 but the Lord laughs at the wicked,
for he sees that his day is coming.
14 The wicked draw the sword and bend their bows
to bring down the poor and needy,
to slay those whose way is upright;
15 their sword shall enter their own heart,
and their bows shall be broken.
16 Better is the little that the righteous has
than the abundance of many wicked.
17 For the arms of the wicked shall be broken,
but the LORD upholds the righteous.
18 The LORD knows the days of the blameless,
and their heritage will remain forever;
19 they are not put to shame in evil times;
in the days of famine they have abundance.
20 But the wicked will perish;

the enemies of the LORD are like the glory of the pastures;
they vanish—like smoke they vanish away.
21 The wicked borrows but does not pay back,
but the righteous is generous and gives;
22 for those blessed by the LORD shall inherit the land,
but those cursed by him shall be cut off.
23 The steps of a man are established by the LORD,
when he delights in his way;
24 though he fall, he shall not be cast headlong,
for the LORD upholds his hand.
25 I have been young, and now am old,
yet I have not seen the righteous forsaken
or his children begging for bread.
26 He is ever lending generously,
and his children become a blessing.
27 Turn away from evil and do good;
so shall you dwell forever.
28 For the LORD loves justice;
he will not forsake his saints.
They are preserved forever,
but the children of the wicked shall be cut off.
29 The righteous shall inherit the land
and dwell upon it forever.
30 The mouth of the righteous utters wisdom,
and his tongue speaks justice.
31 The law of his God is in his heart;
his steps do not slip.
32 The wicked watches for the righteous
and seeks to put him to death.
33 The LORD will not abandon him to his power
or let him be condemned when he is brought to trial.
34 Wait for the LORD and keep his way,
and he will exalt you to inherit the land;
you will look on when the wicked are cut off.

35 I have seen a wicked, ruthless man,
spreading himself like a green laurel tree.
36 But he passed away, and behold, he was no more;
though I sought him, he could not be found.
37 Mark the blameless and behold the upright,
for there is a future for the man of peace.
38 But transgressors shall be altogether destroyed;
the future of the wicked shall be cut off.
39 The salvation of the righteous is from the LORD;
he is their stronghold in the time of trouble.
40 The LORD helps them and delivers them;
he delivers them from the wicked and saves them,
because they take refuge in him.

Psalm 37 illustrates the wisdom psalm well and has many of these standard features. King David, speaking with the wisdom of old age (37:25, 35), lectures a generic "you" (cf. 34:11) with twenty-two sayings that sound like the aphorisms of the book of Proverbs (e.g., cf. 37:1 with Prov. 24:19; Ps. 37:16 with Prov 15:16). Egyptian kings or their viziers wrote similar collections of sayings as early as 2500 BC. Here is an outline of the psalm:

I. Introduction: trust the Lord (37:1–7)
II. Body: retribution of the wicked and care of the righteous (37:8–14)
III. Conclusion: testimonies (37:35–40)

The royal sage teaches that the wicked plot to kill the righteous (37:12, 14, 32) and that for a little while they succeed in unjustly seizing their property (37:7b, 16b). He admonishes, however, not to fret (37:1, 7, 8) but to trust the Lord (37:3, 4, 5, 7, 34) and do good (37:3, 27) by practicing righteousness and justice (37:30–31). He motivates by proclaiming, on the one hand, that the success of the wicked is brief (37:1, 10) and that they will be "cut off" (Ps. 37:9, 22, 28, 34; cf. Gen. 9:11) and, on the other hand, that the Lord will reward the righteous (37:4, 5), especially to "inherit" or "dwell in the land" (37:3, 9, 11, 22, 27, 29, 34), the symbol of life (cf. Prov. 2:21–22). Until then the Lord sustains and blesses the righteous (37:17, 18, 19, 21, 23–24, 26) and will never forsake them (37:28) or condemn them (37:33). These admonitions and motivations are summarized in 37:34, the message of the psalm.

The psalm affirms, as McCann cogently notes, that the Lord rules "in circumstances that seem to deny it." "In short, Psalm 37 is eschatological. For now, the wicked do 'prosper in their way' (v. 7; cf. 1:3). Thus the future tense of the two refrains is significant—'shall inherit' and 'shall be cut off.'" "But to live eschatologically means not only to live for the future but also to live by the future. Living by faith and hope has a profound impact on the present, in terms of emotion and behavior."[8]

## PSALM 15

Psalm 15 is commonly categorized as a psalm that reflects upon Israel's liturgy of worship, but it instructs the worshiper on right living.

A Psalm of David.
1 O Lord, who shall sojourn in your tent?
Who shall dwell on your holy hill?
2 He who walks blamelessly
and does what is right
and speaks truth in his heart;
3 who does not slander with his tongue
and does no evil to his neighbor,
nor takes up a reproach against his friend;
4 in whose eyes a vile person is despised,
but who honors those who fear the Lord;
who swears to his own hurt and does not change;

8 J. Clinton McCann Jr., "The Book of Psalms: Introduction, Commentary, and Reflections, *The New Interpreter's Bible Vol. IV*, ed. Leander E. Keck et al. (Nashville: Abingdon, 1996), 828.

5 who does not put out his money at interest
and does not take a bribe against the innocent.
He who does these things shall never be moved.

## Survey Exposition[9]

Though God in his grace had made Israel his own people, it was made clear from the beginning that he is holy and that the privilege of entering his presence must not be presumed:

> 12 And you shall set limits for the people all around, saying, "Take care not to go up into the mountain or touch the edge of it. Whoever touches the mountain shall be put to death. 13 No hand shall touch him, but he shall be stoned or shot; whether beast or man, he shall not live." When the trumpet sounds a long blast, they shall come up to the mountain. (Ex. 19:12–13)

The book of Hebrews tells us that the worship system God gave to Israel through Moses was designed to teach Israel the unapproachableness of God (Heb. 9:7). Its priesthood, the necessity of sacrifice, the tabernacle itself, the curtain dividing the Holy Place from the Most Holy Place—all this was designed to proclaim the unapproachableness of God: "Stay back! You have no right to be here!" The sacrificial system anticipated the glory of the gospel that through the sacrifice of Christ we are brought beyond that curtain into the very presence of God and accepted.

Still, there are demands on the worshiper. Israel was called to come to the temple for worship, particularly at the time of the three principal feasts (Deut. 16:1–17), but the worship of God must not be understood as mere formalism or empty liturgy. He does not accept the professed

9 This section is adapted from Bruce Waltke, "Psalm 15: An Exposition in Honor of Alan Groves," in *Eyes to See, Ears to Hear: Essays in Honor of J. Alan Groves*, ed. Peter Enns, Douglas Green, and Michael Kelly (Phillipsburg, NJ: P&R, 2010), 17–32; see also Bruce K. Waltke and James M. Houston, *Psalms as Christian Worship: A Historical Commentary* (Grand Rapids, MI: Eerdmans, 2010), chap. 9.

worship of just anyone. Entrance to the Lord's presence is a privilege. There is not only the distance between infinite majesty and finite humanity; there are the ethical barriers reflecting God's holiness.

In Psalm 15 David takes up the question of who may approach God in worship:

> 1 "O LORD, who shall sojourn in your tent?
> Who shall dwell on your holy hill?"

Psalms that take up this question are referred to as "entrance liturgies," and consistently the emphasis in these psalms is that of ethics. These entrance liturgy psalms describe the person who is qualified to participate in the worship of the temple. Psalm 24 is another example:

> 3 Who shall ascend the hill of the LORD?
> And who shall stand in his holy place?
> 4 He who has clean hands and a pure heart,
> who does not lift up his soul to what is false
> and does not swear deceitfully.

So Psalm 15 may be considered a didactic psalm, one that focuses on ethical instruction. But it does so with this question in mind—just who may approach God in worship? The question may have been asked by a priest who protects the sanctity of the temple, not by a sage with the intent to counsel. It envisions the Israelite who seeks to participate in temple festivities responsibly. Some have suggested this psalm was read by the temple warden in "fencing the table," as it were. It is probably better to understand this psalm as appealing directly to the worshiper's conscience, calling for self-examination (cf. 1 Cor. 11:28). In any case, the psalm explicitly connects liturgy with piety and ethics, and it is given to describe the one whose worship of God is acceptable to him. David insists that apart from faith and obedience religious liturgy is mere pretense and an offense (cf. Eccles. 5:1–7; Isa. 1:1–17).

So just who is welcome in God's presence? Psalm 15 may be divided into three parts:

- 15:1 raises the question,
- 15:2–5a answers the question, and
- 15:5b provides a concluding answer in the form of a promise.

The body of the psalm is 15:2–5a—the answer to the question. Of particular interest is that David casts his answer in the form of ten (implicit) commandments—ten ethical requirements of any who would enter God's presence in worship. Here is an analysis of its structure:[10]

I. Question: Who may dwell in the Lord's tent? (15:1)

II. Answers (15:2–5a)

The answer is given in an alternating pattern of virtues and vices

A. Three prescribed virtues (15:2)

1. Who walks (see 1:1) blamelessly (i.e., is totally committed)
2. Who does what is righteous (see 1:5)
3. Who speaks the truth (i.e., reliable words) from the heart (see 7:10)

B. Three proscribed vices (15:3)

4. Who utters no slander
5. Who does no wrong (i.e., something that damages neighbor, whether close or casual)
6. Who does not take up a reproach against his friend. (We might paraphrase, "Who says nothing that would bring his neighbor into disrepute.")

A.′ Two prescribed virtues pertaining to the Lord (15:4)

10 This outline is taken from Bruce K. Waltke, *Concise Commentary on the Psalms*, forthcoming online at The Gospel Coalition, https://www.thegospelcoalition.org/.

7. Who despises a vile person but honors those who fear the Lord (see 2:11)
8. Who keeps an oath (i.e., binds oneself to a future obligation by a curse [e.g., "may the Lord punish me if I renege"], cf. Eccles. 5:1–7) even when it hurts (i.e., damages the vower)

B.′ Two proscribed vices as to money

9. Who charges no interest ("to the poor" [NIV] is added because the Hebrew term refers to the destitute)
10. Who takes no bribe to convict an innocent person (in other cultures of the biblical world bribery was an accepted practice)

III. Conclusion: Covenant keepers will never be shaken off the holy mountain

These directives are not immediately reflective of Moses's Decalogue, but that they are ten does seem intentionally to reflect the Ten Commandments. They artfully move back and forth between speech and action or behavior. And the seventh (15:4a), usually a favored slot in a series, pertains to the fear of the Lord, thus linking behavior to faith. The first three directives demand integrity in behavior and speech (15:2). The next three pertain to specific acts and speech (15:3). The seventh demands a right response to neighbor based on the fear of the Lord, and the eighth cites oath keeping as the test of that fear (15:4). Finally, the ninth and tenth require that money not be used to disadvantage the poor (15:5).

Significantly, David makes no mention of particularly heinous crimes such as murder, adultery, and theft, as in Moses's Decalogue. The prescribed virtues of David's decalogue are more ethically subtle, too small to be caught "in the mesh of the law,"[11] and its proscriptions are commonly violated even by professing Christians—taking advantage of others, gossiping about them, and breaking vows. More

11 Derek Kidner, *Psalms 1–72* (London: Inter-Varsity Press, 1973), 274n6.

fundamentally, the issue is one of the heart, demanding of the worshiper self-examination.

The first three requirements are generalizations, a summary of the virtues required:

> 2 He who walks blamelessly
> and does what is right
> and speaks truth in his heart.

These three descriptions begin in broadest terms: the worshiper must be one whose lifestyle is marked by integrity ("blameless"). The next two directives narrow the first a bit to the (still broad) categories of doing what is right and speaking truth in his heart. The acceptable worshiper is principled in both action and speech—a person marked by integrity and sincerity, and who is without hypocrisy.

David follows up on these three positive descriptions with three negative descriptions, narrowing the focus further. The acceptable worshiper is one

> 3 who does not slander with his tongue
> and does no evil to his neighbor,
> nor takes up a reproach against his friend.

These three pertain to the treatment of others. The acceptable worshiper is one who will not speak harmfully of or do any harm to those with whom he comes in contact but will protect the relationship.

The seventh and critical description pertains to fundamentals: our relationship with God. Here the focus is on the person himself, not just his actions: "who honors those who fear the Lord" (15:4a). God rejects non-God-fearers but honors God-fearers. If we would worship God acceptably, we must honor him by honoring what is good and right and by despising what is evil and wrong. We must identify with and honor the righteous and despise the unrighteous and immoral. We must not idolize the wicked but esteem them as God does. God honors those who honor him. The true worshiper's evaluation of people reflects their own fear of God.

The eighth description pertains to the one who keeps his commitments and abides by his word: "who swears to his own hurt and does not change" (15:4b). That is, the one who enters to worship God is the person who keeps his or her vows—marriage vows and other commitments. Our word must be our bond, and we must honor our promises—even when it "hurts" we must not change our mind. We must be trustworthy.

The ninth and tenth descriptions of the acceptable worshiper relate to his use of and attitude toward money: "who does not put out his money at interest / and does not take a bribe against the innocent" (15:5a, b). That is, if we would worship God acceptably we will not use our money to disadvantage the poor. We will lend as an act of charity, not as an opportunity for investment—to help the needy, not to enrich ourselves. We must be principled in grace and refuse to make profit off another person's misery or create additional burden. Nor will we bear false witness for monetary gain (15:5b). "Whoever is greedy for unjust gain / troubles his own household, / but he who hates bribes will live" (Prov. 15:27). We fear God and seek always to reflect his character and actions in our own.

Finally, David offers a summary benediction on this acceptable worshiper: "He who does these things shall never be moved" (15:5c). This final line answers the introductory question of 15:1. Here is the one who is welcome in God's presence. Significantly, there is no mention of liturgy or ritual, which can be but a cloak of religiosity. The acceptable worshiper is a person of integrity, an integrity that marks all of life. This person "will never be moved." He will enjoy life in God's presence forever.

The Old Testament cultus has covenantal structures. No one can just barge into God's presence, and not just anyone is welcome. God is holy and demands a corresponding holiness on the part of his people. And here again we see the function of the didactic psalms in connection with the temple.

As the psalm functions in the Psalter, it teaches all the people of God to keep covenant. But it has a canonical function also, pointing ahead to David's greater Son who alone has perfectly satisfied these covenant requirements. He is the one in whom God is well pleased (Matt. 3:17). Nothing less than his perfect obedience and sacrifice for his people can secure the eternal inviolability in God's presence this psalm envisions, and this perfect obedience is just what we have in union with Christ. Yet this psalm reminds us that in Christ we have not only justification, acceptance, but also transformation of life, apart from which our worship is unacceptable.

## PSALM 19

A Psalm of David.

1 The heavens declare the glory of God,
and the sky above proclaims his handiwork.
2 Day to day pours out speech,
and night to night reveals knowledge.
3 There is no speech, nor are there words,
whose [heaven's] voice is not heard.
4 Their voice goes out through all the earth,
and their words to the end of the world.
In them he has set a tent for the sun,
5 which comes out like a bridegroom leaving his chamber,
and, like a strong man, runs its course with joy.
6 Its rising is from the end of the heavens,
and its circuit to the end of them,
and there is nothing hidden from its heat.
7 The law of the Lord is perfect,
reviving the soul;
the testimony of the Lord is sure,
making wise the simple;
8 the precepts of the Lord are right,
rejoicing the heart;

the commandment of the LORD is pure,
  enlightening the eyes;
9 the fear of the LORD is clean,
  enduring forever;
the rules of the LORD are true,
  and righteous altogether.
10 More to be desired are they than gold,
  even much fine gold;
sweeter also than honey
  and drippings of the honeycomb.

11 Moreover, by them is your servant warned;
  in keeping them there is great reward.
12 Who can discern his errors?
  Declare me innocent from hidden faults.
13 Keep back your servant also from [the insolent[12]];
  let them not have dominion over me!
Then I shall be blameless,
  and innocent of great transgression.
14 Let the words of my mouth and the meditation of my heart
  be acceptable in your sight,
  O LORD, my rock and my redeemer.
To the choirmaster.

## Genre

Psalm 19 is a hymn, a psalm written in praise of the Lord's creation and his Torah. Here is its structure:

Superscript
I. Praise of God's glory mediated by the heavens (19:1–6)
II. Praise of the beauty and benefits of Lord's law (19:7–10)

12 See Bruce K. Waltke and James M. Houston, *The Psalms as Christian Praise: A Historical Commentary* (Grand Rapids, MI: Eerdmans, 2019), 372.

III. Prayer for salvation from sin within and without (19:11–13)
Dedicatory prayer (19:14)

We consider this psalm here because the praise of the Lord's Torah (19:7–10) thinks in terms of the sage, aiming to give counsel for life. David employs the common vocabulary of the sage—"knowledge" (19:2), "simple" (19:7), "wise" (19:7), and "the fear of the LORD" (19:9), here as a synonym for divine revelation (see p. 417). The warning function of divine revelation (19:11a) echoes the sage also, as does his reference to "reward" for keeping Torah (19:11b). But this psalm does not praise Torah merely—it encourages fidelity to the Torah. It praises Torah and its perfections, but specifically its reliability and value for directing life are in view. The orientation is that of Old Testament wisdom.

Yet there is more to be said regarding genre. The superscript tells us that this is a psalm of David. It was a hymn, presumably to be sung by the people, but the genre is mixed. The first two stanzas are clearly praise—praise for God's general revelation in creation and for his special revelation in Scripture. Both the sun and the Law are essential to life. The Law warns the attentive servant of the deadly danger of breaking it and of the great reward in keeping its judgments (19:11) So the servant humbly prays to be free both of the guilt of hidden errors and also of apostasy prompted by insolent people whom he otherwise cannot resist. Moreover, the hymn differs from the standard praise hymn in that there is no call to praise and no direct address to God. And it differs from the standard petition psalm in that here it moves from praise to petition, not from petition to praise. So the psalm is a combination of wisdom, Torah, praise, and petition.

### Context

As we have mentioned, Psalms 1 and 2 form the introduction to the Psalter. Psalms 3–14 form a single grouping of psalms also, as we mentioned in connection with Psalm 3. Next, the inspired editors of the Psalter seem to have arranged Psalms 15–24 chiastically, with Psalm 19 as the pivot.

- A. Psalm 15 (entrance liturgy)
  - B. Psalm 16 (song of trust)
    - C. Psalm 17 (prayer for help)
      - D. Psalm 18 (royal psalm)
        - X. Psalm 19 (praise psalm: creation/Torah)
      - D.′ Psalms 20–21 (royal psalm)[13]
    - C.′ Psalm 22 (prayer for help)
  - B.′ Psalm 23 (song of trust)
- A.′ Psalm 24 (entrance liturgy)

So Psalm 1 introduces the Psalter in wisdom-praise of the Torah, and now in this grouping of psalms Psalm 19 is at the pivot, the essential point of the collection. Like Psalm 1 it is a wisdom-Torah psalm admonishing us take heed of the Law's teaching.

**Structure**

C. S. Lewis famously wrote of this psalm that it is "the greatest poem in the Psalter and one of the greatest lyrics in the world."[14] Yet he puzzles briefly over the psalm's logical structure. The general structure of the psalm is fairly straightforward. In the first stanza David praises the God who makes himself known and reveals his mind in creation (19:1–6). In the second stanza he praises God's Torah, his special revelation that displays God's moral excellence (19:7–11). Psalm 19:11 functions as a janus, still expressing praise of Torah but turning now to address God in prayer. His prayer is that he would keep God's Torah (19:12–13). Then he concludes with a dedicatory prayer (19:14).

Still, the precise logical relation of these stanzas is not immediately evident. Michael Fishbane observes that the movement has to do with a change of speakers in the psalm. In stanza 1, the heavens speak (19:1–6). In stanza 2, the Lord speaks through his Law (19:7–10). Then in the concluding section, the psalmist speaks with a related petition

13 Psalms 20 and 21 form a pair of royal psalms. Psalm 20 is a prayer for the king going out into battle, and Psalm 21 is praise upon his return from battle.

14 C. S. Lewis, *Reflections on the Psalms* (San Diego: Harcourt Brace, 1958), 56.

(19:11–14).[15] His observation is helpful as far as it goes, but it does not explain the logic of the movement between the stanzas. And we might note that in the first stanza—"heaven speaks"—it is, after all, God himself speaking through his creation. Arnt Meinhold helpfully observes that the psalm moves from a word about God (19:1– 6), to a word from God (19:7–10), and finally to a word to God (19:11–14).[16] This is helpful also, but again, the word about God in the first stanza is, in fact, a word from God.

We might content ourselves with saying that the first two stanzas unite in praise of God—praise for his revelation in creation and praise for his revelation in Torah—and that the third stanza is the psalmist's response (petition). The connection between the first two stanzas, however, may go deeper, as we will discuss below.

## Exposition[17]

### *Praise of God's Glory Mediated by the Heavens (19:1–6)*

The first stanza (19:1–6) praises the display of God's glory and knowledge in the created order. Spurgeon (1834–1892) reminds us that "it is not merely glory that the heavens declare, but the 'glory of God.'"[18] He may have had in mind the naturalist and the scientist Alexander von Humboldt (1769–1859), who the Kaiser at the time thought was the greatest man that ever lived. Von Humboldt led the academic world to extol with awe the glory of the natural order, not "the creation." He never spoke of a Creator.

This first stanza consists of two strophes. The first affirms that the firmament declares the glory of God in his knowledge on display in the heavens (19:1–4b):

15 M. A. Fishbane, *Text and Texture: Close Readings of Selected Biblical Texts* (New York: Schocken, 1979), 86.

16 Craig C. Broyles, *Psalms*, New International Biblical Commentary (Hendrickson, 1999), 109.

17 See also Waltke and Houston, *Psalms as Christian Worship*, chap. 11.

18 C. H. Spurgeon, *The Treasury of David*, vol. 1 (New York: Marshall Brothers, 1883), 270.

1 The heavens declare the glory of God,
and the sky above proclaims his handiwork.
2 Day to day pours out speech,
and night to night reveals knowledge.
3 There is no speech, nor are there words,
whose voice is not heard.
4 Their voice goes out through all the earth,
and their words to the end of the world.

This entire strophe focuses on the declarative function of creation (19:1) that is accomplished without words or sounds (19:3). Creation speaks with an "unspoken eloquence." Though there is no actual speech to be heard by the ear (19:3), the heavens nonetheless declare God's knowledge universally both in time (19:2) and in space (19:4) for all to hear. The heavens declare that they are made, the work of the Creator whose "knowledge" (19:2) in creation is shown to be all-encompassing.

The second strophe focuses particularly on the sun (19:4c–6):

In them he has set a tent for the sun,
5 which comes out like a bridegroom leaving his chamber,
and, like a strong man, runs its course with joy.
6 Its rising is from the end of the heavens,
and its circuit to the end of them,
and there is nothing hidden from its heat.

Here the focus again is on the universality of God's glory in space. The "bridegroom" simile (19:5a) suggests beauty, vigor, and joy, and the "strong man" who "runs [his] course with joy" (19:5b) likens the sun to a strong athlete who is both a sprinter and a long-distance runner who cannot be outrun either in speed or distance. So also the sun bursts its way in every place (19:6).

These first six verses give warrant to Herman Bavinck's famous dictum, "According to Scripture the whole universe is a creation and hence also a revelation of God."[19] Joseph Addison captures this very well in his famous "Ode to the Glory of God," a paraphrase of Psalm 19:

The spacious firmament on high,
With all the blue ethereal sky,
And spangled heav'ns, a shining frame
Their great Original proclaim:
Th' unwearied sun, from day to day,
Does his Creator's power display,
And publishes to every land,
The works of an Almighty hand.

Soon as the ev'ning shades prevail,
The moon takes up the wondrous tale,
And nightly to the list'ning earth
Repeats the story of her birth:
Whilst all the stars that round her burn,
And all the planets in their turn,
Confirm the tidings as they roll,
And spread the truth from pole to pole.

What though, in solemn silence, all
Move round the dark terrestrial ball?
What tho' no real voice nor sound,
Amid their radiant orbs be found?
In reason's ear they all rejoice,
And utter forth a glorious voice,
For ever singing, as they shine,
"The hand that made us is divine."[20]

19 Hermann Bavinck, *Reformed Dogmatics*, ed. John Bolt, trans. John Vriend, vol. 2, *God and Creation* (Grand Rapids, MI: Baker Academic, 2004), 56.

20 M. Tickell, *The Works of the Right Honourable Joseph Addison*, vol. 2 (London: T. Malden, 1804), 465.

*Praise of the Beauty and Benefits of Lord's Law (19:7–10)*

In the second stanza (19:7–11), David moves from the glories of God in creation to the moral excellence of the Torah, in which he delights. "The ever recurring mention of the commands are prized more highly than all creation, including the sun."[21] In these verses David describes both the essence of the Torah and its value—its essential qualities and its benefits to those who read it:

7 The law of the LORD is perfect,
  reviving the soul;
the testimony of the LORD is sure,
  making wise the simple;
8 the precepts of the LORD are right,
  rejoicing the heart;
the commandment of the LORD is pure,
  enlightening the eyes;
9 the fear of the LORD is clean,
  enduring forever;
the rules of the LORD are true,
  and righteous altogether.

In 19:7–9 David seems nearly to exhaust his vocabulary characterizing the moral excellence of the Torah. He refers to God's special revelation under six synonymous terms:

1. "The law of the LORD"
2. "The testimony of the LORD"
3. "The precepts of the LORD"
4. "The commandment of the LORD"
5. "The fear of the LORD"
6. "The rules of the LORD"

21 Hermann Gunkel, *Introduction to the Psalms: The Genres of the Religious Lyric of Israel*, completed by Joachim Begrich; trans. James Nogalski (Macon, GA: Mercer University Press, 1998), 307.

In all these terms the Torah, God's gift to Israel, is in view, highlighting particularly its authoritative direction for life. We might pause to observe that the expression "the fear of the LORD" here refers to God's objective revelation. The human response to this revelation is clearly in view,[22] but the expression is used here to refer to God's law itself. "The fear of the LORD" of course is a prominent theme in the Old Testament wisdom literature. This right estimate of God and corresponding submission to him is the very foundation and principal element of wisdom (Prov. 1:7; 9:10). Here the "fear of the LORD" describes his holy will objectively revealed. To "fear" God is to bow in reverence before his revealed will and live accordingly, and thus that law is itself described here objectively as "the fear of the LORD."

David then characterizes God's Torah with seven adjectives—the seven excellencies of God's word:

1. "Perfect": it is complete. "It is a crime to add to it, treason to alter it and felony to take from it."[23]
2. "Sure": it is utterly trustworthy and reliable, grounded as it is in the omniscience of the Creator.
3. "Right": it is upright. It does not bend or twist but is perfectly smooth and straight. That is, it is flawless and faultless.
4. "Pure": it shines (and thus enlightens).
5. "Clean": it has no impurities, nothing to make it decay.
6. "True": it is firm, steady, cannot be altered or overturned (unlike human judgments).
7. "Righteous altogether": it is in perfect conformity to God's character and will.

Finally, he highlights the value, beneficial function, or reward of the Torah:

22 Derek Kidner, *Psalms 1–72* (London: Inter-Varsity Press, 1973), 117.
23 Spurgeon, *Treasury of David*, vol. 1, 272.

- "reviving the soul" (because it is complete): renews vitality, restores life, is refreshing (cf. Ruth 4:15)
- "making wise the simple" (because it is sure)
- "rejoicing the heart" (because of its moral perfection)
- "enlightening the eyes" (because it shines)
- "enduring forever" (because it has no impurities)
- "true and righteous altogether"

A certain escalation marks the steps of David's praise of God's law—from reviving the soul to making wise to rejoicing the heart to enlightening the eyes. The New Testament emphasizes this remarkable power of God's word in terms of the ministry of the new covenant gospel (Jer. 31:34; Rom. 1:16; 10:13–18; 2 Cor. 3:1–3, 18; 4:3–6; James 1:25).

Finally, in Psalm 19:10–11 David responds in terms of his own valuing of God's word:

10 More to be desired are they than gold,
  even much fine gold;
sweeter also than honey
  and drippings of the honeycomb.
11 Moreover, by them is your servant warned;
  in keeping them there is great reward.

In all this David extols the essence, the moral perfections, and the value of God's revelation in the Torah. God's law is complete, flawless, perfect, and eternal, able then to transform the entire person and direct life successfully and with joy. Its reward, essentially, is life itself. God's law is good for us when embraced in faith and joy, not in grudging obedience to get God's favor and escape his judgment. It is rewarding, refreshing, and sweet. And therefore it is to be treasured. Gold can put food on the table, but it cannot give fellowship at the table. It can buy a house, but it cannot produce a home. It can buy a woman jewelry, but it cannot give the desired love. "Wisdom," divine instruction, can buy a house and a home, food and table fellowship, riches and love. It can enrich all of life. It is therefore of unique value.

Now we are in a position to consider again the connection between these first two stanzas. The created order displays God's "knowledge" (19:2), which is infinite. Wilson suggests that the connecting idea is that of divine authority—established and declared in creation and directing us in Torah.[24] This is a helpful step, but the precise line of thinking would seem to be found in the idea of the revelation of God's mind both in the created order and in his law. Because God is omniscient, he speaks infallibly and with certainty. As Creator he sees the whole; so when he speaks, his word is altogether certain and reliable. His comprehensive knowledge displayed in the created order and his absolute wisdom in governing it establish his wisdom to govern society and human life also. This seems to be the connection between the first two stanzas—God's certain knowledge displayed in the created order and in his law. Lewis comes close to this idea when he observes that in 19:7, as David turns to speak of "something else," it "hardly seems to him something else because it is so like the all-piercing, all-detecting sunshine."[25] The connecting idea is that of God's omniscience in both forms of his self-revelation. Certainty of knowledge depends on comprehensive knowledge. God's knowledge is, in fact, comprehensive, and therefore his word is absolute and altogether certain. His law is good for us because he knows comprehensively and holistically.

This link between God's creation and his law is not unique to Psalm 19. It is the logic of the wisdom literature, both in Job and in Proverbs. In Job's great poem of wisdom in Job 28:12–24, Job gives praise to God's wisdom and acknowledges that such wisdom is inaccessible apart from revelation:

> 12 But where shall wisdom be found?
> And where is the place of understanding?
> 13 Man does not know its worth,

24 Gerald H. Wilson, *Psalms, Volume 1*, The NIV Application Commentary (Grand Rapids, MI: Zondervan, 2002), 365.

25 Lewis, *Reflections on the Psalms*, 64.

and it is not found in the land of the living.
14 The deep says, "It is not in me,"
and the sea says, "It is not with me."
15 It cannot be bought for gold,
And silver cannot be weighed as its price.
16 It cannot be valued in the gold of Ophir,
in precious onyx or sapphire.
17 Gold and glass cannot equal it,
nor can it be exchanged for jewels of fine gold.
18 No mention shall be made of coral or of crystal;
the price of wisdom is above pearls.
19 The topaz of Ethiopia cannot equal it,
nor can it be valued in pure gold.
20 From where, then, does wisdom come?
And where is the place of understanding?
21 It is hidden from the eyes of all living
and concealed from the birds of the air.
22 Abaddon and Death say,
"We have heard a rumor of it with our ears."
23 God understands the way to it,
and he knows its place.
24 For he looks to the ends of the earth
and sees everything under the heavens.

That is to say, God has comprehensive knowledge. He sees and knows everything, and so he can speak with absolute certainty.

We find the same thinking with Agur in Proverbs 30:1–6. Notice how the inspired sage says he obtains knowledge:

The words of Agur son of Jakeh. The oracle.
1 The man declares, I am weary, O God;
I am weary, O God, and worn out.
2 Surely I am too stupid to be a man.
I have not the understanding of a man.

3 I have not learned wisdom,
nor have I knowledge of the Holy One.
4 Who has ascended to heaven and come down?
Who has gathered the wind in his fists?
Who has wrapped up the waters in a garment?
Who has established all the ends of the earth?
What is his name, and what is his son's name?
Surely you know!
5 Every word of God proves true;
he is a shield to those who take refuge in him.
6 Do not add to his words,
lest he rebuke you and you be found a liar.

First, he confesses his ignorance (30:1–2). Then he confesses his inability to have certain knowledge because he cannot go up to heaven to see things whole (30:3)—unless you have comprehensive knowledge, you cannot have certain knowledge. Next, he confesses that the Lord has such knowledge (30:4). Then he confesses that we can gain such knowledge only as we are taught by God: we must be his "son" (disciple, 30:4). Finally, he confesses that God has revealed himself in Scripture (30:5–6).[26]

Woman Wisdom, the personification of Solomon's teachings, connects her life-giving wisdom with her presence at the creation:

The LORD brought me forth as the first of his works,
before his deeds of old;
I was formed long ages ago,
at the very beginning, when the world came to be.
When there were no watery depths, I was given birth,
when there were no springs overflowing with water;
before the mountains were settled in place,
before the hills, I was given birth,
before he made the world or its fields

26 See also Prov. 8:22–36 for this same logic.

or any of the dust of the earth.
I was there when he set the heavens in place,
when he marked out the horizon on the face of the deep,
when he established the clouds above
and fixed securely the fountains of the deep,
when he gave the sea its boundary
so the waters would not overstep his command,
and when he marked out the foundations of the earth.
Then I was constantly at his side.
I was filled with delight day after day,
rejoicing always in his presence,
rejoicing in his whole world
and delighting in mankind.

Now then, my children, listen to me;
blessed are those who keep my ways.
Listen to my instruction and be wise;
do not disregard it.
Blessed are those who listen to me,
watching daily at my doors,
waiting at my doorway.
For those who find me find life
and receive favor from the Lord.
But those who fail to find me harm themselves;
All who hate me love death. (Prov. 8:22–36 NIV)

This is the kind of reasoning we find in Psalm 19. The Creator in heaven has comprehensive knowledge. The created order reveals his omniscience; therefore, he speaks with absolute certainty in his law. This is why David can say that God's law "is sure" (19:7) and that it is "enduring forever" (19:9).

*Prayer for Salvation from Sin Within and Without (19:11–13)*

In the final stanza (19:12–14) David offers his corresponding prayer, asking God to remove past sin, to restrain him from future sin, and to make his life pleasing to him. The structure of Psalm 19 is atypical at this point (as Ps. 139) in that his praise is the basis of his petition, not the result. But for a sincere worshiper having contemplated the comprehensive knowledge of God and the purity of his law with its inherent warnings, this progression of thought is inevitable:

> 12 Who can discern his errors?
> Declare me innocent from hidden faults.
> 13 Keep back your servant also from [the insolent];
> let them not have dominion over me!
> Then I shall be blameless,
> and innocent of great transgression.

In 19:12 David pleads for God's protection from, for awareness of, and forgiveness for hidden sins—sins of which he is unaware. Our heart is such that we are often blinded to our own sins, and so David reminds us to look to God with regard to these "hidden" sins also.

Psalm 19:13 is usually translated in reference to "presumptuous sins," presumably corresponding to the hidden sins of 19:12. But the Hebrew term (זֵדִים) that is used here is a substantival adjective (an adjective used as a noun) that elsewhere consistently refers to "the insolent." It is used to describe those who challenge God (Mal. 3:15), who attack the psalmist (Ps. 86:14), reject Jeremiah's prophecy (Jer. 43:2), mock the pious without restraint (Ps. 119:51), forge lies (119:69), and dig pits (119:85). The psalmist prays that God will put them to shame (119:78) and not let them oppress him (119:122). The Lord is said to rebuke them (119:21) and cause their arrogance to cease (Isa. 13:11; cf. Mal. 4:1). From all the uses of this word elsewhere we should conclude that it refers to *insolent people*—people who from their exaggerated and prideful opinion of their self-importance and sufficiency disregard the Lord, the wise, and revealed truth.[27] This prayer ("Keep me from the

27 Cf. Prov. 21:24, the only occurrence of this word in the singular, which the NIV translates "the proud and arrogant person."

insolent men") is, then, roughly equivalent to Matthew 6:13: "Lead us not into temptation, but deliver us from the evil one" (NIV). The idea is "Keep me from those who would ruin me spiritually." That David's concern in Psalm 19:13a is spiritual failure and apostasy is made clear in 19:13b: "Then I shall be blameless, / and innocent of great transgression." The "great transgression" is that of rebellion (פֶּשַׁע) against the Lord, breaking faith with him. And from such apostasy David asks that God would keep him.

David ends the psalm in 19:14 with a prayer of dedication and plea that God would find him pleasing in both heart and speech:

> 14 Let the words of my mouth and the meditation of my heart
> be acceptable in your sight,
> O Lord, my rock and my redeemer.

The reference here seems to be that of the (divine) royal court. David is asking for favor and acceptance before the King—that God would accept his prayer. He wishes his praise for God's revelation in creation and in his law would be acceptable. He does not ask that this be the ground of his acceptance, however. God himself is his "rock and redeemer." David is grounded in grace.

That David's words were indeed found acceptable to God is evident, for they are preserved for us in the biblical canon. Praise to the God who has given us all-wise, life-giving counsel in his perfect word. Petition to this God for mercy and forgiveness. And praise to him who through his Son—who manifested all the purity of the law and offered himself in sacrifice for sin—has saved us from our sin and who keeps us safely forever. Through Christ, our Rock and Redeemer, we may pray and sing this psalm also, with confidence of our acceptance in him.

## PSALM 73

We have stressed that the unifying element of the Psalter is the establishing of God's kingdom in the earth. This is an entailment of the Psalter's royal orientation, and it comes into sharpest focus in the messianic psalms. God's purpose is to establish his rule in the earth.

One problem related to this theme is the hard reality that evil reigns in high places, error wins the hearts and minds of men, society lives in open rebellion against God, and sin goes so often unchecked. More to our point here, the wicked often seem to prosper while the righteous suffer adversity as though they are cursed. This problem of "theodicy" comes to the fore most prominently in the book of Job, but it is such a common problem that we are not surprised to see it addressed in the Psalms also. This psalm of Asaph concerns his famous crisis of faith and his struggle with the question of why the wicked prosper while the righteous often suffer. And as we will see, it is through the symbolism of the temple that his crisis of faith is resolved and his faith renewed.

In this wisdom psalm Asaph records his crisis, and he has profound questions, but he couches it all in praise and begins with a confession of God's goodness:

A Psalm of Asaph.

1 Truly God is good to Israel,
to those who are pure in heart.
2 But as for me, my feet had almost stumbled,
my steps had nearly slipped.
3 For I was envious of the arrogant
when I saw the prosperity of the wicked.
4 For they have no pangs until death;
their bodies are fat and sleek.
5 They are not in trouble as others are;
they are not stricken like the rest of mankind.
6 Therefore pride is their necklace;
violence covers them as a garment.
7 Their eyes swell out through fatness;
their hearts overflow with follies.
8 They scoff and speak with malice;
loftily they threaten oppression.

9 They set their mouths against the heavens,
and their tongue struts through the earth.
10 Therefore his people turn back to them,
and find no fault in them.
11 And they say, "How can God know?
Is there knowledge in the Most High?"
12 Behold, these are the wicked;
always at ease, they increase in riches.
13 All in vain have I kept my heart clean
and washed my hands in innocence.
14 For all the day long I have been stricken
and rebuked every morning.
15 If I had said, "I will speak thus,"
I would have betrayed the generation of your children.
16 But when I thought how to understand this,
it seemed to me a wearisome task,
17 until I went into the sanctuary of God;
then I discerned their end.
18 Truly you set them in slippery places;
you make them fall to ruin.
19 How they are destroyed in a moment,
swept away utterly by terrors!
20 Like a dream when one awakes,
O Lord, when you rouse yourself, you despise them as phantoms.
21 When my soul was embittered,
when I was pricked in heart,
22 I was brutish and ignorant;
I was like a beast toward you.
23 Nevertheless, I am continually with you;
you hold my right hand.
24 You guide me with your counsel,
and afterward you will receive me to glory.
25 Whom have I in heaven but you?

And there is nothing on earth that I desire besides you.
26 My flesh and my heart may fail,
but God is the strength of my heart and my portion forever.
27 For behold, those who are far from you shall perish;
you put an end to everyone who is unfaithful to you.
28 But for me it is good to be near God;
I have made the Lord God my refuge,
that I may tell of all your works.

Here is the psalm in outline:

I. The theodicy (73:1–17)
  A. Confession of insight: God is good to true Israel (73:1)
  B. Confession of sight: wicked prosper (73:2–12)
    1. Crisis of faith (73:2–3)
    2. Prosperity of the wicked (73:4–12)
  C. Personal conflict and temple epiphany (73:13–17)
    1. Physical pain (ground level) (73:13–14)
    2. Personal conflict (73:15–16)
    3. Entrance into the temple and epiphany (73:17)
II. Asaph's temple epiphany (73:18–26)
  A. Insight into the destiny of wicked (73:18–20)
  B. Insight into self (73:21–26)
    1. Insight into past as a brute (73:21–22)
    2. Insight into God's present grip (73:23)
    3. Insight into future glory (73:24)
    4. Insight into God as all-sufficient and eternal possession (73:25–26)
III. Conclusion (73:27–28)
  A. Destruction of the wicked (73:27)
  B. Commitment to God's care and control (73:28)

Asaph writes as one deeply convinced of God's goodness, which he affirms at the outset (73:1). He does not doubt that God is good to

Israel. He is convinced that God is good and that he upholds his covenant. But this is the point that gives rise to his crisis: his experience seems to contradict this important tenet of faith. This seeming conflict between his theology and his experience presented a near-ruin crisis of faith (73:2), and Asaph relates his steps downward.

First (taking these steps in their logical order), he "saw the prosperity of the wicked" (73:3b). Apparently Asaph held a view of life shaped by his own limited view of the world. This is sometimes called "keyhole theology." Asaph was judging reality by what he could see within the limited horizon of his own lifetime and experience. He saw the prosperity of the wicked (73:4–5), a prosperity such that could embolden them in their wickedness and pride (73:6–12). They were godless, and they were comfortable in it and carefree. And this while Asaph kept the covenant and yet was afflicted. And all this seemed to put God in a bad light. Asaph's mistake, as it is sometimes framed, was that he allowed his problem to define God rather than allowing God to define the problem.

His second step away from God was becoming envious of the wicked (73:3a). He made their prosperity, rather than God himself, his ambition and desire. There is no sin in being perplexed, of course—that is normal Christian experience (cf. 2 Cor. 4:6–8). Failure to understand God's providence is no sin. But to judge God and shape our theology by our limited perception is surely wrong. And to envy and make prosperity our god is to be sinfully discontented with God and mistrusting of his providence.

Asaph's third step down is stated in 73:2: he almost lost his footing. That is, he almost abandoned faith. He began to seriously question the value of his religion and his theological commitments (73:13–16). He does not tell us his specific circumstances, only that his life was not marked by the lack of concern that marked the wicked. His faith did not seem to pay off as expected. And his confusion over this inequity nearly spelled his ruin.

The turning point for him came when he entered the temple, and again Asaph outlines the steps back to a restored faith. First, he could not accept the notion that God actually rewards evil and punishes the good (73:15–16):

> 15 If I had said, "I will speak thus,"
> I would have betrayed the generation of your children.
> 16 But when I thought how to understand this,
> it seemed to me a wearisome task.

His conscience just could not allow such a thought. It is one or the other: Is God good or not? If he is, then he allows suffering for some reason.

His second step back came from what he learned in the temple (73:17):

> 17 until I went into the sanctuary of God;
> then I discerned their end.

He went to the place where he could meet God, and it seems it was the symbolism of the temple that served to restore his faith. It was in the temple that he understood the final destiny of the wicked (73:17–20). There he saw in ritual the symbols of God's holiness, mercy, everlasting life, and final victory. When he saw all of that, he realized that his shortsighted thinking was like that of an animal (73:21–22). A man who knows God should think better. Those symbols of God spoke deeply to him—that is why they were there. And they are recorded for us, that we can see the truths of God in our imagination and see how it all finds final expression in Jesus Christ. We see his death and his resurrection, his triumph over sin, and his kingly reign that will culminate in his glorious return. Those ancient symbols portray realities that enable us to bear up and to understand with Asaph the final destiny of the wicked and our own blessed destiny in Christ.

Finally, in 73:23–24, Asaph transcends "keyhole theology" and recognizes that through all his afflictions God had taken him by the hand—holding him, strengthening him, and leading him to ultimate glory. Just as God took Christ by the hand and took him through the wilderness and through all the temptations and tests to prepare him for his final victories, and just as he took David through his experience of rejection by Saul when he learned to live by faith, so God takes us by the right hand, holding us to himself in Christ, leading us through our crises, and strengthening us until we reach final glory in his presence.

In 73:25–28, Asaph tells us how his crisis of faith resulted in a renewed faith:

> 25 Whom have I in heaven but you?
> And there is nothing on earth that I desire besides you.
> 26 My flesh and my heart may fail,
> but God is the strength of my heart and my portion forever.
> 27 For behold, those who are far from you shall perish;
> you put an end to everyone who is unfaithful to you.
> 28 But for me it is good to be near God;
> I have made the Lord GOD my refuge,
> that I may tell of all your works.

Through this crisis Asaph has come to recognize afresh the deep joy of knowing God and living in his presence. Living under God he has much more than the wealthy wicked. Their joys will fade. Asaph's joy is eternal. And it was the temple symbolism that reminded Asaph of it.

14

# Rhetorical Devices and Structures

RHETORICAL CRITICISM has to do with the poetic devices the psalmist uses to get his message across. This includes the logic of the psalm, how it is put together, and how its construction conveys its meaning. The focus here is not the "form" or genre of the psalm or its motifs. Here we look more narrowly at the poetic techniques by which the psalmists compose their poems. If the psalmists employ certain poetic techniques to convey their meaning, then understanding those techniques is essential to understanding them. As the saying goes, we must first know *how* a text means before we can know *what* it means.

This is the study of poetics, the literary devices that an author uses to construct his composition and to communicate his message. Like the narrator, the poet has a point of view. He has a message, and he communicates his message through artistic forms and methods. Poetics is the study of this artistry. It analyzes the poem itself in full perspective, and from there it proceeds to examine the various components and features:

- poem
- stanzas
- verses/lines
- half-verses/versets/cola

- phrases
- words
- syllables
- sounds

We begin with the entire psalm in perspective. The major components of a given psalm are its stanzas, and the major components of a stanza are its strophes. For example, we saw that Psalm 110 consists of two stanzas: 110:1–3 and 110:4–7. Within the first stanza we noted an introduction (110:1a), a divine citation (110:1b), and a prophetic reflection (110:2–3). Then we observed the same breakdown in stanza two: an introduction to a citation (110:4a), the divine citation itself (110:4b), and the prophetic reflection (110:5–7). These smaller units that make up the stanza are the strophes.

From here the focus narrows to the various literary devices that hold the part together and/or advance the thought of the poem:[1]

- keyword
- refrain
- contrast
- comparison
- logic
- escalation > climax
- patterns (of various kinds)
- janus
- generalization and particularization
- preparation/foreshadowing
- summarization
- interrogation
- *inclusio*
- intercalation

1 See Bruce K. Waltke with Cathi J. Fredricks, *Genesis: A Commentary* (Grand Rapids, MI: Zondervan, 2001), 33–38.

- allusion
- scenic depiction
- naming

### Keyword

A *keyword* is a prominent word that holds the poem together and sheds meaning to other words and to the poem itself. Martin Buber coined the German word *leitwort*, which he defined as "a word or word root that is meaningfully repeated within a text or a sequence of texts or a complex of texts,"[2] the recognition of which illumines the poem.

For example, in **Psalm 2**, the key words are "LORD" and "the King." Every stanza talks about the Lord and the King. The rebellion of the heathen is against the Lord and against the King. It is the Lord who sets his King upon Zion. The King recites the decree of the Lord to enthrone him. The psalmist exhorts the kings to serve the Lord and kiss the Son, who is the King. And once you see that, that begins to open that psalm a little bit more clearly. It's about the Lord and his King and their relationships.

### Refrain

A *refrain* repeats a given phrase or clause. In Psalms 42–43, for example, the king is in exile and longs to return to the temple. Three times he says,

> Why are you cast down, O my soul,
>   and why are you in turmoil within me?
> Hope in God; for I shall again praise him,
>   my salvation and my God. (42:5, 11; 43:5)

All three times, he ends the stanza with this refrain—though he is discouraged, away from the temple and longing for it, he will wait for the Lord, hope in him, and find healing for his distressed soul.

2 Martin Buber, "Leitwort Style in Pentateuch Narrative," in *Scripture and Translation*, ed. Martin Buber and Franz Rosenzweig, trans. Lawrence Alan Rosenwald and Everett Fox (Bloomington, IN: Indiana University Press, 1994), 114.

Psalm 49, a didactic psalm, illustrates the importance of the refrain in a unique way, and we will examine it further below.

### Contrast and Comparison

Often the author will draw attention to his point by means of *contrast* and/or *comparison*. A contrast associates or juxtaposes things that are dissimilar or opposite. A comparison associates or juxtaposes things that are alike or similar. This technique is not unique to poetry but appears in narrative also.

This technique of contrast is used pervasively in Psalm 1. The psalm itself is built with contrasts framing each of the three stanzas. In stanza one (1:1–2) the psalmist contrasts the word of God and the way of the wicked. In stanza two (1:3–4) he contrasts the tree of life and the chaff. And in stanza three (1:5–6) he contrasts the two corresponding outcomes. In this case (Ps. 1), contrast serves to control the shape and message of the entire psalm.

Psalm 23 compares three different settings in which the psalmist enjoys the Lord's care. The Lord is likened to a shepherd who provides for, restores, and protects his sheep (23:1–4). Then he is likened to a wealthy sheik in a large tent (23:5), and here the thought of 23:1–4 is not repeated but escalated: now the Lord provides the psalmist with a table lavishly supplied, he pours oil on his head, and this in the presence of his enemies. So he is well protected. Then 23:6 presents the climactic final scene in which the psalmist rests in God's presence eternally.

### Logic and Escalation

The thought of a given psalm must be traced in terms of its *logic* or logical progression. We must always pay close attention to the logical progression of a psalm, but our point here is that we must observe how the thought develops, how the stanzas hold together, and how the message is made prominent.

The *climax* of Psalm 2:10–12, for example, "Now therefore," signals a cause and effect. The kings and nations of the earth have set themselves against the Lord and against his king in open rebellion (2:1–3). But the

Lord's purpose to rule the earth through his anointed King remains (2:4–6), and his King remains resolved to subdue and inherit the nations as the Lord has promised him (2:7–9). "Now therefore, O kings, be wise" (2:10) marks the climax, and the argument is from cause to effect: because God has enthroned his King, and because the King will surely rule, then there is only one wise course of action: submit to the Son and take refuge in him (2:12).

### Structural Patterns

Chiastic and other parallel literary structures or *patterns* are rare in contemporary English literature, but in the ancient world these are very common, even the expected norm.[3] The ancient author does not simply tell a story or write a poem—he writes it in such a way that the structure of the story conveys its message.

In an *alternating* pattern the thought progresses repetitively:

A<br>
    B<br>
        C<br>
A′<br>
    B′<br>
        C′

This is the pattern we observed in **Psalm 110**:

A. Introduction to the divine citation (110:1a)<br>
    B. The divine citation itself (110:1b)<br>
        C. The prophetic reflection (110:2–3)<br>
A.′ Introduction to the divine citation (110:4a)<br>
    B.′ The divine citation itself (110:4b)<br>
        C.′ The prophetic reflection (110:5–7)

3 See Richard L. Pratt Jr., *He Gave Us Stories: The Bible Student's Guide to Interpreting Old Testament Narratives* (Brentwood, TN: Wolgemuth and Hyatt, 1990), 179–230.

The symmetry is balanced by a simple repetition of structured thought. This alternating pattern is like the waves of the sea hitting the shore with one wave on top of another; with the tide coming in each next wave is more intense than the previous—as in Psalm 110, which climaxes in the King's subduing of the entire earth.

In a *chiastic* pattern the thoughts are repeated but in reverse order:

A
  B
    X
  B′
A′

The chiastic pattern is like throwing a rock into a pond—the ripples go outward from the point of contact in corresponding or concentric waves. And here the critical point is the center, where the rock hits, as it were. This center point is referred to as the "pivot," and it often marks a turning point or point or focus in a poem or narrative.

We observed this in **Psalm 100**:

A. Shout to the Lord.
  B. Serve him . . . with joy/shout
    C. Come (בּוֹא) before him
      X. Know that the Lord, he is God!
    C.′ Enter (בּוֹא) his courts
  B.′ Give him grateful praise with a hymn
A.′ Bless his name

We also noticed this structure in **Psalm 92**:

A. King praises the Lord (92:1–4)
  B. Praise for God's great work and profound thoughts (92:5–6)
    C. All evildoers eliminated (92:7)

X. The Lord is on high forever (92:8)
C.′ All evildoers perish (92:9)
B.′ King rejoices in victory (92:10–11)
A.′ Righteous and king praise the Lord (92:12–15)

In the *concentric* pattern the thoughts are also reversed, but there is no pivot. It is like the tide, which comes in and then flows out:

A
B
C
C′
B′
A′

This pattern can be observed in **Psalm 25**:

A. Introduction: confession of trust in the Lord (25:1)
B. Let me not be put to shame (25:2–3)
C. Show me your ways and forgive my sin (25:4–11)
C.′ The Lord instructs God-fearers in his way (25:12–14)
Janus (25:15)
B.′ Let me not be put to shame (25:16–21)
A.′ Conclusion: petition to redeem Israel (25:22)

**Psalm 32**, apart from an outlying call to praise (32:11), consists of two stanzas of equal length containing within them concentrically structured thoughts:

I. The witness of the forgiven king (32:1–5)
A. Wisdom saying of forgiveness (addressed to congregation) (32:1–2)
B. Testimony of being forgiven (addressed to God) (32:3–5)
II. The prayer and instruction of the king (32:6–10)

B.′ Prayer for godly to escape judgment (addressed to God) (32:6–7)

A.′ Wisdom sayings to repent (addressed to congregation) (32:8–10)

III. Call to praise (32:11)

We should note that though these literary structures may be foreign to us and seem rather ornate, they are not merely artistic—they are structures intended to convey the meaning of the author. Since that is the case, our familiarity with them becomes mandatory.

**Janus or Hinge**

In ancient Roman mythology Janus, a god with faces on the front and back of his head, was the god of gates and doorways. His two faces looked two ways at the same time, back and forth. Our month of January is named after this god—a month that marks a new beginning as it closes the old year and introduces the new. Similarly, a literary *janus* is a device that unites two units by looking both back and forward.

Preachers have often encountered this device when seeking to outline a psalm. A given verse may present difficulty in that it "fits" with the point at hand and yet seems to fit with the following point of thought. There may be keywords or important ideas that are common to both what precedes and what follows. So, does this verse go with, say, point *a* or point *b*? Often this problem is deliberate on the part of the author—it is a transition verse that looks both ways as it progresses to the next thought.

We see this in Psalm 19, where 19:11 is a janus. "By them" (19:11) looks back to "the rules" (19:9), and "is your servant warned" (19:11) looks ahead to the hidden sins and apostasy of 19:12–13. So also "in keeping them" (19:11) looks ahead to "keep back your servant from [the insolent]," and "great [רָב] reward," (19:11) looks back to "much [רָב] fine gold" in 19:10.

We saw this in the chiastic structure of Psalm 92, mentioned above, where 92:8 ("but you, O Lord, are on high forever") pivots the psalm by climaxing one stanza and introducing the next. We also saw this in Psalm 23:4 where David transitions from talking about God (in the third person) as shepherd to speaking to God (in the second person) as his sheik. The use of janus is very common in the Psalter, and recognizing it significantly aids understanding.

### Generalization and Particularization

This technique is just what these terms indicate: a movement in the text toward explication that becomes either more specific or more comprehensive. Psalm 103:2 states its praise in broad, general terms: "Bless the Lord, O my soul, / and forget not all his benefits." But from there David narrows to specifics: forgiveness (103:3), deliverance (103:4), and satisfaction (103:5).

### Preparation and Foreshadowing

This technique refers to the inclusion of material in one part of the text that serves primarily to *prepare* the reader for what will come later in the text. For example, in the lament psalms the psalmist will have an introductory petition that he develops as the psalm unfolds. **Psalm 51** serves as a good example. In 51:1–2, David pleads,

1 Have mercy on me, O God,
according to your steadfast love;
according to your abundant mercy
blot out my transgressions.
2 Wash me thoroughly from my iniquity,
and cleanse me from my sin!

Later in verse 51:7 he begins his main petition:

7 Purge me with hyssop, and I shall be clean;
wash me, and I shall be whiter than snow.
8 Let me hear joy and gladness;
let the bones that you have broken rejoice.

9 Hide your face from my sins,
and blot out all my iniquities.
10 Create in me a clean heart, O God,
and renew a right spirit within me.
11 Cast me not away from your presence,
and take not your Holy Spirit from me.
12 Restore to me the joy of your salvation,
and uphold me with a willing spirit.

The introductory petition prepares the reader for what comes in full later.

### Summarization

A *summarization* offers a synopsis of material that is treated more fully elsewhere. "Surely goodness and mercy shall follow me / all the days of my life" (23:6) is a summarization of the blessedness of living under God's care. There is more to say, but the summary covers it all in broad terms. "The prosperity of the wicked" (73:3) is another example of this technique.

### Interrogation

*Interrogation* is when the psalmist will pose a question or a problem and then follow it up with the answer or solution. Psalm 15:1–2 provides an example:

1 O Lord, who shall sojourn in your tent?
Who shall dwell on your holy hill?
2 He who walks blamelessly and does what is right
and speaks truth in his heart.

### *Inclusio*

An *inclusio* is a repetition of features at the beginning and the end of a unit. This serves to frame a unit, and it emphasizes by repetition. Psalm 8 provides a good example: "O Lord, our Lord, / how majestic is your name in all the earth!" (8:1, 9) frames the entire psalm and asserts its message.

### Intercalation or Insertions

As the terms indicate, an *intercalation* or *insertion* is a technique in which one literary unit is inserted into another. In the midst of developing one thought, the psalmist may suddenly throw in another. We observed this in Psalm 100:

1 Make a joyful noise to the LORD, all the earth!
2 Serve the LORD with gladness!
   Come into his presence with singing!
3 Know that the LORD, he is God!
   It is he who made us, and we are his;
   we are his people, and the sheep of his pasture.
4 Enter his gates with thanksgiving,
   and his courts with praise!
   Give thanks to him; bless his name!

The opening verses (100:1–2) issue the call to praise, as does 100:4. And then 100:5 provides the cause or reason for praise. But between 100:2 and 100:4 is the command of 100:3: "Know that the LORD, he is God." That is, 100:3 interrupts the call to praise with an implied condition for entering the praise of God: Gentiles must know that Israel's God, the Lord, is God and that Israel is his chosen people. With this confession in place, the psalmist continues his call to praise.

**Psalm 24**, the famous enthronement psalm of David, provides another example of intercalation:

1 The earth is the LORD's and the fullness thereof,
   the world and those who dwell therein,
2 for he has founded it upon the seas
   and established it upon the rivers.

We might expect at this point that the "King of glory" would enter the city and be crowned (24:7–10). But instead, 24:3–6 introduces something entirely different:

3 Who shall ascend the hill of the LORD?
And who shall stand in his holy place?
4 He who has clean hands and a pure heart,
who does not lift up his soul to what is false
and does not swear deceitfully.
5 He will receive blessing from the LORD
and righteousness from the God of his salvation.
6 Such is the generation of those who seek him,
who seek the face of the God of Jacob. *Selah*

So now not only is the King entering the city triumphantly but his people are entering with him. But who are his people who enter with him? It is the righteous. Now David can proceed with the triumphant entry of the King:

7 Lift up your heads, O gates!
And be lifted up, O ancient doors,
that the King of glory may come in.
8 Who is this King of glory?
The LORD, strong and mighty,
the LORD, mighty in battle!
9 Lift up your heads, O gates!
And lift them up, O ancient doors,
that the King of glory may come in.
10 Who is this King of glory?
The LORD of hosts,
he is the King of glory! *Selah*

Psalm 24:3–6, then, is an insertion of a new thought, a thought not entirely alien to the thought at hand (enthronement of the King) but subservient to it (the presence and character of his people). And with this intercalation in place the original thought continues. This technique (intercalation) is common in the Psalter.

We might note here also that as the King enters the city, the gates are commanded to lift up their heads (24:7, 9). This is unusual imagery: gates do not lift themselves up, so personification is involved. Moreover, their "heads" do not refer to the top of the gates, as commonly thought, for gates in the ancient Near East, unlike the medieval portcullis gates, do not lift upward but swing on hinges back and forth. Rather, as F. M. Cross, Bruce's professor at Harvard, argued, the picture is probably that of councils of elders who sit anxiously awaiting the return of the king and his army who had gone out to battle. This interpretation is based on Ugaritic texts where the council of the gods is assembled in the mountain of 'El. On the approach of the emissaries of Baal's arch foe, Prince Sea, the gods are bowed and fearful, and in despair. Then Baal, the young king, shouts, "Lift up, O gods, your heads!" So the call to "lift up your heads, O gates" signifies the joy of Israel's elders upon the return of the king in glorious victory.[4]

### Allusion or Intertextuality

Often the biblical writers will pick up passages or themes of earlier biblical writers, and as they do, they often develop those passages and themes further. These connections may be explicit, or they may be simple allusions, and as these intercanonical connections occur we have inspired commentary on those earlier passages and themes.

This is a massively important area of study, but here we just note that this technique is common in the Psalms. We saw previously that Psalm 8 provides a kind of poetic commentary on Genesis 1:26–28. So also in Psalm 2:7, God's declaration to the newly crowned king, "you are my Son; today I have begotten you," the term "Son" alludes to God's promise to David: "I will raise up your offspring after you. . . . I will

4 Frank Moore Cross, *Canaanite Myth and Hebrew Epic: Essays in the History of the Religion of Israel* (Cambridge, MA: Harvard University Press, 1973), chap. 5.

be to him a father, and he shall be to me a son" (2 Sam. 7:12, 14). Thus "son of God" becomes a messianic title.

### Scenic Depiction

The way the biblical writers depict a given scene may also illuminate a passage. God often orchestrates—not in imagination but in real history, in providence—the setting of a given event to make a point. For example, in connection with Psalm 3 we surveyed the background from 2 Samuel 15–16. As David flees from Absalom he meets up with three people: Hushai, Ziba, and Shimei. Hushai is a loyal friend who defeats the counsel of Absalom's adviser Ahithophel. Ziba is somewhat mixed—he is loyal to David, but by being disloyal to his master Mephibosheth. And Shimei hates David, throws rocks at him, and calls him a bloody tyrant because of what he did to his ancestor Saul. It seems beyond coincidence that Hushai, the loyal friend of David, is on the top of the mountain closest to God, Ziba is farther down the slope, and Shimei is at the bottom of the mountain totally removed from God.

As another example, in Psalm 5:3 David prays for justice in the morning. In the ancient Near East, the morning was the time of judgment. The God of justice in the ancient Near East was Shamas, which is the sun. And so the setting in this imagery is the morning sun that gives hope for justice in the light of the new day.

### Naming

Finally, naming is often a significant device in the Psalms. As we saw in Psalm 91, the psalmist uses four names for God: "the Most High," "the Almighty," "the LORD," and "God" (91:1–2). Considering the meaning of the divine names in the context of a given psalm often illuminates its message.

These are some of the literary techniques by which the psalmists convey their meaning. Sometimes the meaning of a psalm is conveyed subtly, and only with these lenses in place will we ascertain all that the psalmists intend for us.

## PSALM 58

Psalm 58 illustrates some of the rhetorical devices we have discussed.

A Miktam of David.

1 Do you indeed decree what is right, you gods?
Do you judge the children of man uprightly?
2 No, in your hearts you devise wrongs;
your hands deal out violence on earth.
3 The wicked are estranged from the womb;
they go astray from birth, speaking lies.
4 They have venom like the venom of a serpent,
like the deaf adder that stops its ear,
5 so that it does not hear the voice of charmers
or of the cunning enchanter.
6 O God, break the teeth in their mouths;
tear out the fangs of the young lions, O LORD!
7 Let them vanish like water that runs away;
when he aims his arrows, let them be blunted.
8 Let them be like the snail that dissolves into slime,
like the stillborn child who never sees the sun.
9 Sooner than your pots can feel the heat of thorns,
whether green or ablaze, may he sweep them away!
10 The righteous will rejoice when he sees the vengeance;
he will bathe his feet in the blood of the wicked.
11 Mankind will say, "Surely there is a reward for the righteous;
surely there is a God who judges on earth."

To the choirmaster: according to Do Not Destroy.

Here David is lamenting the tyranny of evil rulers. The "gods" may have in view what Paul will later call "cosmic powers" (Eph. 6:10) or "rulers and authorities in the heavenly places" (Eph. 3:10; the KJV famously has "principalities and powers") who, in turn, are represented by evil human rulers. The standard components of a lament or petition psalm are evident here, only with some variation:

- lament in form of prophetic accusation against humankind (Ps. 58:1–5)
- address and petition (58:6–8)
- confidence or confession of trust (58:9)
- praise (58:10–11)

From a rhetorical perspective, the psalm is structured as a chiasm:

A. Rulers accused of injustice against humankind (58:1–2)
  B. Reflection and accusation of original depravity (58:3)
  [single line between couplets]
    C. Accusation of injustice and intractability using snake similes (58:4–5)
      X. King of Israel petitions God to smash rulers (58:6) [pivotal line]
    C.′ God's judicial sentence using several similes (58:7–8)
  B.′ Reflection and confidence of justice (58:9)
  [single line between couplets]
A.′ Righteous praise God for justice for humankind (58:10–11)

The couplets of A and A′ frame the psalm by several catchwords:

- "judge" (58:1)
- "mankind" (58:11)
- "gods" (i.e., rulers, 58:1)
- "what is right" (58:1) and "righteous" (58:10, 11)
- "on earth" (58:2, 11)

The single lines of B and B′ stand apart from (see below) and yet are connected semantically with the unified couplets that precede and follow them:

- accusation (58:4–5)
- judgment (58:7–9)

The couplets C and C′ develop the preceding line by similes (i.e., repetitions of "like").

The center line of the psalm is the pivot, expressing petition to God for vengeance. This pivot reverses the mood from the preceding five verses of complaint (58:1–5) to the five verses of hope (58:7–11). The pivot, then, is central to the psalm's message: the king's prayer turns an upside-down world right-side-up. God entrusted control of the world to divine beings in his heavenly court who are represented by the rulers on earth (58:1–2), but they misused their power to benefit themselves, not their subjects (58:3–5). In response to the king's prayer (58:6) the wicked rulers are eliminated (58:7–10), and the righteous are rewarded (58:11a). Thus, all humanity will know that Israel's just God rules (58:11b).

Note also the *inclusio* of 58:1 and 58:10–11 by catchwords:

- "right" and "righteous"
- "gods" and "God"
- "judge"
- "mankind"
- "on earth"

With this *inclusio* the lament that opened the psalm has reversed at the end in terms of confident praise for what God will do in answer to the psalmist's petition.

## PSALM 49

Psalm 49 is a wisdom psalm that grapples again with the problem of evil and the injustices of life, and it does so in a way that illustrates the importance of the refrain.[5]

5 See also "Responding to an Unethical Society: A Meditation on Psalm 49," in Bruce K. Waltke *The Dance between God and Humanity: Reading the Bible Today as the People of God* (Grand Rapids, MI: Eerdmans, 2013), 428–40.

A Psalm of the Sons of Korah.

1 Hear this, all peoples!
Give ear, all inhabitants of the world,
2 both low and high,
rich and poor together!
3 My mouth shall speak wisdom;
the meditation of my heart shall be understanding.
4 I will incline my ear to a proverb;
I will solve my riddle to the music of the lyre.

5 Why should I fear in times of trouble,
when the iniquity of those who cheat me surrounds me,
6 those who trust in their wealth
and boast of the abundance of their riches?
7 Truly no man can ransom another,
or give to God the price of his life,
8 for the ransom of their life is costly
and can never suffice,
9 that he should live on forever
and never see the pit.
10 For he sees that even the wise die;
the fool and the stupid alike must perish
and leave their wealth to others.
11 Their graves are their homes forever,
their dwelling places to all generations,
though they called lands by their own names.
12 Man in his pomp will not remain;
he is like the beasts that perish.

13 This is the path of those who have foolish confidence;
yet after them people approve of their boasts. *Selah*
14 Like sheep they are appointed for Sheol;
death shall be their shepherd,
and the upright shall rule over them in the morning.

Their form shall be consumed in Sheol, with no place to dwell.

15 But God will ransom my soul from the power of Sheol,
for he will receive me. *Selah*

16 Be not afraid when a man becomes rich,
when the glory of his house increases.

17 For when he dies he will carry nothing away;
his glory will not go down after him.

18 For though, while he lives, he counts himself blessed
—and though you get praise when you do well for yourself—

19 his soul will go to the generation of his fathers,
who will never again see light.

20 Man in his pomp yet without understanding is like the beasts that perish.

This psalm has three stanzas:

Stanza 1: 49:1–4
Stanza 2: 49:5–12
Stanza 3: 49:13–20

In a sense, the psalm has just two parts: stanza 1 (49:1–4) is the introduction, presenting the psalm and the author; and stanzas 2–3 (49:5–20) form the body of the psalm, expounding its message.

Notice further that in the body of the psalm, each stanza concludes with a nearly identical refrain, a feature that is crucial to understanding the psalm:

12 Man in his pomp will not remain;
he is like the beasts that perish.

20 Man in his pomp yet without understanding is like the beasts that perish.

With this broad overview in mind we will work our way through the psalm.

*Stanza 1 (49:1–4)*

In the introduction (49:1–4), the psalmist tells us that this is a wisdom psalm. This stanza has two strophes. In the first (49:1–2), the psalmist emphasizes both that his message is for "all peoples" (49:1–2) and that it is of the utmost urgency (49:3–4). This message is one of wisdom, vital for understanding life, and has bearing on everyone—"low and high, / rich and poor together" (49:2). This is typical of wisdom literature, that the sage wishes to teach everyone and so offers his message indiscriminately (cf. Prov. 1:20). His "proverb" (Ps. 49:4a) applies equally to all, even if each may hear it in a distinct way. It both comforts the poor and warns the rich. This proverb will be somewhat enigmatic—it is a "riddle" (49:4b). So this sage's message, important as it is, will be subtle and will require careful consideration.

The second strophe (49:3–4) tells us two important qualifications of the author. First, he is indeed a wise man. He speaks "wisdom" (v. 49:3a), and "understanding" (49:3b), in a "proverb" (or parable, 49:4a), and a "riddle" (49:4b). And, most fundamentally, he is inspired of God. His message is not one he has come up with on his own but one he has received: he "inclines [his] ear" to the proverb (49:4). As Job explains, genuine wisdom for living does not reside in man himself (Job 28:1–11) but comes only from God (28:12–28). In Proverbs the sage says of his wisdom, "For the Lord gives wisdom; / from his mouth come knowledge and understanding (Prov. 2:6). Revelation is required, and the inspired wise man has listened well. It is for this reason that Proverbs emphasizes so prominently that "the fear of the Lord is the beginning of knowledge" (Prov. 1:7) and of "wisdom" (9:10).

*Stanzas 2–3 (49:5–12, 13–20)*

The message of the psalm is given in the two remaining stanzas, and 49:5–6 sets the atmosphere:

5 Why should I fear in times of trouble,
when the iniquity of those who cheat me surrounds me,
6 those who trust in their wealth
and boast of the abundance of their riches?

The psalmist is contrasting himself with the rich. Note that the rich in Scripture, particularly in the wisdom literature, are more than just wealthy. Wealth or riches in the wisdom literature is good and an indication of the exercise of wisdom and of the blessing of God (cf. Prov. 8:12, 17–21). But references to the rich person in Proverbs have negative overtones. The problem is not that they are wealthy but that they use their advantage to abuse others (Ps. 49:5b), "trust in their wealth (49:6a), and "boast" in it (49:6b). In finding their identity and significance in their wealth and trusting in it for their security, it becomes idolatrous (cf. Prov. 18:11; 28:11). And using it to disadvantage others is wrong. Yet rich people so defined seem to have it so well. So, the question of Psalm 49:5–6 is, simply: Given the prosperity and success of the wicked, is there any advantage to the righteous? The psalmist is trying to come to grips with the fact that he lives in an unethical world, and the unethical, in fact, seem to have the advantage.

In 49:7–11 the psalmist pauses to expound somewhat on the limitations of wealth. Specifically, it is of no value when it comes time to die (49:7–10). They may build monuments to their name that will outlast them (49:11), but they die just the same. Whatever streets may be named for them, whatever buildings may bear their name, it is of no value to them. Ultimately it is all folly.

Then we come to the first refrain, the proverbial statement of 49:12:

12 Man in his pomp will not remain;
he is like the beasts that perish.

According to 49:3–4 we are looking for a proverb or riddle of some kind, which the psalmist reveals in the body of the psalm (stanzas 2–3). To catch the subtleties of this riddle requires that we pay close attention to the

Hebrew. The word "proverb" (מָשָׁל, cf. Prov. 1:1) indicates a teaching by way of some kind of analogy—a parable of sorts. So we should look to see how one thing "is like" another. In fact, this is precisely the play on words that Psalm 49 employs, as we learn in the refrain that concludes each stanza:

> 12 Man in his pomp will not remain;
> he *is like* the beasts that perish.

> 20 Man in his pomp yet without understanding
> *is like* the beasts that perish.

Notice the phrase "is like" (49:12, 20). This word in Hebrew is *nimshal* (נִמְשַׁל) and is related to the word "proverb"—*mashal* (מָשָׁל). This word clues us in to the "riddle" we must consider. The "proverb" (49:4) is one of comparison, and in this refrain, twice stated, the psalmist compares people ("is like") to beasts—specifically, beasts that perish. Stanzas 2–3 are given to help us consider its meaning.

There is a further subtlety in the Hebrew of 49:12 and 49:20: the refrain differs in just one word,[6] and this difference is just one Hebrew letter:

> 12 Man in his pomp will not remain [יָלִין, *yālîn*];[7]
> he is like the beasts that perish.

> 20 Man in his pomp yet without understanding [יָבִין, *yābîn*][8]
> is like the beasts that perish.

This one letter of difference between these two words is a kind of pun, and these refrains together will shed light on stanzas 2 and 3.

6 Each of these verses also has a different word for "not" (בַּל, 49:12; and לֹא, 49:20), but this difference is inconsequential, except perhaps to draw attention to the differing words in view: יָלִין (*yālîn*) and יָבִין (*yābîn*).

7 *yālîn*, pronounced "yaleen."

8 *yābîn*, pronounced "yabeen."

As the refrains indicate, stanzas 2 and 3 are about death. People "are like" animals: we all die. And, in fact, stanza 3 begins in terms reminiscent of stanza 1:

13 This is the path of those who have foolish confidence;
yet after them people approve of their boasts. *Selah*
14 Like sheep they are appointed for Sheol;
death shall be their shepherd,
and the upright shall rule over them in the morning.
Their form shall be consumed in Sheol, with no place to dwell.

And the refrain is similar also:

20 Man in his pomp yet without understanding
is like the beasts that perish.

The point is one that "the preacher" in Ecclesiastes makes. Everyone dies, and this makes life seem futile.

But the psalmist emphasizes something more. He talks about two different kinds of people and wrestles with the problem of justice. He positions himself with the righteous, but he is troubled by the reality that the wicked prosper. The wicked make wealth, not God, their goal and thus are idolatrous. Yet they prosper. And in the end, all die. So what is the advantage of the righteous (49:5–7)? The wicked live for what is temporary. In the end they may have buildings and land named after them to be remembered (49:11), but they still die. The righteous also die. And in this respect, we all are like animals (49:12).

But there is a difference.

The discussion of death in stanza 2 has a different tone altogether. Here the psalmist describes the death of the man who trusts in his wealth:

13 This is the path of those who have foolish confidence;
yet after them people approve of their boasts. *Selah*
14 Like sheep they are appointed for Sheol;

death shall be their shepherd,
and the upright shall rule over them in the morning.
Their form shall be consumed in Sheol, with no place to dwell.

All die, but when the fool dies, he dies forever. The simile of 49:14 is vivid—death as their shepherd, leading them to corruption and decay and never to life. They are dead and without hope. But here is the difference between the wicked fool and the righteous wise:

15 But God will ransom my soul from the power of Sheol,
for he will receive me. *Selah*

The difference between the wicked and the righteous will be clear *after death*, when the sheep are separated from the goats (Matt. 25:31–46). The psalmist sees that in a new day the righteous will "rule over" the wicked (Ps. 49:14), for God will ransom the righteous from Sheol (49:15). No man can ransom another out of death (49:7), but God will ransom the righteous from death. Here is the doctrine of life after death in the Old Testament (cf. Job 19:25–26; Isa. 25:8; 26:19; Dan. 12:1–3). The psalmist lacks the full revelation that came to light in the resurrection of Christ, but he is confident that a better day lies ahead of him, even after death. No one can ransom the life of another (49:7–9), but God will ransom the righteous and "receive" or "take" them (לָקַח, 49:15; cf. Gen. 5:24; 2 Kings 2:5, 10).

The psalmist, then, counsels accordingly:

16 Be not afraid [i.e., overawed] when a man becomes rich,
when the glory of his house increases.
17 For when he dies he will carry nothing away;
his glory will not go down after him.
18 For though, while he lives, he counts himself blessed
—and though you get praise when you do well for yourself—
19 his soul will go to the generation of his fathers,

who will never again see light.
20 Man in his pomp yet without understanding
is like the beasts that perish. (49:16–20)

Again, that one-letter difference between these two words in the refrain (49:12, 20) is a kind of pun to draw attention to his point: all die, but when the man "without understanding" dies, he dies without hope.

Notice 49:14 again:

14 Like sheep they are appointed for Sheol;
death shall be their shepherd,
and the upright shall rule over them in the morning.
Their form shall be consumed in Sheol, with no place to dwell.

It is significant that the happy rule of the righteous is said to be "in the morning." This sets a perspective for us. More customarily, our day begins in the morning and ends with the night—first the light and then the darkness. The perspective of the psalmist is the reverse. This life is night—morning comes in resurrection. This verse warns the wicked of their coming fate, but it also establishes a perspective for the righteous.

This psalm also establishes a perspective for the wicked, if they will only hear. To live for today as though today is all there is, is shortsighted.

The tale is told of a rich man who was visited by an angel and was told he could have whatever he wanted. So he asked for a copy of the newspaper to be printed one year from that day. When it was given, he went immediately to the stocks page and planned his investments accordingly. Then while thumbing through the paper his eyes fell on the obituary section where he saw his picture. He lost all interest in the stocks page. That is the lesson of this psalm—to live life from the perspective of the end (cf. Luke 12:13–21).

What this psalm does not spell out for us is how this redemption from death (49:15) will come about. But within the flow of the canon it points us ahead to the Lord Jesus Christ, who is himself the resurrection and the life (John 11:25), the one who died in place of sinners and conquered sin and death in vindication (Rom. 4:25), leading his people out of death with him (1 Cor. 15:20–23). This wisdom psalm teaches us ahead of time the value of Jesus Christ and our need to follow him. We who know Christ may live with the expectant hope that in him we have much more than the little pleasures of today.

15

# The Final Arrangement of the Psalter

*"The prayers of David"*

WE HAVE CONSIDERED various factors or approaches that are important for understanding the Psalms. Matters of historical context, liturgical use, poetry, genre, structure and form, and messianic orientation all are essential, even if some are more particularly relevant in a given psalm than others. In all this our focus has necessarily been narrow, examining the nature of a given psalm and its various components. In this chapter we will take a "big picture" look and seek to understand how the Psalter fits together as a whole.

That the arrangement of the Psalter was intentionally meaningful has been a point of interest for centuries. Some of the early church fathers puzzled over it, and Christian interpreters since have sought to understand it. Since Gerald Wilson's ground-breaking study,[1] significant advances have been made in this area of study, and we will try to explore some of those findings here.[2] The book of Psalms consists of five "books"

1 Gerald Henry Wilson, *The Editing of the Hebrew Psalter*, Society of Biblical Literature Dissertation Series (Chico, CA: Scholars Press, 1985).

2 J. Clinton McMann Jr., *The Shape and Shaping of the Psalter*, Journal for the Study of the Old Testament Supplement Series 159 (Sheffield: JSOT Press, 1993). Norman Whybray, *Reading the Psalms as a Book*, Journal for the Study of the Old Testament Supplement Series 222 (Sheffield: JSOT Press, 1996). David Mitchell, *The Message of the Psalter: An*

of psalms, and we will consider their collections, arrangements, how they all fit together, and how the entire book of Psalms fits in the biblical canon.

## Process of Compilation

The process of collecting these 150 psalms to form a single book of Psalms as we have it today has been helpfully likened to the way a large river is formed—innumerable springs and brooks flowing into small rivers and small rivers into the larger river to give it its full breadth. This illustrates well how the book of Psalms came together—it grew from individual psalms to various collections and finally to the book of psalms as we have it. The vast majority of the psalms were written during the period of the monarchy and first temple—by David, primarily, and others—but over time. Editors—probably Levites[3]—gathered them into an increasing number of collections until finally all 150 were brought together into its final form. The work of the editors at this point was similar to the work of those who put together the book of Proverbs into its final form. We do not know whether there was one or more editors of these earlier collections and of its final form, but we infer more than one because according to Proverbs 25:1 "the men [plural] of Hezekiah" collected Proverbs 25–29.

This final shaping of the Psalter was accomplished by Levites during the exilic or early postexilic period when Persia ruled over Israel. At this point psalms that call the faithful to the temple for worship (e.g., 95:1–2, 6; 100:1–2, 4) take on new meaning and were sung in faith and the hope of a time of renewal. This was a shaping consideration in the collections and ordering of the Psalter. Then the Psalter in its final form became the hymnbook used in the synagogue, which, in turn, influenced the New Testament church.

---

*Eschatological Programme in the Book of Psalms*, Journal for the Study of the Old Testament Supplement Series 252 (Sheffield: JSOT Press 1997).

3 See Susan Gillingham, "The Levitical Singers and the Compilation of the Psalter," in *Trägerkreise in den Psalmen*, ed. F.-L. Hossfeld et al., Bonner biblische Beiträge 178 (Göttingen: Bonn University Press, 2017), 35–59.

This, in brief, was the process of the collection and shaping of the Psalter. Now we will look at that process more closely.

### Stage 1: Individual Psalms for or Away from the Temple

The first stage was the individual psalms. As we have seen, many were composed for use in the temple. The superscript of Psalm 30, for example, tells us that David wrote it specifically for the temple dedication ceremony, and many other of the psalms evidence the temple setting. The hymns, the songs of grateful praise, the coronation psalms, and the laments all have the temple in view. We have observed that most are about the king, making the temple a royal chapel.

### Stage 2: "To the Choirmaster"

The psalms were not composed originally for private but for public use as indicated by the postscript, "To the choirmaster." And they were intended for successive generations. They are mostly abstract (e.g., not naming the enemy) so that they can be used for many historical incidents. David's laments and others that were given to the chief musician may have focused on the king himself, but in giving them to the choir leader for use in the temple, these psalms were given to all the people of God to sing at the temple. Yet they still pertain to the king, not to Mr. Everyman.

### Stage 3: The Collection of Psalms into Groups

The development of the book of Psalms reached a third stage as the psalms began to be collected into groups. There are indications that psalms were collected and grouped according to author:

- 2 Chronicles 29:30: "And Hezekiah the king and the officials commanded the Levites to sing praises to the LORD with the words of David and of Asaph the seer." This would seem to suggest two collections, "the words of David" (cf. Pss. 3–41, except perhaps 33) and "the words of Asaph" (50; 73–83), were in existence in the time of Hezekiah.

- Psalm 72:20 concludes book 2, noting, "The prayers of David, the son of Jesse, are ended." This seems to suggest an earlier collection of the psalms of David.
- Psalms 51–65, 68–70 (the bulk of book 2), 108–110, and 138–145 are Davidic.[4]
- Psalms 42–43[5]–49, 84–85, 87–88 are "of the sons of Korah," also likely reflecting an earlier collection.

There are additional types of groups. Here is a sampling of them:

- The so-called enthronement psalms, framed by Psalms 95 and 100 (see p. 399).
- The "miktam" psalms are grouped together in 56–60.
- The "maskil" psalms are grouped together in 42–46, 52–55, 88–89.
- Morning and evening prayers alternate in 3–6.
- The "Elohistic" Psalter (42–83)[6]
- After the Prologue Book (Pss. 1–2), some identify four sections in book 1: 3–14, 15–24, 25–34, 35–41. Psalms 3–14 seems to consist of two groupings of six psalms (3–8; 9–14), the first

4 This constitutes 75 percent of books 1 and 2. Cf. Pss. 108–110 and 138–145.

5 Pss. 42 and 43 were originally one psalm.

6 The so-called Elohistic Psalter (Pss. 42–83) merits special mention, at least for the difficulties it presents. Outside of these psalms in the Psalter, the psalmists normally refer to God by his name, *Yahweh* ("Lord"). This is his covenant name, the name by which he is known as the God of Israel. But here, *Elohim* ("God") overwhelmingly dominates, the title that highlights his transcendence and infinite power—the one who is God over all. In Psalms 1–41 and 84–150, we find "Lord" 584 times and "God" only 94 times. In this "Elohistic Psalter" (42–83), however, "Lord" appears just 45 times and "God" 210 times. Moreover, the use of the alternate name/title occurs primarily in parallel lines. Outside the Elohistic Psalter the divine name ("Lord") consistently appears in line A, and "God" in line B. Within this Elohistic Psalter, the pattern is reversed. In "synoptic" psalms—psalms with identical or similar verses—those within the Elohistic Psalter use the title "God," while those outside use "Lord." Psalms 14 and 53 provide a clear example: compare 14:2 with 53:2; 14:4 with 53:4; and 14:7 with 53:6. Note that this usage is unrelated to the Wellhausen theory discussed earlier, in which Yahweh and Elohim were assumed to reflect differing source documents, but the reason and significance of this pattern here remain unclear. That this collection of psalms is divided between books 2 and 3 may indicate their earlier collection.

ending with a reflection on mankind's greatest rulers (8:6), the second ending with a reflection on his waywardness (14:3). Psalms 7–9 are linked by celebrating the "name" of the Lord (7:17; 8:1; 9:1–2). Psalms 15–24, 25–34, and 35–41 are thought to form a chiasm.[7] Psalms 15–24 are framed by entrance liturgies and pivot on a torah psalm (see p. 431). Peter Ho notes, among other things, that the superscriptions of books 2–3 form a chiastic Korahite-Asaphite-Davidic-Asaphite-Korahite arrangement.[8]

- David Howard Jr. demonstrated the unified structure of Psalms 93–100 in book 4.[9]
- Book 4 ends with the prayer "gather us from among the nations" (106:47), and book 5 begins with praise: "the Lord gathered us from among the nations" (107:3, authors' translation).
- The Songs of Ascents (120–134), a unified collection that depicts pilgrimage to the temple, pivots on Psalm 127, "by" or "for Solomon" (see p. 105).
- Psalms beginning or ending "praise the Lord" seem to be a corpus of psalms at the end of book 4 (103–106) and of book 5 (146–150).

The editors of the Psalter seem to have arranged the various psalms according to various insights. And it is worth mentioning that the collecting of hymns was not unique to the book of Psalms. The practice in the ancient Near East actually predates David and the Psalter by centuries. In the Psalter, however, under inspiration, the editors grouped psalms with theological-thematic insights that are illuminating for exposition.

7 Peter C. W. Ho, "The Macrostructural Design and Logic of the Psalter: An Unfurling of the Davidic Covenant," in *Reading the Psalms Theologically: Studies in Scripture and Biblical Theology*, ed. David Howard Jr. and Andrew Schmutzer (Bellingham, WA: Lexham, forthcoming 2023).

8 Ho, "The Macrostructural Design."

9 David M. Howard Jr., *The Structure of Psalms 93–100*, Biblical and Judaic Studies 5 (Winona Lake, IN: Eisenbrauns, 1997).

**Stage 4: The Collection of the Psalms into Five Books**

The fourth stage of the development of the book of Psalms is in the formation of the five "books" of the Psalter:

Book 1: Psalms 1–41
Book 2: Psalms 42–72
Book 3: Psalms 73–89
Book 4: Psalms 90–106
Book 5: Psalms 107–150

There are various lines of evidence for the five-book arrangement of the Psalms. First, it seems that each book is intentionally concluded with a psalm that has a doxology:

13 Blessed be the LORD, the God of Israel,
  from everlasting to everlasting!
Amen and Amen. (41:13)

18 Blessed be the LORD, the God of Israel,
  who alone does wondrous things.
19 Blessed be his glorious name forever;
  may the whole earth be filled with his glory!
Amen and Amen! (72:18–19)

52 Blessed be the LORD forever!
Amen and Amen. (89:52)

48 Blessed be the LORD, the God of Israel,
  from everlasting to everlasting!
And let all the people say, "Amen!"
  Praise the LORD! (106:48)

These verses of praise are not boilerplate additions to form the books. They differ and so are original to their respective psalms and therefore seem to have been placed for their concluding doxologies at the close of each book. Book 5 does not have this same kind of doxology—its five concluding psalms (146–150) are themselves praise psalms, seeming to indicate the editorial intention to conclude the entire collection with a crescendo of praise. The ending of each book with a doxology parallels ancient Mesopotamian collections of hymns.[10]

Gordon Wenham notes also that the beginning and end of the five books are marked by blessings (see 1:1; 2:12; 41:1; 72:17; 89:15; 106:3; 144:15), with a gathering of prayers at the end of each book also (see 38–41; 69–71; 86; 88; 102; 140–143).[11]

There are indications that the royal orientation of the Psalter was a shaping consideration of the editors also. For example, the Davidic psalms were not all grouped together, as we might otherwise expect, but spread throughout the Psalter (often in groups). And it has been widely recognized since Wilson that the seams of books 1–3 recall the Davidic covenant (2:7–9; 41:11–12; 72:17; 89:19–37);[12] the close of book 3 laments the seeming failure of the Davidic promise (89); but then book 4—particularly with its reminder in Psalm 90 that the Lord God has always been and remains Israel's refuge, and with the enthronement psalms 93–99—seems intentionally to provide hope and provoke a trusting response.

Rabbinic tradition attests to this five-book division of the Psalter also:

> As Moses gave the five books of laws to Israel, so David gave five Books of Psalms to Israel, the Book of Psalms entitled *Blessed is the man* (1:1), the Book entitled *For the Leader: maschil* (Ps 42:1), the Book, *A Psalm of Asaph* (Ps 73:1), the Book, *A Prayer of Moses* (Ps 90:1), and the Book, *Let the redeemed of the* Lord *say* (Ps 107:2).[13]

10 Wilson, *Editing*, 186.

11 Gordon Wenham, The Psalter Reclaimed: Praying and Praising with the Psalms (Wheaton, IL: Crossway, 2013), 59.

12 It is noteworthy in this connection that book 5 concludes with a final Davidic psalm (145). Psalms 146–150 form the concluding doxology for the entire Psalter.

13 William G. Braude, *The Midrash on the Psalms* (New Haven, CT: Yale University Press, 1954), 40–50.

This tradition is ancient, with explicit testimony appearing in the poorly preserved liturgical fragment of the Qumran scrolls (1Q30), dating to the turn of the Christian era. The Qumran scrolls show much the same form as books 1–3, although books 4–5 vary considerably. That these five books of the Psalms correspond to the five books of Moses has long been widely recognized, as the rabbinic quote above indicates, although no consensus has been reached regarding the nature of this correspondence. C. Hassell Bullock is probably right to observe that it is "designed to emphasize the central place of the law (Torah) in Israel's faith."[14] This correspondence and emphasis may be reflected further in the Psalter's "Torah psalms" (1, 19, 119) and sustained emphasis on Torah (e.g., 40:8; 78:1, 5, 10; 89:30). So also Psalms 1–2 introduce the Psalter with a call to give attention to God's law and acknowledge the righteous rule of God. This would also seem to indicate a corresponding relationship between Moses and David themselves: Moses gave Israel her cultus, and David transformed it into opera.

The change of author at each of the "seams" between the five books evidences this arrangement further. After the introduction (1–2) the next psalm is by David, and virtually the entire first book is Davidic, as we have already noted. The second book begins with a psalm by the sons of Korah (42), the third by Asaph (73), and the fourth by Moses (90). The fifth book begins with an anonymous psalm (107), but the pattern remains nonetheless.

Finally, the initial and concluding psalms of each of five books can be interpreted as *inclusios*.[15] Psalm 1 has long been recognized as the gateway to the Psalter. So also Psalm 150—and perhaps Psalms 146–150—serve as its fitting conclusion, a final doxology. This too seems to reflect an editorial intention in the arranging of the Psalter.

### Stage 5: The Final Canon of the Masoretic Text

The fifth and final stage of development is simply its final shape and its recognized place in the canon itself. We now have a book within a

14 C. Hassell Bullock, *Encountering the Book of Psalms: A Literary and Theological Introduction*, Encountering Biblical Studies (Grand Rapids, MI: Baker Academic, 2001), 58.

15 Wilson, *Editing*, 187–90.

larger book (canon) whose words were those of the king and his people to God. But now it is God's word to us, which we, in turn, sing back to him. And as we sing and preach these psalms, we sing and proclaim God's king, the Lord Jesus Christ.

## The Significance of the Shaping of the Psalter[16]

Delitzsch remarks that the collection of psalms in the Psalter "bears the impress of one ordering mind."[17] He offers two observations by way of preliminary evidence: Psalms 1 and 2 function as the introduction to the entire Psalter, and the closing psalms (146–150) function as a concluding doxology.[18] It seems that editors were responsible for the final collection and arrangement, but Psalms scholarship has not yet achieved a consensus about the unifying principle.[19] Some are skeptical that there is one,[20] but most follow a wisdom/Torah perspective and/or

16 See also Bruce K. Waltke, "Christ in the Psalms," in *The Hope Fulfilled: Essays in Honor of O. Palmer Robertson*, ed. Robert L. Penny (Phillipsburg, NJ: P&R, 2008), 36–37.

17 C F. Keil and F. Delitzsch, *Commentary on the Old Testament*, vol. 5 (Peabody, MA: Hendrickson, 1996), 11.

18 See Tremper Longman III, "From Weeping to Rejoicing: Psalm 150 as the Conclusion of the Psalter," in Schmutzer and Howard, *The Psalms*, 209–30.

19 For a survey, see J. Clinton McCann Jr., ed., *The Shape and Shaping of the Psalter*, Journal for the Study of the Old Testament Supplement Series 159 (Sheffield: JSOT, 1993); Jerome F. Creach, *Yahweh as Refuge and the Editing of the Hebrew Psalter*, Journal for the Study of the Old Testament Supplement Series 217 (Sheffield: Sheffield Academic, 1996); Marvin E. Tate, "Rethinking the Nature of the Psalter," in *Psalms 1–50*, ed. Peter C. Craigie, Word Bible Commentary 19, rev. ed. (Nashville: Thomas Nelson, 2004), 438–72; Nancy L. deClaisse-Walford, ed., *The Shape and Shaping of the Book of Psalms: The Current State of Scholarship*, Ancient Israel and Its Literature 20 (Atlanta: Society of Biblical Literature, 2014); William P. Brown, ed., *The Oxford Handbook of the Psalms* (Oxford: Oxford University Press, 2014); Adam D. Hensley, *Covenant Relationships and the Editing of the Hebrew Psalter*, The Library of Hebrew Bible/Old Testament Studies 666 (New York: T&T Clark, 2018), 6–34; Gert T. M. Prinsloo, "Reading the Masoretic Psalter as a Book: Editorial Trends and Redactional Trajectories," *Currents in Biblical Research* 19, no. 2 (2021): 145–77.

20 See Roland E. Murphy, "Reflections on Canonical Interpretation of the Psalms," in McCann, ed., *Shape and Shaping of the Psalter*, 21–28; John Goldingay, *Psalms*, vol. 1, *Psalms 1–41*, Baker Commentary on the Old Testament Wisdom and Psalms (Grand Rapids, MI: Baker Academic, 2006), 36; Goldingay, *Psalms*, vol. 3, *Psalms 90–150*, Baker Commentary on the Old Testament Wisdom and Psalms (Grand Rapids, MI: Baker Academic, 2008): 11–12; Whybray, *Reading the Psalms as a Book*; Tremper Longman III, "The

a David/Messianic perspective.[21] According to G. Wilson, there were two stages in the development of the book of Psalms: first, Psalm 1–89 ("a royal covenant frame") and then 90–150 (a "wisdom frame," the final frame) in which the psalms were democratized to everyone. David Howard Jr. and Michael Snearly, in a magisterial study to which we are indebted, trace these two major trajectories.[22] Here we follow the Davidic covenant/Messianic perspective.[23]

---

Messiah: Explorations in the Law and the Writings," in *The Messiah in the Old and New Testaments*, ed. Stanley E. Porter (Grand Rapids, MI: Eerdmans, 2007), 23–24; Longman, *Psalms: An Introduction and Commentary*, Tyndale Old Testament Commentaries 15–16 (Downers Grove, IL: IVP Academic, 2014), 33–36; Erhard S. Gerstenberger, "Der Psalter als Buch und als Sammlung," in *Neue Wege der Psalmenforschung: Für Walter Beyerlin*, ed. K. Seybold and E. Zenger, Herders Biblische Studien 1 (Freiburg: Herder, 1994), 3–13.

21 John C. Crutchfield, "The Redactional Agenda of the Book of Psalms," *Hebrew Union College Annual* 74 (2003); 21–47.

22 David M. Howard Jr. and Michael K. Snearly, "Reading the Psalter as a Unified Book: Recent Trends," in Howard and Schmutzer, *Reading the Psalms Theologically*.

23 See also David M. Howard Jr., "The Case for Kingship in the Old Testament Narrative Books and the Psalms," *Trinity Journal* 9 (1988): 19–35; Howard, "Wisdom and Royalist/Zion Traditions in the Psalter," *Structure of Psalms 93–100*, 200–207; Howard, "Divine and Human Kingship as Organizing Motifs in the Psalter," in *The Psalms: Language for All Seasons of the Soul*, ed. Andrew J. Schmutzer and David M. Howard Jr. (Chicago: Moody Publishers, 2013), 197–207; Jerry Eugene Shepherd, "The Book of Psalms as the Book of Christ: The Application of the Christo-Canonical Method to the Book of Psalms" (PhD diss., Westminster Theological Seminary, 1995); David Mitchell, *The Message of the Psalter: An Eschatological Programme in the Book of Psalms*, Journal for the Study of the Old Testament Supplement Series 252 (Sheffield: Sheffield Academic, 1997), 15–65; Richard P. Belcher Jr., *The Messiah and the Psalms: Preaching Christ from All the Psalms* (Fearn, Ross-shire, Scotland: Christian Focus, 2006); Robert L. Cole, *Psalms 1–2: A Gateway to the Psalter*, Hebrew Bible Monographs 37 (Sheffield: Sheffield Phoenix, 2013); Cole, *The Shape and Message of Book III (Psalms 73–89)*, Journal for the Study of the Old Testament Supplement Series 307 (Sheffield: Sheffield Academic, 2000); Jamie A. Grant, *The King as Exemplar: The Function of Deuteronomy's Kingship Law in the Shaping of the Book of Psalms*, Society of Biblical Literature, Academia Biblica 17 (Atlanta: Society of Biblical Literature, 2004); Michael G. McKelvey, Moses, *David and the High Kingship of Yahweh: A Canonical Study of Book IV of the Psalter*, Gorgias Biblical Studies 55 (Piscataway, NJ: Gorgias, 2014); David Alexander Gundersen, "Davidic Hope in Book IV of the Psalter" (PhD diss., Southern Baptist Theological Seminary, 2015); O. Palmer Robertson, *The Flow of the Psalms: Discovering Their Structure and Theology* (Phillipsburg, NJ: P&R, 2015); Carissa M. Quinn Richards, "The King and the Kingdom: The Message of Psalms 15–24" (PhD diss., Golden Gate Baptist Theological Seminary, 2015); Jerome L. Skinner, "The Historical Superscriptions of Davidic Psalms: An Exegetical, Intertextual, and Methodological Analysis" (PhD diss., Andrews University Seventh-Day Adventist Theological

Most significantly, the five books of the Psalter reflect the history of Israel from David to the Exile. Books 1 and 2 are principally by David and represent the triumph of the king. Here we often find David is in crisis, but his psalms always express praise. Book 3 anticipates Israel's exile. This "dark book" of the Psalter laments the failure of the kings, the temple, the nation, and climaxes in the tragic lament that God appears to have forsaken his covenant with David (Ps. 89). Book 4 presents Israel in exile. She has no king, but there is the reassurance that the eternal God is her king. This book ends with a prayer that God would bring Israel back from her exile (106:47–48). Finally, in book 5, restored Israel offers praise to God for her restoration. All is not lost, and the Davidic hope remains. We will track this out a bit further.

### *Introduction: Psalms 1 and 2*

We have noted the verbal links between Psalms 1 and 2, indicating their complementary nature in the minds of the editors. We have also drawn attention throughout this work to the royal orientation of the Psalter; this orientation is reflected in these introductory psalms. Some comparison and contrasts of Psalms 1 and 2 are worth noting again:

- Psalm 1 is a wisdom psalm, extolling the life shaped by Torah; Psalm 2 is a royal psalm, extolling the triumph of the king.
- Psalm 1 is concerned with justice; in Psalm 2, the king dispenses justice.

---

Seminary, 2016); Michael K. Snearly, *The Return of the King: Messianic Expectation in Book V of the Psalter*, The Library of Hebrew Bible/Old Testament Studies 624 (New York: T&T Clark, 2016); Hensley, *Covenant Relationships and the Editing of the Hebrew Psalter*; Peter C. W. Ho, *The Design of the Psalter: A Macrostructural Analysis* (Eugene, OR: Pickwick, 2019); Ho, "The Shape of Davidic Psalms as Messianic," *Journal of Evangelical Theological Society* 62, no. 3 (September 2019): 515–31; Ian J. Vaillancourt, *The Multifaceted Saviour of Psalms 110 and 118: A Canonical Exegesis*, Hebrew Bible Monographs 86 (Sheffield: Sheffield Phoenix, 2019); Andrew Carl Witt, *A Voice without End: The Role of David in Psalms 3–14*, Journal of Theological Interpretation Supplements 20 (University Park, PA: Eisenbrauns, 2021); David Postell, "Does the Book of Psalms Present a Divine Messiah?," in Howard and Schmutzer, *Reading the Psalms Theologically*.

- The wicked in Psalm 1 become in Psalm 2 a cabal of nations.
- The righteous of Psalm 1 becomes the king in Psalm 2.
- Psalm 1 profiles the cause and consequence of the righteous individual against that of the wicked; Psalm 2 profiles the cause and consequence of the rebels against God and his king. The way of the wicked is war against the Lord's rule (Psalm 1) and against his ruler (Psalm 2). Psalm 1 theologically declares that the Lord will destroy the way of the wicked; Psalm 2 politically declares that the Lord's king will destroy their way.

The complementary nature of Psalms 1 and 2 (wisdom and kingship, law and prophecy) seems to have been recognized by the editors. Wilson argues that these twin considerations serve to provide the framework of the Psalter. The inner framework is the Davidic covenant (2; 72; 89; 144); the outer framework is wisdom (1; 73; 90; 107; 145).[24] More broadly, these two psalms establish themes that recur throughout the Psalter. Hearing these "voices" of wisdom and of the king is how the Psalms are to be read and understood. Moreover, Psalm 1 contrasts the righteous who are blessed of God and the wicked who are destroyed in judgment. And in Psalm 1 the difference between these two peoples turns on their relation to God's Torah; in Psalm 2 the difference turns on their relation to God's king. In Psalm 1, a wisdom psalm, the wise are those whose life is shaped by divine instruction; in Psalm 2 "the wise" are those who submit to the king (2:10–12). Placing Psalms 1 and 2 as the introduction to the Psalter, the editors prepare those who meditate on its petitions and praises to interpret them both with respect to the king and to themselves as individuals within his kingdom.

Additionally, Psalm 2 serves to introduce book 1 of the Psalms, the so-called Davidic Psalter (1–41). Psalms 3–41, then, are some-

24 Gerald H. Wilson, "Shaping the Psalter: A Consideration of Editorial Linkage in the Book of Psalms," in McCann, ed., *Shape and Shaping of the Psalter*, 72–82.

times referred to as David's prayer diary. Psalms 1 and 2 lack the attribution of authorship "Of David"; however, both the Vulgate and Acts 4:25 name David as the author of Psalm 2, and in light of the larger Davidic orientation of the Psalter, it is quite possible to understand Psalm 1 as the king's own reflection on the requirements of his righteous rule.

*Books 1 and 2 (Pss. 1–72)*

This royal orientation that marks the beginning of book 1 marks the end of book 2 also (Ps. 72). But there is an escalation: Psalm 2 is a coronation liturgy that announces the ultimate reign of God's King; Psalm 72 describes that reign in terms of its universality in both time and space. The royal orientation continues throughout book 1 with its (almost) exclusively Davidic psalms. There are notes of progression also: Psalm 2 elucidates the promise of the Davidic covenant that the king will inherit the earth, and here the king himself is instructed to pray for it. Psalm 3 begins the king's prayers for that inheritance. The laments that dominate book 1 (3–41) do not sound of despair, for neither the rebellion of the king's own son (3) nor the treacherous nobility (4) can succeed in overthrowing the Lord's anointed.[25]

The king plays a crucial role at the seams of books 1–3. Psalms 3 and 41 reflect the king's assurance of the Lord's protection from his enemies, and Psalm 72 makes petition for the king's universal and endless success. Psalm 72 raises the confident hope that the king's enemies will lick the dust in defeat (Ps. 72:9; cf. Gen. 3:14), and 72:20 reminds us that books 1 and 2 are to be understood as having this royal orientation. Psalm 41 is not a royal psalm, as such, but attending to the needs of the poor (41:1) is the responsibility of king (cf. 72:1–7, 12–14), so Psalm 41 has obvious resonance with the royal psalms.

25 Cf. Stephen G. Dempster, *Dominion and Dynasty: A Theology of the Hebrew Bible*, New Studies in Biblical Theology 15 (Downers Grove, IL: IVP Academic, 2003), 196.

*Book 3 (Pss. 73–89)*

Book 3 is known as the "dark book" of the Psalter, containing the highest concentration of communal laments (see 74; 79; 80; 83; 85; cf. 77; 82; 85; 89:7). Its background is the divided kingdom and, apart from Psalm 86 by David, its composers are temple musicians. In its middle psalms the fall of the northern kingdom is in view, and by its end the southern kingdom has also fallen. The book portrays Israel as collectively questioning her place in God's plan and even questioning, in exile, God's covenant faithfulness. Following on the prayer for the king's reign of justice at the end of book 2 (Ps. 72), book 3 begins with a lament concerning injustice (73) and ends with a lament concerning the seeming failure of the Davidic covenant itself (89).

Asaph's complaint of injustice in Psalm 73 at the beginning of book 3 may indicate the editors' intent to see this personal struggle as representative of a larger, national complaint. Some scholars go so far as to suggest that this book represents the collapse of the Davidic covenant (cf. 89) and prepares the way for God himself to be the true King, as per the "enthronement psalms" that begin book 4. But the continuation of royal psalms in the latter portions of the Psalter suggests that the Davidic covenant has not been lost. The inclusion of one Davidic psalm in this collection, Psalm 86, may be intended to hint at the same. And as we saw in chapter 12, the so-called enthronement psalms have a messianic prospect. Moreover, there is in book 3 an alternating of lament and hope that fosters continued faith in the restoration of a restored Davidic dynasty:

- Psalm 74 laments the destruction of the temple; Psalm 75 asserts God's sovereign rule.
- Psalm 76 asserts God's political rule; Psalm 77 laments that he no longer performs miracles.
- Psalm 78 laments Israel's historic waywardness; Psalm 79 pleads with hope for restoration.
- Psalm 80 pleads for restoration also; Psalm 81 laments Israel's failure to keep her covenant obligations.

- Psalm 82 condemns unrighteous "gods"; Psalm 83 anticipates God's destruction of pagan nations.

We might note further that Psalms 88–89 alternate somewhat also. Psalm 88 is the darkest of the Psalms, and Psalm 89 laments the loss of the Davidic promise (89:38–46). Yet Psalm 89 begins with praise for God's continued steadfast love and his assured promise to David (89:1–4), continues with a rehearsing of the Davidic promise itself (89:19–37), and concludes with more praise and a plea for the restoration of the king (89:46–52). The royal orientation of the Psalter continues even here, and its accompanying hope is not lost.

*Book 4 (Pss. 90–106)*

Most acknowledge that books 1–3 represent the first major step toward a final shaping of the Psalter. And in these three books the hopeful prospect of Psalm 2 has dimmed considerably, as Psalm 89 illustrates. But with book 4 yet another perspective is achieved, opening with "A Prayer of Moses, the man of God" and Israel's great intercessor. Outside of book 4, Moses receives only one mention (77:20), but now the only psalm written by Israel's great deliverer introduces book 4, and he receives mention a total of seven times (90:1; 99:6; 103:7; 105:26; 106:16, 23, 32). This Mosaic perspective seems to signal hope of new beginning. "Just as the previous exile ended, so will this one."[26] If Moses finally brought faithless Israel out of her wilderness exile, the promised Davidic Son will yet deliver Israel again. Moses's psalm itself (90) looks back further to Israel's eternal King, the Lord their God, confessing that he has been Israel's refuge ("dwelling place," 90:1) for all the past ages—long before the monarchy was instituted—and taking trustful encouragement that he will be Israel's refuge now that the monarchy is gone.

Book 4 concludes with two history psalms (105; 106), highlighting God's sovereign rule and faithfulness. It is in this context that we have the

26 Dempster, *Dominion and Dynasty*, 199.

so-called enthronement psalms that we discussed in chapter 12, psalms that anticipate the Lord's future kingship. The Lord God reigns, and he will judge the earth (94:2; 96:10, 13; 98:9). Though the house of David has fallen, God has not failed. Israel's existence does not depend on David: both Israel and David depend upon the eternal God who has always been Israel's refuge and who remains king over all the earth. Yet even here we find included two Davidic psalms (101; 103), both of which are forward looking. The royal orientation of the Psalter continues, and with it a future hope.

Psalm 106 concludes book 4, and it too ends with a doxology and a plea for God's salvation:

47 Save us, O LORD our God,
and gather us from among the nations,
that we may give thanks to your holy name
and glory in your praise.
48 Blessed be the LORD, the God of Israel,
from everlasting to everlasting!
And let all the people say, "Amen!"
Praise the Lord!

*Book 5 (Pss. 107–150)*

Book 5 begins with praise for the Lord's "steadfast love" (107:1), a leading theme of the psalm (cf. 107:3, 15, 21, 31, 43). This reminder of God's unfailing covenant love ties this first psalm of book 5 to the last psalm of book 4 (cf. 106:45) and to Psalms 108–109 that follow (cf. 108:5; 109:12, 16, 21, 26), thus establishing the context for the messianic Psalm 110. Psalm 107 also begins with praise that corresponds to the plea of 106:47–48 "Save us, O LORD our God, / and gather us from among the nations, / that we may give thanks to your holy name / and glory in your praise" (106:47) is answered by a giving of thanks for this very (yet to be accomplished) ingathering:

1 Oh give thanks to the LORD, for he is good,
for his steadfast love endures forever!

2 Let the redeemed of the LORD say so,
whom he has redeemed from trouble
3 and gathered in from the lands,
from the east and from the west,
from the north and from the south. (107:1–3)

The anguish of exile has been overcome, and to remind us of it book 5 includes two groups of Davidic psalms (108–110; 138–145) that express strong messianic hope (e.g., 110). Wilson remarks,

> In Ps 108–110, David emerges as the "wise man" (107:43) who "gives heed" to the cautions of 107:39–42 and relies wholly on the steadfast love of Yahweh. His willingness to sing the praise of Yahweh "among the nations" (108:3) becomes a paradigm of action to be followed, whether by those yet in exile or among those vulnerable returnees surrounded by their foes. David knows that only reliance on Yahweh is effective . . . (108:12). . . . In like fashion to the first group of Davidic psalms, David serves as an example in Ps 138–144 following the plaintive cry of the exiles expressed in the words of Ps 137 which immediately precedes."[27]

The royal orientation of the Psalter continues throughout and to the end, and in this way the Psalms point us to the Lord Jesus Christ who fulfills and exceeds their every hope. Thus the famous cluster of "Hallelujah" psalms (146–150) brings the Psalter to an appropriate conclusion of exuberant praise. Nancy deClaisse-Walford comments,

> But this "unfettered" praise is only possible at the end of the story of the Psalter. The postexilic community must understand where it has come from (the "Who are we?") and where it is going (the "What are we to do?") before it can participate in the praise of YHWH the king. Thus the story of the Psalter become a story of survival in

27 Wilson, *Editing*, 221.

the changed and changing world with which the postexilic Israelite community is confronted.[28]

## Concluding Remarks

The various psalms fit together, and their arrangement suggests insights that serve well to guide us in their interpretation. Connections between neighboring psalms and neighboring groups of psalms, the royal orientation of the psalms, the wisdom of following Torah and of submitting to the Lord's anointed all are factors that illuminate our reading and open the door wide to a reading of the Psalter in light of the larger biblical canon and story in which Christ is the center. Nevertheless, we should take note that they were collected with reference to these different historical settings, not for them. We should not impose this use as the author's original, intended meaning.

Gerald Wilson remarks that our common reference to the Psalter as a "hymnbook," though justified, can leave a wrong impression because the analogy breaks down.[29] The Psalter is not merely a collection of songs randomly assembled, or even topically assembled. It is a book carefully arranged to proclaim a message. The editors' work in arranging the Psalter has long been recognized by the faithful, in both Jewish and Christian communities, as directed by divine inspiration.[30] Given the exilic or early postexilic timeframe, the arrangement of the Psalter reflects the expectant faith of the editors.

It is worth pointing out, as many have, that the lament psalms, though appearing throughout the Psalter, are heavily loaded toward the front, and praise psalms at the end. In this way the book of Psalms moves from lament to praise. What is the message that leads the editors to praise? Palmer Robertson argues at length that we can discern

28 Nancy L. deClaisse-Walford, *Reading from the Beginning: The Shaping of the Hebrew Psalter* (Macon, GA: Mercer University Press, 1997), 103.

29 Wilson, "Shaping the Psalter," 72.

30 Cf. Bruce Waltke, "Textual Criticism of the Old Testament and Its Relation to Exegesis and Theology: Part I—The Reliability of the Old Testament Text," in *New International Dictionary of Old Testament Theology and Exegesis*, 5 vols., ed. Willem A. VanGemeren (Grand Rapids, MI: Zondervan, 1997), 1:51–67.

the message of the Psalter as we read its flow redemptive-historically, pointing us to the consummation of God's kingdom under the rule of the future David:[31]

Book 1: the confrontation of the Davidic-messianic king vs. his enemies
Book 2: the communication of hope amid struggle
Book 3: the devastation of Israel's hope
Book 4: the maturation of hopeful perspective
Book 5: the consummation of the kingdom of God

Mitchell summarizes the Psalter's story in this way:

> The Psalms tell of the Messiah. Because he loves Torah and meditates in it day and night (Ps. 1), the Holy One promises to overthrow every opposition to his rule and to establish his throne on Zion (Ps. 2). He comes as the divine Bridegroom-Messiah to rescue Daughter Zion and raise her to honour (Ps. 45). He issues a command to gather Israel (Ps. 50) and sets up a kingdom like Solomon's which will extend from sea to sea, and from the river to the ends of the earth (Ps. 72). However, his kingdom will be attacked by hostile nations (Pss. 73–83), he will [be] surrounded by enemies and fall into the underworld (Pss. 86, 88). His people bereft of his presence, lament his death, and arraign the Holy One for the failure of his promise (Ps. 89). Israel will be exiled and perish in the wilderness, as they were in Moses' day, as Zechariah foretold (Ps. 90, Zech. 13:7). But the king will be delivered from every evil (Ps. 91) to reemerge from the underworld like a triumphant wild ox (Ps. 92). Thereafter YHVH is praised [in his] rule among the nations (Pss. 93–99). Eventually, Israel regather to the land (Ps. 107), when the Messiah will announce his victory (Ps. 108), anathematize his enemy (Ps. 109), and descend from the right

31 Robertson, *The Flow of the Psalms*; see also Robertson, *The Shaping of the Psalter* (Phillipsburg, NJ: P&R, 2019).

> hand of Power to wage victorious battle (Ps. 110). The deliverance is celebrated in the Hallel Psalms (Pss. 113–117) which recall the joyful triumph of the Exodus. Then he ascends to Jerusalem amidst crowds and joyful celebrations (Ps. 118), while the scattered tribes of Israel, who have strayed like lost sheep, are gathered in (Ps. 119:176). Then the Songs of Ascents represent Israel and the nations ascending to keep the Feast of Sukkot in Jerusalem when, in fulfillment of the promise of Psalm 2, the Messiah is installed on his throne (Ps. 132). Psalms 135 to 137 are a *codetta* to the Ascents collection. Psalms 140 to 144 feature a final attack upon the messianic throne. Evildoers threaten the new David with force, stratagems, and pursuits, but the threat is now easily dismissed. Psalm 145 is a hymn of praise for the victory, and Psalms 146–150 are the grand *coda* of praise to the entire collection.[32]

James Hamilton argues that the Psalter's message can be discerned largely by following the superscripts which highlight David's suffering (book 1), his success (book 2a), his sin and the consequences of it (book 2b), and his slow recovery (book 2c). Book 3 takes us from Solomon to the exile and the seeming collapse of the Davidic covenant, for which book 4 provides the answer, exemplified in the intercessor Moses. And book 5 sounds a note of praise that exults in the certainty that God's promise of salvation will yet be fulfilled.[33] He finds this message in the chiastic structure of the Psalter:

> Book 1: The suffering of the historical David
>     Book 2: The reign of the historical David
>         Book 3: The end of the historical Davidic house
>     Book 4: Moses intercedes for the Davidic covenant
> Book 5: The conquest of the future Davidic King.[34]

32 David C. Mitchell, *The Songs of Ascents: Psalms 120 to 134 in the Worship of Jerusalem's Temples* (Newton Mears, Scotland: Campbell, 2015), 215–16.

33 James M. Hamilton Jr., *Psalms*, vol. 1, Evangelical Biblical Theological Commentary (Bellingham, WA: Lexham Academic, 2021), 8–10.

34 Hamilton, *Psalms*, 64.

The message of the Psalter centers on David, God's covenant promise to him, and the future "David" in whom it will be realized. "The collage of the Psalter is not merely about David's own life but God's purposes in the world and how and where David fits in that wider project."[35] The final editors' placing of Psalm 2 at the head of book 1, and their placing it along with Psalm 1 as introductory to the whole, seems to make their Davidic perspective explicit.

It is likely that David himself is responsible for the shaping of the Psalter in its beginnings—book 1, for example. David understood Israel's past and covenant promises. He understood clearly his own significance in redemptive history and exulted in it. He established psalm singing in Israel's liturgy (1 Chron. 16), he determined the various genres of the Psalms (16:4), and he provided most of the superscripts—all to direct the people of God to understand and rejoice in the message of the Psalms. Later psalms and editors followed, of course. Perhaps Solomon and Hezekiah took part (see 2 Chron. 29:25–30; Prov. 25:1). And there is a long tradition that Ezra and Nehemiah had a finalizing role (see Neh. 12:27–30, 45–47). In any case, the final editors seem to have followed the trajectory set by David himself.[36] Their task was an exegetical one, grounded in God's covenant promise and intended to direct attention to the later David, the Lord Jesus Christ (Luke 24:44–45), the world's only hope.

Brevard Childs offers a fitting ending to our book: "In sum, although the royal psalms arose originally in a peculiar historical setting of ancient Israel . . . they were treasured in the Psalter . . . as a witness to the messianic hope which looked for the consummation of God's kingship through his Anointed One."[37]

35 Hamilton, *Psalms*, 51.

36 Hamilton, *Psalms*, 51–52.

37 Brevard S. Childs, *Introduction to the Old Testament as Scripture* (Philadelphia: Fortress, 1979), 517.

Appendix 1

# Superscripts, Postscripts, or Both

*Bruce K. Waltke*

## I. Introduction[1]

Literary criticism with its emphasis on the text's final form has focused attention on the edited version(s) of the Psalter.[2] From this perspective G. H. Wilson has studied that book's superscripts and postscripts; this has led to rewarding insights into the meaning of the Psalter's final editor(s).[3]

In an essay on the superscripts from a historical perspective, H. M. I. Gevaryahu contended that both in the prophetic books and in the Psalter superscripts were originally written as colophons (that is, as postscripts) to the text and in a later period were transposed to the beginning.[4] In his view the transference of the postscripts to superscripts did not come about through textual corruption but through an editorial decision.

1 This appendix was originally published in *Journal of Biblical Literature* 110, no. 4 (1991), 583–96. Reproduced here with permission along with minor emendation. Translations of Scripture are the author's.

2 L. C. Allen, "David as Exemplar of Spirituality: The Redactional Function of Psalm 19" *Biblica* 67 (1986): 544–46.

3 Gerald Henry Wilson, *The Editing of the Hebrew Psalter*, Society of Biblical Literature Dissertation Series 76 (Chico, CA: Scholars Press, 1985).

4 H. M. I. Gevaryahu, "Biblical Colophons," in *Congress Volume: Edinburgh, 1974*, Vetus Testamentum Supplements 28 (Leiden: Brill, 1975), 42–59.

Gevaryahu based his conviction that "the Superscriptions and Titles in the Bible were originally at the end of the text, but in time they were transferred to the beginning of the text" both on the comparative study of the scriptural headings with Akkadian and ancient Greek literature and on indications within the Bible itself.[5] His first impulse, he tells us, came from W. G. Lambert's review of the corpus of Babylonian-Assyrian colophons by H. Hunger.[6] Lambert described the colophons in those texts as containing the information that the modern Western world puts on the title page. Gevaryahu also noted the Greek literature: "the same method [of colophons] was in use in Greek literature where the name of the author and nature of his book were recorded at the end of the scrolls."[7] C. Wendel thought that the Greek scribes were influenced by the Akkadian colophons through the Arameans.[8] Gevaryahu's internal evidences from the Bible itself were (1) the transference of "Hallelujah" in Psalms 104, 105, and 115 from a postscript, as attested in the MT, to a superscript of the subsequent psalm in the LXX; (2) the preservation of the Hebrew word למנצח (in English translation, "to the choirmaster") at the end of Habakkuk 3; and (3) the preservation of biographical data of the kind found in the colophon at the end of the LXX version of Job, as well as in the original end of Ben Sira, 1:27–29.[9]

Wilson, however, objected to the use of comparative evidence from Mesopotamian sources because the content of their colophons differs from the biblical superscripts. "With very few exceptions," he wrote, "the cuneiform colophons are concerned with items which the biblical s/ss [superscripts] ignore."[10] The "frozen" Akkadian colophons concern themselves primarily with assuring that a text has been accurately copied

5 Gevaryahu, "Biblical Colophons," 51, 52.

6 W. G. Lambert, "Review of H. Hunger, *Babylonische und assyrische Kolophone:* AOAT 2 (Neukirchen-Vluyn: Neukirchener Verlag, 1968)," *Die Welt des Orients* 5 (1970): 290, 291.

7 Gevaryahu, "Biblical Colophons," 51.

8 C. Wendel, *Die Griechische-Römische Buchbeschreibung verglichen mit der des Vorderen Orients* (Halle: Niemeyer, 1949).

9 Gevaryahu, "Biblical Colophons," 52.

10 Wilson, *Editing*, 147.

by the scribe: bibliographical statements, scribal procedure, statements concerning persons involved in the transmission, and other scribal statements. H. Hunger says, "Eine Kolophon ist eine vom Text getrennte Notiz des Schreibers am ende einer Tafel literarischen Inhalts, die Aussagen über Personen, die mit dieser Tafel zu tun haben, enthält."[11] By contrast, biblical superscripts concern themselves mostly with matters of composition: authorship, genre classification, historical circumstance, cultic performance, and function or purpose of the psalm. After analyzing the colophons in question Wilson draws this conclusion:

> This study of the colophons in *BAK* [*Babylonische und assyrische Kolophone*] leads me to question the appropriateness of Gevaryahu's easy equation of biblical s/ss [superscripts] and cuneiform colophons. The colophons seem always to be concerned with the *process* of transmission rather than the actual composition itself.[12]

Wilson, however, addressed neither the Greek colophons nor the internal biblical evidence. One might suppose that if the Greek colophons ultimately took their shape from Mesopotamian sources, they too must be ruled out as significant data. Without attempting to answer Gevaryahu's evidence from the disagreement between "hallelujah" in postscripts of the MT versus their location as superscripts in the LXX, Wilson explained the difference between these textual traditions not as due to a wholesale shift from postscripts to superscripts but to selective editorial activity within the LXX. According to him, the LXX rectified the "nakedness" of Psalm 114 in the MT and Targum by shifting the הללו יה ("praise the LORD") postscript of Psalm 113 to the beginning of Psalm 114, by combining Psalms 114 and 115, and by shifting the postscripts of Psalms 115, 116, 117 to the beginnings of Psalms 116, 117, and 118.[13] In an appendix entitled "The Relationship

11 H. Hunger, *Babylonische und assyrische Kolophone*, Alter Orient und Altes Testament 2 (Neukirchen-Vluyn: Neukirchener Verlag, 1968), 1

12 Wilson, *Editing*, 151.

13 Wilson, *Editing*, 180.

of Habakkuk 3:1+19 to S/S Convention in MT 150," Wilson failed to deal with Gevaryahu's evidence of the postscript in 3:19; his concern is rather to show that, as in the six instances in the Psalter, למנצח ("to the choir master") is followed immediately by בנגינות ("with stringed instruments"). He noted lamely that the postscript in Habakkuk 3:19 "appears somewhat 'truncated' since there is no mention of genre or author, these having been supplied in 3:1."[14]

By failing to confront in this isolated psalm the phenomenon,

> Superscript: תפלה לחבקוק הנביא על שׁגינות ("a prayer of Habakkuk the prophet, according to Shigionoth," Hab. 3:1)
> Prayer: (+ סלה [*selah*] in 3:3, 9, 13) (3:2–19a)
> Postscript: למנצח בנגינותי ("to the choirmaster: with stringed instruments," 3:19b),

Wilson missed the opportunity to shore up the text of the Psalter's superscripts and postscripts, the foundations of his work, and presumably to gain even more rewarding insights into the editing of that book. Habakkuk's composition may be legitimately compared with the psalms in the Psalter for, as W. Rudolph commented, "Das Kapitel [3:1–19] hat eine eigene Überschrift und hat in dieser wie in der Mitte (Sela V.3.9.13) und am Ende liturgische Beischriften, wie sie uns nur in den Psalmen begegnen, die also anzeigen, dass Hab 3 einmal im Gottesdienst Verwendung gefunden hat."[15]

On the basis of Habakkuk 3, J. W. Thirtle proposed in 1904 a largely ignored hypothesis that in the superscripts of the Psalter למנצח + ("to the choirmaster") prepositional phrases were originally not superscripts of the following psalms but postscripts of the preceding ones. Concerning the isolated prayer in Habakkuk 3 he wrote: "Being alone . . . it cannot

14 Wilson, *Editing*, 237.

15 We need not decide here the historical connection of this hymn to the book of Habakkuk. See W. Rudolph, *Micha-Nahum-Habakuk-Zephanja*, Biblischer Kommentar, Altes Testament 13/3 (Gütersloh: Mohn, 1975), 239–41. Wilson also noted the similarity between Habakkuk's superscript and postscript and the received superscripts in the Psalter (*Editing*, 236, 237).

have taken anything from a preceding composition, nor can any concluding words have been misconstrued as belonging to some succeeding composition. It proclaims itself as normal, as a model, a standard psalm."[16] He sought to validate his thesis from the Psalter itself by appealing to the superscript of Psalm 88 and by the correspondence between the superscript of Psalm 56 and the content of Psalm 55:7, 8.[17] New data further corroborate his hypothesis, and no proof has been justly lodged against it.

This essay aims to validate the thesis that in a received "title" to a psalm למנצח ("to the choirmaster") + optional prepositional phrase[18] was originally a postscript of the preceding psalm and the rest of its material introduced the genuine superscript of the following psalm. Moreover, the putative postscript probably includes technical terms for the psalm's performance and the superscription contains matters about the psalm's composition. "Compositional" matters include *lamed auctoris* + author,[19]

16 J. W. Thirtle, *The Titles of the Psalms: Their Nature and Meaning Explained* (New York: Henry Frowde, 1904), 11, 12.

17 Thirtle, *Titles of the Psalms*, 13–15.

18 למנצח ("to the choirmaster") is followed by a preposition with technical notice twenty-four times: *b* ("with") (*ngnwt* ["stringed instruments"]) *ʿl* ("according to") (*hšmynyt* ["The Shimeninith"]/*hgytyt* [The Gittith]/ *mwt lbn* ["Muth-Labben"]/ *ywnt ʾlm rḥqym* ["The Dove of Far-off Terebinths"] / *mḥlt* [mahalath] (*lʿnwt*)/*ʾylt hšḥr* ["The Doe of the Dawn"]// *ššnym* ["Lilies"]/ *šwšn* (*ʿdwt*) ["Shushan (Eduth)"]/ *ngynt* ["stringed instruments"]/*ydytwn* ["Jeduthun"]), *ʾl* ["for"] (*hnḥylwt* ["the flutes"]), *ʾal tšḥt* ["Do Not Destroy"], (ʾ)*l* ["to"] (*ydy(w)twn* [Jeduthun] / *ʿbd yhwh* ["the servant of the Lord"]). These are all in books 1–3. It is followed immediately by author or genre classification, fourteen times each. למנצח ("to the choirmaster") does not occur in book 4, and in book 5 always by itself, bound with ("of David") לדוד.

19 *Gesenius' Hebrew Grammar*, ed. Emil Kautzsch, trans. Arther E. Cowley, 2nd ed (Oxford: Clarendon, 1910), 129c. See Bruce K. Waltke and M. O'Connor, *Introduction to Biblical Hebrew Syntax* (Winona Lake, IN: Eisenbrauns, 1990), 11.2.10d. The almost certain use of the disputed ל in Isa. 38:9 and Hab. 3:1, the customary use of ל in other Semitic languages, especially Arabic, and the clarification of לדוד by a relative clause in 2 Sam. 22:1 (= Ps. 18:1) establishes this point of grammar. J. F. A. Sawyer says, "In the Chronicler's day . . . it can scarcely be doubted that the meaning of *ldwd* was 'by David.' . . . Any attempt to distinguish *l*[ᵉ] *dawid* from the others, or to say that none of them refers to authorship at all, is unsupported by the early evidence and flies in the face of all that we know of early rabbinic methods." J. F. A. Sawyer, "An Analysis of the Context and Meaning of the Psalm-Headings," *Transactions of the Glasgow University Oriental Society* 22 (1970): 26). משה (Moses), איתן האזרחי (Ethan the Ezrhite), הימן האזרחי, (Heman the Ezrahite), אסף (Asaph) ,שלמה ( Solomon), קרח בני (the sons of Korh),דוד (David). M. J. Buss analyzes the

genre classification,[20] historical circumstance behind the composition,[21] and the cultic function for which it was intended.[22] When it is not followed by a prepositional phrase but by "compositional" matters, only למנצח ("to the choirmaster") is to be repositioned as a postscript of the preceding psalm. None of the fifty-five instances of למנצח ("to the choirmaster") + elective prepositional phrases in the received text occurs unbound from compositional matters.

We do not attempt to define the terms pertaining to the psalm's cultic performance and its composition more precisely than their context analysis by J. F. A. Sawyer.[23] He defines למנצח (*lemĕnaṣṣeaḥ*. "to the choirmaster") as "to be recited by the official in charge,"[24] and its prepositional phrase as referring "to elements in or areas of cultic procedure under the direction of the *mĕnaṣṣeaḥ*."[25] Thus *lmnṣḥ lhšmynyt* (Ps. 12:1) means: "to be recited by the official who is in charge of the ritual of *haššĕmînît*." Our lack of a clear, nonhypothetical understanding of the cult presents almost insurmountable difficulties in regaining precisely the significance of what are obvious cultic terms. Nevertheless, by discretely analyzing material into data belonging to superscripts,

---

psalms into three main groups, following the lines of their attribution. See M. J. Muss, "The Psalms of Asaph and Korah," *Journal of Biblical Literature* 82 (1963): 382–92.

20 שיר המעלות ("song of the ascents"), תפלה ("prayer"), תהלה ("praise"), מזמר ("psalm", שירה/שיר ("song"); technical terms are משׂכיל (*maskil*), מכתם (*miktam*), שׁגיון (shiggaion). These nine terms normally occur without the article.

21 See Pss. 3, 7, 18, 30, 34, 51, 52, 54, 56, 57, 59, 60, 63, 142.

22 These more or less nontechnical liturgical terms with ל /l/of purpose are: השבת ליום ("a song for the Sabbath," Psalm 92), לתודה ("For grateful praise," Psalm 100), להזכיר ("for to bring to remembrance," Psalms 38, 70), ללמד ("for instruction," Psalm 60); without ל /l/ are: הבית חנכת ("at the dedication of the temple," Psalm 30), לעני כי־יעטף ולפני יהוה ישפך שׂיחו: ("of the afflicted, when he is faint and pours out his complaint before God," Psalm 102). לענות (Leannoth, Psalm 88) is best not treated as one of these terms because, as C. A. Briggs explains: "*ʿl mḥlt* ["according to Mahalath"] in the title of 53 . . . and *ʿl mḥlt lʿnwt* ["according to Mahalath Leannoth"] in the title of 88 . . . are doubtless the same" (C. A. Briggs and E. G. Briggs, *The Book of Psalms* [ICC; Edinburgh: Clark, 1906] Ixxv). *ʿdwt* (*Eduth*) in Psalm 60 title is also part of the prepositional formula (see Briggs, *Psalms*, Ixxv). *ʿl ʿlmwt* ("according to Alamoth," Psalm 46) is a technical term.

23 Sawyer, "Analysis," 26–38.

24 Sawyer, "Analysis," 36, 37.

25 Sawyer, "Analysis," 36.

which probably pertain to composition, and to postscripts, which probably pertain to performance, the context analysis of these terms will be advanced.

## II. Validation of Thesis

*Regarding Genuine Superscripts*

If it is granted that למנצח ("to the choirmaster") + optional prepositional phrases are "frozen" postscripts originally appended to the preceding psalm, the analysis of the compositional data in the putative superscripts matches well the comparative author and/or genre classification both with the hymns of the ancient Near East and within the Bible itself. Unquestionably Wilson is correct in rejecting Gevaryahu's thesis that these statements about the psalm's composition can be compared with Akkadian colophons. He also established in connection with what he styled "catalogues of hymnic incipits" that genre classification is found in the incipits of Akkadian hymns, a comparison that indirectly supports our thesis. Although the thesis that notices about authorship are also found initially with reference to a psalm cannot be corroborated from comparative Akkadian literature, since they are virtually anonymous,[26] it can be validated from Egyptian hymns and from within the Bible itself.

*Egyptian hymns.* The superscripts to Egyptian hymns mention genre classification and/or authorship. As an example of genre classification consider this superscript to *A Hymn to Amon-Re*: "Adoration of Amon-Re. . . ."[27] The superscripts to *A Universalist Hymn to the Sun* and the famous *Hymn to Aton* mention both genre and authorship. The former's reads: "Praising Amon . . . by the Overseer of the Works of Amon, Seth, and the Overseer of the

26 W. G. Lambert, "Ancestors, Authors, and Canonicity," *Journal of Cuneiform Studies* 11 (1957): 1. In a later article, however, Lambert published a separate catalogue of texts and authors. See "A Catalogue of Texts and Authors," *Journal of Cuneiform Studies* 16 (1962): 59–77).

27 James B. Pritchard, ed., *Ancient Near Eastern Texts Relating to the Old Testament*, 3rd ed. (Princeton: Princeton University Press, 1969), 365 (hereafter cited as *ANET*).

Works of Amon, Horus. They say: Hail to thee . . . ,"[28] and the latter's: "Praise of Re Har-akhti . . . Who is in the Aton-disc . . . (and praise of) the King of Upper and Lower Egypt . . . Akh-en-Aton . . . (and praise of) the Chief Wife of the King . . . Nefert-iti . . . (by) the Fan-Bearer on the Right Hand of the King. . . . He says. . . ."[29] The truncated superscript of *Hymns to the Gods as a Single God*, retains only the author: ". . . the Outline Draftsman of Amon, Mer-Sekhmet. He says: I sing to thee. . . ."[30]

*Biblical hymns*. Within the Bible itself outside of the Psalter one observes similar phenomena. Biblical narrators introduce hymns in a historical context with comment about their genre and author: "Then Moses and the Israelites sang this song to the LORD: 'I will sing . . .'" (Ex. 15:1); "On that day Deborah and Barak son of Abinoam sang this song . . ." (Judg. 5:1); "Then Hannah prayed and said, 'My heart . . .' (1 Sam. 2:1); "From inside the fish Jonah prayed to the Lord his God. He said: 'In my distress . . ." (Jonah 2:1–2); "David sang to the LORD the words of this song when the LORD delivered him from the hand of all his enemies. . . . He said . . ." (2 Sam 22:1–2 [= Ps 18:1]). As we shall see, the synoptic material in the last example shows the transference of introductory material in narrative form to a superscript in hymnic form. Somewhat less precise analogies in narrative can be found in Numbers 21:14–18, 27–30; and 2 Samuel 1:17–27.

A striking comparison with Habakkuk 3, and so with the Psalter, is found in Isaiah 38:9, 10. Concerning the superscript to this "Hezekiah psalm," H. Wildberger said: "In v. 9 the Psalm is provided with its own introduction [better, superscript], which is not at all added smoothly to v. 8."[31] This genuine superscript contains information about genre, author, and historical circumstance. Note the pattern:

28 *ANET*, 367.

29 *ANET*, 370.

30 *ANET*, 371.

31 H. Wildberger, *Jesaja, das Buch, der Prophet und seine Botschaft*, Biblischer Kommentar, Altes Testament 10/3 (NeukirchenVluyn: Neukirchener Verlag, 1982), 1454.

Superscript: A writing (genre) of Hezekiah king of Judah (author)
After his illness and recovery (historical circumstance):
Hymn: I said, In the prime of my life. . . .
Liturgical conclusion: We will sing with stringed instruments. . . .

Instructively, the last line of Hezekiah's psalm contains the liturgical instruction for the temple congregation: וּנְגִנוֹתַי נְנַגֵּן כָּל־יְמֵי חַיֵּינוּ עַל־בֵּית יְהוָה ("we will play my music on stringed instruments all the days of our lives, at the house of the Lord," Isa. 38:20b). The switch from singular to plural in the last line, together with its independent superscription and the radical break between 38:20 and 38:21, shows that this hymn, like Habakkuk 3, at one time had a life of its own in the temple cultus. The resemblance of ונגנותי ננגן ("we will play my music") in the concluding line of the Psalter's optional prepositional phrase, (')בנגינות ("with stringed instruments"), after למנצח ("to the choirmaster"; cf. Ps. 4:1a [Heb]) obliquely supports the notion that the phrase belongs in the putative postscripts, not in the received superscripts.

One is struck by the addition of historical information in these introductions and in this superscript in hymns outside the Psalter, matching the fourteen superscriptions in the book of Psalms with historical notices.

*Regarding Original Postscripts*

In addition to Habakkuk 3, Thirtle's model psalm, our thesis that למנצח ("to the choirmaster") + optional prepositional phrases originally served as postscripts to the psalms preceding them can be validated in several ways: first, by an analysis of the received superscripts of Psalms 3/4, Psalm 18:1/2 Samuel 22:1, Psalms 41/42, 87/88, 108/109, and 138/139; second, by comparing terms of the received superscript of Psalm 56 with the terms of Ps 55:7, 8; third, by noting the differences in titles or incipits to Psalms 104–106, 111–117 in the MT versus the LXX; and finally by calling attention to the postscript of Psalm 145 in 11QPs[a]. The consistency of the data corroborates our observations and analyses. In conclusion it will be argued that the text was ripe for the textual confusion envisioned here and that ample time was available for the corruption and harmonizing editorial activity to have taken place before the extant witnesses to the text.

*Psalms 3/4*. The two introductory psalms of the Psalter—Psalm 1, an introduction to the whole Psalter,[32] and Psalm 2,[33] probably an introduction to books 1 and 2 with a postscript at 72:20—are untitled.[34] The first titled psalm, Psalm 3, exactly matches the proposed model:

Superscript: מזמור ("psalm," genre) לדוד ("by David," author) בְּנוֹ . . . ("when he fled . . . his son," historical notice) (3:1)
Prayer: (+ סלה [*selah*] in 3:3, 5, 9) (3:2–9)
Postscript: למנצח בנגינות ("to the choirmaster with stringed instruments," 4:1a)

This example validates the thesis but does not prove it because למנצח ("to the choirmaster"), though often attested in book 1, is not always present. It could be argued that Psalm 3, like some other psalms, lacked an initial למנצח ("to the choirmaster" + optional prepositional phrase[s]).

*Psalm 18:1/2 Samuel 22:1*. The addition of למנצח לְעֶבֶד יְהוָה ("to the choirmaster by the servant of the LORD"[35]) to the superscript of Psalm 18, lacking in 2 Samuel 22:1, is better explained as a postscript of Psalm 17 than of Psalm 18 that was later transposed to the heading, Gevaryahu's disproved thesis.[36] Once the putative postscript is removed from Psalm 18, the titles of these synoptic texts match much more closely, and their slight differences, וידבר דוד ("and David spoke") versus

32 Brevard S. Childs, *Introduction to the Old Testament As Scripture* (Philadelphia: Fortress, 1979), 513.
33 Wilson, *Editing*, 204.
34 Wilson, *Editing*, 208.
35 The term לְעֶבֶד־יְהוָה in the received titles of Psalms 18 and 36 is not to be taken as syntactically connected with following לדוד, "by the servant of the Lord, David" (see Sawyer, "Analysis," 35); it is better taken as connected with the preceding למנצח.
36 Gevaryahu, "Biblical Colophons," 53.

לְדָוִד אֲשֶׁר דִּבֶּר ("by David which he spoke"), can be readily explained as due to the genre effect of transposing narrative to a hymnic title.

*Psalms 41/42.* Wilson observed that a radical change in authorship coincided with the doxologies dividing the Psalter's books 1–3 (better, 1–4), which have superscripts at their seams.[37] For example, whereas book 1, Psalms 3–41, consists of psalms "by David," book 2, Psalms 42–72, begins abruptly with a collection "by the sons of Qorah." Wilson commented,

> This correspondence of authorship-change with the book divisions and the doxologies which serve to mark them is hardly fortuitous. It must represent conscious editorial activity either to introduce such author-changes in order to indicate disjuncture between such divisions or to make use of such existing points of disjuncture in the division of the Psalter.[38]

He showed surprise, however, that this radical disjunction was blurred between books 1 and 2 by the initial למנצח (*lmnṣḥ*, "to the choirmaster") introducing the received titles of Psalms 39–47. He wrote:

> Here, at the . . . transition from Book I to Book II . . . one would expect to find no resolution of the disjuncture as in the previous cases. Indeed, the break is clearly indicated by author-change and *genre*-change. However, the consecutive repetition of the initial phrase *lmnṣḥ* in eight consecutive superscripts (Ps. xxxix–xlvii) does have a slight softening effect.[39]

Moreover, elsewhere the editor binds material in the superscripts by genre classifications, not by למנצח ("to the choirmaster"). If, however, למנצח ("to the choirmaster") in Psalm 42 is the postscript of Psalm 41,

37 Wilson, *Editing*, 167.

38 Gerald H. Wilson, "Evidence of Editorial Divisions in the Hebrew Psalter," *Vetus Testamentum* 34 (1984): 339.

39 Wilson, "Evidence of Editorial Divisions in the Hebrew Psalter," 348.

then the same radical change in superscripts profiles the separation between book 1 and book 2 as in the disjunctions between the other books in question. The resulting consecutive postscripts may be interpreted as linking the first two books, which probably constitute the original Davidic collection, Psalms 3–72, bound together by the postscript "this concludes the prayers of David son of Jesse" (Ps. 72:20).[40] In any case the linkage of postscripts leaves a different impression from the linkage by initial word. By repositioning למנצח ("to the choirmaster") as a postscript, Psalms 38–41 emerge as a unified collection with the superscript מִזְמוֹר לְדָוִד ("a psalm by David") / לְדָוִד מִזְמוֹר ("by David, a psalm"). In sum, comparative editing techniques within the Psalter validate our thesis.

It may be objected, however, that the למנצח ("to the choirmaster") as a postscript of Psalm 41 is unlikely because it now "unexpectedly" follows another colophon, the doxology of Psalm 41:

ברוך . . . ואמן ("Blessed be . . . Amen," 41:14)
למנצח ("to the choirmaster," 42:1a)

That objection might be valid were the doxology a later addition to the Psalm. Wilson, however, argued quite convincingly that the doxologies concluding the four books of the Psalter were not appended to the psalms by the Psalter's redactor(s), but were a "frozen" part of the psalm from an earlier stage. He based himself on, among

40 This postscript functions like the postscript in Job 31:40c: תַּמּוּ דִּבְרֵי אִיּוֹב ("the words of Job are ended"). That comparative colophon binds together earlier poems by both Job and his three friends (3–31) and separates them from both those of Elihu (chaps. 32–37) and of Yahweh (chaps. 38–41). Likewise, the colophon in Psalm 72:20 separates the earlier collections of books 1 and 2, which accent the triumphs of the kingdom, from book 3, which accents its defeat. P. P. Zerafa rightly defended the postscript in Job 31:40c against commentators who discarded it merely as an editorial note that does not fit into that book's structure: "The author who inserted it did not ignore the three friends, nor did he intend to distinguish Job's speech from that of the other characters of the drama. . . . He only wanted to make sure that Job received what he felt was his due." Peter Paul Zerafa, *The Wisdom of God in the Book of Job*, Studia Universitatis S. Thomae in Urbe 8 (Rome: Herder, 1978), 18, 19.

other arguments, the variations between them—an unlikely situation, he argued, were they added by a later editor—and on the "frozen" nature of the colophons in Sumerian temple hymns.[41] The latter argument is stronger than the former for an editor may have had several doxologies from which to choose. In any case, if the doxology with Psalm 41 is frozen from an earlier period, there can be no objection to the postscript, למנצח ("to the choirmaster"), after it. The case for a postscript after a doxology is put beyond reasonable doubt by the comparative situation at the close of book 2 and book 4. The former's, the colophon to Psalm 72, reads:

> וברוך ואמן . . . (72:19)
> כָּלּוּ תְפִלּוֹת דָּוִד בֶּן־יִשָׁי בן־ישי ("the prayers of David, the son of Jesse, are ended," 72:20);

the latter's, the colophon to Psalm 106, displays,

> ברוך . . . אמן ("Blessed be . . . Amen,"106:48a)
> הללו־יה ("Praise the Lord,"106:48b).

In the light of these other postscripts after doxologies there can be no objection to the restored postscript to Psalm 41. In fact, book 3 now emerges as the only one without a postscript after the doxology.

*Psalms 87/88.* Our thesis finds almost conclusive demonstration by untangling the impossible received superscript of Psalm 88, an old textual *crux interpretum*. That title to this "black sheep of the Psalter" in all texts and versions uniquely contains two or three genre classifications, שיר מזמור ("a song, a psalm) versus משׂכיל (*Maskil*), two authors, לבני קרח ("by sons of Korah) versus להימן האזרחי ("by Heman the Ezrahite"), and exhibits the only instance of the fifty-five occurrences למנצח ("to the choirmaster") that is not placed initially but in the middle of the superscript. If, however, למנצח ("to the choirmaster") + prepositional

41 Wilson, *Editing*, 23, 183–85.

phrase be conjectured as a postscript, these impossible contradictions are resolved. Psalm 87 now has the shape:

Superscript: לבני־קרח מזמור שׁיר ("a psalm of the sons of Korah," 87:1a)
Song: + סלה ([*selah*] 87:3, 6) (87:1b–7)
Postscript: שׁיר מזמור לבני קרח ("A song. A psalm of the sons of Korah ," 88:1aa)
למנצח על־מחלת לענות ("To the choirmaster: according to Mahalath Leannoth," 88:1ab);

and Psalm 88, the pattern:

Superscript: משׂכיל להימן האזרחי ("A Maskil of Heman the Ezrahite," 88:1b)
Prayer: + סלה ([*selah*] 88:8, 11) (88:2–19)

In this reconstruction Psalm 88 is unambiguously "a *maskil* by Heman the Ezrahite," and Psalm 87, "a song, a psalm, by the sons of Qorah." This bisectioning of the title finds further validation in the content of Psalm 88, which is now divorced from the sons of Qorah. M. J. Buss observed, "Ps 88 differs from the rest of the Korah psalms in content."[42] To be sure, we are still left with the anomaly of data pertaining to genre classification and author in both the superscript and the putative postscript of Psalm 87, resembling Ezekiel 19:1, 14. The difference pertains to the order of their presentation: in its superscript, genre classification and author; in its postscript, author and genre classification. Moreover, the genre classification is also reversed from מזמור שׁיר ("A psalm. A song") to שׁיר מזמור ("A song. A psalm"). Two explanations suggest themselves for these reversals. Perhaps this part of its reconstructed postscript preserves an alternative presentation of the genre and author glossed into the text from

42 Buss, "Psalms of Asaph and Korah," 382.

the margin, like later *qĕrê*ʾ readings, even as Babylonian scribes noted liturgical data in their margins.[43] The glossing of marginal materials into biblical texts is too well known to require documentation. Or, less likely, the putative postscript שיר מזמור לבני קרח ("A Song. A psalm of the Sons of Korah") concludes a Qorahite collection (Pss. 83–87) including psalms by Asaph (Ps. 83) and by David (Ps. 86), resembling Psalm 72:20 and Job 31:40.

*Psalms 108/109, 138/139*. In book 5, the psalm introducing the first Davidic collection, Psalms 108–110, and the initial psalm of the final Davidic collection, Psalms 138–145, before the Psalter's final *hallel*, Psalms 146–150, exhibit the expected pattern. Note the patterns of Psalm 108:

Superscript: שיר מזמור לדוד ("A song. A psalm of David," 108:1)
Song: (108:2–14)
Postscript: למנצח ("To the choirmaster," 109:1aa),

And of Psalm 138:

Superscript: לדוד ("Of David," 138:1aa)
Hymn: (139:1ab–8)
Postscript: למנצח ("To the choirmaster," 139:1aa).

Moreover, the psalms preceding them lack the postscript. In short, the data in question of these final Davidic collections in book 5 exactly match the initial Davidic Psalm, Psalm 3, in book 1. In book 2 the psalms introducing the Davidic collections, Psalms 51–65, 68–70, also contain the למנצח ("to the choirmaster") postscript. In contrast to the other examples, however, the preceding psalms also exhibit it. In sum, though these data alone do not prove the thesis, they help validate it, especially since there are no exceptions.

43 W. G. Lambert, "The Converse Tablet: A Litany with Musical Instructions," in *Near Eastern Studies in Honor of William Foxwell Albright*, ed. Hans Goedicke (Baltimore: Johns Hopkins University Press, 1971), 337–39.

*Psalms 56:1/55:7, 8.* The content of the prepositional phrase after עַל־יוֹנַת אֵלֶם רְחֹקִים לַמְנַצֵּחַ עַל־יונת ("to the choirmaster: according to the Dove on Far-off Terebinths") in the extant superscript of Psalm 56 closely matches David's wish in Ps 55:7 [Eng. 55:6]: מִי־יִתֶּן־לִּי אֵבֶר כַּיּוֹנָה אָעוּפָה, "Oh that I had the wings of a dove . . . I would remove myself. . . ." The two texts share the common roots יונה, "dove" and רחק, "afar off." Many commentators heretofore have been at a loss to explain the connection. Our thesis helps explain the linkage and correlatively is corroborated by it.

*Psalms 104–106.* The transposition of the postscript or conclusion, חללו יה ("praise the LORD"), of Psalms 104–106 in the MT to the superscripts or incipits of the following Psalms 105–107 in the LXX (= LXX 104–106), whatever the reason, empirically supports our thesis that transpositions from the end of one psalm to the beginning of another took place in the course of the text's transmission. The same phenomenon can be observed in connection with Psalms 113 and 114. Psalm 113 in the MT has חללו יה ("praise the LORD") both as a superscript or an incipit and a postscript or a conclusion, leaving Psalm 114 naked, but the LXX has חללו יה ("praise the LORD") as a superscript or an incipit of both Psalms 113 (= LXX 112) and 114 (= LXX 113) without a postscript of Psalm 113. Compare and contrast also the MT's postscripts in Psalms 115–117 with the LXX's superscripts in Psalms 116–118 (= LXX 114–117).

*Psalm 145.* Psalm 145 in 11QPs[a] preserves the postscript: לזכרון . . . זיאת . . . , "this is for a memorial." Here we find further empirical evidence for a liturgical postscript in one ancient canonical tradition of the Psalter.[44] Concerning its interpretation Wilson comments: "The fragmentary nature of the context prevents a final interpretation of the text but it certainly indicates the functional concern of the editor(s)."[45] Perhaps significantly it occurs just before the final *hallel* in the Psalter of the MT. . . .

44 The writer opts with Wilson for differing canons of the Psalter at Qumran. See Wilson, *Editing*, 63–92.

45 Wilson, *Editing*, 137.

*Psalms 148/149*. R. A. F. Mackenzie contended that what is now Psalm 148:14b,c originally introduced Psalm 149.[46] If he is correct, his reconstructed texts of these two psalms further corroborates the confusion of the endings and beginnings of successive psalms at a stage earlier than the earliest extant texts and versions, even though it is in the reverse direction from the textual corruption defended in this essay.

*The consistency of the data*. In contrast to the switching back and forth between author and genre classification, למנצח ("to the choirmaster) always occurs as the first element in the superscripts of the present Psalter, with the exception of the textually corrupt superscript of Psalm 88.[47] This consistency supports the thesis. In the title of Psalm 46 the technical term על עלמות ("according to Alamoth"), so similar—though importantly not identical—to the technical prepositional phrases after למנצח ("to the choirmaster") is syntactically placed after לבני קרח ("of the sons of Korah") and so might be urged as an objection to our thesis. One could argue that since the technical prepositional phrases, normally placed after למנצח ("to the choirmaster"), can be placed just as well after the notice of author, which belongs to the genuine superscript, these phrases are, after all, part of the superscripts. But the same phenomenon in Habakkuk 3, תפלה לחבקוק הנביא על שגינות ("a prayer of Habakkuk the prophet, according to Shigionoth), negates the objection. In fact, the superscript of Psalm 46 is the only one that comports in this respect to our paradigm model![48]

*Regarding causes of conflation*. Both unintentional scribal error and deliberate editorial activity were involved in the transposition from the postscript of one psalm to the initial position in the next. The prose

46 R. A. F. Mackenzie, "Ps. 148:14b, c: Conclusion or Title?" *Biblica* 51 (1970): 221–24.

47 See "Appendix C: Distribution of Technical Terms in the Psalms Headings," in Wilson, *Editing*, 238–44.

48 Possibly על עלמות ("according to Alamoth") sets up an *inclusio* with a postscript of Psalm 48. Both F. Buhl (in *Biblia Hebraica*) and H. Bardtke (in *Biblia Hebraica Stuttgartensia*), respectively, want to emend על מות ("until death," NAB) at the end of Psalm 48 to על־עלמות ("according to Alamoth") as in 46:1. While that is possible, they err in proposing to attach their emended text as a superscript to Psalm 49 rather than as a postscript to Psalm 48, for that conjecture creates the difficulty of explaining the dislocation of על־עלמות ("according to Alamoth) before למנצח ("to the choirmaster").

of these editorial notices butting up against one another versus the poetry of the psalms themselves contributed to their textual conflation. Whether the psalms were transmitted in texts employing stichometry or without noting versification, as is mostly the case in the Qumran scrolls, it was almost inevitable that the two prose appendages would be linked, even though the psalms were separated by various spacing techniques at least as early as in the Qumran texts.[49] The opportunity for scribal error was further exacerbated by the scribes' ignorance of למנצח + ("to the choirmaster") prepositional phrase. The LXX translator rendered למנצח ("to the choirmaster") as εἰς τὸ τέλος ("for the end"), and Jerome, *in finem* ("unto the end").

This ignorance also establishes the necessary chronological gap between the time of composition and our extant evidence of the text for the conflation of the postscript with the superscript to have taken place.[50] Gevaryahu claims that the meaning of the musical terms was forgotten during the Babylonian exile.[51] With the exception of Psalm 67, למנצח ("for the choirmaster") + prepositional phrases occurs only with psalms whose superscriptions present authors, namely, קרח בני ("sons of Korah"), דוד ("David"), and לדוד ("of David"). It never occurs in book 4, in any postexilic psalms, and only with לדוד ("of David") in book 5. The combined evidence shows that it is appended only to preexilic psalms. Since the versions and the earliest attested texts and versions of the psalms date to about mid-second century BCE, the conflation could have taken place over a course of several centuries, ample time for the consistent repositioning of the putative postscript to the received superscript. In sum, the similarity in prose form of the putative postscripts and superscripts, combined with later scribal ignorance of the former's meanings and functions, created a situation ripe for textual confusion during the extended, unattested period of their textual transmission.

49 Malachi Martin, *The Scribal Character of the Dead Sea Scrolls*, 2 vols. (Louvain: Institut Orientaliste Université de Louvain, 1958).

50 See Mitchell Dahood, *Psalms I, 1–50: Introduction, Translation, and Notes*, Anchor Bible (Garden City, NY: Doubleday, 1966), xxx.

51 Gevaryahu, "Biblical Colophons," 52n36.

Another contributing factor to the transposition could have been the attitude of the scribes toward these prose appendages. They felt no compunction at breaking up earlier collections of psalms and redistributing their contents according to different considerations.[52] It is well known that the editors within the Greek tradition unquestionably added material to the superscripts.[53] The alternative canons of the Psalter at Qumran show that collectors rearranged the psalms.[54] In short, postscripts and superscripts were handled less carefully than the psalms themselves throughout the attested course of the text's history up to the present. This more cavalier attitude toward the postscripts and superscripts, together with a textual milieu already overripe for textual confusion, further contributed to conflating the postscript with the succeeding superscript. Once the confusion took place, the scribes would have been forced into the habit of joining them.

The conflation occurred earlier than mid-second century BCE for none of the thirty-plus distinct texts of the Psalms at Qumran gives evidence of what we believe to have been the text of the original psalm.[55]

## III. Conclusion

To be sure, the thesis that למנצח ("to the choirmaster") + optional prepositional phrases in the superscripts of the received psalms were originally postscripts of the preceding psalms, a thesis probably entailing the correlative notion that originally superscripts pertained to composition and postscripts to performance, rests on conjecture and so must always remain less than absolutely certain. The comparative data, however, both in extrabiblical literatures and within the Bible convincingly validate the thesis. In the cognate biblical literature one observes compositional elements, genre classification, and author in the superscriptions, and matters pertaining to performance, preservation, and collections in the postscripts. Within the Bible one finds the

52 Wilson, *Editing*, 142.

53 Albert Pietersma, "David in the Greek Psalms," *Vetus Testamentum* 30 (1980): 218.

54 Wilson, *Editing*, 63–92.

55 Wilson, *Editing*, 96–116.

same pattern, Habakkuk 3 being the parade example. The thesis finds numerous confirmations within the Bible, both apart from the Psalter and in the varying canons of the Psalter, especially in resolving the *crux interpretum* of the superscript of Psalm 88. The texts of the psalms restored according to this thesis are much superior to those received by tradition. E. Würthwein, who lays down extremely conservative criteria for deciding the so-called original text, says: "A conjecture may be justified if textual corruption has entered the tradition so early that it antedates the earliest versions."[56] There was ample time in a textual milieu conducive to corruption for the conflation to have taken place.

This thesis is foundational to future philological studies on the meaning of terms in the Psalter's superscripts and postscripts and to winning new insights into the structure and meaning of its edited form(s).

56 Ernst Würthwein, *The Text of the Old Testament* (Grand Rapids, MI: Eerdmans, 1979), 117.

Appendix 2

# A Canonical Process Approach to the Psalms

*Bruce K. Waltke*

DR. CHARLES LEE FEINBERG is one of our Lord's rare and precious gifts to His church.[1] He uniquely brings to the proclamation of Jesus as Messiah those strengths of his commitment to the Christian faith, his many spiritual gifts, his Jewish heritage, and his studies with W. F. Albright. As I thought about offering a small token of my affection and appreciation for Dr. Feinberg, who preceded me in the teaching of Semitic languages and Old Testament exegesis at Dallas Theological Seminary, it seemed fitting that it pertain to the proclamation of Jesus as Messiah and to the exegesis of the Old Testament.

Throughout the history of the church, Christians have found meaning and significance in the Old Testament in the conviction that the Old Testament foretold an age of salvation to come, and that this age had come with the advent of Jesus of Nazareth. That conviction that the Old Testament promised an age of salvation, including a regenerated

1 This appendix was originally published in John S. Feinberg and Paul D. Feinberg, *Tradition and Testament: Essays in Honor of Charles Lee Feinberg* (Chicago: Moody Press, 1981), 3–18. Reproduced here with permission, along with minor emendation. Translations of Scripture are the author's.

people under a restored king of the Davidic line, is based solidly on the teaching of the New Testament. For example, Peter said in his Temple sermon: "Indeed, all the prophets from Samuel on, as many as have spoken, have foretold these days" (Acts 3:24; see also 1 Pet. 1:10–11).

The writers of the New Testament saw Jesus as the fulfillment of prophecies not only in the prophetic literature *sensu stricto*, but also in specific statements in the book of Psalms that they treated as though they belonged to the prophetic literary genre. The early church, for example, regarded the sufferings of Christ at the hands of Herod and Pontius Pilate as the fulfillment of Psalm 2:1–2 in precisely the same way as they saw His death on the cross as the fulfillment of Isaiah 53. After rehearsing the psalm,

> Why do the nations rage
>   and the peoples plot in vain?
> The kings of the earth take their stand
>   and the rulers gather together
> against the Lord and against his anointed one (Acts 4:25–26),

they concluded: "Indeed Herod and Pontius Pilate met together with the Gentiles and the people of Israel in this city to conspire against your holy servant Jesus, whom you anointed. They did what your power and will had decided beforehand should happen" (Acts 4:27–28). At Pentecost, Peter regarded Psalms 16 and 110 to be just as prophetic as Joel 2 and used all three texts indiscriminately to prove that God predicted Jesus' death, resurrection, ascension, and the pouring out of His Spirit.

But since the apostolic era, the church has not agreed about the extent and the nature of the psalms that speak of Jesus Christ. Those who employ the allegorical method of imposing Christian doctrine upon the psalms without considering their meaning and significance to the audiences for whom they were originally composed have tended to see Jesus in almost every verse of every psalm. Augustine, who dominated all subsequent interpretations of the Psalter in the Western church, was never surpassed in seeing Christ everywhere. According to Augustine, our method of interpretation should be "Him first, Him last, Him midst and without end."[2] Thus, for example, he says that the blessed man of Psalm 1 "is to be understood of our Lord Jesus Christ."[3] Adhering to the same approach, Bonaventure commented on Psalm 3:5,

> I laid me down and slept
> and rose again:
> for the LORD sustained me,

"Our blessed LORD is speaking. He laid him down in the sepulchre. He slept His sleep of three days; He rose up again on the third day from the dead."[4]

Those scholars, on the other hand, who reject the unrestrained Alexandrian method of interpretation and who opt instead for the Antiochian principle that every passage has only one literal, historical meaning, have tended to minimize the messianic element in the psalm. Those employing this approach, which is the most widely accredited method among Protestants, can be classified further into three broad categories: the precritical or noncritical expositors, the literary-historical critics who deny any real predictions, and the literary-historical critics who see the psalms cited in the New Testament with reference to Jesus as containing both direct prophecies and indirect prefigurements of Christ.

The precritical or noncritical expositors—represented by such writers as E. W. Hengstenberg,[5] A. C. Gaebelein,[6] David Baron,[7]

2 John Mason Neale and Richard Frederick Littledale, *A Commentary on the Psalms: From Primitive and Mediaeval Writers* (London: John Masters, 1884), 77.

3 Saint Augustin, *Expositions on the Book of Psalms*, vol. 8 of *Nicene and Post-Nicene Fathers*, ed. Philip Schaff (New York: Christian Literature, 1888), 1.

4 Neale and Littledale, *Commentary on the Psalms.* 107.

5 E. W. Hengstenberg, *Christology of the Old Testament* (1828; repr., Grand Rapids, MI: Kregel, 1970).

6 Arno Clemens Gaebelein, *The Jewish Question* (New York: Our Hope, 1912).

7 David Baron, *Types, Psalms and Prophecies*, 3rd ed. (1907; repr., New York: American Board of Mission to the Jews, 1948).

David Cooper,[8] and the late J. B. Payne[9]—tend to limit the number of messianic psalms to the approximately fifteen psalms cited in the New Testament with respect to Jesus Christ, and they regard them as direct prophecies of Christ. J. B. Payne divided these psalms into two groups: those that predict the Messiah in His glory (Pss. 2; 8; 45; 72; 89; 110) and those that foretell His passions (Pss. 16; 22; 40; 41; 69; 109).

But most scholars today disdain an approach that ignores a psalm's historical context and meaning. Noncritical scholars by their "proof-texting" actually discredit the claims of Jesus in the eyes of literary and historical critics.

The literary and historical critics who deny there is any real prediction in the Psalter explain the messianic element in the psalms, which they limit to statements about an ideal, future son of David, as reflections of the natural and nationalistic aspirations of the late postexilic Jewish community who hoped for the return of the Davidic political conditions. Wellhausen wrote: "The theocratic or messianic hope was the hope that the conditions of David's times might return." Moreover, for him prophecies are "not predictions . . . but announcements of aims."[10] Most recently R. E. Clements continued to show Wellhausen's influence when he wrote: "The main essential of the 'messianic' hope was . . . derived from the expectation of the restoration of the Davidic family to the kingship of a renewed Israel after the Babylonian exile."[11] He then added: "We find that not one of the texts which the New Testament appeals to in support of such a hope can, from a strictly historical-critical

8 David Cooper, *Messiah: His First Coming Scheduled* (Los Angeles: Biblical Research Society, 1939).

9 J. B. Payne, "Psalms," in *Zondervan's Pictorial Encyclopedia of the Bible*, ed. Merrill C. Tenney (Grand Rapids, MI: Zondervan, 1975), 940–43.

10 Julius Wellhausen, *Prolegomena to the History of Israel* (Edinburgh: A. & C. Black, 1885), 415. See also George R. Berry, "Messianic Predictions," *Journal of Biblical Literature* (1926): 232–38.

11 Ronald E. Clements, *Old Testament Theology: A Fresh Approach* (London: Marshall, Morgan and Scott, 1978), 150.

point of view, be held originally to have been intended in the way in which it was later taken. . . . Yet, in spite of this certainty about their original meaning, it is precisely these texts which have formed the seedbed of the messianic hope."[12]

Whereas the noncritical approach tends to discredit the messianic claims of Christ by its neglect of history, this approach discredits the New Testament by untying, or at least loosening, the bond connecting the New Testament with the original meaning of the Old Testament.

The literary-historical critics who see the messianic psalms pertaining to the sufferings and the glories of the Christ as containing real predictions and indirect prefigurements of Jesus, reject both the Montanistic theory of inspiration, which represented the biblical writers as passive instruments of the divine Spirit, and the attack upon the credibility of the New Testament witness. These men insist on the literal, historical sense as the only proper sense, but they recognize that the psalms contain real predictions in that they present an ideal that was only partially real in ancient Israel, but which became actual in the life of Christ. C. A. Briggs put it this way: "The psalms embraced the vision of a reality beyond the impression of the senses, a vision which guided Israel to an ever deeper understanding of the reality."[13] H. H. Rowley found the vision of a king whose kingdom would extend to "the ends of the earth" (Ps. 2:8), whose "divine throne [is] for ever and ever" (45:6[7]), and who would "live while the sun endures, and as long as the moon, throughout all generations" (72:5) went beyond pious optimism or flattering hyperbole. He wrote, "While they may have been royal psalms, used in the royal rites of the Temple, they were also 'messianic.' They held before the king the ideal king both as his inspiration and guide for the present, and as the hope of the future."[14]

12 Clements, *Old Testament Theology*, 150.

13 Charles Augustus Briggs, *Messianic Prophecy: The Prediction Of The Fulfillment Of Redemption Through The Messiah* (New York: Charles Scribner's Sons, 1886), 63.

14 Harold Henry Rowley, *The Faith of Israel: Aspects of Old Testament Thought* (Philadelphia: Westminster, 1957), 192.

Franz Delitzsch,[15] followed closely by Kirkpatrick,[16] analyzed the messianic psalms into five classes: (1) typical, that is, psalms that refer primarily to the circumstances of the time but which God also intended to prefigure some feature in the life of Christ (see Pss. 34; 69); (2) typico-prophetic psalms, not only were the sufferings of the psalmist typical of Christ's sufferings, but the records of them were so molded by the Spirit of God as to predict the sufferings of Christ even in circumstantial details (see Pss. 22; 40); (3) Jehovic psalms, that is, those that prepared men's minds for God's incarnation in this world and his victory over evil (Pss. 18; 50; 58; 93; 96–98); (4) indirectly messianic psalms, those that pertained to David's seed and thus indirectly to Jesus Christ as the son of David (see Pss. 45; 72); and (5) purely predictive (Ps. 110). Concerning this last reference Delitzsch wrote: "Among all the Davidic psalms there is only a single one viz. Ps cx, in which David . . . looks forth into the future of his seed and has the Messiah definitely before his mind."[17]

But while this approach maintains a balance between history and prophecy, yet it fails to give a consistent and comprehensive method for identifying the messianic element in the psalms. For the most part these expositors limit the typical element in the psalms to those cited in the New Testament, because apparently they are afraid of allowing the typical method of interpretation to degenerate into the unrestrained allegorical method. But this method cannot adequately explain why, for example, the New Testament (John 2:17) cites Psalm 69:9, "zeal for your house consumes me," as a reference to Christ but not Psalm 3:1, "How many are my foes." In all fairness, it seems as though the writers of the New Testament are not attempting to identify and limit the psalms that prefigure Christ but rather are assuming that the Psalter as a whole has Jesus Christ in view and that this should be the normative way of interpreting the psalms.

15 C. F. Keil and F. Delitzsch, *Commentary on the Old Testament*, vol. 5 (Peabody, MA: Hendrickson, 1996), 68–71.

16 A. F. Kirkpatrick, *The Book of Psalms: Books I* (Cambridge: Cambridge University Press, 1912), lvii–lxvii.

17 Keil and Delitzsch, *Commentary on the Old Testament*, 66.

I conclude, therefore, that both the nonhistorical and undisciplined allegorical method of interpreting the psalms and the Antiochian principle of allowing but one historical meaning that may carry with it typical significance are inadequate hermeneutical principles for the interpretation of the psalms. In place of these methods, therefore, I would like to argue for a canonical process approach in interpreting the psalms, an approach that does justice both to the historical significance(s) of the psalms and to their messianic significance. Indeed, I shall argue that from a literary and historical point of view, we should understand that the human subject of the psalms—whether it be the blessed man of Psalm 1, the one proclaiming himself the son of God in Psalm 2, the suffering petitioner in Psalms 3–7, the son of man in Psalm 8—is Jesus Christ.

By the canonical process approach, I mean the recognition that the text's intention became deeper and clearer as the parameters of the canon were expanded. Just as redemption itself has a progressive history, so also older texts in the canon underwent a correlative progressive perception of meaning as they became part of a growing canonical literature.

My indebtedness to Childs'[18] canonical approach is obvious. But I distinguish the approach advocated here from his, especially as he represents it in *Introduction to the Old Testament as Scripture* (1979), in at least these three ways:

1. Childs does not clearly distinguish the stage of literary activity in the development of the text from changes that take place through scribal activity on the text. This is due to the fact that he has no clear definition of inspiration. But by the "canonical process approach" I have in mind that development of the text and canon that took place under the Spirit's inspiration in contrast to those changes that took place through scribal copying.

2. Childs reckons with tracing the development of the tradition through historical criticism, another term he does not define, though

18 Brevard S. Childs, *Biblical Theology in Crisis* (Philadelphia: Westminster, 1970).

recognizing that all too often the procedure is arbitrary and as such leads to inconclusive and nugatory results. One of the frequent presuppositions underlying historical criticism is the denial of supernatural activity as a cause effecting an event. Childs allows the possibility of a divorce between Israel's religious history and the canonical witness to that history. By canonical process I have no such division in mind and clearly affirm God's supernatural intervention in Israel's history.

3. Childs lays emphasis on the authority of the Jewish text achieved at about AD 100. I lay emphasis on the meaning of the Hebrew Scriptures within the context of the New Testament.

In contrast to canonical criticism—represented also in the writings of J. Sanders[19] and R. E. Clements[20]—according to which the ancient texts were reworked in the progressive development of the canon in such a way that they may have lost their original historical significance, the canonical process approach holds that the original authorial intention was not changed in the progressive development of the canon but deepened and clarified. I agree with Childs' emphasis on the unity of the text and the value of rhetorical criticism, and with his minimizing the recovery of original literary unities apart from their canonical form, but I would emphasize that canonical texts in their earlier stages in the progressively developing canon were just as accurate, authoritative, and inspired as they are in their final literary contexts.

The canonical process approach is similar to the approach known as *sensus plenior* in that it recognizes that further revelation brought to light a text's fuller or deeper significance, but it differs from that approach in several ways.

First of all, in contrast to the normal sense of *sensus plenior* that God intended a fuller meaning in a text than that intended by the human author,[21] the canonical process approach does not divorce the human

19 James A. Sanders, *Torah and Canon* (Philadelphia: Fortress, 1972).

20 Ronald E. Clements, *Old Testament Theology: A Fresh Approach* (London: Marshall, Morgan and Scott, 1978), 150.

21 Raymond E. Brown defined *sensus plenior* as "that additional, deeper meaning, intended by God but not clearly intended by the human author, which is seen to exist in the words of a Biblical text (or group of texts, or even a whole book) when they are studied in the

authorial intention from the divine intention. According to the canonical approach, the original poets presented their subjects in ideal forms, that is, in prayer and in praise fully acceptable to God. Progressive revelation, however, fleshed out this vision and made more clear the exact shape of the ideals always pregnant in the vision.

Second, *sensus plenior*, although insisting that the text's true historical significance was always present in the mind of God, tends toward an allegorical method of interpretation by regarding later writers as winning meanings from the text quite apart from their historical use and significance. By contrast, the canonical process approach underscores the continuity of a text's meaning throughout sacred history along with recognizing that further revelation won for the earlier text a deeper and clearer meaning.

And third, the canonical process approach consciously recognizes and represents the distinct stages in that winning of the clearer and deeper significance of older texts through the discernment of the stages in the development of the canon rather than viewing the New Testament writers as "supernaturally" discovering the fuller, divine meaning of the text.

In the case of the Psalms we can identify at least four distinct advances in the meaning and significance of many specific psalms, and the exegete must keep these four stages in view in his interpretation of them. We can liken the four stages to four lookout points on a mountain. From each successively higher vantage point the vista becomes more full or complete. So also in the four successive stages of the canonical approach to these psalms the text's significance becomes more and more complete and at the last stage the fullest meaning of the text is finally won.

The four distinct points in the progressive perception and revelation of the text occasioned by the enlarging of the canon are: (1) the

---

light of further revelation or development in the understanding of revelation." Cited by William Sanford LaSor, "The *Sensus Plenior* and Biblical Interpretation," in *Scripture, Traditional Interpretation*, ed. W. Ward Gasque and William Sanford LaSor (Grand Rapids, MI: Eerdmans, 1978), 270.

meaning of the psalm to the original poet, (2) its meaning in the earlier collections of psalms associated with the First Temple, (3) its meaning in the final and complete Old Testament canon associated with the Second Temple, and (4) its meaning in the full canon of the Bible including the New Testament with its presentation of Jesus as the Christ.

I was surprised recently in rereading Delitzsch's commentary on the Psalms to discover that he had come to a similar position almost a century ago. He wrote:

> The expositor of the Psalms can place himself on the standpoint of the poet, or the standpoint of the Old Testament church, or the standpoint of the church of the present dispensation—a primary condition of exegetical progress is the keeping of these three standpoints distinct, and, in accordance, therewith, the distinguishing between the two Testaments, and in general between different steps in the development of the revelation, and in the perception of the plan of redemption.[22]

Unfortunately, however, Delitzsch too sharply distinguished the standpoints and failed to recognize the genetic and organic connection between them in the development of the revelation. But in recognizing three distinct stages in the revelation he anticipated my own awareness of the need for identifying stages in the progress of revelation and apprehension of many psalms.

This canonical process approach to the interpretation of the Psalms rests on at least four convictions.[23]

First, it assumes that the people of God throughout history are united by a common knowledge and faith (certainty in the knowledge).

22 Keil and Delitzsch, *Commentary on the Old Testament*, 64.

23 I am partially indebted here to Adolf Schlatter, "The Theology of the New Testament and Dogmatics," in *The Nature of New Testament Theology: The Contribution of William Wrede and Adolf Schlatter*, ed. Robert Morgan, Studies in Biblical Theology, 2nd ser., 25 (London: SCM, 1973), 117–66.

Although the community's knowledge is expanded during the time that the canon is taking shape, the former knowledge and faith is not changing. To preserve the "givenness" of its faith, Israel was instructed to remember her heritage both by recital and ritual at the Passover and Firstfruits festivals in the spring and at the Tabernacles festival in the fall (Ex. 12:26–27; 23:14–17; Deut. 16:1–17; 26:1–11; 31:10–13). Moreover, the people of God preserved other tokens of their history by preserving relics such as an omer of manna (Ex. 16:32) and by erecting memorials such as the stones at Gilgal (Josh. 4:20–24). From the call of Abraham to the close of the Old Testament era, each succeeding generation passed on its common faith by circumcising its male infants. In short, each succeeding generation of the believing community was shaped by its unchanging past history, and the knowledge added to it was consistent with that heritage. This is one reason we can confidently say that the progressive revelation by clearer perceptions of earlier texts was an organic and genetic unity.

Second, this approach accepts the biblical witness that God is the ultimate author of the progressively developing canon. He inspired elect individuals to add to that revelation already received through their own unique experiences with God in the progress of sacred history. Because of that common, divine inspiration we have further reason for affirming the continuity in the progressive revelation and grasping of the canonical literature. Moreover, because God is the author of the whole Bible, any piece of literature within it must be studied in the light of its whole literary context.

Third, this approach rests on the conviction that as the canon developed, lesser and earlier representations were combined to form greater units that are more meaningful than their component parts. Therefore, the full meaning of an earlier and smaller text cannot be gained without interpreting it in the light of the entire Bible.

Finally, this approach presupposes that the canon closed with the addition of the last book of the New Testament. Thus the received Scriptures constitute the final literary framework within which any given text must be interpreted.

Now that we have broadly sketched the canonical process approach with its four organically connected stages of interpretation and the four convictions that undergird it, let me now apply the approach to the Psalms.

First of all, we ask what the psalm meant to the original poet. Here it is important to note that the human subject of most of the psalms is a king. Two lines of evidence lead to this unmistakable conclusion: the external evidence of the so-called superscriptions and the internal evidence of the psalms themselves. The Masoretic text identifies King David as the author, and presumably the human subject, of seventy-three psalms; the LXX attributes eighty-four psalms to him.

There are many good reasons for accepting Gesenius-Kautsch-Cowley's (par. 129 *c*) contention that the preposition *l*ᵉ in the phrase *ledāwid* in these headings designates authorship even as in Arabic, and that the phrase accordingly should be translated "by David." First, many Old Testament traditions from both the pre-Exilic and post-Exilic periods present David as a composer and a promoter of Israel's psalmody. In the book of Samuel, for example, it is claimed for the psalm numbered as Psalm 18 in the English version that "David sang to the LORD the words of this song" (2 Sam. 22:1). The same statement is found in the heading to Psalm 18 after the phrase לְדָוִד (*le dāwid*). Moreover, the superscriptions of fourteen psalms specify the incident in David's life that prompted him to write the psalm. The Chronicler claims that David assigned the Levites to various musical guilds in order to beautify the Mosaic ritual with music and associates David with Israel's psalmody (1 Chron. 16:1–43).[24] Then too, one of Israel's earliest writing prophets complained that the men of the Northern Kingdom whiled away their time strumming on their harps like David (Amos 6:5). The same persuasion regarding Davidic authorship persists in both the early Jewish tradition and the New Testament. Ben Sirach

24 William Foxwell Albright, *Archaeology and the Religion of Israel* (Baltimore: Johns Hopkins, 1953), 125–26, and Helmer Ringgren, in *Theological Dictionary of the Old Testament*, vol. 3, ed. G. Johannes Botterweck and Helmer Ringgren (Grand Rapids, MI: Eerdmans, 1975), 164, also connect David with Israel's psalmody.

(c. 190 BC) put the tradition into poetry: "In all that he [David] did he gave thanks to the Holy One, the Most High, with ascription of glory; he sang praise with all his heart, and he loved his maker" (Eccl. 47:8–9; cf. Josephus, *Contra Apion* VII:305–06). The New Testament cites David as the author of Psalms 2, 16, 32, 69, 109, 110. In the case of the last reference, Jesus identified the Messiah as greater than David on the assumption that David wrote it (Matt. 22:43–44). There is no need to chronicle the numerous contributors to this orthodox opinion after the close of the canon.

Furthermore, the literature from the Ancient Near East tends more and more to support this unanimous biblical and ancient tradition by pointing to the antiquity of the Psalms. Gunkel demonstrated that Israel's hymns closely parallel in their forms the hymns of ancient Egypt and Mesopotamia.[25] Parallel Sumerian hymns contain musical notations as unintelligible to Sumeriologists as the musical notations in the Psalter are unintelligible to Hebraists.[26] S. Mowinckel has demonstrated from internal evidence that the psalms were sung in the cultus of the First Temple,[27] and M. Dahood backed up his conclusion with linguistic evidence from the Ugaritic texts, though he marred his work by overextending the argument.[28]

In addition to the evidence of the superscriptions that King David is the author of about half the Psalter, and presumably the human subject of these psalms, there is the internal evidence of the psalms themselves. None disputes the form-critical researches of H. Gunkel that Psalms 2, 18, 20, 21, 45, 72, 89, 101, 110, 132, 144 are royal psalms. But more significantly John Eaton[29] has followed up the work of H. Gunkel,

25 Hermann Gunkel, *Einleitung in die Psalmen*, completed by Joachim Begrich (Gottingen: Vandenhoeck & Ruprecht, 1933).

26 Samuel Noah Kramer, *The Sumerians: Their History, Culture, and Character* (Chicago: University of Chicago Press, 1963), 207.

27 Sigmund Mowinckel, *The Psalms in Israel's Worship*, 2 vols. (New York: Abingdon, 1962).

28 Mitchell Dahood, *Psalms I, 1–50: Introduction, Translation, and Notes*, Anchor Bible (Garden City, NY: Doubleday, 1966),

29 John H. Eaton, *Kingship and the Psalms*, Studies in Biblical Theology, 2nd ser., 32 (Naperville, IL: Alec R. Allenson, n.d.).

S. Mowinckel, and others in showing that the supplicator in the so-called psalms of lament (c. fifty psalms) is also a king. Eaton wrote,

> Gunkel identifies the following. All nations attend to the psalmist's thanksgiving (Pss. 18:50; 57:10; 138:1, 4; 119:46). His deliverance has vast repercussions (22:28f.). He invokes a world-judgment to rectify his cause (7:7, 9; 56:8; 59:6; 59:9; cf. 43:1). He depicts himself as victorious over the nations through God's intervention (118:10–12). He confronts armies (3:7; 27:3; 55:22; 56:2f.; 59:6; 72:4; 109:3; 120:7; 140:3, 8). He is like a bull raising horns in triumph (92:11).
>
> To these items from Gunkel . . . we may add considerably. The speaker vows continual psalmody. He stands out before the vast festal congregation (22:33, 26; 40:10f.). His head is raised on high. . . . His glory receives special mention. . . . He is blessed with superabundant life. . . . His designations of God as his helper are often related to warfare. . . . Enemies, military and national in character, aim at him personally rather than at his country and people.[30]

We conclude, therefore, that transcending the various types of psalms so laboriously analyzed and classified by Gunkel stands the more significant fact that in the original composition the king is the human subject of the psalms, whether they be lament, acknowledgment, praise, or belonging to various other types of psalms.[31] Furthermore, we must

30 Eaton, *Kingship and the Psalms*, 23–24.

31 Although we have argued here that לְדָוִד (*le dāwid*) means "by David," other proposed interpretations of the phrase do not undermine the thesis that the original composition had an ideal king in view. Mowinckel argued that *dawidum* originally meant a chief or king, especially among seminomadic groups. See Mowinckel, *Psalms in Israel's Worship*, 1:77ff.; 2:98–100. Elsewhere he argued that the phrase meant "destined for the (cultic) use of David" (i.e., the reigning king). See Mowinckel, "Psalm Criticism between 1900 and 1935," *Vetus Testamentum* 5 (1955):18. D. R. Ap-Thomas also read *dwd* as a title of office, more specifically "deputy, ruler, governor." See D. R. Ap-Thomas, "Saul's 'Uncle,'" *Vetus Testamentum* 11 (1961):244ff. Eissfeldt interpreted the word with the phrase "in praise of David's exploits." See Otto Eissfeldt, *The Old Testament: An Introduction* (San Francisco: Harper, 1965), 451. Dalglish interpreted the preposition *l* more vaguely "of David." Accordingly, it could mean: "a collection belonging to David," a psalm "for David," etc. See Edward Dalglish, *Psalm Fifty-One: In the Light of Ancient Eastern Patternism* (Leiden:

bear in mind that the king is presented idealistically and prays to God and praises Him through the inspiration of God's Spirit.

We now move to the second standpoint in our canonical approach to the Psalms by asking the question, What did these psalms mean in their earlier canonical collections mentioned in such passages as 2 Chronicles 29:30 and Psalm 72:20 and used in connection with the worship of the First Temple? Here too we come to the conclusion that the living king continued to be understood as the human subject of many of these songs of praise and petition.

First, the Davidic covenant, alluded to several times in the Psalms—most especially Psalm 89—provides us with a firm basis for the conviction that the individual in view in many psalms was the son of David. According to this covenant, God promised David a son whose house and kingdom would endure forever before God and whose throne would be established forever (2 Sam. 7:12–16). In the light of such a promise, it would be most surprising if David did not intend his many and varied types of royal psalms to be used by and for the house of David at the house of the Lord. Almost certainly, these royal psalms had a royal significance in Israel's cultus.

Second, those scholars sensitive to the extensive royal interpretation of the psalms universally recognize that the king represented the people. Mowinckel wrote, "All that concerned him and his cause also concerned the people; nothing which happened to him was a purely private affair."[32] It would be utterly foreign to the culture of preexilic Israel to suppose that the psalms were democratized in their interpretation. Such an interpretation would be appropriate for texts in our democratic, twentieth-century Western societies, but it would be unthinkable during the monarchy in preexilic Israel

Third, we believe the living king was understood to be the human subject of most psalms, because in the Ancient Near Eastern literature the king was the patron of the foreign cults (exactly as is the case in Israel) and was the subject of numerous hymns. Gunkel noted that the

Brill, 1962), 240. Waltke is indebted here to his student Gordon Brubacher, who wrote a thesis on the structure of Psalm 68, for bringing these references together.

32 Mowinckel, *Psalms in Israel's Worship*, 1:42–61.

extant prayers and laments of the Mesopotamian kings are "extraordinarily numerous."[33] Why, then, should we think that Israel would have reinterpreted the psalms at this early period in Israel's history as a reference to the common man or some other individual than the son of David? Directly reinforcing this argument is the universal recognition among students of Ancient Near Eastern languages and literatures that the king played a central role in the religions of the Ancient Near East.[34]

Fourth, it is sufficiently clear that in many psalms not ascribed to David the king is the human subject of the psalm. For example, in Psalm 44, associated with the sons of Korah, is it not most likely that the king represents the defeated army of Israel in prayer before God? Who is a more likely candidate than the king as the speaker of the line, "I do not trust in my bow, my sword does not save me" (44:6)? It is also instructive to note that in this psalm, as in many others, there is a fluid interchange between the plural pronoun "we" and the singular pronoun "I." This psalm begins, for example, "We have heard with our ears . . . our fathers have told us what you did in their days" (44:1), followed by "You are my King and my God, who decrees victories for Jacob" (44:4). This change can best be explained on the assumption that the human subject is the king representing the people. In short, although the psalm is assigned to the sons of Korah, the human subject is a king. Does not this also suggest that other psalms not assigned to David were composed for Israel's king?

Fifth, Birkeland[35] has shown that in many psalms, the enemies are Israel's international political enemies and that this indicates, as Kraus[36] also argued, that the individual subject is a king.

33 Gunkel, *Einleitung*, 161. Mowinckel makes the same observation: "All this points to the fact that in Israel, as in Babylonia and Egypt, the psalms . . . were originally intended, not for all and sundry, but for the king and the great." Mowinckel, *Psalms in Israel's Worship*, 1:77.

34 For a critique of Mowinckel's notion of an annual enthronement festival for Yahweh, of the myth and ritual school, and of the comparative phenomenology approach of the Uppsala school, see Bruce K. Waltke, "Israel, Religion of," in *The New International Standard Bible Encyclopedia*, II.

35 Harris Birkeland, *The Evildoers in the Psalms* (Oslo: I. Kommisjon has J. Dybwad, 1955), 12ff.

36 H. J. Kraus, *Psalmen*, 1, Biblischer Kommentar Altes Testament Band XV/1 (Neukirchen: Neukirchen Verlag, 1961): 40–53 (excursus 2).

We conclude, therefore, that most psalms had a royal significance in their cultic use at the First Temple.

Now it is important to note that each living successor to David's throne was clothed in the large, magnificent, purple mantle of the messianic vision attached to the House of David. Each king became the son of God through his anointing with Yahweh's Spirit. Of these historical kings Ringgren wrote: "The king is Anointed of Yahweh, he is setup by him and proclaimed his son, he shall maintain right and righteousness in the country, he conveys to his people divine blessings, rain and fertility, he defeats in divine power all enemies, he rules over the whole world, and his throne shall stand eternally."[37] We should also add that ideally he also suffers on behalf of the kingdom of God and wrestles with God in prayer in accordance with the divine imperative: "Ask of me [my son], and I will give the nations as your inheritance" (Ps. 2:8). H. Gressman[38] pointed out that Israel's association of the reigning monarch with messianic significance found its counterpart in Egypt where the pharaoh was also associated with messianic expectations. But none of David's successors up to the time of the Captivity had shoulders broad enough to fill this ideal mantle that was laid upon him at his coronation as Yahweh's king over Israel.

We conclude, then, that the many types of psalms composed for the First Temple and used in it and constituting a part of Israel's canonical literature had a messianic meaning and significance that none of David's successors satisfied up to the time that the house of the LORD was destroyed and the House of David was deported to Babylon.

A third vantage point in interpreting the psalms is gained by now asking the question, What did these royal psalms mean to the editors who gave the Old Testament canon its received shape and substance? Or, to put the matter another way, What do these psalms mean in the broader context of the Old Testament canon compiled during the postexilic period, probably between 400 BC and 200 BC?

37 Helmer Ringgren, *The Messiah in the Old Testament* (Chicago: Allenson, 1956), 20.
38 Hugo Gressman, *Der Messias* (Gottingen: Vandenhoeck & Ruprecht, 1929), 1–7, 415–23.

Haggai makes it sufficiently clear that the exiles who returned from the Captivity continued to associate the living House of David with the messianic hope. This perception of the matter inherited from the preexilic period is apparent in the LORD's address to the House of David through Haggai:

> Tell Zerubbabel governor of Judah that I will shake the heavens and the earth. I will overturn royal thrones and shatter the power of the foreign kingdoms. I will overthrow chariots and their drivers; horses and their riders will fall, each by the sword of his brother. "On that day," declares the LORD Almighty, "I'll take you, my servant Zerubbabel son of Shealtiel," declares the LORD, "and I will make you like my signet ring, for I have chosen you," declares the LORD Almighty. (Hag. 2:21–23)

In sum, the two institutions—the House of David and the house of the LORD—providing Israel with its greatest sense of continuity were revived at the beginning of the postexilic era.

But Zerubbabel and apparently his descendants continued to fall short of the messianic expectation laid upon them, and by about a century later the last of the Old Testament canonical prophets, Malachi, projected the vision of Israel's golden age, when the LORD would come to His people with healing in His wings, to an age beyond his own temporal horizon and on into the eschatological future. Thus, when the Old Testament canon closed, no son of David was sitting on Yahweh's throne, and no living scion of David's line was associated with that hope. Accordingly, we may safely conclude that the royal psalms in the final shape of the Old Testament canon must have been interpreted prophetically precisely as we found them interpreted in the New Testament. This prophetic interpretation of these old texts is not a reinterpretation of them away from their original, authorial meaning; rather, it is a more precise interpretation of them in the light of the historical realities. Aage Bentzen noted, "It must, however, be acknowledged that the difference between the 'cultic' and the 'eschatological' interpretations of the Enthronement [*sic*, royal] Psalms is not very great."[39] If one keeps in mind the genetic and organic unity in the progressive apprehension of these psalms, the following statement by R. E. Clements might prove helpful:

> From the point of view of the messianic interpretation of certain psalms it appears most probable that the same stimulus towards a new dimension of interpretation has been felt. It is in fact possible that those editors who incorporated into the Psalter the texts of royal psalms, which must have appeared obsolete at a time when Judah had no king, do so out of a genuine hope that Israel would again need them. In this case, a dimension of hope was present in the act of retaining compositions which the contemporary political scene made inapplicable in their original sense [*sic*]. The formation of the canon, therefore, must have had its own part to play in projecting the ideas and images associated with the kingship into the future.[40]

The intertestamental literature and the New Testament make clear, however, that the royal dimension of the lament psalms became lost during this period of time, and thus Israel lost sight of a suffering Messiah. Perhaps these psalms now become democratized in the synagogues and interpreted as references to Everyman, as Mowinckel theorized.[41] But that was not their original meaning and significance, and Jesus had to correct Israel's understanding back to their original intention. In brief, the New Testament does not impose a new meaning on these old psalms but wins back for them their original and true significance. We cannot be sure how the editors who compiled the final form of the Old Testament interpreted the lament psalms. It seems plausible to me to suppose that they continued to understand them according to their original meaning. I draw that conclusion on

39 Aage Bentzen, *King and Messiah*, Lutterworth Studies in Church and Bible (London: Lutterworth, 1955), 37.

40 Clements, *Old Testament Theology*, 151.

41 Mowinckel, *Psalms in Israel's Worship*, 1:78–80.

the basis that the progressive development of the canon is a genetic and organic unity, on the recognition that later prophecies, such as Isaiah 53, made it abundantly clear that the one to be exalted by Yahweh over all the nations must suffer and die, and on the certainty that the protoevangelium was understood as a reference to the suffering and triumph of the Messiah over Satan.

Thus we conclude that at this third stage in the development of the canon, the psalms continued to have a royal and messianic significance, but they now carried a predictive meaning as well. Israel must now wait in hope for a future son of David worthy to pray and sing these psalms.

With the advent of Jesus Christ this hope was satisfied. Accordingly, within the literary context of the New Testament the psalms find their final and full meaning and perception. From this fourth and highest vantage point we win the full significance of the psalms. Jesus of Nazareth, son of David and Son of God, fulfills these psalms. Those elements in each psalm presenting the king as anything less than ideal, such as his confession of sins, are the historical eggshells from the preexilic period when the psalms were used for Israel's less than ideal kings.

We conclude, then, that the Psalms are ultimately the prayers of Jesus Christ, Son of God. He alone is worthy to pray the ideal vision of a king suffering for righteousness and emerging victorious over the hosts of evil. As the corporate head of the church, he represents the believers in these prayers. Moreover, Christians, as sons of God and as royal priests, can rightly pray these prayers along with their representative Head. Dietrich Bonhoeffer also reached the conclusion that Jesus Christ is the one praying in the psalter. "The Psalter," he wrote, "is the prayer book of Jesus Christ in the truest sense of the word."[42]

42 Dietrich Bonhoeffer, *Life Together*, trans. John W. Doberstein (New York: Harper and Brothers, 1954), 46.

Appendix 3

# Summary of Psalm Forms

## Hymns or Descriptive Praise Psalms

- form:
  - call to praise
  - cause or reason for praise
  - conclusion or renewed call to praise
- common identifiers:
  - "praise"
  - "psalm"
  - "song"
  - the use of musical instruments
  - the note of rejoicing

## Lament Psalms

- direct address
- lament or complaint
- confidence
- petition
- conclusion or praise

## Individual Psalms of Grateful Praise or Declarative Praise Psalms

- Proclamation: "I will praise the Lord"; sometimes just the praise itself, as in 116:1: "I love the LORD."
- Introductory summary statement of what God has done: "for he saved me."
- Reflection on past need and deliverance: "I cried, he heard, he answered."
- Praise: "Come join with me in praise."

## Songs of Trust[1]

- declaration of trust
- interior lament
- invitation to trust
- basis of trust

1 C. Hassell Bullock, *Encountering the Book of Psalms: A Literary and Theological Introduction*, Encountering Biblical Studies (Grand Rapids, MI: Baker Academic, 2001), 168–70.

# Bibliography


Alexander, Joseph Addison. *The Psalms.* Edinburgh: John Greig and Son, 1864.

Archer, Gleason L. *A Survey of Old Testament Introduction.* Chicago: Moody Press, 1974.

Augustin, Saint. *Expositions on the Book of Psalms.* Vol. 8 of *Nicene and Post-Nicene Fathers,* First Series. Edited by Philip Schaff. New York: Christian Literature, 1888.

Augustine. *The Confessions of St. Augustine.* New York. Wiley and Putnam, 1844.

Bavinck, Herman. *Reformed Dogmatics.* Edited by John Bolt. Translated by John Vriend. Vol. 2, *God and Creation.* Grand Rapids, MI: Baker Academic, 2004.

Beale, G. K. *The Morality of God in the Old Testament.* Christian Answers to Hard Questions. Philadelphia: Westminster Seminary Press; Phillipsburg, NJ: P&R, 2013.

Belcher Jr., Richard P. *The Messiah and the Psalms: Preaching Christ from All the Psalms.* Fearn, Ross-shire, Scotland: Christian Focus, 2006.

Bonar, Andrew. *Christ and His Church in the Book of Psalms.* London: James Nisbet, 1859.

Braude, William G. *The Midrash on the Psalms.* New Haven, CT: Yale University Press, 1954.

Briggs, Charles A. *A Critical and Exegetical Commentary on the Book of Psalms.* New York, Scribner's Sons, 1906–1907.

Brown, William P., ed. *The Oxford Handbook of the Psalms*. Oxford: Oxford University Press, 2014.

Broyles, Craig C. *Psalms*. New International Biblical Commentary. Grand Rapids, MI: Zondervan, 1999.

Buber, Martin. "Leitwort Style in Pentateuch Narrative." In *Scripture and Translation*. Edited by Martin Buber and Franz Rosenzweig. Translated by Lawrence Alan Rosenwald and Everett Fox. Bloomington: Indiana University Press, 1994.

Bullock, C. Hassell. *Encountering the Book of Psalms: A Literary and Theological Introduction*. Encountering Biblical Studies. Grand Rapids, MI: Baker Academic, 2001.

Calvin, John. *Commentary on the Book of Psalms*. Translated by James Anderson. Vol. 4. Baker, 2003.

Carr, David M. *Writing on the Tablet of the Heart: Origin of Scripture and Literature*. Oxford: Oxford University Press, 2003.

Childs, Brevard S. *Introduction to the Old Testament as Scripture*. Philadelphia: Fortress, 1979.

Clifford, Richard J. *Psalms 1–72*. Abington Old Testament Commentaries. Nashville: Abingdon, 2002.

Cole, Robert R. *Psalms 1—2: Gateway to the Psalter*. Hebrew Bible Monographs 37. Sheffield: Sheffield Phoenix, 2013.

Cole, Robert R. *The Shape and Message of Book III (Psalms 73–89)*. Journal for the Study of the Old Testament Supplement Series 307. Sheffield: Sheffield Academic, 2000.

Collins, C. John "Introduction to the Psalms." In *ESV Study Bible*. Wheaton, IL: Crossway, 2008.

Compton, Jared. *Psalm 110 and the Logic of Hebrews*. Library of New Testament Studies, 537. New York: Bloomsbury T&T Clark, 2015.

Creach, Jerome F. *The Choice of Yahweh as Refuge in the Editing of the Psalter*. Journal for the Study of the Old Testament Supplement Series 217. Sheffield: Sheffield Academic, 1996.

Cross, Frank Moore. *Canaanite Myth and Hebrew Epic: Essays in the History of the Religion of Israel*. Cambridge, MA: Harvard University Press, 1973.

Crutchfield, John C. "The Redactional Agenda of the Book of Psalms" *Hebrew Union College Annual* 74 (2003): 21–47.

Dahood, Mitchell. *Psalms*. 3 Vols. Garden City, NY: Doubleday, 1965–1970.

deClaisse-Walford, Nancy L. *Reading from the Beginning: The Shaping of the Hebrew Psalter.* Macon, GA: Mercer University Press, 1997.

deClaissé-Walford, Nancy L., ed. *The Shape and Shaping of the Book of Psalms: The Current State of Scholarship*. Ancient Israel and Its Literature 20. Atlanta: Society of Biblical Literature, 2014.

Dempster, Stephen. *Dominion and Dynasty: A Theology of the Hebrew Bible*. New Studies in Biblical Theology 15. Downers Grove, IL: IVP Academic, 2003.

Driver, S. R. *Studies in the Psalms*. London: Hodder and Stoughton, 1915.

Eaton, John H. *Kingship and the Psalms*. Studies in Biblical Theology, Second Series, 32. Naperville, IL: Alec R. Allenson, n.d.

Eaton, John. *The Psalms: A Historical and Spiritual Commentary with an Introduction and New Translation*. New York: Continuum, 2005.

Ferguson, Sinclair. *Deserted by God?* Grand Rapids, MI: Baker, 1993.

Flournoy, Parke P. "The Psalms Not Post-Exilic." *The Bible Student* 3, no. 1 (January 1901).

Futato, Mark D. *Interpreting the Psalms: An Exegetical Handbook*. Handbooks for Old Testament Exegesis. Grand Rapids, MI: Kregel, 2007.

Gerstenberger, Erhard S. "Der Psalter als Buch und als Sammlung," in *Neue Wege der Psalmenforschung: Für Walter Beyerlin*. Edited by K. Seybold and E. Zenger. Herders Biblische Studien 1. Freiburg: Herder, 1994.

Gillingham, Susan. "The Levitical Singers and the Compilation of the Psalter." In *Trägerkreise in den Psalmen*, 35–59. Edited by F.-L. Hossfeld et al. Bonner biblische Beiträge 178. Göttingen: Bonn University Press, 2017.

Glenn, Donald G. "An Exegetical and Theological Exposition of Psalm 139." In *Tradition and Testament: Essays in Honor of Charles Lee Feinberg*. Edited by John S. Feinberg and Paul D. Feinberg. Chicago: Moody Press, 1981.

Goldingay, John. *Psalms*. 3 Vols. Grand Rapids, MI: Baker Academic, 2006–2008.

Goodacre, Robert, ed. *The Psalms and Hymns of the Late Isaac Watts.* London: n.p., 1821.

Grant, Jamie A. *The King as Exemplar: The Function of Deuteronomy's Kingship Law in the Shaping of the Book of Psalms.* Society of Biblical Literature, Academia Biblica 17. Atlanta: Society of Biblical Literature, 2004.

Gundersen, David Alexander. "Davidic Hope in Book IV of the Psalter." PhD diss., Southern Baptist Theological Seminary, 2015.

Gunkel, Hermann. *Introduction to the Psalms: The Genres of the Religious Lyric of Israel.* Completed by Joachim Begrich. Translated by James Nogalski. Macon, GA: Mercer University Press, 1998.

Hamilton Jr., James M. "David's Biblical Theology and Typology in the Psalms: Authorial Intent and Patterns of the Seed of Promise." In *Reading the Psalms Theologically: Studies in Scripture and Biblical Theology.* Edited by David Howard Jr. and Andrew Schmutzer. Bellingham, WA: Lexham, forthcoming 2023.

Hamilton Jr., James M. *Psalms.* 2 Vols. Evangelical Biblical Theology Commentary. Bellingham, WA: Lexham Academic, 2021.

Hensley, Adam D. *Covenant Relationships and the Editing of the Hebrew Psalter,* The Library of Hebrew Bible/Old Testament Studies 666. New York: T&T Clark, 2018.

Ho, Peter C. W. *The Design of the Psalter: A Macrostructural Analysis.* Eugene, OR: Pickwick, 2019.

Ho, Peter C. W. "The Macrostructural Design and Logic of the Psalter: An Unfurling of the Davidic Covenant." In *Reading the Psalms Theologically: Studies in Scripture and Biblical Theology.* Edited by David Howard Jr. and Andrew Schmutzer. Bellingham, WA: Lexham, forthcoming 2023.

Ho, Peter C. W. "The Shape of Davidic Psalms as Messianic." *Journal of the Evangelical Theological Society* 62 (2019): 515–31.

Henry, Matthew. *Matthew Henry's Commentary on the Whole Bible: Complete and Unabridged in One Volume.* Peabody, MA: Hendrickson, 1994.

Hilber, John. *Cultic Prophecy in the Psalms.* Beihefte zur Zeitschrift für die alttestamentliche Wissenschaft 352. New York: Walter de Gruyter, 2005.

Hogenhaven, Jesper. "The Opening of the Psalter: A Study in Jewish Theology." *Scandinavian Journal of the Old Testament* 15, no. 2 (2001): 169–80.

Howard Jr., David M. "The Case for Kingship in the Old Testament Narrative Books and the Psalms," *Trinity Journal* 9 (1988): 19–35.

Howard Jr., David M. "Divine and Human Kingship as Organizing Motifs in the Psalter." In *The Psalms: Language for All Seasons of the Soul*, 197–207. Edited by Andrew J. Schmutzer and David M. Howard Jr. Chicago: Moody Publishers, 2013.

Howard Jr., David M. *The Structure of Psalms 93–100*. Biblical and Judaic Studies from the University of California, San Diego 5. Winona Lake, IN: Eisenbrauns, 1997.

Hurvitz, Avi. "The Chronological Significance of 'Aramaisms' in Biblical Hebrew." *Israel Exploration Journal* 18 (1968).

Ker, John. *The Psalms in History and Biography.* Solid Ground Christian Books, 2006.

Keil, C. F., and F. Delitzsch. *Commentary on the Old Testament.* Vol. 5. 1866, reprint. Peabody, MA: Hendrickson, 1996.

Kidner, Derek. *Proverbs*. Downers Grove, IL: InterVarsity Press, 1964.

Kidner, Derek. *Psalms 1–72*. London: Inter-Varsity Press, 1973.

Kidner, Derek. *Psalms 73–150*. London: Inter-Varsity Press, 1975.

Kirkpatrick, A. F. *The Book of Psalms: Book I.* Cambridge: Cambridge University Press, 1892.

Kirkpatrick, A. F. *The Book of Psalms: Books IV and V.* Cambridge: Cambridge University Press, 1912.

Kuntz, J. Kenneth. "Continuing the Engagement: Psalms Research Since the Early 1990s." *Currents in Biblical Research* 19 (2012): 321–78.

Leupold, H. C. *Exposition of the Psalms.* Grand Rapids, MI: Baker, 1969.

Lewis, C. S. *A Grief Observed.* New York: Harper One, 1961.

Lewis, C. S. *Reflections on the Psalms.* Orlando: HBJ, 1986.

Longman III, Tremper. *How to Read the Psalms.* How to Read Series. Downers Grove: InterVarsity Press, 1988.

Longman III, Tremper. "The Messiah: Explorations in the Law and the Writings." In *The Messiah in the Old and New Testaments*, 13–34. Edited by Stanley E. Porter. Grand Rapids, MI: Eerdmans, 2007.

Longman III, Tremper. *Psalms: An Introduction and Commentary.* Tyndale Old Testament Commentaries 15–16. Downers Grove: IVP Academic, 2014.

Lovitt, Harriet. "A Critical and Exegetical Study of Psalm 139." UMI dissertation series, 1964.

Mays, James L. *Psalms.* Interpretation: A Commentary for Teaching and Preaching. Louisville: John Knox, 1994.

MacLaren, Alexander. *The Psalms.* 3 Vols. New York: A. C. Armstrong and Son, 1904.

Martin, Chalmers. "Imprecations in the Psalms." *Princeton Theological Review* 1, no. 4 (1903).

McMann, J. C. *The Shape and Shaping of the Psalter.* Journal for the Study of the Old Testament Supplement Series 159. Sheffield: JSOT Press, 1993.

McCann, Jr., J. Clinton. "The Book of Psalms: Introduction, Commentary, and Reflections," *The New Interpreters Bible.* Vol. 4. Edited by Leander E. Keck et al. Nashville, TN: Abingdon, 1996.

McKelvey, Michael G. *Moses, David and the High Kingship of Yahweh: A Canonical Study of Book IV of the Psalter.* Gorgias Biblical Studies 55. Piscataway, NJ: Gorgias, 2014.

McNeile, A. H. *The Psalms.* Vol. 1 of *A New Commentary on Holy Scripture.* Edited by C. Gore, H. L. Goudge, and A. Guillaume. New York: Macmillan, 1942.

Metzger, Bruce. *Textual Commentary on the New Testament.* 2nd edition. New York: American Bible Society, 1994.

Miller, Patrick D. *Interpreting the Psalms.* Philadelphia: Fortress, 1986.

Mitchell, David C. *The Message of the Psalter: An Eschatological Programme in the Book of Psalms.* Newton Mearns, Scotland: Campbell, 2003.

Mitchell, David C. *The Songs of Ascents: Psalms 120 to 134 in the Worship of Jerusalem's Temples.* Newton Mears, Scotland: Campbell, 2015.

Moberly, R. W. L. "Lament." In *New International Dictionary of Old Testament Theology and Exegesis.* 5 vols. Edited by Willem A. VanGemeren. Grand Rapids, MI: Zondervan, 1997: 4:866–84.

Moberly, R. W. L. *Old Testament Theology: Reading the Hebrew Bible as Christian Scripture.* Grand Rapids, MI: Baker Academic, 2013.

Motyer, Alec. *A Christian's Pocket Guide to Loving the Old Testament: One Book, One God, One Story,* Pocket Guides. Fearn, Ross-shire, Scotland: Christian Focus, 2015.

Motyer, Alec. *Look to the Rock: An Old Testament Background to Our Understanding of Christ.* Grand Rapids, MI: Kregel, 1996.

Motyer, Alec. *Treasures of the King: Psalms from the Life of David.* Nottingham, UK: Inter-Varsity Press, 2007.

Motyer, J. A. "The Psalms." In *New Bible Commentary.* Edited by Gordon J. Wenham et al. Downers Grove, IL: IVP Academic, 1994.

Murphy, Roland E. "Reflections on Canonical Interpretation of the Psalms." In *The Shape and Shaping of the Psalter*, 21–28. Edited by J. C. McCann. Journal for the Study of the Old Testament Supplement Series 159. Sheffield: JSOT Press, 1993.

*NIV Study Bible: Fully Revised Edition.* Grand Rapids, MI: Zondervan, 2020.

Perowne, J. J. Stewart. *The Book of Psalms.* Vol. 1. Andover: Warren F. Draper, 1879.

Perowne, J. J. Stewart. *The Book of Psalms.* Vol. 2. 4th Revised Edition. 1878; repr., Grand Rapids, MI: Zondervan.

Prinsloo, Gert T. M. "Reading the Masoretic Psalter as a Book: Editorial Trends and Redactional Trajectories." *Currents in Biblical Research* 19 (2021): 145–77.

Poythress, Vern. *Reading the Word of God in the Presence of God: A Handbook for Biblical Interpretation.* Wheaton, IL: Crossway, 2016.

Pratt, Richard L. *He Gave Us Stories: The Bible Student's Guide to Interpreting Old Testament Narratives.* Brentwood, TN: Wolgemuth and Hyatt, 1990.

Pratt, Richard. "Historical Contingencies and Biblical Predictions," in *The Way of Wisdom: Essays in Honor of Bruce K. Waltke.* Edited by J. I. Packer and Sven K. Soderlund. Grand Rapids, MI: Zondervan, 2000: 180–203.

Pritchard, J. B. *Ancient Near Eastern Texts Relating to the Old Testament.* 3rd Ed. Princeton: Princeton University Press, 1969.

Richards, Carissa M. Quinn. "The King and the Kingdom: The Message of Psalms 15–24." PhD diss., Golden Gate Baptist Theological Seminary, 2015.

Robertson, O. Palmer. *The Flow of the Psalms: Discovering their Structure and Theology.* Phillipsburg, NJ: P&R, 2015.

Robertson, O. Palmer. *The Shaping of the Psalter: An Introduction to the Flow of the Psalms.* Phillipsburg, NJ: P&R, 2019.

Ross, Allen P. *A Commentary on the Psalms.* 3 Vols. Kregel Exegetical Library. Grand Rapids, MI: Kregel, 2011–2016.

Prothero, Rowland E. *The Psalms in Human Life.* 1903; repr. Vestavia Hills, AL: Solid Ground Christian Books, n.d.

Ryken, Leland, et al., eds. *Dictionary of Biblical Imagery*. Downers Grove, IL: InterVarsity Press, 2000.

Sawyer, J. F. A. "An Analysis of the Context and Meaning of the Psalm-Headings," *Transactions of the Glasgow University Oriental Society*, 22 (1970): 26–38.

Scroggie, W. Graham. *The Psalms.* Revell, 1978.

Shepherd, Jerry Eugene. "The Book of Psalms as the Book of Christ: The Application of the Christo-Canonical Method to the Book of Psalms." PhD diss., Westminster Theological Seminary, 1995.

Skinner, Jerome L. "The Historical Superscriptions of Davidic Psalms: An Exegetical, Intertextual, and Methodological Analysis." PhD diss., Andrews University Seventh-Day Adventist Theological Seminary, 2016.

Shead, Andrew, ed., *Stirred by a Noble Theme: The Book of Psalms in the Life of the Church.* Nottingham, UK: Apollos, 2013.

Snearly, Michael K. "The Return of the King: Book V as a Witness to Messianic Hope in the Psalter." In *The Psalms: Language for All Seasons of the Soul.* Edited by Andrew J. Schmutzer and David Howard Jr. Chicago: Moody Publishers, 2013.

Snearly, Michael K. *The Return of the King: Messianic Expectation in Book V of the Psalter*. The Library of Hebrew Bible/Old Testament Studies 624. New York: T&T Clark, 2016.

Spurgeon, Charles Haddon. *The Treasury of David.* 6 Vols. New York: Marshall Brothers, n.d.

Steinmetz, David C. "Luther as an Interpreter of the Bible," in *Archiv für Reformationgeschichte* 70. Beiheft: Literaturbericht, 1973.

Stott, John. *Favorite Psalms.* Chicago: Moody Press, 1988.

Tate, Marvin E. "Rethinking the Nature of the Psalter." In *Psalms 1–50*, 438–72. Revised Edition. Edited by P. C. Craigie. Word Bible Commentary 19. Nashville: Thomas Nelson, 2004.

Tate, Marvin E. *Psalms 51–100*. Word Biblical Commentary 20. Dallas: Word, 1990.

Tickell, M. *The Works of the Right Honourable Joseph Addison*. Vol. 2. London: T. Malden, 1804.

Trible, Phyllis. "Wrestling with Words, Limping to Light." In *Why I (Still) Believe: Leading Bible Scholars Share Their Stories of Faith and Scholarship*. Edited by John Byron and Joel N. Lohr. Grand Rapids, MI: Zondervan, 2015.

Trueman, Carl. *The Rise and Triumph of the Modern Self: Cultural Amnesia, Expressive Individualism, and the Road to Sexual Revolution*. Wheaton, IL: Crossway, 2020.

Vaillancourt, Ian J. *The Multifaceted Saviour of Psalms 110 and 118: A Canonical Exegesis*. Hebrew Bible Monographs 86. Sheffield: Sheffield Phoenix, 2019.

Waltke, Bruce K. "Biblical Theology of the Psalms Today: A Personal Perspective." In *The Psalms: Language for All Seasons of the Soul*. Edited by Andrew J. Schmutzer and David M Howard Jr. Chicago: Moody, 2013.

Waltke, Bruce K. "A Canonical Process Approach to the Psalms." In *Tradition and Testament: Essays in Honor of Charles Lee Feinberg*. Edited by John S. Feinberg and Paul D. Feinberg. Chicago: Moody Press, 1981.

Waltke, Bruce K. "Christ in the Psalms." In *A Hope Fulfilled: Essays in Honor of O. Palmer Robertson*. Edited by Robert L. Penny. Phillipsburg, NJ: P&R, 2008.

Waltke, Bruce K. *Concise Commentary on the Psalms*. The Gospel Coalition, forthcoming. https://www.thegospelcoalition.org/.

Waltke, Bruce K. *The Dance between God and Humanity: Reading the Bible Today as the People of God*. Grand Rapids, MI: Eerdmans, 2013.

Waltke, Bruce K. *Genesis: A Commentary*. Grand Rapids, MI: Zondervan, 2001.

Waltke, Bruce K. "The NT Interpretation of the Psalms." In *New International Dictionary of Old Testament Theology and Exegesis*. Vol. 4. Edited by Willem A. VanGemeren. Grand Rapids, MI: Zondervan, 1997.

Waltke, Bruce K. *An Old Testament Theology: An Exegetical, Canonical, and Thematic Approach*. Grand Rapids, MI: Zondervan, 2007.

Waltke, Bruce K. "Psalms." In *New International Dictionary of Old Testament Theology and Exegesis*. Vol. 4. Edited by Willem A. VanGemeren. Grand Rapids, MI: Zondervan, 1997.

Waltke, Bruce K. "Psalm 15: An Exposition in Honor of Alan Groves." In *Eyes to See, Ears to Hear: Essays in Honor of J. Alan Groves*. Edited by Peter Enns, Douglas Green, and Michael Kelly. Phillipsburg, NJ: P&R, 2010.

Waltke, Bruce K. and James M. Houston. *The Psalms as Christian Praise: A Historical Commentary*. Grand Rapids, MI: Eerdmans, 2019.

Waltke, Bruce K., James M. Houston, and Erika Moore. *The Psalms as Christian Lament: A Historical Commentary*. Eerdmans, 2014.

Waltke, Bruce K., and James M. Houston, with Erika Moore. *The Psalms as Christian Worship: A Historical Commentary*. Grand Rapids, MI: Eerdmans, 2010.

Waltke, Bruce K. "Superscripts, Postscripts or Both." *Journal of Biblical Literature* 110, no. 4 (1991): 583–96.

Weber, Beat. "Bibliography of Psalms and the Psalter since 1990." Academia.edu (website). Accessed September 27, 2022. https://www.academia.edu/5910732/BiblioPss1990ff_Bibliography_of_Psalms_and_the_Psalter_since_1990.

Weiser, Artur. *The Psalms: A Commentary*. The Old Testament Library. Philadelphia: Westminster, 1962.

Wenham, Gordon J. *Psalms as Torah: Reading Biblical Song Ethically*. Grand Rapids, MI: Baker Academic, 2012.

Westermann, Claus. *Praise and Lament in the Book of Psalms*. Atlanta: John Knox, 1981.

Whybray, Norman. *Reading the Psalms as a Book*. Journal for the Study of the Old Testament Supplement Series 222. Sheffield, UK: JSOT Press, 1996.

Wilson, Gerald H. *The Editing of the Hebrew Psalter*. Society of Biblical Literature Dissertation Series. Chico, California: Scholars Press, 1985.

Wilson, Gerald H. *Psalms Volume 1*. NIV Application Commentary. Grand Rapids, MI: Zondervan, 2002.

Wilson, Robert Dick. "The Headings of the Psalms." *The Princeton Theological Review* 24, no. 1 (January 1926): 1–37.

Witt, Andrew Carl. "A Voice without End: The Role of David in Psalms 3–14." *Journal of Theological Interpretation Supplements* 20. University Park, PA: Eisenbrauns, 2021.

# General Index

# Scripture Index